MARGERY KEMPE
AND HER WORLD

THE MEDIEVAL WORLD

Series editor: Julia Smith
Founding editor: David Bates

MARGERY KEMPE AND HER WORLD

ANTHONY GOODMAN

An imprint of **Pearson Education**

London · New York · Toronto · Sydney · Tokyo · Singapore · Hong Kong · Cape Town
New Delhi · Madrid · Paris · Amsterdam · Munich · Milan · Stockholm

PEARSON EDUCATION LIMITED

Head Office:
Edinburgh Gate
Harlow CM20 2JE
Tel: +44 (0)1279 623623
Fax: +44 (0)1279 431059

London Office:
128 Long Acre
London WC2E 9AN
Tel: +44 (0)20 7447 2000
Fax: +44 (0)20 7240 5771
Websites: www.history-minds.com
www.pearsoneduc.com

First published in Great Britain in 2002

© Pearson Education Limited 2002

The right of Anthony Goodman to be identified as Author
of this Work has been asserted by him in accordance
with the Copyright, Designs and Patents Act 1988.

ISBN 0 582 36809 X

British Library Cataloguing in Publication Data
A CIP catalogue record for this book can be obtained from the British Library

Library of Congress Cataloging in Publication Data
A CIP catalog record for this book can be obtained from the Library of Congress

10 9 8 7 6 5 4 3 2 1

Typeset in 10.5/13pt Galliard by Graphicraft Limited, Hong Kong
Printed and bound in Malaysia

The Publishers' policy is to use paper manufactured from sustainable forests.

For Heather Hawkes and Robert Rose,
companions in historical explorations

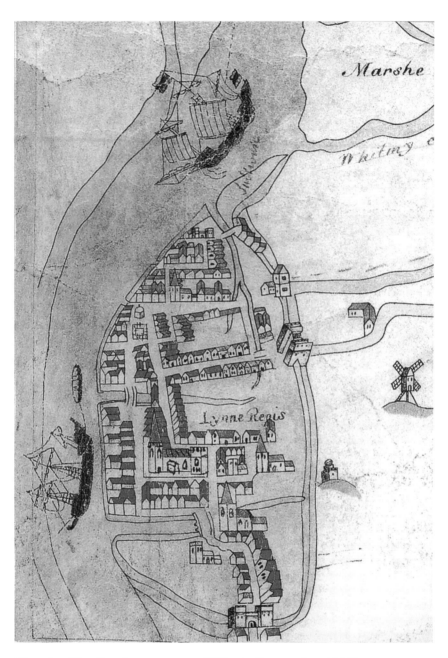

Plate 1 The first known map of King's Lynn, *circa* 1588.
Norfolk Record Office, BL 71

CONTENTS

CONTENTS

SERIES EDITOR'S PREFACE

The *Book of Margery Kempe* is the recollections of a devout lay woman with no formal education, committed to writing by scribes on her behalf in the 1430s. Controversial and often misunderstood in her own day, Margery is now one of the best known Christian mystics of the late Middle Ages. In recent years, many scholars have studied her remarkable spiritual insights and passionate outbursts of devotion, her struggles to negotiate her way through the patriarchal expectations of urban oligarchy, the Church and marriage, or her apparent personality disorder marked by histrionic and hysterical behaviour. In this latest addition to the Medieval World Series, Anthony Goodman deploys a lifetime's expertise in the history of late medieval England and Europe to provide a different appraisal of Margery Kempe. By exploring her external world in its social, political, ecclesiastical and topographical richness, he situates her interior, religious world with sympathetic precision in the context of her own family, home and travels. This attractively wide-ranging study takes the reader from the flourishing East Anglian port of Lynn (now King's Lynn) to Venice, Jerusalem and Rome. Goodman brings these milieux alive through a wealth of documentary research, much of it using unpublished material from English and Italian archives, and thus establishes a far more secure historical context for Margery than hitherto available. With his assistance, we meet the people Margery met. We are also encouraged to probe the attitudes and gender expectations of provincial English urban oligarchies in the fourteenth and fifteenth centuries; the experience of pilgrimage and travel across the length and breadth of Europe; the shrines and saints' cults of the late Middle Ages; the problems of medieval childraising; the textual complexities of the *Book of Margery Kempe*, and much more besides. Skilfully keeping Margery's *Book* as his point of reference, Anthony Goodman ranges through aspects of late medieval history all too frequently studied in isolation from one another. The great strength of his book is to integrate them so as to illuminate Margery Kempe and her world. I am delighted that this is the first volume to appear in the Medieval World Series under its new editor.

JULIA M.H. SMITH

AUTHOR'S PREFACE

I was first spurred into writing about *The Book of Margery Kempe* by Professor Derek Baker: his enthusiasm gave me the courage to undertake an amateurish canter. Since then (over twenty years ago) the field of Margery Kempe studies has become formidably larger, so, as an old drayhorse now put out to grass, I am being foolhardy in attempting a gallop. That is my excuse for having sought out so busily the help of friends, colleagues and strangers, who have responded with unfailing good humour, and who have saved me from many errors, introduced me to texts and suggested lines of enquiry.

I owe particular thanks for commenting on chapters to Professor Christopher Allmand, Dr Gary Dickson, Professor Barrie Dobson, Ms Ann Kettle, Dr John Law, Dr Alison McHardy and Professor Nicholas Orme, and for commenting on sections of chapters to Mrs Katherine Parker and Dr Richard Mackenney. Kate Parker, currently engaged in research for a Ph.D at the University of East Anglia on 'Lordship, Liberty and the Pursuit of Politics in Lynn, 1370–1430', has been generous with her knowledge and advice. Professor John A.F. Thomson read the whole manuscript and was meticulously helpful with comments and advice.

Dr Stefano Piasentini helped me to find my way around the Archivio di Stato, Venice, and gave me references to sources there and in the Biblioteca Marciana which I would not have been able to find. Dr Jane Laughton kindly allowed me to use her research on the portmote rolls of Melton Mowbray. A number of scholars have put unpublished papers at my disposal – Dr James G. Clark, Ms Kettle, Mrs Parker, Mr Harry Schnitker and Ms Janice Smith (of the York Glaziers Trust).

Besides those mentioned, a host of scholars have benefited me in the task, some with advice, some with references – Dr Patricia Allerston, Professor Michael Angold, Ms Andrea Briehle, Dr Stephen Boardman, Dr Andrew Brown, Professor Donald Bullough, Professor John Burrow, Dr Gianfranco Dogliani, Dr Alastair Dunn, Professor Christopher Dyer, Mr Owen Dudley Edwards, Ms Tina Eriksson, Dr Adam Fox, Mr Peter Gibson (former Superintendent and Secretary of the York Glaziers Trust), Ms Lynne Hainsworth, Dr Elizabeth Hartley (Keeper of Archaeology, the Yorkshire Museum), Dr John Jurica (Assistant Editor of *The Victoria County History of Gloucestershire*), Dr Margaret Laing, Dr Katherine

Lewis, Dr Philip Morgan, Mrs Deidre Mortimer (and other Friends of York Minster), Dr Graeme Small, Professor David Smith, Professor Lynn Staley and Professor Tom Scott.

My understanding of the problems posed by *The Book of Margery Kempe* as autobiography has benefited greatly from a lecture given by Professor Felicity Riddy, 'Getting a Life: Margery Kempe as Auto-biographer', at a conference on 'Medieval Biography and Biographers, Northern Europe in the late Middle Ages', held under the auspices of the University of Edinburgh at St George's School, Edinburgh in May 2001.

I learned too late to make use of it of Samuel Fanous's D.Phil. thesis (University of Oxford, 1998), 'Biblical and Hagiographical Imitatio in *The Book of Margery Kempe*'. Dr Fanous is to publish a book based on the thesis, entitled *Piety and Posterity: Margery Kempe and the Late-Medieval Culture of Religious Fame*. I am grateful to him for sending me a synopsis of his book, which will, I am sure, provide a definitive inter-pretation of problems involved in interpreting the presentation of Margery's spiritual persona.

I owe thanks to many librarians and archivists, especially at Edinburgh University Library and The National Library of Scotland, and also at Bristol Record Office, The Borthwick Institute, University of York, The College of Arms, London, Gloucestershire Record Office, National Monuments Record Centre, Swindon, Tyne and Wear Archives Service and Worcestershire Record Office. Mr Christian Daw, former archivist of the Venerabile Collegio Inglese, Rome, responded helpfully to my enquiries, and his successor, Mr Nicholas Schofield, shared his know-ledge of medieval churches and congregations in Rome. Above all, Ms Susan Maddock, Principal Archivist at Norfolk Record Office, has helped me over several years with her unrivalled knowledge of the Borough Archives of King's Lynn, of which she is custodian.

I owe a particular debt of gratitude in my research for this book to my wife Jackie, who has given me many scholarly insights into the text and was eagle-eyed in reading the final version. Together we have fol-lowed in some of Margery's footsteps, but, thankfully, not in the mutual spirits of Mr and Mrs Kempe on the road to Bridlington. I am grateful to my daughter, Emma Goodman, and to Mr Michael Pacey, who have patiently backed up my shaky computer skills.

LIST OF ILLUSTRATIONS

LIST OF PLATES

Plate 1   The first known map of King's Lynn, *circa* 1588.
Norfolk Record Office, BL 71
Plate 2   Bench end from St. Nicholas' Chapel, King's Lynn, with carvings of fifteenth-century ships.
© V&A Picture Library
Plate 3   St Nicholas' Chapel, King's Lynn, Norfolk
Used by kind permission of The Churches Conservation Trust/ Christopher Dalton
Plate 4   Thomas Arundel, Archbishop of Canterbury
The Bodleian Library, University of Oxford, MS Laud Misc. 165 fol. 5
Plate 5   Entrance to the Chapter House, York Minster. Margery Kempe describes how she was examined by clerics on her way of life and her faith in the Chapter House.
Plate 6   Supplicant asks the executed Richard Scrope, Archbishop of York, for his prayers. From The Bolton Book of Hourse, *circa* 1420– 30.
© Dean and Chapter of York: reproduced by kind permission
Plate 7   Figure of pilgrim who was devoted to Santiago de Compostela, formerly in St Saviour's church, York, now in former St Mary's Church (*YORK STORY*)
Plate 8   Gentile Bellini (*circa* 1429–1507) Procession in St Mark's Square, 1496 (oil on canvas), Galleria dell' Accademia, Venice, Italy/ Bridgeman Art Library
Plate 9   Jan van Scorel (1495–1562) Members of the Jerusalem Guild of Utrecht, *circa* 1535
© Centraal Museum Utrecht

CHRONOLOGY OF THE LIFE OF MARGERY KEMPE*

c. 1373	Birth of Margery Brunham.
c. 1393	Margery's marriage to John Kempe.
1413	The couple visit Yorkshire and decide to take vows of chastity; their interviews with Philip Repingdon, Bishop of Lincoln and Thomas Arundel, Archbishop of Canterbury.
c. 1413–15	Margery's great pilgrimages: itinerary via Norwich, Great Yarmouth, Zierikzee, Constance, Bologna, Venice, the Holy Land, Venice, Assisi, Rome, Middelburg, Norwich.
1417–18	Margery's pilgrimage to Santiago de Compostela, embarking at and returning to Bristol; visit to Hailes abbey; arrest and examinations in Leicester; stays at Melton Mowbray; visits York; examination by Henry Bowet, Archbishop of York at Cawood; goes to Bridlington and Hull; arrested at Hessle; imprisoned in Beverley and examined there by Bowet; passes through Lincoln on way to West Lynn; visits London; passes through Ely on way back to King's Lynn.
c. 1431	Deaths of Margery's son and her husband.
1433–4	Margery's journey to Prussia: itinerary via Norwich, Ipswich, Norway, Danzig (Gdansk), Stralsund, Bad Wilsnack, Aachen, Calais, Dover, Canterbury, London; visit to Syon abbey (Middlesex).
23 July 1436	The third amanuensis of the text of Margery's *Book* (the cleric) starts to make a copy of Book One.
28 April 1438	The same amanuensis starts to write down Book Two.

* This is based principally on the reconstructions in *B.M.K.*, xlviii–li and Windeatt, 29–30.

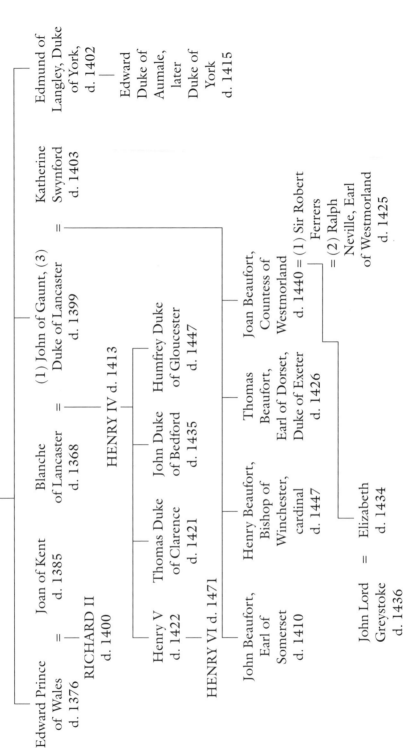

EDWARD III d. 1377

Edward Prince of Wales d. 1376 = Joan of Kent d. 1385 | RICHARD II d. 1400

(1) John of Gaunt, (3) Duke of Lancaster d. 1399 = Blanche of Lancaster d. 1368 | HENRY IV d. 1413

Katherine Swynford d. 1403

Edmund of Langley, Duke of York, d. 1402 — Edward Duke of Aumale, later Duke of York d. 1415

Henry V d. 1422 | HENRY VI d. 1471

Thomas Duke of Clarence d. 1421

John Duke of Bedford d. 1435

Humfrey Duke of Gloucester d. 1447

John Beaufort, Earl of Somerset d. 1410

Henry Beaufort, Bishop of Winchester, cardinal d. 1447

Thomas Beaufort, Earl of Dorset, Duke of Exeter d. 1426

Joan Beaufort, Countess of Westmorland d. 1440 = (1) Sir Robert Ferrers = (2) Ralph Neville, Earl of Westmorland d. 1425

John Lord Greystoke d. 1436 = Elizabeth d. 1434

Lancastrian kings and some of their forbears and kinsfolk

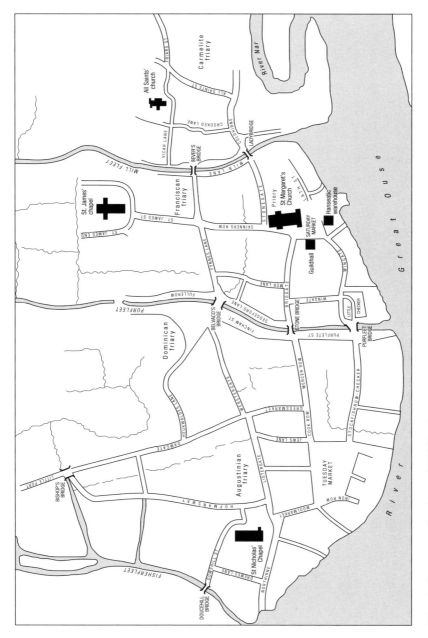

King's Lynn in the later Middle Ages

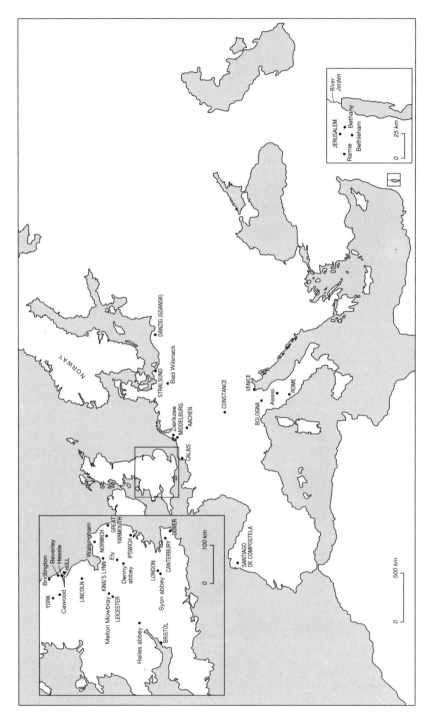

Places visited by Margery Kempe

ABBREVIATIONS

Asshebourne   Owen, M.D. (ed.) (1981), *William Asshebourne's Book. King's Lynn Corporation Archives 10/2*, Norwich: Norfolk Record Society, xlviii

A.S.V.   Archivio di Stato, Venice

A.V.C.I.R.   Archive of the Venerabile Collegio Inglese, Rome

Bodl.   The Bodleian Library, University of Oxford

B.M.K.   Meech, S.B. and Allen, H.E. (eds.) (1940) *The Book of Margery Kempe*, London: E.E.T.S., original series, 212

C.C.R.   *Calendar of Close Rolls*

C.I.M.   *Calendar of Inquisitions Miscellaneous*

C.P.   C[okayne], G.E., new edition, Gibbs, V. *et al.* (eds.) (1910–59) *The Complete Peerage of England, Scotland, Ireland and Great Britain and the United Kingdom*, 13 vols, London: St Catherine's Press

C.P.R.   *Calendar of Patent Rolls*

Derby's Expeditions   Toulmin Smith, L. (ed.) (1894) *Expeditions to Prussia and the Holy Land made by Henry Earl of Derby*, Camden Society, new series, lii

E.E.T.S.   Early English Text Society

E.H.R.   *English Historical Review*

Harrod   Harrod, H. (1874) *Report on the Deeds and Records of the Borough of King's Lynn*, King's Lynn

H.M.C., Lynn   'The manuscripts of the corporations of Southampton and King's Lynn' (1887) *Historical Manuscripts Commission. Eleventh Report*, Appendix, part iii, London

Ingleby   K.L.R.O., KL/C7/29: Ingleby, H. (trans.) (1924) 'King's Lynn corporation minutes, Book I, 1422–50' (translation of KL/C7/2; Hall Book)

J.E.H.   *Journal of Ecclesiastical History*

K.L.R.O.	King's Lynn Record Office
m	mark (monetary unit of account, one mark being equal to 13s 4d)
N.R.O.	Norfolk Record Office
Owen	Owen, M.D. (1984) *The Making of King's Lynn. A Documentary Survey*, London: British Academy
P.R.O.	Public Record Office
R.R.	Ingleby, H. (ed.), Isaacson, R.F. (trans.) (1919–20), *The Red Register of King's Lynn*, 2 vols, King's Lynn: Thew and Son
S.A.C.	Galbraith, V.H. (ed.) (1937) *The St Albans Chronicle 1406–20*, Oxford: U.P.
Test. Ebor.	*Testamenta Eboracensia*, 3 vols (1836–65), London and Durham: Surtees Society
Windeatt	Windeatt, B.A. (trans.) (1985) *The Book of Margery Kempe*, London: Penguin

GLOSSARY

basilica	A church of an early Christian type, designed on classical lines. In Rome, the term is applied especially to seven principal churches founded by the Emperor Constantine.
baxter	Baker.
beguine	An unmarried working woman who lived devoutly with similar women in a beguinage; the movement flourished in the Low Countries.
brasier, brazier	An artisan who worked in brass.
Candlemas	Feast of the Purification of the Virgin Mary, celebrated by lighting many candles.
coifmaker	Maker of caps.
dragoman	An Arabian guide and interpreter in the Holy Land. The term was used for such guides elsewhere in the Middle East.
edicule	Term used for the Chapel of the Holy Sepulchre, a distinct building within the Church of the Holy Sepulchre, Jerusalem.
fletcher	A maker of or dealer in bows and arrows.
Hanseatic League	A long-lasting alliance of cities, towns and districts as far apart as the Rhineland and the Baltic ports, a principal aim of which was to secure common trading privileges in the countries where they did business. Some members were intent on consolidating control of some major shipping lanes across the North Sea and the Baltic.
inferioris non burgensis	Term used in King's Lynn to describe a male secular inhabitant who was not a burgess and was of low social status.
lector	Lecturer.
Lollard	A later medieval English heretic. The varying beliefs of Lollards were strongly based on unorthodox interpretations of the New Testament, available to them in their unique translations into the vernacular. They were heavily influenced by

	the teachings of John Wycliffe (d. 1384), and his and their tenets anticipated fundamental Protestant doctrines and attitudes.
Mamluk	One of the elite group of warriors and officials who defended and governed Egypt and Syria (including the Holy Land), drawn from among the freed slaves of the sultan and amirs.
mediocris	Term used in King's Lynn to categorise a burgess who was not in the highest status group of burgesses there.
morrowspeech	Meeting of gild members the day after they had celebrated a gild feast.
potencioris	Term used in King's Lynn to describe the most honoured and wealthiest burgesses there.
scuola	A religious gild in Italy; in Venice the leading gilds, the *scuole grandi*, played important social roles.
souter	Shoemaker or cobbler.
studium generale	Institution for higher education.
utensilia	Appurtenances for home and/or for domestic production.
webster	Weaver.
writ	A letter of command issued by Chancery. Various sorts of judicial writs initiated or directed the course of legal processes.

chapter 1

INTRODUCTION

T he subject of this study is an account, unique in character, of the
life in devotion of a medieval Englishwoman, Margery Kempe, of
King's Lynn, Norfolk, who was born in the early 1370s and was alive
in 1438. A manuscript volume which the Butler-Bowdon family, of
Pleasington Hall, Lancashire, found among their possessions in 1934
was identified as *The Book of Margery Kempe*. It is now in the British
Library (Additional MS 61823).

The manuscript dates from the mid-fifteenth century; the writing is in
a neat and clear hand, and the language is Middle English in a Norfolk
dialect of the period.[1] This is not the original manuscript but a fair copy,
probably copied directly from the original, with some personal and place
names probably abbreviated. The scribe is called Salthows.[2] The only
indication of early ownership is the inscription in a late fifteenth-century
hand, 'Liber Montis Gracie', which identifies it as having been in the
library of Mount Grace priory (Yorkshire, North Riding), a Carthusian
house.[3] A prominent set of marginal annotations of the text (of an
approving and devout nature) has been attributed to a monk of the
house.[4]

A few other manuscripts from the priory's library have been identified.
Dom David Knowles concluded from their subject matter, and evidence
of the literary activities of some of the monks, that this priory most fully
exemplified the engagement of the Carthusian Order in England with
late medieval English spirituality in the last phase of monasticism.[5] At
this devotional powerhouse, *The Book* appears to have been reverenced.
There is not much evidence that *The Book* made an impact anywhere else
except within this community of remote and exceptionally austere monks
– though they constituted a large and probably devotionally influential
community, twenty-seven strong at the dissolution of the priory in
1539.[6] However, no copy of *The Book* has been identified among those
surviving from the libraries of two monasteries which had extensive

collections of devotional manuscripts in the fifteenth century – the Charterhouse of Sheen (now Richmond, Surrey) and the Briggetine convent of Syon (Middlesex).[7]

Yet we must bear in mind how deeply impoverished our perceptions of late medieval English spirituality are as a consequence of the enormous destruction of religious texts during the Reformation. It may betoken a more widespread valuation of *The Book* that, after the dissolution of Mount Grace, a pensioned-off monk or a religiously conservative lay person considered the work to be a precious devotional testimony, and that subsequent Roman Catholics risked preserving a compromising work which might have been used to support accusations of subversiveness. There is evidence that extracts from the text had circulated at the end of the fifteenth century and, indeed, continued to be regarded as spiritually uplifting in subsequent decades. The London printer Wynkyn de Worde put together excerpts taken from nineteen passages in *The Book*, c. 1500, under the title *A shorte treatyse of contemplacyon taught by our lorde Ihesu cryste, or taken out of the boke of Margerie Kempe of Lynn*. It is not clear whether Worde was printing from Salthows's copy: the printed extracts are in contemporary London English. As Professor Sanford Meech pointed out, all seven pages of them are meditative, excluding descriptions of experiences in the secular world with which they are interlarded in *The Book*.[8] Worde probably judged that his readership would find meditations devotionally rewarding, but that they might be indifferent to, or even repelled by, the accounts of their author's worldly tribulations. Moreover, aspects of *The Book* – its bewildering chronological jumbles and its homely loquacity – might have jarred on some potential readers in a period when humanist canons were influencing the form and content of vernacular literature and educational curricula. Besides, in the early Tudor period, public discourse insisted with increasing emphasis on the propriety of harmonious obedience to hierarchical prescriptions. Women should know their place – which, *The Book* shows, some of Margery's contemporaries thought on occasion she did not. Besides, there were renewed concerns about the spread of Lollard heresies. In this climate of opinion, *The Book*'s harping on its subject's defiances of ecclesiastical and lay authorities, and on her susceptibility to charges of heresy, would have ruffled some sensibilities. To the conventionally devout, the repeated need for *The Book*'s role model to be distinguished from Lollards might then (when their profiles were very clearly established) have seemed puzzling, perhaps, indeed, alarming. However, Worde's meditative extracts may have been well received, though only one copy survives; another London printer, Henry Pepwell, reprinted them in 1521, in a volume containing seven devout treatises.[9]

The first modern translation of the text was published in 1936 by Colonel Butler-Bowdon: he acknowledged that the American scholar Hope Emily Allen had identified firmly the 'authoress' as the hitherto obscure Margery Kempe of King's Lynn. There is only one reference to her full married name in *The Book*, 'Mar. Kempe of Lynne', but a number of times she is referred to by her Christian name. She is also identified as 'John of Burnamys daughter of Lynne', and elsewhere in the text he is said to have been 'mayor five times of that worshipful borough and alderman [of Holy Trinity Gild] also many years'.[10] The original text, with a full scholarly apparatus, was published four years later by Professor Sanford Meech and H.E. Allen.[11] This exemplary edition is the foundation for studies of *The Book*. Its introductory material, footnotes and appendices contain a mass of information, indispensable to students of the subject. Dr B.A. Windeatt published a modern version in 1985, which has brought knowledge of *The Book* to a much larger readership.[12] However, for the three decades or so after Meech and Allen's publication of the text, studies of it were fitful. It may be that the editors' mastery of the subject for some time had the effect of ring-fencing it. Historians tended to 'cherry pick' examples from it, though paying the text the compliment of accepting what it said literally.

Perhaps some of the main thrusts in the historiography of fifteenth-century England for long sidelined *The Book* as a historical source. K.B. McFarlane, doyen of historians of later medieval England, put studies of the nobility to the forefront, using as prime source material the documentary evidence of their own and other relevant archives, with a heavy prosopographical emphasis. Though McFarlane's works on John Wycliffe and the Lollards produced a new understanding of the social significance of the heretical movement, he was steely in his secular approach to devotional matters and steered clear of using *The Book* as evidence.[13] So, perhaps surprisingly, did the growing numbers of British historians interested in exploring *mentalités* – with the electrifying example of Emanuel Le Roy Ladurie's reconstitution of the Pyreneen community of Montaillou in the later thirteenth and early fourteenth centuries, based on an inquisitorial register, as an encouragement.[14]

The Book is unique in the nature and richness of the testimony it gives as a construction of a town dweller's mentality in medieval England. Its scope is remarkable. It has a huge cast (though mostly anonymous and unidentifiable) and reflects on experiences in major English cities and some of the great cities of Christendom. However, urban historians have preferred to reconstruct religious and other aspects of their societies by using record evidence. Wariness in using *The Book* is understandable, for, though (as the selection of documents printed by Dr Owen shows),

King's Lynn is rich in documentation from the period, it remains difficult to position *The Book* within its social and cultural milieux and hazardous, therefore, to use it as evidence for urban mentality, except in the most general ways. Documentation has not even yielded information placing Margery Kempe securely within broad family and social networks. The disappearance of the records of most wills made in King's Lynn in the fifteenth century has robbed us of a vital source. Lynn was an ecclesiastical 'peculiar', with its own court, outwith the ordinary diocesan jurisdiction of the see of Norwich. The records of the Lynn court do not appear to have survived: we have only a few stray wills proved before and recorded by diocesan officials.[15] Meech and Allen made identifications of Margery's father and her husband from the borough records, but the figure of *The Book* still remains, as a consequence of the dearth of other evidence, one which floats detached from much of what we know about Lynn society.

From the 1970s onwards, studies of *The Book*, particularly by American scholars and by scholars of literature, have proliferated. Medievalists have seen it as an important piece of evidence in a variety of related contexts, notably those of gender, individual consciousness and religious sensibility.[16] The figure of Margery, in this post-*Annaliste* historiographical climate, has taken on a rich significance which it lacked in the perception of its earliest modern commentators. Father Thurston, S.J., who reviewed Butler-Bowdon's edition in *The Tablet* and more fully in *The Month* in 1936, was cautious in his assessment of the significance of the devout personality projected in *The Book*. He wrote in *The Tablet* that 'it is impossible to forget the hysterical temperament revealed in every page of the narrative portions'. In *The Month* he asserted: 'That Margery was a victim of hysteria can hardly be open to doubt, for apart from her weeping fits, she was constantly subject to mysterious illnesses from which she suddenly recovered.' However, he showed appreciation of the good qualities of 'these queer mystics', especially their genuine love of God.[17] These judgements have a 'modern' flavour, but also reflect the Church's traditional distrust of unusual manifestations of religious enthusiasm, using a fashionable medical term to express some of the adverse judgements which, according to *The Book*, were made about Margery's disturbing exhibitions of devotion at the time. However, Father Thurston's diagnostic bent is one which has been followed more recently as a consequence of the burgeoning studies on the history of medicine. *The Book* has a good deal of evidence about the illnesses and disfunctionality of its subject, particularly intriguing for the psychologist. It projects Margery's growing inability to fulfil with equanimity some basic normal requirements of society. The visions which are at the heart of its subject matter might be judged, from some modern viewpoints, as delusional. The descriptions of trance-like ecstasies emphasise the accompanying physical symptoms. Spiritual progression is described within the context of mental and bodily ills, and physical symptoms (such as ringing in the ears or spots before the eyes) are given a spiritual significance. A temptation nowadays would be to put the Margery of *The Book* on the couch or in the surgery.[18]

Let us now consider aspects of the composition of *The Book*. The text is divided into two parts; the first, the bulk of the work, comprising eighty-nine short chapters, the second, ten. The text in the form we have it was first written down in 1436, copied from an earlier, badly written version. The copying, we are told, commenced on the day after the feast of St Mary Magdalene (23 July). The date was probably symbolic, associating the depiction of Margery as a reformed sinner embraced by Christ with its supreme female role model.[19] The circumstances of the first book's composition are explained in a very brief preface and are amplified in the preceding, more expansive proem. The preface starts off rather laconically: 'A short treatise of a creature set in great pomp and pride of the world, which since was drawn to our Lord by great poverty, sickness, shames, and great reproofs in many divers countries and places, of which tribulations some shall be showed after, not in order as it is fallen but as the creature could have mind of them [remember] when it were written.'[20] The proem had input from the priest who transcribed the existing text, in order to 'express more openly' what it was about than was done in the earlier introduction. It is much more eloquent and well considered, beating the drum for Margery's spiritual struggles and attainments, and providing an ambitious rationale for the work. It commences: 'Here beginneth a short treatise and a comfortable one for sinful wretches, wherein they may have great solace and comfort to them and understand the high and unspeakable mercy of our sovereign Saviour Christ Ihesu, whose name be worshiped and magnified without end, that now in our days to us unworthy deigneth to exercise his nobility and his goodness.'[21] The proem appears to reflect a change of intention for the text, perhaps made at the behest of her clergyman-amanuensis and his superiors. For Margery had contracted with the previous scribe (a briefly engaged second amanuensis) that he was 'never to reveal it [the book] as long as she lived'.[22] She had, therefore, intended publication after her death, in the hope, one assumes, of posthumously confirming her holiness. Presumably, when the opaque content of the first draft (which had been written down in a semi-literate scrawl) at last became clear to the better educated clergyman who became her amanuensis and his and to Margery's mentors among the clergy, they impressed upon her the desirability of instant publication.

My assumption is that the good news conveyed in *The Book* was thought to merit it. In the proem, the treatise is advertised as a utilitarian one, a helpful spiritual handbook which demonstrated Christ's continued benevolent bustling down orthodox channels – at a time when heretics were claiming to have authoritatively rediscovered the true route to his grace. The proem is also strongly justificatory, emphasising that Margery's spirituality has the imprimatur of impeccably orthodox clerical authorities, and that some of the great and the good among them had long urged her to have a written account made.

The second book was a new composition recorded by the same clergyman-amanuensis, by then a seasoned collaborator with Margery. Unlike the first book, it does not have separate introductions, but in its first chapter the writer recorded that he commenced work on the feast of St Vitalis Martyr (28 April) 1438. Vitalis had been a Roman bureaucrat, a family man who spoke out against the persecution of Christians, declared his own faith and accepted his martyrdom with dignity – a good role model, perhaps, for borough officers and chaplains in Lynn who thought their superiors were behaving wickedly.[23] This writer of the second book 'held it expedient to honour of the blissful Trinity that his holy works [the Saviour's] should be notified and declared to the people, when it pleased him, to the worship of his holy name'.[24] The book dwelt on events in Margery's life in the 1430s which were not covered in Book One. Its concluding chapter consisted of a well-composed set of her prayers, which handily distils the essence of her devotion. The intention here was presumably to show the *moyen homme sensuel* and his female counterpart, and how they might relate to and benefit from the vaulting devotion of the treatise.[25]

Why was an extended second book composed? The first amply – and often repetitively – demonstrated the special character of Margery's devotional life and its background. In its sequel there were no extended dialogues with Christ or visions of sacred scenes; it is mostly concerned with her family affairs and the hazards she encountered on her further travels. The accounts of these travels (and of earlier ones) have similar vibes to those of the heroes of romances and the travellers' accounts of their experiences which were in vogue. One explanation for its composition, assuming that the copying of the first book was finished well before this was commenced, may be that the former was well received by 'the people' and that the writer was catering for a demand for more. On the other hand, the first book may have had a mixed reception – some people may have had a problem in accepting the presentation of Margery as a holy paragon in view of what they had heard about her treatment of her family, her impulsive and forbidden embarkation across the North

Sea, and wanderings on the continent, often without female company, in more recent years. However, it may be significant that, at the start of the first chapter of the second book, the writer introduced it briefly with jaunty self-confidence and none of the laboured justifications which characterised the proem composed for the first. That suggests that Margery and her clerk were buoyed up by at least some of the reactions to the latter.

In the proem and the introductory passage in the second book, it is made abundantly clear that Margery did not write down *The Book* herself. She was dependent, it is emphasised, on the availability of amanuenses and for long endured frustrations in getting the job done because of the inadequacies and hesitations of those whom she engaged to do it. We may safely infer from this that, when a mature woman, she lacked the skill to write at a level appropriate to literary composition. This was the assumption apparently made previously by worthy and worshipful clerics who 'proffered to her to write her feelings with their hands'.[26] The fact that she is shown relying on others to write correspondence for her suggests that her writing skills, if she had any, were minimal. A master of divinity writes a letter for her to a widow on spiritual matters.[27] She gets a layman to write to her husband, asking him to fetch her home.[28] Had Margery any reading ability? *The Book* attributes to her a remarkable knowledge of Scriptures and devotional treatises. Dr Margaret Aston has reviewed the evidence for lay literacy in the period, which suggests how it had increased, but Dr Aston also shows how illiterate layfolk could gain a well-informed and even sophisticated grasp of religion by a variety of means.[29] *The Book* illustrates one aspect of these by describing how a priest read to Margery in private from the Bible, from commentaries on it and devotional works, for the most part of seven or eight years, though she concluded (one may think, rather smugly) that this prolonged seminar course was 'to great increase of his cunning and of his merit' – rather than to hers![30] If she did have some reading knowledge, she is more likely to have had it in the vernacular than in Latin. After she was arrested in Leicester and brought before its steward, he spoke in Latin to her, 'many priests standing about to hear what she should say and other people'. She replied prudently: 'Speak English, if thou liketh, for I understand not what thou say.'[31]

Technical literacy (the ability to read and write in Latin) may have been a rare skill among Lynn burgesses. A leading one, William Erl (well known to Margery's putative father), is recorded in an ecclesiastical record as *litteratus*.[32] Nevertheless, occasional citations in *The Book* suggest that Margery was well versed in key scriptural passages. Awed by the Word of God, without any formal grammatical training or expertise, she seems to have learnt the meaning of key Latin words and phrases, just as generations of Roman Catholics did apropos of Mass before it came to be said in the vernacular. After Christ assured her that her frequent experience of spots before the eyes betokened the presence of angels, she had the knowledge and wit to turn the phrase 'Benedictus qui venit in nomine domini' into a greeting for them.[33] She recalled with pleasure that when a 'great clerk' in York asked her to explain a verse from *Genesis* which he cited in Latin, she had expounded it to his satisfaction.[34] In Germany she quoted from the Psalter to her angry companions after she had dismayed them by her lachrymose reaction to the exposure of the Blessed Sacrament in a friary.[35] So Margery (who seems to have had a facility for picking up dialects and languages)[36] may have learnt many Latin verses from Scripture by heart from hearing their recitation, and grasped their meaning in a learned way from the expositions of clerics.

It is unclear whether she was able to read with facility in the vernacular. For well-to-do burgesses of Lynn (especially, perhaps, merchant venturers) who relied on the help of wife or daughter in business affairs, it would surely have been useful if their womenfolk had some literacy and numeracy.[37] Moreover, Margery became frustrated when there was no suitable confessor available for her to consult or when she had no good sermon to look forward to.[38] Though in such circumstances meditation was a joyful refuge for her, one might expect that she would have liked to scan devotional texts too. However, there may have been a good reason for not alluding in *The Book* to skills in literacy, if she possessed any. As it attests, pertness in Scripture, generally considered highly inappropriate in a woman, brought down on her suspicions that she was a heretic. Lollard women had a reputation for being learned; the steward of Leicester's question to her in Latin (shrewd temptation to the vanity of a suspected autodidact) was probably designed to elicit evidence that she was likely to be one of them.[39] It was important for *The Book* to demonstrate that, though she had become exceptionally eloquent in bearing testimony to Christ's compassion, she derived her religion from the precepts of well-respected priests with impeccably orthodox reputations. Her inability to write down her 'feelings' and eventual reliance on a priest to do so reinforced her profile as dependent on the Church.

However, Margery's first amanuensis was a layman. Usually, devout women had their revelations from God recorded by a cleric, but Margery had refused offers from clerics to write for her. This course of action perhaps reflects an initial fear that a cleric might try to tone down some of her more robust comments. Her decision nearly scuppered the project. The layman who first wrote down Book One, 'nearly four years or more' before 1436, died before he could complete it. An Englishman, married with a child, he had lived for some time in 'Dewchland' (Germany or the Netherlands). He wrote in a mixture of English and German and was, presumably, used only to writing commercial letters and accounts in German or in a melange of the vernaculars. His writing skills were gravely defective.[40] It has been suggested that he was the son of Margery discussed in *The Book*, who returned to Lynn with his wife and child after living and marrying in Prussia.[41] The fact that the amanuensis was a layman – and especially if he was Margery's son, portrayed in the second book as a penitent sinner – implies that he was likely to have painstakingly and unquestioningly recorded her pronouncements. For the son, the writing would have been an act of both penance and filial piety, which he needed to get right.

The relationship between author and first scribe has helped to preserve Margery's modes of expression: a distinctive voice is one of the striking characteristics of *The Book*. However, his transcription was clearly inadequate. Margery persuaded a priest she knew (the final amanuensis) to look at the text. He found it difficult to understand ('for it was neither good English nor Dewch') or to decipher, but he promised to try to transcribe it. However, he backed off from doing so as there was 'then so evil speaking of this creature and of her weeping that the priest durst not for cowardice speak with her but seldom'.[42] He advised her to consult a 'good man' who had known the first amanuensis well and who had received letters from him in Dewchland – presumably, this 'good man' was a merchant venturer of Lynn for whom the first scribe (perhaps his apprentice) had acted as an agent abroad. This second layman's agreement to transcribe the text was a commercial transaction. He gave up after managing to copy only one folio! This is curious, since he was used to reading the first scribe's handwriting. Perhaps it had deteriorated as a result of ill-health, or he found the content of the book alarming or not to his taste.

The priest came to Margery's rescue; he now found it easier to read the text. 'And so he read it over before this creature every word, she sometime helping where any difficulty was' (perhaps by deciphering the script or by filling in the indecipherable with substitute phrases and passages?).[43] No suggestion is made that this amanuensis played any part in modifying the content. He was not, apparently, of high status and authority in the clerical hierarchy of Lynn.[44] However, he does appear on occasion in the first book as witness to the 'truth' of her 'feelings'.[45] This raises the possibility that these passages were inserted and that other modifications were made at his prompting. Clearly, his co-operation had become vital to the success of the project. It is even more probable that he influenced the content of the second book, since he was no longer working from a text but 'after her own tongue [at her dictation]'. By then, they had established a relationship of mutual confidence as regards composition, and Margery (apparently then in her sixties) may have come to rely on his judgement.[46] There were good reasons for him to minimise any input; the text gained in authority if presented in the authentic voice of a holy woman. Moreover, especially as regards the publication of the first book, he may have feared adverse repercussions, which might be minimised if he could present himself as essentially a mere copyist.

It is the contention of the present work that the content and argument of *The Book* were, from long before its commencement, shaped by the precepts of a clerical coterie in Lynn, though they may not have always realised what effects they would have, what the end product would be, or entirely approved of the contents. It is notable that the last events recorded in *The Book* were the condemnation by her confessor of her failure to consult him about her journey abroad and her reconciliation with him and her friends. The Margery we are presented with would never have launched herself into the literary deep without having been freighted with the spiritual guidance and learning of her confessors. At the end, she is shown peacefully at anchor at the feet of the survivor among them.[47]

The Book of Margery Kempe has often, as I have said, been treated at face value as an autobiographical fragment. Autobiographies from any age pose peculiar problems for the historian, not only from deliberate falsification and lapsed and false memory, but from the basic urge to construct the evolution of a distinct personality filtered through the necessarily subjective interpretation of experience. This urge, as we shall see, had a particular imperative in what was the leading genre of medieval autobiography, the religious sort. The period, though not prolific by post-Renaissance standards in the production of autobiographical writing, does have some notable examples. The *apologia pro vita sua* composed by, or written in the name of, a public figure, a genre of classical origins, was not unknown. A fourteenth-century example, concerned with politics, war and diplomacy, is the *Vita Karoli Quarti imperatoris ab ipso Karolo conscripta*, in which the Emperor Charles IV (d. 1380) described his early political and military struggles.[48] More commonly, autobiographical fragments are found inserted in chronicles and biographies, describing episodes in which the author had participated or had witnessed. The anonymous chaplain who wrote the *Gesta Henrici Quinti* vividly recollected the emotions which he had experienced during Henry V's great victory over the French, the battle of Agincourt (1415).[49]

There is, indeed, a good deal which is similarly descriptive of incident in *The Book* – one reason for its modern appeal. However, in essence it is an example of autobiographical genres which are more characteristically medieval, and some of which had notable female practitioners. These sorts focused on exploring and analysing the motives and states of mind of their subjects, albeit within a religious frame. Self-examination in the context of God's providential scheme was encouraged by the elaboration of the practice of confession. Professor Colin Morris has traced the process by which contrition, which required self-knowledge, became essential to penance, and how penitential motivation came to inspire autobiographical writing.[50] For changes to be wrought in the soul, it was necessary to analyse the roots of past failings in their deepest recesses, by reconstructing past life. This was often seen in terms of distinct phases – the insouciant frolicking on the broad highway to damnation, the experience of conversion to a better way, the struggles with temptation and the joyful progress along the narrow and difficult path, led by the light of Christ's grace.

Confessional autobiographical fragments are related to this mentality. An overtly penitential example is the work written in 1354 by Henry of Grosmont, Duke of Lancaster (cousin of Edward III), *Le Livre de Seyntz Medicines*, which may have been written, Kenneth Fowler suggests, as a task set for him by his confessor. It is an allegory, 'in which the author, after taking stock of himself, reveals to the Divine Physician and his assistant the *Douce Dame* the wounds of his soul, that is his five senses, each of which is infected by the seven deadly sins . . . and then suggests and prays for the remedies appropriate to each cause of infection'. He incorporated into the work many experiences from his career.[51]

A related and deeply introspective vein of autobiography sprang from the development (and spread, particularly from the twelfth century onwards) of the kind of devotion known as 'contemplative'. In the fourteenth and fifteenth centuries lay elites, who had increasing access to devotional texts in the vernacular, showed enthusiasm to learn about and indeed practise contemplative devotion. Exemplary and instructional texts (and, doubtless, priestly guidance) enabled the devout to essay its techniques. Through analysis of one's sinfulness, and progressive and affective meditation on aspects of the deity, the aim was to free the soul from the clog of sensual desires, redirecting thought and emotion to a deep understanding of the love of God, from which flowed an austere and charitable way of life. Some spiritually privileged 'contemplatives' were vouchsafed revelations in their soul, in the form of divine messages and sacred visions. Dr Michael Clanchy has noted the exhortation to his readers by St Bernard of Clairvaux to turn their attention inwards and read in 'the book of experience': 'He asked whether any of his monks had received the intimate experience of a kiss from the mouth of Christ'.[52]

To give others the benefit of such divine intimations, it was desirable to have revelations written down accurately and to help to validate them by relating something of the recipient's spiritual circumstances. From the twelfth century onwards holy women were among the foremost in developing this sort of devotion and having it recorded. However, their autobiographical reflections are often so single-minded in their intro-spectiveness that they provide few indications of the subject's exterior circumstances. As in the case of Margery's contemporary Dame Julian of Norwich, we may be left with sketchy impressions of their lives, unless the contemplative wrote other kinds of works, or works were written about him or her. We have, besides, lives of female contemplatives and ascetics who left no autobiographical writings, written by a priest to promote the cause of their sanctity; these painstakingly attempt to reconstruct a good deal of the subject's spiritual insight because this was at the core of their sanctity.[53]

The Book is to be placed within these devotional genres. It has often struck readers familiar with contemplative literature as distinctly odd and eccentric in its combination of highly coloured anecdotal recall of the worldy vicissitudes of its subject and rapt accounts of inner congress with the deity and the sacred. Yet autobiographical genres were not well established and firmly fixed; this freed 'unlearned' layfolk in particular to work to a model with which they felt comfortable and were able to develop to fit their circumstances. Henry of Grosmont may have taken as his model a work by Robert Grosseteste, bishop of Lincoln (d. 1253), which compared the body to a castle. However, Henry 'adapted the metaphor to his subject in an altogether independent way'.[54] What may appear to us bizarre and garishly colourful about *The Book* (though contemporaries are unlikely to have reacted in this way) arises from its particular, highly personal combination of the two devotional autobio-graphical genres – the confessional and the contemplative.

This combination produces a rich brew of evidence about experience and personality, whose verisimilitude is enhanced by the strong authorial voice, exuberant and quirky, but impressively consistent and seemingly artless. However, we must take into account the insistent concern the author doubtless felt to conform to stereotypes of the penitent and the contemplative, and to refrain from bucking the trends presented by her literary exemplars. In *The Book*, experience has been carefully selected and crafted, honed over many years to project a didactically driven, complex and coherently constructed model of a personality. It would be wise to start reading *The Book* with the working premiss that what we have is a tantalisingly artificial image of the 'real' Margery Kempe, even as regards (rather, especially as regards) her spiritual personality. In this, *The Book*'s prime sphere, some splashes of subjectivity would be welcome: apparent spontaneity is controlled by the rigid justificatory and didactic purposes. The interpretations put upon relationships and the accounts of incidents must be treated with a high degree of historical scepticism. For instance, we have so far no independent evidence that, as *The Book* relates, Margery was examined by Archbishop Arundel of Canterbury and twice by Archbishop Bowet of York. Indeed, the general circumstances in which the alleged interviews took place make it entirely plausible that they actually happened. However, *The Book*'s accounts of their tenor, and the words and attitudes attributed to the participants, may be highly fictionalised in order to enhance its agenda concerning the truth of her revelations and the persecutions she endured, and to tickle the fancies of the intended readership.

There is a factor conditioning *The Book* which guarantees that it provides a sort of autobiographical verisimilitude. The assumption is made here that the intended auditors and readers of *The Book* included people from Lynn. For the holiness of the devout woman to be generally accepted, it had to be recognised in the society where she normally functioned. In a community the size of a large modern English village, in which Margery, from one of its most prominent families, lived for most of her long life, she must have been a well-known figure. If *The Book* was to carry any conviction there, the figure of Margery it presented needed to be a credible one. Care had to be taken to make her conversation and behaviour recognisable. More interestingly, their rationale had to be expounded in terms and ways which fitted in with the cultural norms and aspirations of the elite and populace. For the historian, it is *The Book* as a notable achievement of urban culture which is of supreme importance. Here we have a striking expression of mentalities in King's Lynn in the 1430s, whose artifice, and whose unconscious assumptions, give us insights into the minds of its intended public as well as its promoters.

Why produce yet another book about Margery Kempe? My interest comes from the angles of social and political history. I am intrigued about the social contexts within which *The Book* was produced and in which it positions Margery's adventures of mind and body. My enquiry is directed principally to understanding the possible ways in which knowledge of these contexts can augment our understanding of *The Book*, and the extent to which *The Book* can be used to illuminate them. I do not wish to underestimate the work that others have done in relating *The Book* to its socio-cultural environment. Above all, the notes which Meech and Allen provided for their edition are a mine of information. However, hopefully there is space for a book on the subject. Hopefully, too, focus on it will help to supplement the research of fellow workers in the field, advancing understanding of the ways in which *The Book* can be useful to readers by relating it to the outlook and concerns of men and women on the staithes of Lynn and along the highways and byways of Christendom.

The plan which I have followed is to sketch out first at some length the social and political background in Lynn in the later fourteenth and early fifteenth centuries, then to relate Margery's family and mentality to it. This leads on to a consideration of her social roles. An outline of the position of the Church in Lynn leads on to a discussion of the piety of *The Book*. Thereafter Margery is launched on her travels, from the perspective in particular of what they tell us about a provincial society's view of and relations with the world.

I have adhered to the chronological framework to Margery's life worked out by Meech and Allen, though because of the nature of the text, question marks remain about the dates and sequence of many events described in it.

chapter 2

LYNN AND THE BRUNHAM FAMILY

The Lynn of Margery Kempe was one of England's leading ports. Its population in 1377 has been estimated as 4,691, about 1,300 less than that of Norwich, which, with York and Bristol, ranked as the largest and most populous English towns after (a long way after) London. The sizes of loans which the community of Lynn made to the Crown on occasion suggest that it had one of the largest concentrations of urban wealth in England; for instance, in 1386 the loan made by Lynn to Richard II equalled that lent by Norwich, and was less than the amounts lent by only five other urban centres. In 1426, a group of influential parishioners estimated the number of communicants as around 3,900 – they are likely to have excluded children below the age of at least ten.[1]

The principal burgesses had a strong sense of their stake in the borough's hallowed corporate rights and mercantile privileges. They considered that they had governing responsibilities and an elitist status, reflected in their roles in communal ceremonies, secular and religious, and in their grandiose lifestyle. They cultivated a variety of collective and individual links with kings, magnates, the gentry society of Norfolk and comparable mercantile elites. Some of them were particularly well known in Norwich, London and Danzig (now Gdansk). It is typical of their aspirations to cosmopolitan sophistication and their hierarchical pretentiousness that the brass of Robert Braunche (d. 1364) and his wives, Letitia and Margaret, in St Margaret's church, is one of the largest brasses surviving from medieval England and was probably made in Tournai and imported through Bruges. It was of a type popular with Hanseatic merchants. Robert and his ladies (each with her lapdog at her feet) are richly and elegantly dressed. Below the three imposing figures, the scene of a royal banquet is engraved, with birds fit for a king and his nobles – peacocks – being served.

The eminent of Lynn thought they knew all about gracious living. Concern for the minutiae of status, bound up with office-holding, is reflected in the unregenerate Margery's reproaches to her husband that she was come of 'worthy kindred' and that he should not have married her, for her father had been mayor and alderman of the Trinity Gild. She was determined to maintain 'the worship of her kindred' and had 'full great envy' that her neighbours should be arrayed as well as she.

Presumably she continued to wear 'pompous array', such as 'gold pipes on her head and her hoods with the tippets were dagged [slashed]. Her cloaks also were dagged and laid with divers colours between the dags that it should be the more staring to men's sight and herself the more be worshipped'. Yet despite the disparagement of her husband's family, they belonged to the same status group in Lynn, the highest.[2]

In the decades before *The Book* was written, Lynn and its elite in particular had endured difficult times. Relations with the overlord of the borough, the bishop of Norwich, had gone through one of their periodic crises, and there had been a prolonged and bitter struggle within the borough community over the form of constitution, complaint focusing on the degree of control exercised by a rich and close oligarchy, and on the policies which they had pursued. Margery had been born into this oligarchy; *The Book* makes clear that she had strong views about the standing and achievements of her family. The background of secular life and trends in Lynn needs to be explored in order to understand the position of Margery's family and the formation of the social mentality displayed in *The Book*, facilitating an appreciation of its sometimes opaque evidence about this urban society.

Environment, economy and society

Lynn is situated on the North Sea coast, to the south of the great inlet, the Wash. It is on the east bank of the estuary of the broad and highly navigable River Ouse, at a point where a number of rivers and streams discharge into it, forming a pool, or 'lynn'.[3] Before the Norman Conquest, salt workings (salterns) were well established on some of these tidal outlets; there were settlements at Wootton, Gaywood, South, East and North Lynn. In 1086, Domesday Book records, there were twenty-nine salterns on the bishop of Thetford's 'lynn', in his demesne of Gaywood. By the last decade of the eleventh century, the salt marsh running adjacent to the bank of the Ouse between two streams, the Purfleet and, to the south of it, the Millfleet, was sufficiently vigorous in commerce, and populous, to have a market on Saturdays and a fair on St Margaret's day (20 July), which was said in Henry I's charter of confirmation of these marketing rights (1106) to last for three days.[4] About ten years before, Bishop Herbert Losinga (who transferred the seat of his bishopric from Thetford to Norwich) had instituted a parish to serve the inhabitants of his marsh, for which a splendid new church was built. By the mid-twelfth century a port was flourishing on the estuary just north of Purfleet and a distinct settlement was clustering behind it, with its own large marketplace where market was held on Tuesdays. This area (Newland) formed the other main component in the nucleus of the town called until 1537 Bishop's Lynn, and often, simply, Lynn.

Before the end of the thirteenth century, the Holy Trinity Gild (Lynn's pre-eminent gild) had a gildhall to the north of the parish church, St Margaret's, facing it across Saturday Market; this was on the site of the present Guildhall, built substantially in the early fifteenth century, with a bold façade of chequered flint and stone and a great window of seven lights. There the Holy Trinity brethren held their sessions, and so did the borough's governors, the mayor and jurats, sitting in congregation with their fellows councillors and presiding over the Monday court. There were amenities hereabouts. By the mid-fourteenth century there was a conduit in Saturday Market; in 1309 a public latrine had been built near the west end of the church.[5]

Lynn was vulnerable to attack from sea and land; its rapid expansion in the twelfth and thirteenth centuries made it of great value to the bishops and the Crown. Grants of murage (the right for town corporations to tax their inhabitants in order to build defensive walls) were made by Henry III in 1266 and Edward I in 1294. Walls were constructed which enclosed much more than the built-up strip along the Ouse, to take advantage of banks and river lines and to provide protection for watercourses and agrarian land. Only traces of the walls remain; there is the impressive South Gate, whose Tudor rebuilding disguises the fact that it is a structure of the fourteenth and fifteenth centuries.[6]

A prominent feature of Lynn's townscape, which developed in the thirteenth century, was the building of quays (staithes) along the Ouse waterfront, constructed of timber on silt and spoil which had accumulated against the old salt mounds. The staithes were difficult to maintain in good repair and there was dense encroachment on them with the building of warehouses, dwellings and shops. Building plots in Lynn lacked uniformity in size; water courses influenced their configuration. One cannot escape water in the old town of Lynn, as the flood levels in recent centuries marked on the west door of the parish church bear witness. Plots were mostly long and narrow. The houses of the well-to-do were generally constructed out of a mixture of stone and brick rubble, with a considerable degree of timber framing. According to Dr V. Parker, the evidence indicates that 'the standard house plan was "L" shaped, with a long range at right angles to the street, containing the hall, and a short cross-range on the street which probably once contained shops and solars. The front range bridged an entry passage which usually ran the whole length of the tenement, giving access not only to the house, but to the warehouses and outbuildings beyond'. The street façade might have decorative features, such as the fourteenth-century window with delicately sculpted cusps at Number Nine, King Street, projecting wealth and status.[7] One surmises that Margery grew up in a house of this kind, furnished with luxurious imported goods to which merchant venturers had easy access.

Earlier generations of immigrants to Lynn had been attracted largely by the salt workings, but by the end of the fourteenth century their economic importance had been thoroughly eclipsed by opportunities provided by the trade in a variety of commodities, which by c. 1200 was attracting immigrants not just from neighbouring regions but in considerable numbers from across the North Sea. The trade of Lynn flourished in the general expansionary conditions of the twelfth and thirteenth centuries, particularly as a consequence of Lynn's commanding position at the confluence of waterways.[8] Navigation was possible far inland, for example, to Huntingdon, Wisbech and Cambridge: this facilitated the transport of heavy cargoes in bulk, such as grain.

Lynn merchants were great suppliers and purchasers of a variety of commodities across this hinterland. In the 1380s Bishop Arundel of Ely bought fish and timber at Lynn, and sold grain there.[9] In 1392 Henry of Bolingbroke fitted out ships for his voyage to Prussia on the waterfront; merchants and traders in the town supplied him with ships' gear, utensils, victuals and cloth.[10] In 1406–7 Holy Trinity Gild sold millstones (probably imported as ballast in seagoing ships) to the abbess of Denney (Cambs.).[11] In 1407–8 the gild sold a millstone each to William Grene of Mildenhall (Cambs.) and Alan Hubberd of Cambridge, and a consignment of them to John Hake of London.[12] Margery expected to find a boat at Lynn to take her to Waterbeach for one of her visits to Denney abbey, but when she came to the waterfront, she found that all the boats going towards Cambridge had left.[13] Lynn had close trading links with Norwich and London, cities where Margery was on occasion well received. Some Lynn men had business and family links in London and were to be found residing there.[14] John Wesenham was a prominent burgess of Lynn in 1379; he was also a citizen of London.[15] A gruesome and tragic incident in 1417, recorded by a monk-chronicler of St Albans, illustrates the links between Lynn and London. Three beggars kidnapped three little children in Lynn and mutilated them. They intended to exploit the children's misery, begging in London. However, one little boy recognised and shouted out to his father, a merchant visiting the city, who rescued him and had the beggars arrested. They confessed and were hanged for their crimes.[16]

Seagoing trade connected up with Lynn's river system. Ships from Newcastle brought coal and fish, and laded goods for the coastal route to London.[17] The principal thrusts of Lynn's trade abroad in Margery's lifetime were over the North Sea and into the Baltic. Lynn's export staple in these regions was cloth; furs, oil, wax, iron, brass and timber were principal imports. Other goods imported were tables, hats and purses.[18] Grain was an important commodity. William Asshebourne, common clerk of the borough, recorded (undated) an early fifteenth-century petition from the 'merchants of England', requesting that the king, in his reply to letters from the Grand Master of the Teutonic Order (the crusading Order which ruled Prussia), should take into account the scarcity of corn in England and the fact that none of the ample Prussian stocks had been allowed to be exported thither.[19]

German merchants were well established in Lynn. In 1310 the mayor and burgesses had confirmed their privileges as a community and, indeed, some of them had burgess-ship. A group of merchants of the Hanseatic League became established in the town.[20] Relations between the Crown and the League were perennially fraught, mainly as a consequence of conflicts of interest between English traders and the League's North Sea and Baltic members, who were generally backed by the local rulers. The English resented the preferential customs dues paid by the Hanseatics in England, and their attempts to restrict access to the areas in which they tried to maintain a monopoly of trade, such as Iceland.[21] In 1415 the Hanseatics, backed by Eric IX of Denmark and Norway, accused Lynn merchants of having traded illegally at Bergen. This was the staple port to which all fish caught off the Norwegian coast had to be brought, where it was heavily taxed. Trade at Bergen was dominated by Hanseatics, who were trying to squeeze the English out.[22] At Congregation in Lynn on 28 May 1428, all the merchants frequenting Norway entered the Guildhall together and complained that they had been forced to flee by ships threatening them in a warlike manner.[23] Long before then, John Kempe, whose son Margery was to marry, and her putative kinsman, Robert Brunham had experienced the problems of trading in Hanseatic spheres. Kempe was one of the many Lynn men among English merchants trading in Prussia who petitioned the king in 1388 about the alleged ills they had suffered there, especially seizure of their goods.[24]

Yet it would be unwarranted to conclude that hostility was the keynote of relations between Lynn and men from Hanseatic towns. They had rubbed along together, co-operating and squabbling about trade, for generations. Margery's son made a career in Prussia and married locally;

earlier, as an apprentice to a merchant of Lynn, he may have been sent there to learn the business. If he was, it is likely that his master was replicating well-established patterns of mercantile behaviour in Lynn. In Congregation on 14 November 1428, William Style, Thomas Wursted and John Wesenham sought burgess-ship for their respective apprentices, John Heyward, William Curson and Richard Sparke, who were all in Prussia.[25]

Apprenticeship was an important element in the recruitment of Lynn burgesses. There were, indeed, three ways in which they were customarily recruited: through paternity (as in the cases of John Brunham senior and John Kempe junior), through apprenticeship, or by payment of a fine of 40s. In the period from 1342 to 1395, those claiming by paternity never rose above 42 per cent.[26] This suggests that the burgess community had to an extent to open their ranks in order to keep up numbers and sustain communal wealth. Many of those who attained burgess-ship by apprenticeship or purchase came from outside the town. Perhaps the burgesses as a group were barely maintaining their succession in the male line, as, indeed, seems to have been the case with John and Margery Kempe.[27]

The recurrence of epidemic disease probably had significant effects. Lynn was one of the ports of entry for the Black Death in 1349; its ravages were long remembered there. The Franciscan annalist of Lynn noted an epidemic of pestilence in East Anglia in 1361, in which many boys, young people and the rich died. Professor Gottfried has traced a region of endemic disease to the south of the town in the fifteenth century.[28] In Lynn itself, perhaps large-scale storage of stockfish (dried cod and herring) facilitated outbreaks by attracting rats. Christ said to Margery: 'Thou shalt be eaten and gnawed by the people of the world as any rat gnaweth stockfish.' Pestilence, however, is not a preoccupation in Margery's book; it is mentioned only three times. It was among a list of signs which Christ sent people to make them heedful. He told her once when one outbreak of plague was going to occur. When she was unwilling to go to Denney abbey in time of pestilence, He reassured her. This apparent casualness about plague may indicate how normal a feature of life in Lynn it appeared to the composer and potential readers of *The Book*. Fear of storms and fire are much more to the fore, echoing in fearful tone the Franciscan annalist's awed and gloomy notes on the dire effects on Lynn and its neighbourhood of the great wind of 1362, the lightning strike of 1363, the thunderstorm of 1364 and the terrible storm and flood of 1374.[29]

Little evidence has so far been adduced about craft gilds and their roles in the commerce and government of the town. The old gild merchant, the Holy Trinity Gild, traditionally had a close relationship with communal government. It may be that in most trades, gilds were embryonic. Dr Owen concluded that craftsmen there functioned principally to serve the needs of the inhabitants, and those of the port and shipping. Artificers in a variety of trades engaged in popular agitation against urban government in the 1410s, but they did not, apparently, conspire together as brethren of craft gilds. Craftsmen in particular trades may not have been concentrated in sufficiently large numbers to form gilds which attained a high economic and political status. The flow of a wide selection of finished goods through the port, much of whose carrying trade was controlled by the merchants, may have provided stiff competition for denizen craftsmen.

One area of specialisation in Lynn which Dr Owen has identified was that of weavers making coverlets for beds (a commodity doubtless much in demand in Lynn's blustery climate).[30] Only one of the gilds surveyed in 1389 was a craftsman's gild, that of the Ascension (coifmakers), though there were gilds of young merchants (Nativity of St John the Baptist) and shipmen (Exaltation of Holy Cross). Merchants seem to have comprised a large part of the wealthiest section of society in Lynn. In the surviving fragment of the poll tax return for Lynn in 1379, the merchant John Wesenham was assessed at the highest individual amount to be paid in the borough (13s 4d); the two men who paid 6s 8d were mercers, and similarly styled were nine out of the ten men who paid 3s 4d. The highest amount at which 'great merchants dealing with stock and other trade' were assessed throughout the realm was 6s 8d, and 3s 4d may have been the assessment for 'sufficient' merchants.[31]

Communal government and relations with overlords

By the later fourteenth century the government of Lynn had what seemed to be a reasonably settled and stable constitution, apart from difficult and contentious issues connected with the rights of its principal overlords, the bishops of Norwich. The community of the burgesses nominated twelve jurats who on 29 August annually elected the mayor and the four chamberlains (officials entrusted with the borough's financial administration) and various other officials, who took office a month later for twelve months. They also elected a further twelve councillors. The jurats and councillors (the 'Twenty-Four') with the mayor and the alderman of the Holy Trinity Gild formed the 'community of Lynn', entrusted with its government. Meeting frequently in Congregation in the Guildhall, this 'community' acted as a judicial and regulatory tribunal, and as a council considering the implementation of royal mandates and the policies to be pursued towards the outside world. Congregation made leases, appointed tax collectors, assigned revenues, looked after and improved amenities. They elected members of parliament.[32]

Lynn was no exception to the trend that oligarchical rule, characteristic of boroughs, produced popular discontent in the thirteenth and early fourteenth centuries. Dr Owen has noted that grievances were expressed over the imposition of taxation by Congregation, raised to meet the costs of royal subsidies and to carry out works on amenities.[33] The costs of the Hundred Years War pressed heavily on major ports; they had to maintain their defences in good order, and their merchants and shipmen risked trading losses through the impressment of ships and crews, and through enemy attacks at sea. Besides, Lynn had ongoing special needs – the maintenance of water courses and staithes could be costly. What is surprising is that, though its government was dominated by a small group of rich merchants (of whom Margery's putative father, John Brunham senior was a prime example in the later fourteenth century), it was only, it appears, in the 1400s that internal constitutional confrontation became a recurrent feature of borough politics, continuing into the 1420s. A variety of reasons can be put forward for this. As we have seen, there were few strong craft organisations, whose lesser masters and journeymen might provide a natural constituency for articulating grievances. The fact that Lynn was a nodal point for trade along inland waterways may to some extent have cushioned losses and contractions in overseas and coastal trade, mitigating hardships. Moreover, there was a factor in Lynn politics which might have deflected anger away from the ruling elite, and united rich and poor in shared indignation – the sometimes abrasive assertions of the episcopal franchise, in ways which were seen in secular society in Lynn as unjustified and oppressive.

In 1204 King John had granted to the men of Lynn a free borough and gild merchant and the right to hold the two fairs on the feasts of St Margaret and St Nicholas. So Lynn was, albeit in a limited sense, a royal borough, holding some privileges directly from the Crown – one reason for the continuing close relations between Crown and borough, and for the personal interest which some kings (notably, the Lancastrians) took in its affairs.[34] In a sense, it was 'King's Lynn' for centuries before the bishops' franchise was abolished. However, King John's charter had acknowledged and reserved the customs enjoyed by the bishops (and a share held by the Earl of Arundel) and their successors and heirs. The following year the bishop granted the burgesses the liberties held by the town of Oxford, saving his own liberties. The connection was reflected in the community of Lynn's consultation (c. 1410) with their Oxford counterparts over a moot point about the trading rights of 'foreign'

merchants in their charter. The latter's response was that these could only
sell wholesale, to gildsmen and important people, and in times of market
and fair.[35] In the fourteenth century, the bishops exercised a very extensive
franchise. This included jurisdiction over all staithes, water courses and
unbuilt plots. They shared equally with the Earl of Arundel's heirs the
profits of toll, the markets and other customs such as mooring charges.
In 1337 Edward III granted the reversion of a quarter of the Tolbooth
(appurtenant to the castle and manor of Rising) to his son Edward (the
Black Prince). As part of the newly created duchy of Cornwall, it was to
be held by the eldest son of the king, reverting to the Crown when
there was no son. Each toll owner appointed a bailiff to preside in
the Tolbooth (traditionally said to be on the Bishop's Staithe, now the
King's Staithe) – a daily reminder to passers-by of what many regarded
as the irritatingly intrusive power of the bishop.[36] The situation was not
always grasped by those one might expect to have been well informed;
in reply (1399?) to a complaint from the prior of Ely about the tolling
of purchases made by members of his household, the mayor wrote
to him explaining that the Tolbooth was not under the borough's
jurisdiction.[37]

By the later fourteenth century there was an ancient history of friction
with the borough community over the bishop's more extensive (and
probably more consistently and vigorously exercised) franchises. The
burgesses attempted to redefine and curtail episcopal claims, and a watch-
ful eye was kept on what were sometimes claimed to be the over-zealous
and unjust activities of the bishops' officers – a flashpoint for conflict.
Professor Mark Ormrod has outlined the Crown's handling of the
prolonged and thorny issue of the franchise, disputed between Bishop
Bateman and the burgesses from 1346 to 1348, and Edward III's grant
in favour of Bateman in 1350, as an act of grace.[38]

For the first three decades or so of Margery's life the see of Norwich
was occupied by the high-born Henry Despenser, who held it from
1370 until his death in 1406. He was a notably tough-minded prelate,
always on the lookout for opportunities to exercise his martial talents.
In 1377 he was involved in a serious incident in Lynn, which badly im-
paired his relations with the community and was damaging to its finances
and reputation. Thomas Walsingham gave a vivid account of it, perhaps
based on one circulated by the leading burgesses of Lynn in an attempt
to exculpate themselves. For this account squarely puts the blame for
the riot which ensued on the bishop's pride and hotheadedness, and
portrays Lynn's governing elite as prudent and prescient.

According to the chronicler, Despenser visited the town soon after
Easter (Easter Day occurring on 29 March). He was not content with

receiving the customary honours which his predecessors had done, but sought that, as lord of the borough, he should be treated in public with the same honour as the mayor, who was preceded by a macebearer. The cautious response of the *majores* (Mayor and Congregation?) was that they were happy to acquiesce in the bishop's request as long as he sought a grant of this custom from the king or his council, and if it could be introduced without offence to the community. Some of them said they feared the reactions of the common people, since they were fickle and inclined to malice; they felt that they would risk being stoned by a mob. On bended knees they begged the bishop to desist from his intention. The mayor, Richard Houtone, is likely to have been among the *majores* who tried to moderate the bishop's demands; so probably were Margery's future father-in-law, John Kempe, then second in precedence among the jurats, and her putative father, Brunham, who had been elected one of the councillors to assist the mayor and jurats in 1376.

The bishop, being, according to Walsingham, 'young and headstrong', like Rehoboam (the Biblical archetype of the immature ruler), contemptuously rejected their plea and asserted his determination to proceed, despite any opposition from those whom he loftily termed 'ribalds'. He reproached the *majores* for having a timid attitude towards the commons. They replied diplomatically, emphasising that they did not wish to obstruct his rights but that they feared that, if he went ahead, their lives would be put at risk because the people would put the blame on them. The bishop brushed aside their objections and ordered one of his men to bear a mace ahead of him. The procession had not got far before the commons, declaring that his action was contrary to their liberties, closed the town gates, bent their bows and shot at him. It may be that they only intended to scare him off. The account noted that it was in the fading evening light that he was hit, and his horse and one of his men injured. Some of his retinue then fled, abandoning him.[39] One notable feature of this account is its emphasis on the *majores'* apprehensions about the commons, though they may have exaggerated these in the mistaken hope of swaying the bishop's intent. However, if the report was accurate, it provides evidence that tensions existed between the *majores* and commons, anticipating the confrontations between the *potenciores* and the *inferiores non burgenses* which were to erupt in the early fifteenth century.

The version of the riot which Despenser gave in a petition to the Crown, not surprisingly, stressed the violence and evil intent of the rioters. The burden of his complaint was reflected in the terms of a commission of oyer and terminer appointed on 12 June, which was to enquire into his allegations that twenty-one named assailants and others had assaulted him in the town, pursued him into the priory (to which the parish church was attached) with the alleged intention of killing him, besieged him there, killed twenty of his horses (perhaps deliberately targeted rather than their riders) and assaulted his servants.[40] The mayor had to appear before the king's council to answer the bishop's charges against the townsmen. Fortunately, the borough was able to enlist the help of various lords and, above all, the intercession of Joan, Princess of Wales, the mother of Richard II, who, aged ten, succeeded his grandfather Edward III on 21 June 1377.[41] Feelings ran high in the town about the riot. This was one of the few incidents which the Franciscan annalist at Lynn thought worthy of note: he recorded that certain foolish people (*fatuos*) had attacked the bishop and that, as a result, Lynn was put under interdict from 9 June to 9 August.[42] Some burgesses had been involved in the troubles, for in October Congregation appointed a group headed by Brunham (recently elected mayor) to negotiate compensation for two burgesses, William Holmestone and Thomas de Sparham, for the injuries they had received at the hands of members of the bishop's household.[43] These burgesses were not named in the bishop's petition, so it may be that they were either attacked by his men when trying to restore order during the assault or in a separate incident. The grant of compensation certainly suggests that, in the view of the ruling group in Lynn, the violence was not one-sided.

As a result of this lamentable affair, Lynn started the new reign under a cloud, its name for good order besmirched and its communal finances depleted by the need to pay travelling expenses to London, legal fees, and substantial gifts to win the maintenance of great folk.[44] It was perhaps a tribute to the reputation which Brunham had for sound sense, diplomatic skills (which his putative daughter did not inherit) and the possession of contacts in high places that he was elected mayor in August 1377 in these difficult circumstances. It was a tribute to his success as mayor that he was, unusually though not uniquely, re-elected for a further year in 1378.

The disputes with Despenser seem to have been quiescent for the rest of Richard's reign. In his account of the Peasants' Revolt of 1381, the Lynn Augustinian, John Capgrave in his later chronicle noted outrages at Bury, Norwich and Ely, among other places, but none in his home town. It is not clear whether there were disturbances there, but it may be significant that a quarter of the body of Geoffrey Litster, the Norwich dyer hailed as 'King of the Commons', was displayed there. He had been captured and condemned to a traitor's death by Despenser. Men from Lynn were alleged to have been active elsewhere as rebels in Norfolk, exhorting, menacing, extorting and killing. John Coventry, bowyer, sent a message to Nicholas de Massyngham, justice of the peace and collector of poll tax, demanding that he send £10 to the town. John Spanye, *soutere* (cobbler) and cordwainer in the Grassmarket at Lynn, was said to have gone to Snettisham with a band of thirty armed men and incited the men of the vill to rise and search for Flemings (a frequent target of wrath in 1381), to kill them. Ralph Panton, threatened with death by Spanye, promised to pay his servant 10s. Spanye inflicted loss on victims elsewhere. Other Lynn men said to have been 'out' in 1381 were two tailors (Thomas Colyn and Pinchebek), two glovers (Henry Cornish and Walter Prat), John Whetewong, webster, a certain Sadelere, who lived in Cook's Row (*Cokrowe* – near Tuesday Market), Thomas Paynot's son of the same name, and the intriguingly named John Bokeleerplayer. Colyn, Prat, Whetewong and Paynot junior had all been accused by the bishop in 1377 of rioting against him. The Sadelere of 1381 may have been Adam le Sadelere from the Grassmarket, also accused in 1377. Among the artisans of Lynn were men quick to take up arms over public issues and exploit them to their profit. The *majores* of Lynn had reason to fear the 'fickleness' of close neighbours who had strong opinions and limited respect for law.[45]

In this politically volatile period the leading burgesses may have hoped for the protection rather than the wrath of their awesome overlord. They maintained official courtesies with him: in the 1380s he was the recipient of mayoral hospitality.[46] It was not only Despenser's fiery temperament that made him a difficult man to challenge. He had good connections with Norfolk knightly families: some of these may be reflected in the remaining coats of arms (the bishop's and those of several such families) which originally framed what has been termed the Despenser Retable, in Norwich cathedral. This altarpiece comprises five exquisitely painted panels of the Passion and Resurrection.[47] Moreover, the bishop's nephew, Thomas Despenser, was one of Richard II's favourite nobles in his last years, created by him Earl of Gloucester in 1397.

The usurpation of Henry of Bolingbroke in 1399 seems to have triggered a new and prolonged period of confrontation between the bishop and Lynn. This time it was much more serious for him, as the challenges to the ways in which the episcopal liberties were exercised were spearheaded by the *majores*, whose approach contrasted markedly with the mode of humility adopted by their predecessors in 1377. Presumably they were more confident of winning favour from the Lancastrian dynasty. In 1392, as we have seen, Bolingbroke had had his crusading expedition fitted out at Lynn and, before sailing for Prussia from Heacham nearby, had made pious offerings to some of the deserving in the town – an anchoress, the Carmelites and the poor. Foreign threats early in his reign made him specially reliant on the leading maritime communities. The leading men of Lynn organised naval expeditions, with some gratifying results. On 19 May 1400 four Lynn shipowners – John Brandon, William Gideney, Thomas Trussebut and Robert Brunham – were licensed by the Crown to arrest two more ships, in addition to their own, which were at sea by the king's command in order to attack Scottish and Frisian shipping. They had each fitted out their ship (Brunham's was *le Holygost*). A week later, off Berwick, the fleet captured a Scottish ship. Among the prisoners were Sir Robert Logan, Scottish admiral, and David Seton, Robert III's secretary. The exploit was chronicled at St Albans abbey.[48]

On 12 July Henry IV wrote to the mayor (Edmund Belleyetere) and community of Lynn, rejoicing in and giving thanks for their success and asking for their assistance in victualling by sea the army with which he intended to invade Scotland.[49] By contrast, the bishop was out of favour; he had been one of the very few nobles who had raised a military retinue in order to oppose Bolingbroke's challenge to Richard II in 1399. Having mustered a retinue of 62 men-at-arms and 130 archers, he vainly attempted to attack Henry, but had to surrender and was imprisoned briefly. He was suspected of complicity in the plot of January 1400, the aim of which was to restore Richard, and received a pardon.[50]

The new dynasty's benevolence towards Lynn and wariness of Despenser may have emboldened the burgesses to attempt to enlist royal support for their grievances against him. Apparently Belleyetere's successor as mayor, John Wyntworth, and the community petitioned the Crown. On 6 December 1401 the royal council appointed a commission headed by Norfolk knights to enquire about offences allegedly committed against the inhabitants by the bishop and his officers, hindering the mayor and aldermen from enjoying the liberties granted by the king's progenitors. In particular, there was his failure to repair 'le Bysshopstathe', resulting in floods.[51] The commission failed to resolve the issue; on 2 March 1403 a much more high-powered one was appointed to terminate what was described as a long-standing dispute over the staithe between the parties. It consisted of Henry Percy, Earl of Northumberland, his brother Thomas, Earl of Worcester, and two notable Lancastrian servants, the Norfolk knight, Thomas Erpingham and the Keeper of the Privy Seal, Thomas Langley.

The Percies were a new power in East Anglia as a result of the custody which they had received of the Mortimer honour of Clare.[52] Henry IV wrote to the bishop about the commission, asking him to be at Gaywood (his house outside Lynn) on 12 March to meet the commissioners, and telling him that the mayor (Thomas Brygge) and community had agreed to abide by their decision. If the bishop would not comply, Henry said, he would provide a remedy with the advice of his council. Brygge's mayoralty (1402–3) was characterised by hostility to the ways in which episcopal rights were exercised. In reply to an undated letter from the bishop, complaining that Brygge had seized distresses from the latter's Tolbooth officers, taken by them for non-payment of stallage in Tuesday Market, Brygge said it was customary for men and women selling goods there to carry their forms and stools under their arms to and from their houses, without making any payment. He asserted that he had delivered the distress to the bishop's steward, to await his judgement, and he protested that he had no intention of abrogating any of the bishop's rights.[53] Another letter to the bishop from a mayor and the community (whose surviving text is also undated) may relate to this episode. In this, the right of the mayor to govern the market, setting the sale price of herrings and surveying victuals and stalls there, was asserted. Complaint was made about the activities of William Oxenforde and other episcopal officials. They had confiscated stalls and victuals from the market and piled them up inconveniently and obstructively in front of the bishop's gaol. They had set the price of herrings and had charged Lynn merchants toll at the East Gate on beasts bought for their own use at the bishop's fair, held in his manor of Gaywood. These activities, the letter asserted, were against their franchise and custom. They asked the bishop to allow the mayor to have control of the market.[54]

However, Brygge seems to have pursued too aggressive a policy and on one occasion got his fingers burned. It may have been in connection with these events that Henry Prince of Wales (the future Henry V), who was granted his share in the Tolbooth as Duke of Cornwall in 1403, wrote to the bishop: he said that Brygge had appeared before his council and had acknowledged the offence which he had committed against the court of Tolbooth. He had been ordered to make amends to the bishop, the bishop's steward, and to others whom he had offended. The prince asked Despenser to deal leniently with Brygge, as he had submitted humbly. Either Brygge had enlisted the help of the prince's council to mediate on his behalf with the bishop, or the bishop had succeeded in lining up their support. If the latter was the case, their attitude may have reflected admiration on the prince's part for the old ecclesiastical warhorse, the lone survivor of Richard II's few staunch defenders. The prince retained a reverence for Richard's memory. Mayor and community seem to have been anxious to modify the exercise of the prince's stake in their affairs. They petitioned the king to allow them to have the parcel of the Tolbooth held by the prince at farm, as had been the case under its previous holders for a long time. Henry IV acceded and wrote to the prince's council in these terms.[55] He may have been keen to weaken this point of common interest between his son and the bishop.

Henry IV had difficulty in bringing the bishop to make peace with the burgesses of Lynn. He wrote to the bishop acknowledging the latter's notification of an accord which he had made with the commissioners appointed in 1403; the king emphasised that he should carry this out.[56] However, recent events may have reinforced Despenser's obstinacy, whose continuance casts light on the weakness of the authority of a king who was repeatedly treated by leading subjects early in his reign as a usurper. The bishop seems to have been determined to press on with lawsuits against the mayor and community over their alleged seizure of his properties in Lynn. The battle of Shrewsbury (July 1403) at least temporarily asserted Henry's authority over those inclined to rebel. However, the deaths of the Earl of Worcester and Northumberland's son, Sir Henry Percy as traitors terminated the Percy family's influence in Norfolk, perhaps to the bishop's relief. Although in the parliament which met in January 1404, he agreed to cease all process at law against the mayor and community, to Henry's evident irritation he proceeded to do the opposite. He successfully prosecuted an assize of novel disseisin (a form of legal action resting on a claim of unjust dispossession) against the mayor, John Wyntworth, and community, recovering jurisdiction over a large acreage of land and receiving the huge award of 1,000 marks in damages, putting them utterly at his mercy. These matters are outlined in an angry letter which Henry wrote to him, dated 14 July 1404. The king expressed surprise that the bishop had not replied to his letters asking him to suspend the suit, and informed him that the execution of the verdict was in abeyance. He forbade any further action against the mayor and commonalty until the matter was settled with the royal council's advice.[57]

So it appears that in Henry's early years the burgesses of Lynn took an unwontedly bold line in harrying the bishop's officers and challenging his franchise – presumably expressing long pent-up resentment against him personally as well as against the episcopal franchise, in a political climate more favourable to them. Despenser proved a wily and determined opponent, prepared to ignore the king's will. The aged bishop, in his last years, seems to have felt that he had nothing to lose by throwing caution to the wind in defending episcopal rights. A letter which he wrote to a Norfolk justice of the peace suggests that he hoped to rally the support of the gentry, and that he regarded his Lynn tenants as behaving in as disobedient and riotous a manner as they had done in his youth. He wrote that, in a plea between himself and the people of Lynn, they had purchased a writ of *Nisi prius*. Jurors of the country empanelled for the assize to be held in the town were excusing themselves, in fear of their lives, since people in Lynn were uttering dire threats in case they brought in a hostile verdict. His council were similarly reluctant to go to Lynn. Despenser asked his correspondent and other members of the bench to be there with him on the day of the assize to uphold the law.[58] Despite his age, he was prepared once more to confront a mob. His intransigence was to cost his principal opponents, the *majores*, dear. They may have won some measure of popular support for their stand, but the expenses of the litigation involved burdened the community as a whole and were a factor behind the coming internal challenge to their rule. Despenser taught them that in the long run, co-operation with the overlord was more comfortable than confrontation.

The three bishops installed within ten years of his death in 1406 seem to have been inclined to assuage tensions with the burgesses. They were Alexander Tottington (d. 1413), Richard Courtenay (1413–15) and John Wakeryng (1415–25). On 15 June 1414 Henry V's uncle, Thomas Beaufort, wrote to Courtenay reporting the good disposition of the men of Lynn and asking him to be a good lord to them.[59] On 10 July Beaufort wrote to the mayor (Bartholomew Petypas) and burgesses urging them to make a settlement with the bishop; he had been appointed to arrange this.[60] There was a problem in 1425 over the activities of John Newark, bailiff at the Tolbooth, concerning control of the sale of oysters and cod. On 16 March the mayor (John Permonter) informed Congregation that Beaufort had given sentence that mayor and community should have their measure until Newark could prove that they did not have the right to it. The bailiffs were not to take oysters or certain sorts of fish; Beaufort promised to communicate with them and the bishop (Wakeryng) about the matter. Congregation agreed that John Waterden should ride with Beaufort to the bishop with a petition to recover the fish seized by the Tolbooth bailiff; on 2 April, the mayor reported how Waterden had spoken to the bishop in Beaufort's presence about the episcopal bailiffs' seizure of oysters and cod. The bishop agreed that they should desist.[61] The strong personal interest and involvement which Beaufort had developed in the town's affairs was one reason for the bishops to tread warily. There is ample reason for believing John Tilney's words in Congregation on 15 December 1416 about Beaufort's goodwill: 'ther nys no toune in Englond hym wer lother to greve ne take agayn than Lenn'.[62] Moreover, the high-born Bishop Courtenay, during his brief episcopate, was much preoccupied with national affairs. He was heavily involved in diplomacy, and died outside Harfleur during Henry's siege of the port. As one of the king's favourite clerics, he was unlikely to have offended his master's concern for good order by becoming embroiled with the men of Lynn.

In addition, there were now pressing reasons why the latter were anxious to avoid confrontations with Despenser's successors. By the 1410s consensus among the burgesses about the borough constitution had broken down badly, weakening their position and giving bishops as well as the Crown legitimate cause for intervention. Internal peace in the 1420s remained fragile, potentially in need of external support. Another matter of concern for the inhabitants was the need to repair and improve water courses, which required episcopal co-operation.[63] In 1424 Congregation was preparing to do due honour to Bishop Wakeryng as overlord. On 7 April it agreed to present him with a pipe of wine and twenty coombs of oats on his intended arrival in the town.[64] At Congregation on 25 April, it was determined that the community should pay the costs of his visit and that he should dine at the mayor's table. The mayor (Permonter) and his brethren of the Gild of Corpus Christi were to ride out to meet him, clad in scarlet, and the town's macebearer would summon the rest of the community to meet him on foot.[65] Wakeryng is one of only two bishops of Norwich mentioned by name in Margery's book, in a vignette of him visiting the town which presents him in a benevolent light, as an inspiring preacher and compassionate pastor.[66]

Relations with kings and nobles

The Lynn elite appreciated the importance of good relations with kings and nobles. As we have seen, in 1377 they relied in part on the help of the youthful Richard II's mother, Joan Princess of Wales (d. 1385), widow of the Black Prince: Joan Holand, Duchess of Brittany (d. 1384), who in 1384 procured a favour from the Crown for John Brunham, was her daughter. Joan's husband, Duke John, had in 1378 been granted by the Crown the castle and manor of Rising, near Lynn, and the attached share in the Tolbooth of Lynn.[67] This was during Brunham's mayoralty. Perhaps he had made personal links with the princess and the duchess in connection with their husbands' successive tenancies of the Tolbooth. In 1362, as executor of John de Sustede of Lynn, who had leased the prince's share of the Tolbooth, Brunham had made suit to his council concerning £15 owed for the farm: the prince, as a gift, had discharged him of it as executor.[68] Richard II himself does not seem to have made any special ties with Lynn, though he appears to have visited it with his queen, Ann of Bohemia, during the mayoralty of Henry de Betele (1382–3), probably during their progress through Norfolk in June 1383.[69] It may have been in connection with this visit that the Duchess of Brittany procured the favour from the king, her half-brother, for Brunham; the date of the exemption was 8 July.

For most princes and nobles, there were no compelling reasons for visiting Lynn frequently, if at all. It was not on the habitual itineraries of most of them, but it was a convenient place to pass through or stay for pilgrims visiting the shrine of Our Lady at Walsingham, for travellers to and from some parts of Lincolnshire, and for embarkation to ports in northern Europe. Thomas Arundel, bishop of Ely, when based at his castle of Wisbech in August 1383, went for a brief excursion to Lynn, staying overnight.[70] In 1410–11 the town chamberlain accounted for 3s 4d for sweet and red wine provided for Lord and Lady Willoughby during their stay, 'for the honour of the town'. William Lord Willoughby (c. 1370–1409) of Eresby (Lincs.) was a staunch supporter of Henry IV; his wife, Joan Holand, was the niece of Brunham's late benefactress, and former wife of Edward III's son, Edmund of Langley, Duke of York. The chamberlain also accounted in 1410–11 for gifts to other noble visitors, the Yorkshire landowner, William Lord Roos (whose family's devotion to St William of York was to be shared by Margery) and the Northamptonshire landowner, Thomas Lord Zouche.[71] In 1420/21 another Lincolnshire lord formed a close connection with Lynn: the aged Thomas Lord de la Warr (d. 1427), who was a priest (exceptionally for a baron), was received into the Holy Trinity Gild.[72] The Norfolk baronial family whose castle and honour was near Lynn were the Bardolfs: some traces of Wormegay castle remain. Thomas Lord Bardolf (d. 1386) willed to be buried in the Carmelite house at Lynn. His son and heir, Thomas was appointed on a commission of array for Lynn in December 1399, soon after Henry IV's usurpation – John Brunham was one of his four fellow arrayers. However, in 1405 Bardolf joined the Earl of Northumberland in rebellion against Henry; on its failure he fled with the earl to Scotland. He died in 1408 of wounds received at the battle of Bramham Moor (Yorks.), when once again trying to stir up rebellion.[73]

Henry IV and some of his close kinsmen and leading officials seem to have taken a considerable interest in the affairs of Lynn, as their visits to the town suggest. John Capgrave, Augustinian friar of Lynn and chronicler, recalled how he saw Henry's daughter, Philippa (aged twelve), set sail from the port in August 1406; she was on her way to marry Eric IX of Denmark and Norway. The alliance is likely to have been welcomed in Lynn by those interested in North Sea fishing and trade. To see Philippa off, Henry, his queen, Joan of Navarre, his sons, Henry, Thomas and Humfrey, and many other lords and ladies stayed in Lynn for nine days.[74] In 1409 or 1410 the Chancellor of the Realm (Thomas

Arundel, archbishop of Canterbury) was in Lynn, where he dined with the mayor at the borough's expense.[75] His visit was probably in connection with the town's internal disputes, which were long to remain of concern to Lancastrian kings and their councillors. At Congregation on 4 September 1413, it was reported that Thomas Duke of Clarence (Henry V's brother), his wife (Margaret Holand) and their retinue were expected to stay in the town.[76] Henry V was on pilgrimage to Walsingham when he visited the town on 18 April 1421.[77] On 17 July 1424 Congregation discussed arrangements for the reception of the archbishop of Canterbury (Henry Chichele), the Chancellor (Henry Beaufort, bishop of Winchester) and the late Henry V's youngest brother, Humfrey Duke of Gloucester.[78] Henry VI was treading well-worn family paths when he stayed at least one night in Lynn (1 August 1446), coming from Walsingham and on his way to St Edmunds abbey.[79]

The member of the House of Lancaster who visited Lynn most, and who became deeply involved in the borough's affairs, was Thomas Beaufort (1377–1426), half-brother of Henry IV and also younger brother of the bishop of Winchester. The Beauforts were the children of John of Gaunt, Duke of Lancaster (d. 1399) and his mistress Katherine Swynford (d. 1403), who were legitimised in 1397 after their parents' marriage. Thomas Beaufort was highly valued by his royal kinsmen for his military talents and probably too for his upright and austere character. Henry IV had him created Earl of Dorset in 1412, and Henry V elevated him as Duke of Exeter in 1416, trusting him so fully that he willed that he should be his son's guardian. How did Beaufort's close connection with Lynn come about? Part of the answer may lie in his specialisation in naval administration, in a period in which war at sea intensified. On 28 November 1403 he was appointed admiral to the north, an office which he held till 28 April 1406, and on 21 September 1408 he was appointed admiral to the north and to the west for life.[80] The co-operation of the Lynn elite in providing and paying for shipping was valuable to him, especially for duties in the North Sea. On 17 August 1424, the mayor told Congregation that the duke had sent messages that ships needed to leave port to fight enemies who were at sea. There was agreement that the mayor should offer him on the town's behalf one barge and one balinger (similar to a whaling boat). An animated discussion ensued, and it was concluded that the duke should be informed that the merchant adventurers would bear the charge of provisioning the ships. Four days later the mayor related to Congregation that he had spoken to the duke, who was agreeable that an indenture should be made on these terms. The burgesses decided that proclamation be made, assuring volunteers of free provisions and announcing that *Le Goost* and *Le Iamys* were to be prepared, each to have a complement of eighty soldiers and mariners. Arrangements were made for taxing the merchant adventurers.[81]

Beaufort's early connection with Lynn had been strengthened by the grant to him for life in 1405 of Lord Bardolf's forfeited castle, honour and manor of Wormegay, with appurtenances, a grant which in 1408 was converted into one including the heirs of his body. By 1416 he had a house and staithe in Lynn: he then sought remedy from the mayor and burgesses for their poor state, alleging that damage was being done to his property through the flow from the town's mill. No effective measures seem to have been taken, for on 16 December his servant, John Tilney appeared in Congregation, protesting about neglect of previous complaints, 'wherfor he preyeth you with alle the hart possible that ye may certifie my lord your avis and purpos in this cas ye or nay'.[82] His first official appointment concerned with the internal affairs of the borough was apparently that of 7 February 1406, soon after his acquisition of Wormegay. This commission was to enquire into disturbances – an early phase of the dissensions which wracked the town for so many years.[83] Beaufort was to be heavily involved in trying to resolve these. When he was Chancellor (31 January 1410–20/21 December 1411), he summoned the burgesses to appear before him, and on 14 June 1415 the mayor, Robert Brunham, and the community submitted all their differences to his and Bishop Courtenay's arbitration and bound themselves to observe the award.[84] In December 1417, Beaufort was appointed to head the commission of peace for Lynn, but he was not to be reappointed when a new commission was made out in February 1422.[85]

The patronage of a great lord of the blood royal, highly esteemed by both Henry IV and Henry V, was of great value to the urban community and to individual members of it. The community lobbied Beaufort for support for favours from the Crown, especially when he was Chancellor. For instance, on 11 July 1410 the mayor (John Brandon) and the alderman (of Holy Trinity Gild, petitioned him for a reduction of the community's contribution to a grant to the Crown.[86] On 16 April 1410 or 1411, the mayor, alderman and burgesses, addressing him as Chancellor, wrote concerning their attempts to obtain commissions about nuisances, and the appointment of justices of peace for the liberty.[87] Individual members of the Lynn elite sometimes successfully sought Beaufort's intervention in suits within the borough. In Congregation on 11 August 1424, the mayor, John Wesenham, and Robert Springwell, executors of Robert Brunham, declared how Edmund Benet had injuriously arrested the mayor's goods for a debt owed to him by Brunham. At Benet's insistence, Beaufort had sent a mandate ordering the executors to render account.[88] In Congregation on 2 April 1425, Beaufort's letter to the mayor (John

Permonter) and jurats was read, ordering them to make an end of the suit pending between Margaret Galyon and Thomas Middilton.[89]

The community was assiduous in courting Beaufort with presents and entertainments. Possibly in 1410–11, they sent wine to him at Hardwick on his way to Lynn, and more for him to drink at Bawsey pond, where he fished. His wife, Margaret was also entertained in the town.[90] On 25 November 1410, the mayor (Robert Botekesham) gave dinner to Beaufort, and on 4 July 1412 the latter wrote to the mayor (Roger Galyon) and community, recommending to them his minstrel, Grene Piper.[91] In July 1424 Congregation determined the order and array in which the borough officers were to meet Beaufort and decided to present him with twelve cygnets, twenty-four young herons, the same number of bittern and, for his dogs, four capons.[92] The burgesses were keen to enlist his help in their long quest to secure repayment of a loan of 400 marks which the borough had made to Henry V in 1415; later in the month, the mayor and two other burgesses (one of them William Herford, who had been executor to John Brunham) were deputed by Congregation to ride to him to discuss the matter, together with citizens from Norwich, which had also made a loan to Henry V.[93] Beaufort, indeed, had many other interests and involvements besides Lynn: he was heavily engaged in the Lancastrian enterprise in France. His will of 1426, made at his manor of Greenwich, reflects his familiarity with London and his landed interest in Suffolk; he had arranged for his burial in St Edmunds abbey. His many pious bequests to religious houses included a number in Norfolk, but none specifically in Lynn, which is not mentioned in the will, though other evidence suggests that he may have had cordial relations with at least one friary there.[94] An undated list of members of his household includes a good number of Norfolk knights and esquires, but no servants, it appears, from the borough. However, John Tilney, Bachelor of Civil Law, who was to serve for a number of years as his deputy in his court of admiralty, had been member of parliament for Lynn twice in 1413, in 1414 and 1415.[95] *The Book of Margery Kempe* contains a tantalising hint that Beaufort's links with the burgess elite may have had a cultural side, bringing about interchanges in religious modes between courtly and bourgeois circles.[96]

Internal conflicts

It was fortunate for Lynn that during its time of internal troubles it acquired such an eminent and well-regarded secular patron. Major tensions between apparently well-defined status groups became a set pattern in the 1410s, and continued more sporadically into the next decade. The conflicts centred on constitutional and financial issues. Specifically in dispute were the terms of admission to the burgess-ship, and qualifications for participation in mayoral elections and related appointments, and for election as a jurat. Accusations were made about the ways in which borough funds had been spent, and about the claims made on them by individuals for compensation. Broadly speaking, agitation was directed at constitutional reform to undermine the domination of urban government by a closely connected group of wealthy burgesses, and at their alleged exploitation of office more in their own interest than in the whole community's.[97] They were defined in contemporary Lynn urban records as *potenciores*, the discontented as *mediocres* and *inferiores non burgenses*. The prolonged breakdown in the customary degree of harmony necessarily drew in interested external parties – the Crown, the bishops of Norwich, magnates and gentlefolk. A fractured, disordered society in a leading town adversely affected the reputations of its lords, patrons and well-willers, as well as those of its community and of individual burgesses. It was a weakness to the realm. Opinions about the issues among interested outside parties varied: in this period, royal councillors and lords did not necessarily jerk their knees in favour of oligarchical rule in towns. Those initially under attack, the *potenciores*, had to lobby hard for outside support, as, indeed, did their critics.

In a memorandum drawn up for the mayor and community in 1412, after control of government by *potenciores* had been ousted, it was said that controversies had arisen over oppressions allegedly committed by Robert Botekesham (who had recently died) and certain *potenciores* during his mayoralty (1410–11).[98] However, it did not mention that there had been riots and unlawful assemblies several years before, in which artificers from a variety of crafts had participated, some of them well-to-do. Grievances aired may have been a foretaste of those which were to polarise opinions later. A petition by a group to king and lords in parliament relates to these earlier troubles. John Oxenford, John Cressyngham, Thomas Hal[l]e, William Wygenhale, Robert Smyth, Thomas Capmaker and William Cole said that they had been before the royal council to seek a remedy for the dispute between the 'grauntz Gentz de la Ville' and themselves and other 'povres communes' of the town. However, the great men had procured a commission which resulted in the suppliants' imprisonment. They asked to be delivered, to answer any charges and to give information to redress ills, for the common profit of the town. The response was that they were to be delivered. Some (probably all) the agitators were craftsmen; Oxenford was a fuller, Cressyngham a skinner, Halle a webster, Wygenhale a tailor. In February 1406 the king wrote to his council, enclosing a petition from the mayor and burgesses concerning the rebellion of Cressyngham and others of Lynn. Henry ordered the Council to examine the petition and ensure the punishment of the rebels.[99]

In Easter term following, the case of an indictment by jury for riot and conspiracy in the town and its suburbs was dealt with in the court of King's Bench. According to the record of the case, Cressyngham, Halle, Robert Clipston, smith, Capmaker, Wygenhale and others (unknown) to the number of 300 men of the town (the number probably a formulaic exaggeration) had on 21 October 1405 risen up there and continued to riot for three days, despite proclamation by the mayor, John Wyntworth, Robert Botekesham, one of the keepers of the peace in the town, and other keepers. The alleged rioters had the common bell rung to attract support, and paraded around, seeking out and uttering threats against Thomas Brygge, Richard Kent and other burgesses. Brygge, who armed himself to go to the mayor's assistance, was menacingly confronted by the rioters, but some of those present saved him from harm. The rioters focused on preventing the export of corn laded in a ship by Robert Brunham, Kent and other burgesses for the relief of Bordeaux. With the consent of the burgesses, the mayor proclaimed that the corn was to be sold in Lynn at sixpence a bushel. But the rioters were not content with this: they insisted on a market price of fivepence. They tried to pressure Wyntworth into having it proclaimed that no one was to initiate legal process over their proceedings. They said that if anyone brought letters patent ordering that the corn should be handed over, they would make him eat the seal attached to the letters. Over the three days they intimidated the burgesses by their perambulations, with a trumpet playing before them.

This account of events suggests that new life was breathed into the demonstrations during the following week by the arrival of the fuller, John Oxenford and John Wynke, pattenmaker, who had been out of town. They apparently tried to turn what had basically been a food riot into a scheme for constitutional change in the borough. At a series of meetings there and in the suburbs the pair allegedly masterminded a conspiracy to subvert the mayoral authority and the liberties and privileges of the burgesses, as granted by kings. They aimed, too, to destroy Brygge, Kent and other 'burgenses potenciores' who might resist their plans. The record goes on to recount how the five named as instigators of the first riots made appearances in King's Bench. In May they pleaded not guilty. In September they were released by the court on sureties. They were told that they would receive pardons. Letters patent recording pardons to them, to Oxenford and also to Edmund Goldsmyth, as well as John Maydeston and Thomas Feltwell, both goldsmiths, were dated 14 October 1406.[100] The association of goldsmiths with more menial craftsmen foreshadows the alliance against the *potenciores* which was to emerge so strongly; some of the ringleaders in this earlier agitation were to participate in that alliance. The skinner, Cressyngham and the tailor, Wygenhale were among the *inferiores* involved in the attempt to make a settlement with the *potenciores* in 1411. So was the goldsmith, Thomas Feltwell who was to be denounced in 1416 as an incorrigible plotter against the *potenciores*.[101]

As we have seen, tensions once more became critical during Botekesham's mayoralty, royal summonses being issued in 1410–11 for the appearance of the parties before Thomas Beaufort as Chancellor. Burgesses emerged as critics of the establishment: the troubles of 1405 may have suggested to the discontented among them ways in which popular feeling could be exploited. Their heavy and long-lasting involvement in agitation was to give the movement to oust or modify the control exercised by a powerful coterie a coherent constitutional programme. A burgess who early on may have become prominent for his criticism of the governing *potenciores* was Bartholomew Petypas. By a mandate dated 18 July 1410, he was summoned before king and council to answer charges against him.[102] In August 1411 Roger Galyon (*mediocris*), who stood for the popular interest, was elected mayor, and in December *potenciores, mediocres* and *inferiores* bound themselves to abide by the ordinance to be made for government by a group of eighteen drawn from each of their groups. Among these were Robert Brunham (*potencioris*) and John Brunham the elder's executor, William Herford. John himself was second named among the *potenciores* who went surety, and John Brekeropp, who married the widow of Margery's brother-in-law, Simon, was among the *mediocres*. First-named among the *inferiores* was John Wyrham, possibly the 'good man' who figures fleetingly in an important incident in *The Book*, which occurred ten years later.[103] However, a John Wyrham, mercer, became a burgess in the year 1411–12.[104]

At a meeting at the Guildhall on 8 April 1412 it was decreed that decisions taken by a quorum of at least ten of the Eighteen would be valid – a modification which was to work in favour of the 'popular' interest. The quorum speedily reached partisan conclusions. It disallowed claims for expenses in office of five recent mayors – Edmund Belleyettere, Thomas Waterden, John Wyntworth, Thomas Brygge and the late Robert Botekesham.[105] When Belleyetere had been made a burgess in 1364, he had been an apprentice of John Brunham; at his death in 1416/17, Robert Brunham was one of his feoffees.[106] The quorum denounced Robert, among other mayors, for having spent large sums in the conflict with Bishop Despenser without the consent of the community and to its prejudice and impoverishment. In future, they decreed, there would be financial controls on mayoral expenditure. Also, the *inferiores* were to enjoy the episcopally bestowed privileges which had been denied to them. These ordinances, agreed by a majority of the Eighteen, were set down in a document dated 20 May, on which day they were assented by the mayor (Galyon) and community; in July members of the three status groups made separate written confirmations. The memorandum recording these proceedings, mentioned above, concludes with a note of their submission in Chancery and confirmation by decree of the Chancellor, now Archbishop Arundel, dated 17 November 1412. The borough constitution had been effectively changed to allow a wider participation in decision-making.[107] In August Galyon had been re-elected mayor, and he was succeeded in 1413 by Petypas (*mediocris*), who had been one of the Eighteen. Petypas came to be regarded by his opponents among the *potenciores* as the prime fomentor of faction, the ringleader of a 'gang of four' named in indictments of 1415 as William Hallyate of Gaywood, John Bilney of South Lynn (*mediocris*, 1411–12), and John Tilney the younger, of Lynn. The first three were said to be merchants, but Tilney was styled 'husbandman' – perhaps insultingly, and certainly so if he was the John Tilney associated with Bishop Courtenay and Thomas Beaufort or his son.[108]

The settlement of 1412 did not bring lasting peace; some *potenciores* proved implacable. They seem to have become particularly incensed by the new regime's widening of opportunities for admission to the burgessship. The series of indictments made in 1415 by two juries at Swaffham (Norfolk) reflect their partisan views. According to one jury, the 'gang of four' had procured Galyon's subsequent nomination and election as mayor in 1412, flouting the customs granted by King John, supported forcefully by a large crowd of burgesses and others. They had maintained Galyon unlawfully in office for two years, and during his mayoralties they had admitted inhabitants of the town (*forinsecos*) of small worth or repute to the liberty without the due consent of the burgesses. It was also alleged that, during Petypas's mayoralty, they had used the town's common seal in the Guildhall, without the consent of the burgesses or previous mayors, in order to make out letters of attorney to two of them, Bilney and Tilney, and others, empowering them to initiate certain suits and release common debts of the town.[109]

According to the other Swaffham indictment, the 'Four' had led an attack on the brethren of Holy Trinity Gild on 18 June 1413. In the run-up to the 1414 election, on the evening of 20 August, Thomas Waterden, John Wyntworth, Thomas Brygge and John Spicer were with other 'honourable gentlefolk' in John Warner's tavern. Allegedly the 'gang of four' approached them, menacingly arrayed and accompanied, and presumably broke up their meeting. As Waterden and his companions went to their lodgings, with links borne before them, they were ambushed and assaulted by persons unknown to the jurors, except for a glazier and a spurrier. The gaolkeeper, John Frevylee, alerted by the disturbance, arrested the assailants and took them off to the town gaol. But whilst he was absent, Petypas and the other three indicted, accompanied, as was usually alleged in the indictment, by a great multitude, came to the gaol and released those arrested. Nine days later, a Privy Seal letter was dated which ordered the sheriff of Norfolk, Edmund Oldhall, and local gentle-folk to scrutinise the forthcoming election. If the jurors are to be believed, this really rattled the popular party and its leaders. When Oldhall and his fellows arrived, the 'Four', together with a large, armed crowd, menaced and insulted them and the 'good' burgesses. They were further terrorised when the bridges were broken down and armed guards put on the town gates – to prevent any more gentlefolk from coming to the sheriff's aid, according to the jurors. The sheriff and 'good' burgesses were denied access to the Guildhall, the usual place of election. Feelings were presumably running high against the presence of outsiders who were clearly thought to be unsympathetic to the popular cause and whose presence might embolden *potenciores* to attempt to disregard the 1412 ordinance. So the election in 1414 was held in the house of Augustinian friars, instead of in the Guildhall, as was customary, 'in contempt of the king and the liberties of the town'. In fact, the mayor who emerged, John Lakynghith, was an elderly and infirm *potencioris*, aged about seventy-five. Whatever the truth of the lurid accusations made by the jurors in 1415, it seems that Petypas and his allies were concerned to appease hostile opinion; perhaps they thought that the arthritic Lakynghith could be manipulated.[110]

Nevertheless, the factions remained at loggerheads. *Potenciores* were doubtless behind an attempt to discredit Master John Tilney, Bishop Courtenay's clerk. On 1 October 1414 he was released from imprisonment on sureties (who included Petypas, Hallyate and Galyon). Accusation had been made against him to Henry V in person; he, the mayor and burgesses were pledged to appear before the king.[111] On 25 January 1415, according to the second Swaffham indictment, Petypas, abetted by Hallyate, Bilney and Tilney, among others, assaulted the mayor and other good burgesses in Guildhall, with his dagger (*baselard*) drawn. Lakynghith was thrown to the ground and trampled, to the terror of the 'good' burgesses and former mayors. Petypas and his allies continued to be so unpleasant on a daily basis to Lakynghith and his colleagues that they did not dare hold Congregation in Guildhall. This last allegation receives some support from records of the proceedings of Congregation, according to which, two days after the alleged trampling of Lakynghith, he summoned a group of *potenciores* to his house. The first-named of these was Robert Brunham, the alderman of Trinity Gild. Lakynghith wanted advice about how to punish those who had suddenly left the Guildhall on the 25th (presumably when Congregation was in session) and made a clamour in St Margaret's church to raise the people. They were identified as Walter Caundeller, John Taillour and Richard Essex, tailor, none of whom had figured among the long list of sureties who several years before had agreed to abide by the ordinances of the Eighteen. Order was made to Robert Beer, macebearer, to imprison two of the accused; with well-considered humanity, Taillour was spared on account of old age.[112]

As in Henry IV's later years, in 1415 the Crown once more embarked on strenuous efforts to compose the divisions. Lakynghith was summoned to appear before the king's council on 10 February, but as he was in his seventies and suffering from arthritis, he deputed Robert Brunham to appear in his place.[113] The Council failed to secure agreement between the factions.[114] Back in Lynn, the mayor and his allies attacked recent reforms. In Congregation on 7 March, in the presence of the prior of Lynn (Thomas Hevenyngham, perhaps representing the interests of Bishop Courtenay) and a large number of burgesses, Lakynghith proposed the administration of an oath to burgesses admitted during the mayoralties of Galyon and Petypas, in order to ascertain whether they had paid the customary entry fee. Robert Brunham was absent from Congregation, allegedly ill.[115] On 10 May the royal commission to enquire into dissensions, which produced the Swaffham indictments, was issued. Its text exasperatedly recited the failure of the parties to respond satisfactorily to the efforts of the king and council to settle matters; they remained puzzled, the writ asserted, as to the true cause of the dissensions. The government, apparently heartily sick of the affair, and preoccupied with the intensification of confrontation with the French Crown, had remitted matters to a rather low-powered group of Norfolk gentry.[116] They and their jurors seem to have acted wholly in the interests of the *potenciores* for, as we have seen, the jurors mounted a comprehensive attack on the conduct of the leaders of the popular party, accusing them of committing and inciting serious breaches of the peace.[117] This was no solution. In June, Bishop Courtenay and Beaufort were appointed to make an award in the disputes. They failed. The choice of mayor in August was apparently marked by controversy. John Bilney was elected with 'popular' support, but against the royal will.[118]

The commotion of 30 September 1415 and its aftermath

The man who became the focus for this new crisis was Margery's possible kinsman, Robert Brunham, who had been occupying the office of mayor, presumably because Lakynghith had become too debilitated. On 26 September 1415 three royal writs were issued: one ordered Brunham to continue as mayor, another ordered Bilney not to meddle with the mayoralty, and a third ordered Brunham to cite a group of twelve, including Bilney, Petypas and Hallyate, into Chancery.[119] Mayhem erupted when these writs were delivered to Brunham. This was on 30 September, when he was in the Holy Trinity Gild Chapel in St Margaret's parish church, to hear Mass. William Asshebourne, common clerk, who was at the centre of events that day, drafted a vivid account of them. Brunham ordered the two writs concerning the mayoralty to be read out in the chapel by Asshebourne, and gave the other one to Robert Beer, the doorkeeper, for him to execute. Voices were raised; people flowed in and out of the chapel, clamouring that the town's liberties should be preserved. Prior Hevenyngham (who, *The Book* said, proved sympathetic to Margery's piety) intervened after the procession of the clergy, ordering the crowd to be quiet and leave so that the service was not interrupted. He invited Brunham to hear Mass in the chancel. In the stalls there were John Littlebury, a Lincolnshire knight who had performed distinguished service in the chamber of Henry IV's household, and none other than Bartholomew Petypas! Was he lobbying for support at court and in ecclesiastical circles?

Despite the prior's exhortation, the crowd in the body of the church had grown. After the blessing, Petypas bluntly urged Brunham to go to Guildhall for the ceremony to take the customary oath of Bilney as mayor. Brunham replied that the Chancellor (Henry Beaufort, bishop of Winchester), when he was last in Lynn, had ordered him to continue in office until further order from the Council and that the order had now been repeated under penalty of £1,000. He referred to the writ addressed to Bilney and explained that he had given it to Beer for delivery. Requests were apparently being made for a Congregation to be held in Guildhall, but Brunham expressed a prudent reluctance to go there whilst the people were so aroused. When Petypas asked him for the door key, he prevaricated. He insisted that he would continue in office – he did not intend to lose £1,000. Brunham was in a fearful dilemma. 'Ignorant people' were coming in and out of the church, making remarks which Asshebourne felt were inappropriate to record. At the prompting of Littlebury and Petypas, Brunham agreed to go to his house in 'le Mercerrowe' (near the former residence of Margery's father) to collect the key as long as his safety was assured. But when he left the church and was in the street;

> the peple gederid so thikk and so meche that with strengthe the thrast hym forthe and the commune clerc [Asshebourne] bothe to the Gildhald door and dede calle to hym John Mordon belleman of Lenne and made the meyre send Hym for the keyes of the Gildhald doers agayn the meyres will and made the Belman whan he come to unschyt the doer and then Robert of Brunham mayre was borne doune with strengthe of peple and lay ther long in perile and defoiled never mayre so that men herden tellen of and also the commune clerc. And after that Robert of Brunham meyre was thrast up the greces [stairs] with grete power and strengthe of mene in to the Gildhald and sette hym doun on the lowe benche in the southe corner of the Gildhald and [he] . . . was in is tribulacion and passion . . .

Bilney – whom Asshebourne described as mayor elect, legitimately chosen according to the royal charter and the new ordinance – arrived and sat in the hall on a lower bench. He had been held up by the debilitating effects of fever and other infirmities. Asshebourne, pressured by the clamour, reluctantly administered the oath to him as mayor. Only then did Beer, the doorman deliver the writ to Bilney forbidding him not to meddle with the mayoralty. Bilney performed an instant volte-face, asserting that he would obey the writ and ordering Asshebourne to read it out loud. Brunham asked Beer why he had delayed so long and failed to deliver the writ as ordered. The doorman said that he had gone to Bilney's house but was unable to speak to him. On returning to the Guildhall, he had found difficulty in getting in because of the crush at the door. Brunham was in 'agony' or 'perplexity'. The prior of Lynn, Littlebury, Bartholomew Systerne, jurat (*potencioris* in 1411), and John Permonter, burgess (*mediocris* in 1411), managed to give him some protection and attempted to mediate on his behalf. Demand focused on his surrender of the keys to the muniment chests and custody of the royal charter, the common seal, and the mayoral sword and seal of office. Eventually Brunham agreed to the surrenders, apart from the sword, with the consent of Systerne and Permonter, and in accordance with the advice of the prior and the knight. He protested that he was forced to do so against his will. A burgess wrested the mayoral sword from his servant. Bilney asserted that the proceedings were against his will and that he would in no way assume office. He as well as Brunham opposed the giving of the key to the chest and the mayor's seal into Littlebury's safekeeping, under the seals of Systerne and Petypas, with the consent and precept of the community.[120]

At this point Asshebourne's account ends abruptly. The extent to which he massaged his version of events is unclear: it is certainly credible that he and leading burgesses had had to perform a delicate balancing act, facing the present anger of the crowd, but aware of the wrath of the Crown to come. Asshebourne goes straight on to record the consequences. The Crown's response to these defiant proceedings was rapid. A flurry of royal writs was issued on 6 October. Edmund Oldhall (deputy sheriff of Norfolk) was commissioned to bring those suspected of leading the riot to be examined in Chancery – presumably to answer Bishop Beaufort. They were named as Thomas Middleton, tailor, Thomas Baryngton, goldsmith (*inferior* in 1411), Thomas Emmede, tacker, and Thomas Bekham, hosier.[121] These sound as if they were scapegoats, small fry with large mouths, not the more calculating and formidable leaders of the 'popular' party. Brunham seems to have recovered his nerve. In Tuesday Market on 14 October, and next day in Saturday Market, he had writs proclaimed, addressed to him as mayor, which, while recognising Bilney as mayor elect (a sop to the popular cause), enjoined Brunham to continue exercising office. Asshebourne noted the presence with him on these occasions of groups including the past 'potencior' mayors Thomas Waterden and Thomas Brygge and, in Tuesday Market, John Brekeropp, *mediocris* in 1411.[122]

However, Brunham, may have been agitating for discharge from an office whose exercise in the present climate of opinions had reduced him to terror a few weeks before. The Crown now took a firmer line. A writ dated 18 October, addressed to Thomas Hunte, who had recently supported Brunham at the proclamations, ordered him to exercise the office of mayor for the remainder of the mayoral year (until 29 September 1416); he was regarded hopefully by the Crown as zealous for peace.[123] This roused up the 'popular' party. On 3 December a commission was appointed, headed by the distinguished Norfolk landowners, Thomas Lord Morley and Sir Simon Felbrigge, and including Edmund Oldhall and the sheriff, William Paston. They were ordered to enquire into who, with thirty-eight named individuals, was obstructing Hunte's exercise of his office. The list included prominent agitators in recent years, such as Thomas Feltwell, Thomas Baryngton, Thomas Emnede, Walter Caundeller, William Wygenhale and Richard Essex.[124] Two days later, the Constable of the Tower of London was ordered to receive one of those named, John Sherman (*mediocris* in 1411–12), and the *inferior* John Wyrham (perhaps Margery's friend).[125] In January 1416 two of the commissioners, Oldhall and Thomas Derham, held an inquisition in Lynn, at which a jury which included some notable *potenciores* indicted their opponents. According to a King's Bench roll of proceedings in the current Hilary term, the jury had alleged that, at the Chancellor's behest, a royal sergeant-at-arms, John Drax, was detailed to deliver to

Hunte the commission ordering him to hold office as mayor, and various writs. When, on 29 November, Drax was in the Guildhall to proclaim the appointment, he and Hunte were menaced by forty-five named individuals and 300 unknown men of the town, incited by Hallyate, Petypas, Bilney and Richard Thorp (*potencioris* in 1411). The crowd of rioters was said to have seized the letters from the hands of Drax and Hunte. Thirty alleged rioters were brought into King's Bench and fined.[126] Hallyate, Petypas and Thorp, arrested on charges of treason, were to receive pardons dated 10 April 1416.[127]

The *potenciores* were back in the saddle, but they remained nervous. In July the mayor, Hunte and the 'good men' of the community wrote to the sheriff, John Spenser, to enlist his help against their defeated opponents. In one letter, Hunte declared that it was well known in Lynn that Thomas Feltwell, goldsmith, had been indicted of rising and riot. He had made no real effort to seek the community's intercession, but he remained obstinate, 'full of yvell will'. Hunte and his colleagues had information that Thomas Hardwell, Thomas Emnede and other misdoers resorted to Petypas, and that they were planning to secure a summons to Hunte to answer charges before the king or his council. Spenser was requested to find out the truth of this, and, if it was true, to try to put a stop to it. The letter makes clear that payment and rewards were on offer for Spenser in return for his co-operation.[128] In the eyes of the *potenciores*, Petypas was still a dangerous man, with highly placed friends: less than a fortnight later, Hunte again wrote on the community's behalf to Spenser, asking for his help in preventing Petypas from becoming customs officer in Lynn, on the grounds that the town had suffered from the disorders which he had caused.[129] However, the Crown had now swung behind the agenda of the *potenciores*. A mandate under the Privy Seal (28 July) ordered a return to the traditional way of electing mayors.[130] This was the procedure followed on 29 August 1416. Careful precautions were taken. On election day, at about nine o'clock, proclamation was made on behalf of the Crown and bishop that no artificers and labourers who were inhabitants of Lynn should open shops and stalls or work at their craft, except burgesses, and that travellers should leave the liberty, in order to prevent gatherings and riots. A meticulously detailed record of procedure in Congregation was made by the clerk, noting that only the burgesses were present, that assent was given to the customary form of election now prescribed by the Crown, and that this was adhered to. The *potencioris* John Wesenham was elected, and the election and appointment of officials was scrutinised by members of the council of the recently consecrated bishop of Norwich, John Wakeryng, including Prior Hevenyngham of Lynn and Edmund Oldhall, Duchy of Lancaster receiver in the region and justice of the peace. Jurats and burgesses, 'with happy countenance' (*hilari vultu* – a phrase which had been implausibly used to describe Richard II's facial expression when he renounced the Crown), rejoiced that proceedings had been conducted peacefully.[131]

However, discontent over the restoration of elite rule rumbled on, though it never seems to have reached the intensity of the 1410s. According to an indenture to which Bishop Wakeryng was a party, dated 20 April 1420, a new ordinance was made for the government of the borough, following further dissensions there.[132] In 1429/30 Bishop Alnwick was party to an indenture intended to settle the long-standing disputes. There were to be annual elections of burgesses in each of the borough's nine constabularies. They were to form a council of twenty-seven, which was to play a part in decision-making together with the mayor, the alderman and the Twenty-Four.[133] This provision of fuller and more direct representation for *mediocres* and *inferiores* may have succeeded in further reducing tensions.

The causes of the internal conflicts in Lynn were examined by Dr Michael Myers in his thesis. He highlighted the deleterious effects on economy and society of the fall in wool exports from the port in the first decade of the fifteenth century, which resulted from the realm's conflicts with the French and some of the leading Hanseatic towns. Evidence of Lynn's economic decline in the period, Myers shows, is to be found not only in the customs accounts of the port but in the tally of admissions to the burgess-ship (which rose sharply), the borough's rental accounts, and the rise in its communal debt. The resulting tensions, he argues, turned into a full-blown political crisis, when wool merchants who were among those who had dominated government, sued the borough for the large expenses which they had incurred. The chamberlains' accounts reveal the high costs which had arisen from negotiating over the issue of the borough's relations with the bishop and over problems with the Hanseatics. The impetus for political attacks on the *potenciores* and their system of control through the oligarchically skewed constitution came primarily from younger merchants who were more concerned with the growing cloth exports. They were supported by the *inferiores non burgenses*, disenfranchised artisans who, Dr Myers claims, came from the bishop of Norwich's adjacent manor of Gaywood.[134]

It would perhaps be a mistake to treat those listed in the concords of 1411–12 as belonging to the status groups as all constituting members of three solid factions. One can, indeed, identify a variety of links between many of the members of each group (especially among the *potenciores*), including prominent political activists. However, there were kinship and other ties across the groups (especially between *potenciores* and *mediocres*).

It can be assumed that there were those in all three groups who, though glued in solidarity at times of high tension, at heart wanted to see concord restored – as it eventually was. It is notable that, despite all the accusations of verbal and physical intimidation (often in accordance with legal formulas), no one, apparently, was killed in any of the allegedly tense and large-scale disturbances.

The compromise assented to by Archbishop Arundel as Chancellor was a victory for the *mediocres* and *inferiores*, establishing the basis for a regime with a reformed constitution, favourable to their aspirations to have a greater say in key elections and fuller financial control, and facilitating the further opening up of admissions to the liberty. It may well be the case that Bishop Tottington, Bishop Courtenay and Thomas Beaufort supported and promoted the reformers; the bishops in reaction to the *potenciores'* opposition to episcopal liberties a few years before and in order to promote their manorial tenants' aspirations; Beaufort perhaps because he judged that the elitist regime had grown prodigal, self-serving and isolated, possibly undermining the town's ability to help to defend the realm, for which he bore a heavy regional responsibility. However, the attitude of king, nobles and councillors changed notably early in Henry V's reign, leading to restoration of control by the *potenciores* and the abolition of the reformed constitution. The 1412 settlement had not produced concord but a hardening of opinion among discontented *potenciores* and (if hostile indictments are to be believed) riotous behaviour by hot-headed *inferiores*, incited or condoned by the reform leaders. Possibly, *potenciores* with a lifetime of contacts in government and gentry circles were trying hard to pull in favours in order to discredit their opponents. They seem to have won crucial external support over the 'public order' issue.

What were the reactions of Courtenay and Beaufort? Courtenay's death in 1415 may have deprived the reformers of a leading ally. However, both of them had apparently gone along with the Crown's increasing distrust of the popular faction. This culminated in the measures taken against the reforms and their supporters by John Duke of Bedford, custodian of the realm during his brother's absence in France in 1415, measures which involved Beaufort's brother, Bishop Henry, who had succeeded Arundel as Chancellor. A key to understanding the failure of Courtenay and Thomas Beaufort to prop up the Lynn reformers, whatever their past attitudes may have been, probably lies in the close relationships which each of them had with Henry V. As king he would not tolerate disorder, not least because it might threaten concentration on the war with his French adversaries. The Crown's overriding of electoral process by imposing its own candidate as mayor in 1415, and nullification of the reformed constitution in 1416, were policies which contrasted markedly with the royal search for consensus and appeasement of popular agitation in Henry IV's last years. A harsh pro-elite policy under Henry V effectively stamped out disorder, at least for the time being. However, it is likely that the *potenciores* were chastened, despite their opponents' defeat. The revival of their reputation as the rightful governors depended, in the eyes of the world at large, on their ability to restore and maintain peace and concord, a policy which required co-operation in government with the richer and more forceful of their critics among the *mediocres*, and constitutional adjustments to defuse a legacy of popular resentment.

The arrangements for John Permonter as mayor to greet Bishop Wakeryng at the head of the Corpus Christi Gild in 1424 symbolised the need to parade and instil a sense of unity. Though there were to be future dissensions, there were feelings in Lynn by the mid 1420s that much had been achieved to restore harmony. Congregation had a record made of the achievements as mayor of Permonter, categorised as *mediocris* in 1411–12 and elected to the office in 1423 and 1424.[135] He had, it was alleged, 'amicably, humanely and discreetly established firmly peace and tranquility among all the estates of the town'. A detailed account was made of how he had carried on the process of procuring a supply of fresh water to run into the ditches around the town walls, also irrigating its fields. He had secured royal licence and the assent of Bishop Wakeryng and of the chapter of Norwich cathedral priory for the borough's control of the land through which the water course flowed. 'In the whole time of his mayoralty he brought great honour to the town above all others, whose fame spread far and wide.'[136]

The Brunhams

It is clear, then, that for much of Margery's early life, the traditional governing elite was involved in conflicts to sustain and enhance its concept of the privileges and customary constitution of Lynn, and that, when Margery was a mature woman starting to flex her spiritual muscles, this elite confronted a crisis which saw it swept from the governing role which the leading families considered their birthright, but was then restored to a somewhat uneasy control. The identification of Margery as the daughter of a particular John Brunham by Meech and Allen, from references to her father in *The Book*, if it is accepted, positions her as born into the highest rank of the *potenciores*, part of the tightly knit network of wealthy merchants who controlled the government in the later fourteenth century and up to the revision of the constitution in 1411–12.[137]

Who were the Brunhams? Their origins are obscure, as are the blood relationships of most of those whose surname it was who appear to have been residents of Lynn in the later fourteenth and early fifteenth centuries.[138] It is likely that Margery's forbears originated in the manor of Burnham, not far from Lynn. Margery's apparent forbear, Ralph de Brunham is first mentioned in the *Red Register* of Lynn in 1320 and had established himself within its elite by the 1340s; he was among the jurats in 1342–3 and 1346.[139] Ralph appears to have been alive on 23 March 1353, when his son, John was admitted to the freedom of the borough. John may have been a vintner.[140] He is the Brunham whom Meech and Allen identified as Margery's father. A distinction between an elder and younger John Brunham was made in the Lynn borough records from 1394, about twenty years after Margery's birth. Her putative father had made the first of many appearances as jurat in 1354.

In terms of taking part in elections to office, holding borough and royal offices, sitting on and testifying before commissions and giving pledges, John Brunham was to become the most eminent and one of the most active Lynn burgesses of the later fourteenth century. He was selected as one of the four chamberlains in 1355, 1361 and 1367, and as mayor in 1370, 1377, 1378, 1385 and 1391.[141] He was one of a small group of burgesses at the heart of Lynn's public affairs. The mayoralty made him responsible, in the eyes of leading royal officials, for ensuring that Lynn met the demands of the Crown and its obligations to the realm. For instance, in May 1386, as mayor he was appointed to head the commission from the king's council to array the men of Lynn 'in view of imminent invasion by the French and others'.[142] The invasion threat was posed by the huge army and fleet concentrated in Flanders by the government of Charles VI of France that summer. Frantic defence preparations were made in England; luckily for the English, the fleet never sailed. Brunham had, doubtless, already gained a reputation beyond Norfolk as a safe pair of hands. He had represented the borough in parliaments summoned to Westminster in January 1365, May 1368, January 1380, February 1383 and November 1384.[143] He may have feared that he was becoming too useful a workhorse for the Crown and his fellow burgesses, as he procured in 1383, at the Duchess of Brittany's supplication, an exemption for life from being put on assizes or being made a royal minister, on the grounds that he was 'too old to labour'.[144] This did not deter him from twice more accepting the office of mayor. He was almost certainly the John Brunham who was alderman of the Holy Trinity Gild from 1394 to 1401, which ex officio entailed close involvement in the business of borough government. He may also have been the John Brunham who was importing shipments of wine into

Lynn in the period 1389–91.[145] If these references are to the same John Brunham as the one admitted to the liberty in 1353, he must have lived to a ripe old age. Since Margery was apparently born c. 1373, she may well have been his younger child by a second or even a third wife. On 19 December 1412, Brunham's executor, William Herford (a goldsmith, admitted to the liberty in 1395, with a John Brunham as one of his pledges) attended Congregation in place of John and said that he was in bed, poorly (*languidus*), and so old that he could not by any means attend.[146]

Brunham had died by 16 October 1413, when his son John quitclaimed to Herford and others a messuage with buildings and appurtenances called 'le vought', next to the stone bridge, which his father had bequeathed to him. This bridge, over the Purfleet, was about midway down what is now the High Street; so Margery may have been brought up in an area where many of the richest merchants lived.[147] John Brunham junior, presumably Margery's brother or half-brother, had been admitted as a burgess on 19 December 1394. Brunham junior may have been a hosier.[148] Both Brunhams (and John and Simon Kempe) were brethren of the prestigious Corpus Christi Gild in 1404–5.[149] John Brunham junior remains a shadowy figure and does not appear to have held offices in urban government. He was probably the John Brunham who was a brother of the Gild of St Giles and St Julian in 1410 and as late as 1 July 1431.[150] The gild had been founded in the 1380s, and its brethren seem not to have been well-off in 1389, since they offered a farthing at Requiem Masses (half the statutory amount offered by many gild members in Lynn). They had a concern for travelling brethren; attendance was obligatory at the funerals of those who died within ten miles of the town.[151] Perhaps John Brunham travelled around peddling his wares. His membership of the fraternity certainly suggests that he was a parishioner of the chapel of St James, which was its cult centre – in contrast to Margery, who worshipped in the parish church and who strongly objected to the attempts by the parishioners of Lynn's other chapels to encroach on the rights of the mother church. As we shall see, she was banned by a friar from attending his sermons at St James – particularly embarrassing for her brother if he was a parishioner there.

In contrast to John junior, Robert Brunham, as we have seen, emulated the career of John senior. He had a high and at times stormy profile in overseas enterprises and later in borough politics and administration. However, no firm evidence has been found either that he was a son of John Brunham senior or, indeed, that he was related to him and Margery. He was older than Margery and John Brunham junior, for he was described as a vintner in 1388 – a trade which he may have had in common with Margery's father. From 1392 he exported cloth from Lynn; he was also a grain exporter and wine importer, and in 1405–6 had a partnership in this business with William Herford. A shipowner, he made a fortune, despite the hazards and vicissitudes of overseas enterprise: in 1410 he lent the Crown 200 marks for naval defence. Robert Brunham was elected chamberlain in 1395, 1401 and 1405, and mayor in 1406 and 1408. He represented Lynn in parliament in 1402 and 1417, and from 1411 he was the alderman of Holy Trinity Gild. He was not alone among Lynn burgesses in having connections with landowners, for whom he acted as a feoffee.[152] He died before 11 August 1424.[153]

Despite Margery's elitist background, *The Book* does not refer to the prolonged political strife in Lynn. It is unlikely that townswomen, though excluded from public office, failed to take an interest in and express opinions about the vital issues. This was especially so in Margery's case, as her father was among the most eminent of Lynn burgesses (as she was proud to point out): in his last years he was involved in the process of constitutional change, at least nominally. One might surmise that then she would have shared his views about the growing conflict, as she appears to have done strongly about the long-standing issue of whether the parochial rights of St Margaret's should be diluted in favour of the borough's chapels. Her putative kinsman, Robert Brunham came to be in the thick of the political controversy. Very occasionally, *The Book* shows her to have been well attuned to what one might term political gossip in the town. She discussed whether Prior Derham would join Henry V in France, a move cancelled by the king's death in 1422, and she pondered a rumour that Bishop Beaufort had died.[154] Indeed, one might expect that in a devotional treatise, specks of earthly controversy would be ignored. Yet her prime exemplar St Bridget had made the castigation of the wrong-doings of rulers and elites an integral part of her spirituality.[155] However, Margery's background and circumstances were very different from Bridget's: in the context of Lynn in the 1420s and 1430s, *The Book*'s silence on political matters may have a certain eloquence. For judgements about Margery's devotion are likely to have been swayed by her birth into an elite whose claims to rule for the public good had come under repeated and sustained attack, both respectable and popular. It may be significant that the fears expressed in Yorkshire that she might gain a hold over the common people and lead them astray were not replicated in the case of Lynn – in that context *The Book* had to face the issue of her recurrent unpopularity and accusations that her conduct was disruptive, disreputable and even malignant.

There are odd parallels between the political vicissitudes of the *potenciores* in Lynn in the early decades of the fifteenth century and *The*

Book's account of its subject's unregenerate individualism, the savage opposition she endured, the suspicion of her attempts to reform, and the eventual widespread acceptance of her goodness. This presentation of Margery's pious trajectory may therefore have aroused secular resonances which produced a 'feel-good' factor in the calmer 1430s. Indeed, the recollection of how her pious antics were originally received in Lynn may well have recalled too its time of troubles, for in that context they may have increased scorn and fear of the *potenciores* and abashed some of the latter. Her conduct c. 1413 (a time of humiliations for the *potenciores*) seems to have been widely unpopular.[156] After her return from her overseas pilgrimages in 1415 (the year of the commotion in St Margaret's and the Guildhall), there was widespread condemnation of her wearing of white clothes and her cryings, leading those who had given her meat and drink to ban her from their premises. Her friends were in despair, as carefully accounting burgesses would have been, at what they regarded as her reckless practice of charity, which had left her in debt.[157] However, *The Book* attempted to set the record straight on all these matters, putting her behaviour in its 'true' context, that of spirituality.

Arguably, *The Book* attempted to reflect and promote the sense of communal harmony which its subject's behaviour seemed to have helped to subvert. The degree of anonymity it preserves for most of its huge cast of individuals is notable. Only three Lynn laymen (and no women) are mentioned by name – Margery's father and husband, and John Wyrham, witness to her miraculous escape from death or injury. Yet many other Lynn layfolk appear, such a sick 'lyster' (dyer), a friend who was a 'worshipful' burgess, described as a 'mayor's peer' (possibly a jurat) and his wife, a 'worshipful' burgess who was a future mayor, and a 'worshipful' burgess's wife.[158] Most of Margery's key spiritual advisers, past and present, were either named or were easily identifiable from the text. These clerics were necessary witnesses to the truth of her 'feelings'. One reason for *The Book*'s reticence about the layfolk of Lynn may have been a desire to avoid the reactivation of partisan feeling by highlighting individual *potenciores* and their former opponents. So in this respect, as in others, *The Book* has the right 'mood music' for the mid-1430s. In spiritual parallel to the political evolution, Margery is presented as one who had been reformed, transcending the dross of arrogant and avaricious individualism which had polluted her previous life in the early 1400s. Here was a stem of the archetypal stock of the *potenciores*, an aged, often vilified widow, now authoritatively revealed as humbled, punished, transformed, the radiant refractor of divine benevolence. Despite any appearances to the contrary, and hostile interpretations of them, Margery had become truly community-minded, going about town doing good works to high and low, and encouraging their godly instincts, powered by high-octane spiritual fuel, which enabled her to outpace the ministrations of any traditional Lady Bountiful. The *Sturm und Drang* of the Lynn housewife and Lynn politics had now alike seemingly been calmed.

The Book generally presents Lynn in a favourable light. It is not an anti-urban tract, castigating the particular wickedness and spiritual blindness of the inhabitants. The community's sense of unity and religious reverence are projected in references to the solemn public processions on feast days and the performance of the liturgies. 'Worshipful' burgesses and their wives and widows are shown as full of good and merciful impulses. The people flock to hear good preachers. However, some of the latter (and some of their superiors) are (as in other towns) prone to misjudge hastily and fearfully signs of the numinous – producing vicious denunciation and treatment of Margery. This is one issue that rouses controversy. (A contrasting, commendable one is intense attachment to one's church.) *The Book*, whilst castigating manifestations of sin in Lynn, on the whole takes a kindly view of its society. Whereas the Franciscan annalist of Lynn in the later fourteenth century had catalogued the series of disasters with which God had afflicted the town, *The Book*, whilst recording Christ's dire warnings of similar punishments to be visited on Lynn (and other) folk, elaborates the countervailing good news that He had permitted His special servant, in whose soul He, the Holy Trinity, the Blessed Virgin and the company of Heaven on occasion lodged, to dwell in their midst.

Any attempt to relate the tenor of a devotional treatise to its politico-social background is hazardous and necessarily involves a good deal of speculation. We are on surer ground in trying to tease out a text's incidental and unselfconscious evidence about the assumptions, tastes and routine habits of its author, providing, in this case, a window into some of the social norms and minutiae of a bourgeois society. Margery, born into a powerful elite, as we have seen, defined her status with pride, with reference to her father's office-holding in the borough, and not apropos her husband. She retained a strong sense of her hierarchical status, recalling more than twenty years later how, in Bishop Repingdon's household, she had been 'set to meat with many worthy clerks and priests and squires of the Bishop's'.[159] The passage has a certain similarity with the hierarchical seating plans for a noble's hall drawn up by her contemporary John Russell, a domestic officer of Humfrey Duke of Gloucester.[160] Her joy on this occasion was increased when the bishop courteously sent her fare 'from his own mess'. *The Book* mentions how, on a visit to a monastery, she was 'set at meat' with the abbot and impressed him by her devout table talk.[161] Margery appreciated fine food and drink. She enjoyed eating meat and treating herself to 'pyment' (wine infused with honey and spices).[162] As became a probable vintner's daughter, she purchased good wine for herself in Rome. As a penance, she exchanged it for the sour wine which the poor old woman she was serving had for herself.[163] When relying on charity in Rome, Margery noted that Dame Florentyn, a principal benefactress, had, in alms, filled her bottle with good wine.[164] Margery customarily used a spoon – silver spoons seem to have been status symbols among the Lynn elite, sometimes useful as pledges.[165] She had a keen eye for tableware – she noted that a poor woman who gave her hospitality in Rome served her wine in a cup made of stone.[166] Margery was fastidious and modest, hating the flea infestations she acquired abroad and shrinking from participation in naked communal ablutions in Germany.[167] Though she enjoyed reciting homilies in public, and came to accept the spiritual necessity of submitting to alarming and repellent physical symptoms, in other respects she shrank (doubtless in accordance with her upbringing) from making a spectacle of herself. She hated being dressed as a Fool (as well as being hierarchically degraded at meals) by fellow pilgrims.[168] She was worried that she might disgust another group of pilgrims if she succumbed to seasickness.[169] She did not wish to be recognised in London in mean raiment.[170] *The Book* amply illustrates her delight in well-appointed lodgings and surroundings, and the distress she endured when sampling the lifestyles of the poor or travelling with straitened funds.[171] She sometimes thought that she had three cushions in her soul for the Holy Trinity to sit on – one of gold (presumably gold thread), another of red velvet, and a third of white silk.[172] She was disgusted by ooze and muck in the gutter.[173] The gutters in the centre of Lynn may have been especially filthy because of the combination of rubbish-tipping in the Purfleet and other streams, and the frequent flooding; perhaps she had the Purfleet (near places where she had probably lived) particularly in mind.

Margery was clearly at home in the politest society. She was spiritually uplifted 'if she saw a prince, a prelate, or a worthy man of estate and degree whom men worshipped and reverenced with lowliness and meekness'.[174] As we have seen, there were ample opportunities for her to have viewed the official reception of great folk in Lynn, especially in the Lancastrian period. One may imagine that, when she was a girl, her father introduced her to visiting ladies and their *domicellae* so that she could learn about good manners and conversation, rather like the knights in Sir Bertilak's castle in the poem *Sir Gawain and the Green Knight*, eager to observe Gawain's courtliness.[175] Certainly Margery seems to have been at ease with practically the highest in the land, such as Henry

IV's sister and niece, and the Earl of Arundel's son. When elderly, she may have spiced her conversation with the occasional French word, in the pretentious spirit which Chaucer had attributed to his Prioress in The Prologue to *The Canterbury Tales*. Genteel as well as homely talk presumably went down well in aspiring Lynn circles.[176]

The incidental ways in which mundane aspects of Margery's personality emerge in *The Book* suggest that she had high consumption standards and valued courtliness. In these respects the 'Margery of the Book' can be taken as paradigmatic of her status group: other women born into the elite of Lynn by implication had similar expectations and standards. They saw themselves as a worthy estate in the hierarchy of nobility. Their self-imaging in this fashion was probably often promoted by their fathers and husbands as an expression of status, and they themselves are likely to have played significant roles in refining the concept of urban nobility. Some of the more artless expressions of Margery's personality in *The Book* suggest how deeply ingrained the *potenciores'* sense of their worthiness was, a self-esteem which was a formidable force, sustaining their belief in their superior qualities and their will to rule in the face of formidable challenges.

chapter 3

MARGERY AND URBAN
GENDER ROLES

Medieval views about the nature of gender and about appropriate gender roles have been the subject of intense historical scrutiny in recent decades. There is, indeed, considerable evidence about the contemporary rationale for laws and customs regulating these matters, and about the legal frameworks in place. The Bible and the works of the Church Fathers provided a bedrock for sharp stresses in canon law, and in clerical discourse, on the religious significance of gender differences. As regards English cities and towns, collections of urban customs and gild regulations and records of the proceedings of borough courts reflect insistent distinctions between the legal and customary rights of men and women.[1] One effect of the generally lower status accorded to women in these contexts has been to obscure them in large measure from the view of historians. As named individuals they appear, occasionally and fleetingly, in a variety of capacities in the records of borough courts. They appear, too, in the more sparsely surviving records of diocesan courts, among whose responsibilities under canon law was the protection of the rights of both parties in marriage.[2] Thus on 18 March 1408, in a certain high chamber in Archbishop Bowet's residence at Cawood, near York (with which Margery was to become painfully familiar), in his presence and that of many witnesses, Sir William Rither subscribed by oath to certain articles contained in a schedule. Here is the tenor of part of the document, as entered in Bowet's Register:

> thes er the articles that henry be the grace of god archebisshop of york askys that Sir William of Rither sall make to hym for Sibelle his Wyfe. ffirst that the fforsayd Sir William hir lord ne sall noght do ne gat do hir ne bodily harme ne hir mahyame ne bete ne enprisone bot kepe hir in full ffredom als a man of his degre hayth to do to his Wyfe wyth outen doying or saying that may be reproue or velany to hir person. Also that hir forsayd lorde sall voyd Marion of Gryndon out of his compaigne and out of his and hir forsayd Sibelle . . .

. . . compaigne als longe als the forsayd sibell lyues ne neuer to haue at do
with the forsayd Marion be way of synne.

The document contains further provisions intended to ensure Sibelle
Rither's welfare.[3]

Wills can be an important source of information: husbands sometimes
made elaborate provisions about the disposition of property, money and
chattels with regard to their wives and daughters. A considerable number
of wills made by widows survive; those of married women are sparser
and generally shorter since, as Ann Kettle has explained, the law did not
clearly endorse their freedom to make wills and bequests: 'It seems that
in general the testamentary capacity of the married woman was dependent
on the permission and the co-operation of the husband.'[4]

Unfortunately, Margery Kempe's name has not yet been found in any
court record, nor has a will made by her or one of her kinsfolk, nor a
mention of her or any of them in someone else's will. Even taking account
of the disappearance of so much documentary evidence, it aptly symbolises
the exclusion of women from so many of the public rights held by men
that her name (presumably) is known to appear in only two documents,
account rolls of the Holy Trinity Gild.[5] Yet this was a woman who by
birth belonged to the highest status group in one of the leading English
towns and who, according to her Book, made a considerable stir on her
home ground and in the wider world.

The historian of medieval women, perforce much reliant on literature
strongly shaped by the prominent *topoi* on the subject (in writings mostly
by men), on records of laws framed by men, and on court judgements
made by them, has his or her work cut out to reconstruct their individual
and collective gender experiences. *The Book* is valuable for its projection
– ostensibly – of a woman's reactions and sensibilities. We must not
expect it to yield too much. The information which it contains about
daily life and mundane social relations is fitful and haphazard, though
nonetheless valuable. As we have seen, the work is didactic and polemical
in purpose. It is only in a limited sense autobiographical. It does not
provide a rounded pen-portrait of its subject, a history of her sentimental
attachments or of her secular careers as housewife and businesswoman.
Such matters are, indeed, discussed or alluded to, but only insofar as they
illuminate various spiritual planes and states. The work is modelled on
religious genres, and the mentality which is presented is one heavily
influenced by their themes and conventions. Within the literary framework
set up by Margery, emphasis on feelings about parents and kin, husband
and children, was not only for the most part beside the point but would

detract from it. Indeed, Margery is represented as praying for grace for her husband and children, but her devout concerns came to embrace the whole of Christendom. Christ said to her soul: 'You make every Christian man and woman your child in your soul for the time, and would have as much grace for them as for your own children.'[6] The presentation of Margery's familial relationships is partial and distorted by the agenda of *The Book*. However, the selectivity itself is significant and, because the preferred devotional model had a high degree of social interaction built into it, a good deal about such relations may be glimpsed or inferred, as it can about more mundane aspects of behaviour in Lynn.

Before discussing Margery's apparent familial and secular roles, let us rehearse some contemporary views about gender and review the position of women in urban society, with Lynn particularly in mind.[7] A huge weight of authority in past discourse enforced the precept that it was proper, in the normal course of affairs, for women to be subordinate and obedient to men. This was revealed in the Scriptures and evident in the order of nature, as expounded in the Hippocratic system of medicine. The predominant 'humours' in men's bodies inclined them to rational thinking as well as physical strength, whereas 'female' humours characteristically produced light-mindedness as well as bodily weakness. Consequently, women, by their nature, had an urgent impulse to seek for sexual intercourse in order to procure regenerative male infusion as a remedy for their 'humoural' deficiencies, as well as to fulfil their procreative urge. Men's sexual desires distracted them from the natural exercise of reason. In the eyes of the canonists, in the words of Professor Brundage, 'sexual desires were inextricably entwined with lust – an infirmity of the flesh which contaminated the soul'.[8] Since, according to weighty tradition in clerical discourse, women were the occasion of weakness, it was proper that they should not generally exercise governing roles and that their activities should be supervised constantly. Their access to power had to be restricted and they had to be policed, through male control of their bodies, property and chattels. Institutions upholding such gender hierarchy were seen as providing a framework of social order within which men and women could more easily seek salvation. In marriage, it was the husband's duty to regulate his wife's and his own sexuality, so that neither of them should fall into venial sin through concupiscence, such as by engaging in excessive and passionate intercourse or by indulging in intercourse at all during the periods of abstinence prescribed by the Church.

In this strongly entrenched system of beliefs, with its heavily slanted definitions of gender, there were opportunities for exaltation for both sexes, though in sermon and discourse much emphasis was placed on the female need to strive for virtue, through virginity, chaste living and motherhood. The Virgin Mary and a canon of female saints and martyrs provided exemplars to be reverenced by both men and women. The legendary accounts of females suffering at the hands of wicked pagans, punctuated by signs of divine approval for these holy ladies, and their triumphant apotheoses, had a widespread appeal to both sexes and are likely to have consoled and inspired many women besides Margery who were unhappy or unfulfilled in their lives. Such themes are projected in the sculptured panels of Nottingham alabaster illustrating the life of St Katherine of Alexandria, now in the Ca' d'Oro in Venice. There was, indeed, a long-established clerical mode of denunciation of feminine frivolity, but conscientious clerics accepted their particular duty (as well as laymen's) in assisting women in their supposedly more heroic struggle to retain their virtue – and to achieve their potential for spiritual illumination. This potential was equal to men's; past and recent models suggested that some women might achieve it in a remarkable and distinctive way. Hence the great pains which some of Margery's confessors are described as having taken with her, and the earnestness with which they and some leading prelates listened to her descriptions of her 'feelings'. On first meeting her, Richard Caister, vicar of St Stephen's, Norwich was sceptical as to whether a woman could speak for an hour or two about the love of God, but he was soon taking her words on it very seriously.[9]

Let us now consider briefly aspects of women's rights and restrictions in boroughs and some evidence about their roles in Lynn, before assessing what light *The Book* throws on these and other gender-related issues. Any property and chattels which a woman brought to her marriage by inheritance and gift, or acquired during the course of it, were in the husband's care and control. A widow might normally look forward to receiving substantial provision for her welfare made by her spouse.[10] Since women were normally barred from apprenticeship, they could not progress to mastery of a craft and consequently gain eligibility to hold office in urban government and craft gilds. However, such gilds were sometimes prepared to allow a widow to carry on her husband's business and to admit her to gild membership.[11]

Random surviving wills from Lynn in the fifteenth century cast a little light on the material expectations and circumstances of married women and widows, though they do not necessarily illuminate their circumstances and expectations to the full. The burgess John Slegge, in his will of 1414, left his wife Isabelle her present dwelling house for one year after his death, with the necessary furnishings. All his other extensive properties in and out of the town were to be sold immediately for the health of his soul and that of his previous wife.[12] Robert Salesbury, burgess of Lynn, in 1429 bequeathed his wife Agnes all his domestic furnishings (*utensilia*).

His son Thomas was to receive the tenement where he lived and a sum to be used for the good of his and Agnes's souls. John Roper (1439) left his wife Isabella the furnishings of his house in Lynn, though his brother Roger was to receive silverware and his best 'ffedyrbed' and the fittings. Katherine, the wife of John Cook (1447), was to hold his tenement in Briggate until her death, when it was to be sold for the good of their souls. Likewise the messuage in Wiggenhall, which Helena, wife of Edmund Mechyll (1447), was to receive, was to be sold after her death for the same purpose. Katherine Cook was appointed an executor by her husband, as had been Johanna Silisden by her husband William in 1410, Agnes Salesbury by her husband Robert in 1429, Margaret Spicer by her husband John in 1430, and Elizabeth Slynghelant by her husband Theodoricus in 1448.[13] Two women's wills survive – one married (Joanne Blocke, 1411) and one a widow (Katherine Curson, 1415). Joanne Blocke had her own seal and was allowed free disposal of her goods by her husband, whom she appointed as her executor, 'so that he makes disposition for my soul as he perceives the better to please God and raise up my soul'. She had money at her disposal for pious bequests.[14] In the will made by Katherine Curson, 'in my pure widowhood', she reveals that she had a good deal of inherited property which was to be sold for the good of her soul. She possessed a lavish amount of expensive plate, much of which she bequeathed to her daughters. Katherine wished to be buried in the Lady Chapel of St Nicholas' chapel, next to her husband Thomas; £10 was set aside for two chaplains to celebrate for their souls for a year after her death. She appointed her sister Margaret as one of her executors, but Margaret handed over the task to her two male colleagues.[15]

Burgesses, besides making provision for their widows, are likely to have been generally inclined to allow their wives control over at least some of their own assets, since not only were they dependent on their goodwill and co-operation in this life but, as there was a good chance that they would predecease their wives, in the next. A nostalgically affectionate widow was more likely to say regular prayers for the deceased and ensure that the provisions which he had made for the health of his soul (often with a hefty financial investment) were carried out and maintained. Well-to-do women in Lynn could also make a mark in business and social life, sometimes in partnership with their husbands – and, indeed, were probably often expected and needed to do so. Some cases which came before Congregation reveal the community's underlying assumptions that wives had a duty to respect and promote the interests of their husbands and to ensure that they acted conformably to the common good. In 1416 the mayor, Thomas Hunte, writing to the sheriff of Norfolk, alleged that the wife of the stubbornly recalcitrant goldsmith Thomas Feltwell, indicted of rising and riot, had interceded on his behalf.[16] In 1428 William Scarlett's ship was laded in the port and sailed out with a non-burgess's merchandise, without payment of the necessary fine to the mayor. Scarlett excused himself in Congregation on the grounds that 'it was done without his knowledge but that it was done by order of his wife'.[17] The wife of John Draper appeared before Congregation and asked that her alien-hating husband should be released from prison. She offered to find pledges for his good behaviour.[18] Burgesses' wives doubtless had a variety of roles to play in protecting or promoting the family interest, especially when their husband was incapacitated (as was Margery's permanently in his last years) or absent on business. Sometimes, too, they were well placed to oil wheels for those running borough affairs. In 1416, as has been recounted, Mayor Hunte wrote urgently to the sheriff, John Spenser, seeking his political support in the borough's internal affairs. He exclaimed effusively, 'And, sir, Elizabeth my wife commendeth her to you 1,000 times' – a remark which conjures up a cosy world of entertainment in the mayoral household.[19] Married women as well as widows, such as Margery, were received as members of the 'top people's club', the Holy Trinity Gild in the period. Many of the certificates of Lynn's gilds from 1389 allude to membership by sisters as well as brethren, though where the names of a gild's alderman and *custodes* are given, they are men. Of the twenty-two members of the gild of St Edmund listed then, twelve were married couples and three were women listed without husbands.[20]

What can be gleaned from *The Book* about the social roles to which Margery was expected to conform and about how they moulded her behaviour? The text does not reflect a general burden of complaint about the lot of women or present its author as a victim or critic of the subjection of women. Accusations that she disrupted a noble marriage,[21] and that even when just passing through a town as a stranger she might be credited with the ability and intention to induce wives to leave their husbands, are presented as unjustified criticisms by wicked individuals who were attempting to discredit her.[22] In worldly terms, Margery realised that she had a good deal to be thankful for, as *The Book's* frequent recognition of the miseries of the poor, the destitute and the diseased suggests. The elite wives of Lynn expected to be pampered and svelte hostesses, like those who model fashionable clothes on the Walsokne and Braunche brasses in St Margaret's. Such ladies were accustomed to be treated with courtesy by their social superiors, with respect by their husbands and with deference by their inferiors, as *The Book's* projection of Margery amply bears witness.[23]

Before focusing on the evidence about Margery's marriage in *The Book*, let us consider her childhood. What we can infer about it either from *The Book* or from general sources is slight. The subject of female childhood, especially at any level of society below that of the nobility, is hard to illuminate for this period. Professor Nicholas Orme has noted that few medieval writers had much to say about children. The Church did little to distinguish their status. It laid at baptism the obligation on godfathers and godmothers to ensure that the parents should provide physical care and basic religious instruction for the child and arrange for its confirmation. Meal times were often occasions for instruction through the children's saying or leading graces – or, at least, the boys doing so.[24] Infants were frequently taken to church services. In Margery's time, children were admitted to communion and confession at the age of twelve or soon afterwards.[25] Merchants' daughters may have been 'brought up to pray daily and to visit churches, using the basic prayers'.[26] Manuals of instruction on the upbringing of children were above all concerned with training for adulthood; evidence for the culture of children is sparse. Nicholas Orme has written illuminatingly about this culture – about the dolls which girls may have had and the games they played. Holy dolls and toys helped to teach the Gospel story. In Amsterdam's Historisch Museum there is a miniature set of models for the Stable of Bethlehem, made in pewter, and dating from the fifteenth century – perhaps made for a child. Adults continued to cherish and play with holy toys. In Italy Margery accompanied a woman who had an image of Christ, which she set 'in worshipful women's laps in cities, which they would put shirts on and kiss as if it were God himself'.[27]

Margery's views on how children should behave were conventional, as expressed in Christ's words to her soul: 'There was never child so buxom to its father as I shall be to you to help you and keep you.'[28] She was a true daughter when she studied to please Him.[29] We may infer from *The Book*'s picture of Margery as an adult that she was an attractive and perhaps over-talkative child – silence in the presence of adults being a mark of good behaviour. It would be unwarranted to surmise that she was inclined to be meek! She had a vivid imagination; if she watched the performance of religious plays in Lynn, such as the one put on at Corpus Christi in 1385 and the play of St Thomas of Canterbury, she doubtless responded with strong sympathies. The notable grasp that the 'Margery of *The Book*' had of the tenets of the Faith suggests that children were well instructed in the Brunham household. Her striking ability as an adult to memorise and understand Scripture and devotional literature implies that not only her skill at learning by rote but an ability to understand what she had learnt as well had been developed from an early age. Her intellectual capacity had probably been stimulated to the limit thought proper for a merchant's daughter of Lynn. Whether she was taught to read (or even write) in the vernacular remains a moot point, as we have seen.[30]

Conflict from early on in life between a well-developed sense of duty and a natural waywardness can be read into Margery's repentance for her 'unkindness' (with respect to God) since her childhood.[31] Her adult defiances of some of the precepts of her confessors, and unwillingness on occasion to obey those which Christ dictated to her soul, may have replicated juvenile acts of insubordination. Perhaps as a teenager she found it a particularly hard struggle to reconcile sexual impulses with a strong sense of religious duty. *The Book* implies that as an adult she had a vigorous sexuality to which as a young married woman she gave uninhibited expression, in defiance of the Church's teaching. She blames herself for the delectable thoughts, fleshly lusts and inordinate love which she had then had for her husband's person – a riotous confession revealing apparently what has probably been the perennial failure of canonists to police the marriage bed.[32] Allegedly, on one occasion she had been tempted to commit adultery.[33] Some time after her conversion, during a period of self-doubt, when she was prey to diabolical temptation, she had a vivid fantasy of priests and laymen displaying their penises to her and of being ordered to prostitute herself to all of them, the one she liked best first.[34] However, perhaps one should not take these references to scarcely bridled, unregenerate lust, and even reversion to it after her conversion to contemplation, too seriously. This sounds like the practised stuff of confession, an acceptance of the clerical notions of the weakness of women's nature, arrestingly illustrated with penitential relish.[35] At the least, *The Book*'s presentations of its subject's sexuality show how powerfully the Church's precepts might fashion a woman's self-imaging, and suggest that those aspects of her image were considered plausible and readily acceptable for its potential readers and auditors.

Another fantasy – this time one that was commendable – was that she should daily be drawn naked on a hurdle from town to town and have filth thrown at her, for the sake of Christ, as long as this did not arouse scandal.[36] This scenario may have borne traces of the Passion, the martyrdoms of saints, and of accounts which Margery had heard of the execution of traitors, such as Geoffrey Litster, 'King of the Commons', in Norfolk in 1381, whose traitor's death, as we have seen, was hideously illustrated and well remembered in Lynn.[37] This must have made quite a stir in the town when Margery was a little girl. Her flight of imagination about the humiliation of her body might suggest to us ambivalent feelings towards it, a desire to punish it and to be degraded through it, mingled perhaps with masochistic sexual pleasure. Yet here again one must be cautious about imposing the aperçus of pseudo-psychology. This imagining can be viewed too as a stereotypical contemporary response, if a particularly dramatic one, to the 'pulp fiction' of hagiography.

It is not clear from *The Book* what sort of practical skills Margery was taught as a girl. The prime ones may have been those needed to supervise the running of a household, though it is not clear that she could scrutinise, let alone compile, accounts. In the businesses which she set up, her role was supervisory: male servants did the manual work. Margery as a married woman was used to having maids to look after her domestic needs, though as a young wife she unlocked the buttery with her own set of keys and helped herself to food and drink.[38] In Rome she was to act as menial servant to a poor person as an act of self-abnegation. A similar motive (rather than impoverishment) lay behind her washing of her husband's soiled linen when he became senile. In her meditations, she joyfully projected herself in role reversal, being maidservant to the Virgin Mary as a child, up to the age of twelve, and to the new-born Christ. In both imaginary and real roles Margery is represented as a practical and conscientious servant; she is complimented on her work for the Blessed Virgin by St Elisabeth. This contrasts with her strictures on some of her real-life maids.[39] In the remaining records of the poll tax return for Lynn in 1379, the occupational designation most frequently given to women is that of 'servant'; even many artisans and labourers who were taxpayers at the basic rate had female servants. In the passages on domestic service, *The Book* provided a role model for any maidservants of Lynn who heard it being recited; putatively, they might be uplifted by learning how Margery the Supermaid, after the birth of Christ, by begging procured cloths, bedding and food for Him and His Mother, and found lodgings on the flight into Egypt (intrepid traveller into the unknown as she was in mundane life). After He was laid in the Sepulchre, she made a bedtime drink for His Mother.[40] So Margery is variously represented as of a status to be waited on, with a keen sense as to how service should be performed, and as possessed of an ability to do the job herself in a practical and frugal way. A possible inference is that her mother gave her a good example of how a merchant's household should be run. Margery's interest in setting up businesses (admittedly failures), in travel and in going about and out of the town suggests that if she was taught the arts of embroidery (as one might expect), she did not ply them with the skill and attention which engrossed generations of genteel women. Her talents were forensic and practical – she was at ease on the soapbox or at the washtub – and part of the unintended poignancy of *The Book* lies in the implication that a woman of her status had few opportunities to develop a variety of such talents, physical as well as mental.

Who was Margery's husband and what light does *The Book* throw on their marriage? Documentary evidence about the Kempes from the Lynn records was collated by Meech and Allen, and some of the relevant documents were printed by Dr Owen. Her husband (who may have been born c. 1370) appears to have been a younger son of John Kempe, skinner, who was admitted to the burgess-ship of Lynn on 29 January 1351. The father was probably the John Kempe elected as one of the four borough chamberlains in 1372 and 1381, and one of those elected as a subcollector of the parliamentary subsidy in January 1374.[41] The assumption is made here that he, and not Margery's husband, was the John Kempe who was prominent in Lynn's international trade in the 1380s and early 1390s. In 1388 he had the largest claim for compensation (£300) made by those from Lynn among the English merchants listed in a complaint by the Crown that they had suffered losses as a result of the seizure and forcible sale of goods by the authorities in Prussia.[42] John Kempe was singled out for mention in letters written in 1389 by Richard II to the Duke of Pomerania and the town of Lübeck about commercial grievances; Kempe was said to have been imprisoned at the suit of a merchant of Stralsund. A customs account for Lynn (1389–91) shows him to have imported cargoes (mainly of stockfish, but also beer and spars) in a variety of ships, including ships of Bremen, Danzig, Wismar and Osterdam. He also had a cargo of wine on a ship of Lynn in which John Brunham had a similar cargo laded. In 1392–3 Kempe paid subsidy on three cargoes of cloth and wool, freighted for export in separate vessels, two from Lynn and one from 'Kampe'.[43] John Kempe senior had died by 5 June 1393: in the annual account (ending on that date) of the treasurers of the gild of Corpus Christi (of which he and his sons Simon and John were brethren), payment is recorded to the Lynn Franciscans for a trental (Requiem Mass thirty days after burial) for his soul.[44]

The admission of Margery's husband and his elder brother to the burgess-ship was recorded in a notice of the proceedings of Congregation dated 28 May 1393.[45] In Congregation held on 8 October 1395, John Kempe 'junior' was elected as one of the jurats, an office which his father had held and to which Simon had been elected.[46] Simon was to play an active role in urban government, but the younger John does not appear to have been mentioned again in connection with it.[47] Nor does he appear to have developed a career as a merchant venturer.[48] Simon Kempe, Meech and Allen showed, died between 14 June 1408 and 22 May 1410. He had held a considerable amount of property – tenements in the mercantile centre, in Purfleet Street and Briggate, and in Damgate, where there was a good deal of craft production, not far from Tuesday Market.[49] He left a widow, who in 1416–17 was married to a prominent burgess, John Brekeropp.[50]

John and Margery probably married c. 1393, when she was past her twentieth year (if one can trust her later statements about her age). Dr Jeremy Goldberg has argued that this is not out of line with other evidence about the age of female marriage in towns.[51] The marital home may have been in Burghard's Lane (now New Conduit Street), overlooking the Purfleet: in 1391,1398–9, 1401–2 and 1425 one John Kempe held a tenement there.[52] According to *The Book*, the couple had fourteen children.[53] After the birth of her first child, Margery became deeply depressed, despairing of salvation because of an unconfessed sin. The insensitive reaction of her confessor triggered a complete breakdown, which necessitated her being put under restraint because she was inflicting injuries on herself.[54] It may have been directly after the birth of her last child that, despite feeling weak, she travelled to Norwich to consult Richard Caister, the vicar of St Stephen's. The visit was prompted by Christ's assertion that she should bear no more children and His command that she should visit Caister.[55] However, it would be carrying surmise too far to conclude that Margery's urge to end sexual relations with her husband was caused by apprehension about recurrent post-natal depression or any other problems which she experienced in connection with childbirth. It is, indeed, noteworthy that the text puts important spiritual impulses and experiences in the contexts of the birth of children and of postnatal depression or debility, but on the evidence it would be unwarranted to posit from this physical and psychological cause and spiritual consequence.

The Book provides little information about the Kempes' children. It would be easy to construct a theory that Margery was indifferent as a mother on its testimony that she was frequently out of the house and, indeed, out of town when one might have expected some of them to have been young. However, in this period of recurrent epidemics (especially in a region prone to outbreaks), it would not have been untypical if few of her children survived infancy.[56] No documentary evidence has come to light that any of them outlived her, though *The Book* mentions one who reached adulthood. In fact, Margery did recall anxiety about the upbringing of a child; when Christ informed her that she was pregnant, she expressed concern about arranging for the 'keeping' of the infant and He reassured her that He would 'ordain for a keeper'.[57] Apart from this recollection of concern, she saw no need to defend her role generally as a mother: the criticisms of her family role in Lynn were concerned mainly with her as a wife. Maybe wives from leading burgess families there, like those among the nobility, were expected to have only a remote or narrowly defined role in the upbringing of their children. Perhaps she was able to imagine herself as having an affectionate relationship with the Virgin Mary, as her maid when the latter was a child, because that replicated familial relationships in prestigious Lynn households. Above all, as has been suggested, *The Book* does not dwell on her role as mother, or on her children, because these subjects were largely irrelevant to its purposes. The behaviour of an adult son was described at length because it provided an analogy to St Bridget's concerns about her son Karl, an edifying tale of repentance and an explanatory background for Margery's visit to Danzig. Also, Margery needed to defend herself against accusations that she had brought illness on her son by cursing him. This 'tall' young man was apprenticed to a 'worshipful' burgess engaged in overseas trade. He rejected his mother's example and precepts – perhaps in reaction to their austerity or out of embarrassment at her controversial behaviour. When he went overseas on business, he fell into the sin of lechery. He also developed a disfiguring skin complaint and his master, after he returned home, dismissed him, thinking that he had contracted leprosy. The burgess had probably sent him to complete his apprenticeship in Prussia, as we have seen in other cases.[58] Margery's son repented and received his mother's blessing. He amended his way of life and recovered his health. He lived for many years and married in Prussia, having a daughter. He brought his family to Lynn, where he died about a month later, a reformed character. *The Book* records his death in a matter-of-fact way.[59] There appears to be no surviving record of her son's admission to the liberty, presumably because his apprenticeship was terminated as a result of his illness. However, he had probably acquired expertise in commerce whilst serving his apprenticeship abroad, and the steadiness of character which he subsequently exhibited may have led to his employment as a factor in Prussia by Lynn merchants. The number of pilgrimages which he undertook, which impressed his mother, suggests that he had done well financially and had time for leisure and money to spend.

The Book does provide some clues to Margery's maternal feelings in her meditations on the Holy Family, especially in her description of her role as the Virgin's maid. In visualising herself in this way, she was replicating stereotypical behaviour found in a well-established genre of devotional literature, which had invented apocryphal incidents and anecdotes to supplement the Gospels. This genre had been developed by the friars to promote among the clergy and laity a more vivid realisation of the sufferings of Christ and His Mother, and an intensification of love for them. The emotional relations and reactions within the Holy Family were leading subjects of sculpture and painting, stimulating especially representations of the Nativity and the Virgin and Child. Gospel and legendary literature on such themes, and their visual representations, provided models for burgess and other families, encouraging compassionate behaviour. They are likely to have influenced Margery's attitudes to her children. In the example given in *The Book* of her behaviour as a parent, she is represented as a mother who in the opinion of some lacked compassion, but who was in fact dedicated to helping her son achieve salvation and proud of his emergence (paralleling hers) from a worldly to a devout way of life.

Margery rejoiced in her son's marriage, a means of keeping him from the sin of lechery. The nature and problems of her own marriage are a recurring theme in *The Book*; they suggest that she had been brought up with a strong sense of its obligations. This sense of obligation is reflected in Christ's words to her about the nature of their spiritual union: 'It belongeth to the wife to be with her husband and to have no true joy till she comes into his presence.'[60] And elsewhere in *The Book*: 'It is appropriate for the wife to be homely with her husband . . . they must lie together and rest together in joy and peace.'[61] A tract which set out to denigrate and undermine the wholesome and blessed nature of marriage would have been speedily condemned by the clergy and burgesses of Lynn. However, according to *The Book*, Margery came to find the sexual side of her marriage repugnant and to desire ardently that holy precepts might reform and purify her relationship with her husband. She had, apparently, an arduous struggle to persuade him to give his consent to mutual chastity. We may perhaps, with some confidence, regard her mystical visions of the holy household and of herself as the bride of Christ as, in a sense, ineffable compensation for the problems within her marriage, and the consequent break-up of the Kempe household. In *The Book*, as we have seen, marital problems are not blamed on difficulties with childbirth. Nor are they on grief at the possible illnesses and deaths of her infants and children, but on the obligation to have sexual intercourse with her husband. For several years, during which she continued to bear children, she wanted to end this.[62] She developed a revulsion for John's attentions. They appeared to her as an insuperable obstacle to the development of her spiritual life. In the view of the canonists, and in clerical discourse, chaste marriage was the purest form of an institution designed partly to contain human frailty. The Church laid down that chastity in marriage required mutual agreement to forego legitimate requests to fulfil the 'marital debt', and a commitment to total sexual abstention.

Margery's change of heart – as we have seen, she had seemingly had great enthusiasm for John's body – seems to have had a profound psychological effect on him, particularly as her conversion led to other unsociable habits. He was upset by the fact that she engaged in a complete fast on Fridays, whereas she had hitherto eaten and drunk with him. Possibly on 26 April 1413, his desire to possess her was 'slain' when she said 'Jesus, help me' as he approached.[63] For eight weeks he did not touch her when they were in bed. His resentment boiled over in the very hot weather they experienced whilst travelling from York, probably on 26 June. Margery vividly remembered the scene: she was carrying a bottle of beer and he had a cake 'in his bosom'. He accused her of being a bad wife, but his bewildered feelings about her behaviour are evident in his confession that it was fear that had restrained him from touching her. To repel his advances, she clung in prayer to a conveniently nearby wayside cross. She asked him to agree to their taking vows of chastity. At first he refused her request, on the grounds that her proposed chastity would lead him to commit mortal sin. She refused to resume eating and drinking with him on Fridays, which so incensed him that he declared that he would make love to her again. However, at heart he seems to have already conceded defeat. He agreed to her wish for a chaste marriage and she relented from her obduracy about the Friday fast. They prayed together 'and afterwards they ate and drank together in great gladness of spirit'.[64] To the modern reader, with his or her referential framework of satirical comedy sketches, *The Book*'s description of this scene has unfortunately hilarious overtones, but in essence it is perhaps the most affecting terrestrial one in it. Not long afterwards the Kempes proclaimed their intention by announcing it before Bishop Repingdon, with a view to taking the public vows of chastity.[65] In *The Book*'s presentation of their dilemma and bruising resolution of it, what comes across (Margery recollecting when John was an invalid or dead) is how, underlying the brutal frankness and wounding anger, there was a deep well of mutual respect and affection. There is no suggestion that John had punished her for disobedience, or that he threatened to do so, yet canon law and social custom sanctioned physical chastisement of wives by husbands, as long as it was not disabling.

John Kempe thereafter countenanced and supported his wife in her spiritual endeavours, difficult and painful as this may have been for him at times. He was with her when she sought a privilege at Lambeth Palace, and (presumably silent) during her lengthy communing with Archbishop Arundel in his garden there, 'till stars appeared in the firmament'.[66] When they went together on pilgrimage to Canterbury, John was conspicuously absent when she was accused of Lollardy and menaced.[67] Prudently, he did not accompany her on any of the other pilgrimages mentioned in *The Book*. He must have given his permission for her to go abroad without him, a course of action likely to besmirch their honour – and, indeed, a rumour reached England that she had given birth whilst abroad. He dutifully met her when she returned from Yorkshire in 1417/18 and accompanied her to London to procure a confirmation of her privilege from Archbishop Chichele. In view of the mixed views about her religiosity in Lynn, her presence there probably caused more problems for John than her absence. They broke up their household, taking separate lodgings lest people impugned their adherence to their vows. However, when, aged over sixty, John fell down stairs and injured his head badly, people said Margery should be hanged if he died as she had not looked after him properly. She subsequently took him back home and they once more shared a roof, though he was a semi-invalid, mentally enfeebled and suffering from incontinence. *The Book* presents Margery as preoccupied with his welfare in the years until his death, c. 1431.[68] Whereas as a sinful young woman she is presented as having failed as a wife and householder, *The Book* argues against her critics that in holy old age she became a perfect mother and spouse.

The text throws a little light on the couple's financial arrangements and the extent to which Margery had some independence. It seems that John allowed her to control her possessions and to treat her acquisitions as her own. Since he disapproved of the extravagant raiment she wore, it is likely that she purchased it herself.[69] According to *The Book*, she took up brewing, becoming one of Lynn's leading brewers for three or four years until she lost a lot of money by it. Perhaps she faced stiff competition from imports of beer. This enterprise seems to have been undertaken against John's advice; it was again on her own initiative that she later set up a horse-mill. Her business failures had a bad effect on her reputation, and so must have reflected adversely on his too.[70] Margery does not appear on the Leet and Husting Roll among the brewers listed, but John does appear as such for the two accounting years from September 1403 onwards.[71] So he was nominally responsible, it appears, for any debts she incurred as a brewer in this period. After the termination of her enterprises, she still had resources which John treated as hers, for in 1413, as the price of chastity, she agreed to settle his debts,[72] which may have taken a large chunk of her assets.

John would not or could not fund her overseas pilgrimages. It took her over two years to raise the large sum she required to go to Jerusalem. Then, after the parish priest had asked in the pulpit if 'any man or woman' claimed a debt against her husband or herself, she satisfied their claims before she left.[73] She was confident in Rome that she would be able to repay the loan made to her there soon after her return to England, and indeed fulfilled this promise.[74] We do not know whether she or John funded her separate household establishment. Costs were reduced when the Kempes lived together again, though they did so with a certain frugality; Margery complained about the high expenditure on heating the water to clean his clothes constantly. When widowed, living without ostentation as a devout vowess, her financial position was probably adequate to her needs. Some time in the early 1430s, maybe when she was a widow, she granted a layman 'a great sum of good' (from her *utensilia?*) as payment to transcribe *The Book* (a task he was unable to fulfil).[75] It would have accorded with the affection and respect for his wife which *The Book* attributes to John if he had bequeathed her adequate lodgings or rent and goods, though we cannot be sure how well-off he was at the time of his death. When she set off for Danzig about two years later, she was probably inadequately supplied because she had not planned to go. She may have acquired funds for her further travels from her daughter-in-law, the latter's kinsfolk, or Lynn merchants in Danzig. On her return she was confident of raising a loan in London, which suggests that her credit was good.

However, it is the accounts of her financial and business dealings when married which provide more significant evidence. Indications of her control of funds as wife are provided for the most part incidentally, and it is not suggested that this was reprehensible or needed explanation or justification. Her business ventures are said to have aroused widespread condemnation, but only after the collapse of her second one. The businesswoman who had failed spectacularly could expect to have her reputation picked over! It was not anticipated that readers of *The Book* would be surprised or angered by an account of a wife who was allowed such liberties by her husband. We may conclude that marital arrangements of this kind were familiar in Lynn. However, we must note the public restrictions on the sorts of enterprises Margery could pursue. The ones she could pursue seem to have been unfamiliar to this merchant's (possibly vintner's) daughter. Her inexperience in brewing (an occupation as much second nature to many a village wife as spinning) lost her a lot of money and, when it came to horse-milling, she seems to have lacked some essential equine expertise. Yet the accounts of how she coped with practical arrangements when a solitary pilgrim abroad suggest that, if girls had been admitted as apprentices to merchant venturers, she might have been in her element dispatching cargoes in a foreign port.

Though John Kempe appears not to have exercised his legal right to control all the possessions which his wife brought to the marriage or acquired during its course, matters of finance – bound up closely with those of status in the urban environment – may have placed strains on the marriage before Margery's conversion and concomitant physical rejection of John. Margery may well have grown resentful that John could not maintain her in the state that Brunham womenfolk expected in marriage. She was to recall regretfully that when he had urged her 'to leave aside her pride, she answered sharply and shortly and said that she was come of worthy kindred – he should never have wedded her. . . . And therefore she would save the worship of her kindred, whatever any man said'.[76] As we have seen, Margery's father had had a distinguished office-holding career in the borough, and John Kempe's early promise in this sphere faded. Margery's resort to business ventures suggests that John was failing to generate the income commensurate with the lifestyle she considered to be appropriate to her status. If we take her account of her failings as a young wife as being basically factual rather than an overegged confessional confection, her behaviour may have dashed any prospects he had in business and government. His standing is likely to have been damaged by the reputation she acquired for pride, luxury and frivolity, and by his failure to moderate her behaviour. The temperamental differences between them, which *The Book* frequently underlines, may have worked against material success in the marriage, a failure in worldly terms which would have disillusioned both of them. In this theoretical model, Margery's working-out of the consequences of her conversion might be viewed as a brilliant sleight of hand, the reinvention of a troubled marriage on a different plane.

Margery's ability to reinvent herself has made her a gender icon in modern times. However, perhaps a lot of saints have had a long-suffering human doormat to stamp on. To take an outrageously modern line, I would suggest that John Kempe emerges from *The Book* as the real saint. To say the least, it cannot have been easy for him to adjust to and accept his volatile spouse's dizzying blast-off to spiritual heights – her deep communing with learned men, her development of startling meditations, her public manifestations, alarming to many, shameful to some. Besides, her illumination presumably eclipsed the role that society expected him to play as spiritual head of the household. In *The Book* his attempts to discipline his wife in her wayward phases are shown as ineffective, and it is his wife who disciplines their wayward son. She usurps masculine prerogative by seizing the initiative in regulating sexuality in the marriage. He fails to assert what contemporaries considered the natural authority of husbands – in peasant society such failures could bring down public rituals of humiliation upon husbands considered to be inadequate by the community.[77] It is hardly surprising that John's sexual desire for her was quenched, in wilting recognition of the stellar wrench which had pulled her from the mundane scene which was all he knew, undermining his marital authority. Yet they remained married for about thirty-eight years – presumably an unusual feat in the eyes of Lynn society.

Since male life expectancy was shorter than female, and bridegrooms were often older than their brides (though not clearly more so in this case), some women troubled in their marriages might have realistically looked forward to the probability of widowhood. Then they could avoid any pressure to marry again by taking a vow of chastity before a bishop, similar to the one which Margery took.[78] Some such vowesses, particularly when devotionally inclined, retired to anchorholds (cells for recluses). Why did not Margery, with John's permission, do the same? A monk in Canterbury Cathedral said that an anchorhold would be the best place for her.[79] There may have been various hindrances. Well-established and well-endowed anchorholds were limited in number; when a vacancy arose, patrons may have preferred to appoint a nun or an unmarried or widowed vowess. They might well have baulked at housing a married woman with a controversial reputation, who might lack stability or fail to attract adequate offerings for her keep.[80] Moreover, Margery may have hesitated over commitment to the requisite confinement, which would have, to some extent, cut her off from communal religious experiences, the fix of public rejection, and the performance of some of the works of mercy, which became integral components of her spirituality. Besides, she retained a sense of obligation to her husband, perhaps sharpened by the slurs on her performance of wifely duties.

Though the Kempes' marriage became gravely disfunctional, certainly from a conventional early twenty-first-century viewpoint, and probably in some contemporary eyes, *The Book* projects some shining, positive memories of it – of the couple's long-lasting mutual affection. When, early in the marriage, she was recovering from a breakdown, John, 'ever having tenderness and compassion for her', overruled the advice of her keepers and maids that she was unfit to be allowed responsibility for herself again.[81] After her conversion, 'he was ever a good and an easy man with her. Though he sometimes for vain dread left her alone for a time, yet he resorted evermore again to her, and had compassion for her, and spoke up for her as far as he dared for dread of the people . . . And always her husband was ready when all others failed, and went with her where our Lord would send her, always trusting that all was for the best and should come to a good end when God willed'.[82] A Panglossian *avant la lettre*! These comments on the hapless Kempe sound to our ears self-righteously condescending, but the text is testimony about one in whose soul Christ and the Company of Heaven lodged and, incidentally, testimony as to how Margery uncomfortably spoke her mind. I prefer to see these remarks as evidence of how mutual love pierced and obliterated past painfulness. It is evident that Kempe, who knew better than anyone about Margery's shortcomings and who could have blown away her pretensions, gave her, in his apparently hesitant and crablike way, the precious gift of his faith in her. Without the support of John Kempe, there could have been no *Book of Margery Kempe*.

So *The Book* presents a picture of a woman who, when married, apparently came to behave in ways which, taken together with her eccentric devotional flamboyance, seemed alarming to some – insisting on a vow of chastity, criss-crossing the known world without her husband and, at times, without a suitable chaperone, wearing puzzling clothes, and living in the secular world separately from her husband. Can her transformations be regarded as one solution to problems created for women which were inherent in the medieval concept and practices of marriage? It is clear that the Margery presented in *The Book* did develop problems in fulfilling some of the legal obligations and conventional expectations of a married woman, but it is difficult to be certain what the root causes and the course of these problems were. According to *The Book*, the relationship between husband and wife was changed not as a result of the variety of physical and pyschological problems touched on but because of the development of Margery's religious personality. We should beware of reductionist gender-orientated speculation when dealing with the literary expression of spiritual phenomena. In the light of this caveat, it would be dangerous to regard the invention of Margery as a religious personality as a means of breaking free from the general constraints of medieval marriage, as paradigmatic of predominant agonising dilemmas and, indeed, of oppressions supposedly the common lot of married women in the period. Men as well as women grew up subjected to rigid hierarchical constraints and heavily constricting role prescriptions. For both sexes, choice of favourite cults and devotions in the public world, and the opportunities available to some, if so temperamentally inclined, to develop concomitantly a rich interior devotional life, provided the means to cultivate a private garden of personal autonomy. Moreover, at the risk of generalising from one piece of evidence, I surmise that the story about Margery which is presented suggests that other married ladies in Lynn might have had a good deal of *de facto* control over their inherited assets and their acquisitions. Such *grandes dames* may also have had a good deal of freedom of movement and activity, which peer pressure doubtless constrained them, for the most part, to use in highly circumscribed ways, but which they had the leisure to use. Margery seemingly went back and forth to the churches, in and out of private houses. She may have made religiously motivated journeys frequently in her region; *The Book* mentions a visit to a local shrine beyond the town walls and visits to Norwich and Cambridgeshire.[83] Medieval journeys always had their pious aspect. Might not the more secular-minded among the ladies of Lynn have set out on 'devotional' trips which were excuses for socialising, shopping and sexual adventure? Religious activities appear to have facilitated women's cultivation of their autonomy in a variety of ways. Going to services could be realistically shown in *The Book* as providing opportunities to flirt and, indeed, to make illicit assignations.[84] Here it hints at a world of discreet trysts among respectable urban ladies. The remark made to Margery, that alarming pilgrim, by the mayor of Leicester, that he and his fellows feared that she would lead their wives away to follow her example (presumably of wandering about far from home with strange men), is, in terms of modern feminist discourse, redolent of male oppressiveness.[85] Perhaps one should see it too as an expression of male insecurity, an admission that the underprivileged and controlled status of the burgesses' wives of Leicester did not prevent them from aspiring to a good deal of disturbing freedom and autonomy.

The Book's evidence about medieval marriage – and it provides only doubtful slivers of evidence about one marriage – does not support a scenario of marital oppression by a husband but of problems experienced by a couple within marriage. What exacerbated the problems that arose for Margery and her husband were the current doctrines that marriage was an inferior state to virginity and that sexual pleasure ought not to be indulged. It may be that the latter problem was not so evident in many arranged marriages. Nevertheless, for some, dilemmas over the spiritual consequences of the loss of virginity and the enjoyment of sex in marriage may have been heightened when the abstract law of the Church was publicised and humanised in the period by increasing numbers of saints' lives written in the vernacular, and by the diffusion of similarly accessible texts about contemplative devotion. This was heady stuff, with an electrifying appeal to certain temperaments. How were devotees to reconcile familial and canonical obligations within marriage with the imitation of the saints and the attainment of glimpses of spiritual perfection now temptingly on offer? This was not just Margery's dilemma, nor was it solely the dilemma of women. Margery and, we may infer, her clerical mentors did not think that her desire for chastity was unusual among married women. Christ said to her: 'Daughter, if thou knew how many wives there are in this world that would love me and serve me right well and duly, if they might be as freely from their husbands as thou art from thine, thou wouldest see that thou wert right much beholden unto me. And yet are they put from their will and suffer full great pain'.[86] It sounds as though some of them had confided in Margery, who is likely to have talked up the marital grumbles of her gossips. The sentiment is likely to have echoed confessional themes familiar too to Margery's clerical cronies. Perhaps we have a glimpse of a coterie of pious groupies of the parish on the occasion when Master Aleyn the Dominican dined with 'a worshipful woman who had taken the mantle and the ring', becoming a vowess, like Margery. Master Aleyn, forbidden to commune with the latter by his Order, had been given permission to speak to her by his Provincial (Thomas Netter) and invited her to the dinner, at which they had a spiritual, uplifting encounter. 'There was a dinner of great joy and gladness, much more ghostly than bodily, for it was savoured and sauced with tales of Holy Scripture.' Afterwards, in token that he would once more stand by Margery in God's cause, he presented her with a pair of knives.[87]

Let us now briefly consider some slight evidence about men's marital problems and spiritual dilemmas. The case of Thomas Tuddenham of Oxborough (1401–62) and his wife Alice Wodehouse was, indeed, very different from what we know about the marriage of the Kempes. According to the evidence presented before Bishop Alnwick's commissaries (including Margery's confessor Robert Spryngolde) in St Margaret's, Lynn on 22 November 1436, he had not had sexual intercourse with Alice in the eight years of marriage which had ended in separation in 1425. Alice, now a nun, was among the witnesses and among those who testified that the child born during the marriage was fathered by her father's chamberlain. Clearly there may have been, if the parties are to be believed, exceptional circumstances leading to non-consummation.[88] It is a curious coincidence that what must have been a celebrated case involving carnality, abstinence and a vow of chastity was tried in Lynn a few months after the recopying of *The Book* commenced. The circumstances of the Tuddenham marriage were, indeed, singular. Yet here was a respected married gentleman (a future patron of Capgrave) who had allegedly failed to consummate the marriage, though living a long time with his wife, a scenario accepted by the episcopal court. Indeed, men who wished to live chastely had more opportunities to seek stability outside marriage in a religious Order, since there were many more places available for them in monasteries than for women. We have evidence that some noblemen who stayed in the secular world tried to subdue their sexual desires (as well as doing penance for other sorts of sins) by habitually chastising their flesh in a way that Margery tried for a time. Capgrave alleged that Henry of Grosmont, Duke of Lancaster (d. 1361) 'beneath a somewhat splendid and, according to the fashion of the kingdom, rich apparel . . . wore a concealed hair-cloth, and thus effectually compelled the flesh to be subservient to the spirit'.[89] The keynote of this expedient (which was to be adopted by such diverse characters as

Henry VI, Edward IV's brother-in-law Earl Rivers, and Sir Thomas More) was its genteel discretion. Maybe its practitioners attempted to fulfil the marital debt abstemiously and abstractedly, exhorting their wives to show likeminded detachment. Wills often echo aspects of the spiritual concerns that were among the central points of mutuality in 'good' medieval marriages – above all, concerns to help one's partner to escape the Devil's wiles, to make a good death, and to minimise the pains of Purgatory. As regards these overriding preoccupations, Margery is presented as having eventually concluded that lovemaking (especially with an enthusiastic husband) was a dark, mutual hindrance. Her solution to the marriage dilemma was distinguished by being uncompromising and extreme: in daring it equalled the forays of Lynn merchant venturers. Through their privations they came back with their cogs laden with cargoes of cod; her gruelling spiritual quests filled her soul with the Company of Heaven.

One remarkable aspect of Margery's character, as presented to us, was her determination to fulfil her ambitions: *The Book* makes the remarkable claim that, consequently, she became a star. It illustrates the constraints imposed according to gender in that society, but it also shows how some folk thought that one woman had been empowered by Christ and that others could be encouraged to use their freedoms to construct a more virtuous way of life. Those who had helped Margery to develop her way, and to have her experiences and feelings transcribed, probably comprised a coterie of reforming clergy of different stripes in Lynn, united in their enthusiasm for mystical devotion, and perhaps influential with other ladies of the parish, wives, widows and anchoresses, and with some of the menfolk, such as the hapless John Kempe. John Capgrave, in his *Liber de Illustribus Henricis* (c. 1446), dedicated to the monk-like but recently married Henry VI, praised the worthiness of the institution of marriage, in refutation of 'those who praise the single life to such a degree that they seem as it were to condemn matrimonial alliances'.[90] Might he not have had partly in mind inspirers and admirers of Margery's Book? They may have pushed a somewhat puritanical agenda on marital issues. The likelihood that *The Book* reflects such a slanted viewpoint should be borne in mind when it is used as evidence for what widespread current views of ideal and actual gender relations then were.

chapter 4

ECCLESIASTICAL AUTHORITY
AND RELIGIOUS CULTURE
IN LYNN

An exploration of the roles of the Church and religion in Lynn is essential to an understanding of the tenor of *The Book* and the attitudes ascribed in it to Margery. *The Book* is an expression of religious mentalities and concerns in Lynn in the 1430s. The work was presumably intended in the first instance for a Lynn readership and audience. It refers offhandedly to what was familiar to them, in homely terms tailored to their preoccupations and ways of expressing themselves. In order to explore the seedbed of the work, and to determine its value as evidence about piety in the town, let us then consider the framework and character of religion there in its subject's lifetime.

Lynn, as we have seen, was under the secular jurisdiction of the bishops of Norwich. As is found in some other places dominated by bishops as landowners, pastoral jurisdiction over the inhabitants was exercised by a special court and they were not subject to the normal jurisdiction of deans and archdeacons, as elsewhere in the diocese. The borough of Lynn was thus distinguished in an important respect from the neighbouring parishes.[1] Notably singular in matters of ecclesiastical jurisdiction, Lynn was unusually unitary for a leading English town in its parochial structure, though this situation did, as we shall see, induce long-lasting internal tensions over matters of jurisdiction. In the early years of the twelfth century, Bishop Losinga had a new church with parochial rights built to serve the burgeoning population clustering on the spits of land along the Ouse. The church's dedication was 'in honour of St Margaret and St Mary Magdalene and of all holy virgins'. Losinga granted the church in appropriation to Norwich cathedral's Benedictine priory. A cell of the monastery, a small priory, was developed together with the parish church. The claustral buildings were to the south of the church; all that can now be seen of them is a quite impressive residential range. The cure of souls was carried out by the appointment of a vicar, who is likely to have been assisted by some of the chaplains serving side altars. The prior of Lynn exercised direct jurisdiction over secular priests in the parish. This is reflected in the concern expressed to Margery by a priest whose 'good master' was the prior (probably Thomas Hevenyngham) as to whether the latter would be recalled to Norwich and replaced, and in 1422, soon after his death and replacement by a 'well worshipful clerk, a doctor of divinity' (John Derham), in the concern of a priest who held an office from him as to whether the new prior would fulfil a proposed mission to go to Henry V in France.[2] The prior and a few other monks from Norwich (four in 1426) were usually resident. St Margaret's priory possessed property in the town, rented out. Since long before Margery's time, the priory had not had any of those sorts of secular jurisdiction within the borough which in some other cities and boroughs created traditions of hostility and friction between clerks and layfolk.

In Lynn the relations of the small community of monks with the borough authorities and with the inhabitants in general seem to have been normally cordial.[3] Lynn burgesses, like burgesses elsewhere, often set aside a sum in their wills for tithes owed to St Margaret's which they had neglected to pay.[4] The monks apparently sided with their Norwich confreres in opposing the plans of groups of parishioners which, on occasion, threatened the integrity of parochial rights. Demarcation problems might arise between the prior and the parishioners over responsibility for the fabric of St Margaret's.[5] The chancel was the monks' choir and the parishioners worshipped in the nave and in side chapels, though leading burgesses might be invited to worship in the choir, and some of Margery's most intense sensations occurred there.[6] Prior Hevenyngham showed his sympathy for Margery's devotion and did the parishioners a good turn by allowing her to receive communion from the parish priests in the prior's chapel so that she was out of their earshot. However, he had to rescind this arrangement as a new brother sent from Norwich objected to her presence there.[7] Hevenyngham may have been the 'worshipful Prior', whose sermon one Good Friday moved Margery to tears, and who bore her demonstrativeness during it 'meekly'.[8]

St Margaret's, despite past vicissitudes, still displays the lineaments of a truly magnificent medieval church, which must have dominated fifteenth-century Lynn. Sufficient remains of how it appeared then for us to appreciate some of the reasons why it was the object of Margery's pride and affection, a worthy centre for the expression of her piety by one who must have seen some fine urban churches on the continent, such as St Lievens Monster at Zierekzee, San Petronio at Bologna and the Marienkirche at Stralsund. Built of white limestone, St Margaret's is 235 feet long, with lofty and wide chancel, nave and aisles. The building of the present church commenced in the mid-twelfth century, but there was a substantial rebuilding in the following century, and considerable works continued to be done in Margery's lifetime and later in the fifteenth century, financed by both private and communal contributions. Mayors and Congregations took their duties as the collective executive of the parishioners of Lynn very seriously, including their responsibility to maintain the nave and the western parts of the fabric. The state of St Margaret's reflected civic worth and pride. The most striking external features of the church today are the two western towers at the end of the nave, which display stonework from the earliest period of building. The low tower at the crossing formerly had as a canopy an octagonal, lead-covered wooden lantern, apparently rather like Ely cathedral's. This was taken down soon after the great storm of 1741, when much of the south-western tower, with its spire, crashed down on the nave and its aisles. So the interior, as we see it today, is to a large extent a rebuilding of the eighteenth and nineteenth centuries. The church has lost other distinctive medieval features, its outer north aisle, and the glass which filled, among others, its great eastern and western windows.[9]

Medieval St Margaret's, as an urban parish church, was probably particularly rich in its sculptured images and its furnishings, since it was the only church in the borough with full parochial rights. It attracted burgesses' bequests, and it was the focus for many of the gilds' religious activities.[10] Before 1300 a chapel in honour of the Blessed Virgin, known as the Gysine, was established at the north-east end of the nave. A priest assigned by the prior to serve the Gysine heard Margery's confession on many occasions. The word 'Gysine' is apparently derived from the Old French word for childbirth (*gesir*), a highly appropriate association since St Margaret gave aid in childbirth, according to the interpretation commonly put on her legend. In fact, St Margaret had her own chapel.[11] Margery, during her frequent pregnancies, like other young wives of the parish, had ample reason to haunt the church.

A notable feature of the interior was probably the chapel of the Holy Trinity Gild. Typically, in the mayoral year 1406–7 this very rich gild (a considerable property owner in the town) had appointed several chaplains to celebrate there, and another one in the church of St James.[12] There were images in St Margaret's in 1389 of St John the Baptist, St Antony, St Katherine, St George and St William of Norwich, among others, which were honoured by particular gilds seeking the patronage of the saint.[13] The church, besides being the centre for much of Lynn's communal, associative and individual piety, was a venue for ecclesiastical suits, and a good deal of secular business may have been unofficially settled within its walls, especially in the Holy Trinity Chapel. As we have seen, the dramatic political confrontation of 30 September 1415, centring on Robert Brunham, started to unfold within the church, where Prior Hevenyngham protected him from insult and tried to moderate the crowd's disorderly behaviour.[14]

It is likely that the images in the church, as well as the performance of the liturgies there and the processions to and from it on the most solemn feast days to which Margery frequently alludes, had been crucial in her early religious education.[15] Before her full conversion, we are told, there was the occasion in the church when her mind was so consumed with the allure of adultery that she could not concentrate on listening to evensong, or on saying the Paternoster, or on any good thought.[16] The reconstructed Margery was apparently a familiar figure there, kneeling or lying, perhaps in some periods almost as much a fixture as the images of the saints. *The Book* recalls many such occasions which were memorable in her devotional life.[17] There was the occasion during Mass (probably in 1413) when a stone from the vault and the attached end of a beam fell on top of her – the parish church was clearly in particular need of the bequests to its fabric fund that well-to-do townsmen frequently made.[18] Then there was the time when Bishop Wakeryng (who held the see from 1416 to 1425) preached and was patient with her ecstatically disruptive reactions to his words.[19] In 1421 there was a fire in the Guildhall. Sparks drifted through the clear air across Saturday Market towards the church, threatening to ignite the lantern vault over the crossing tower – Margery, entering the church, saw sparks drifting down from the lantern. According to *The Book*, a miraculous snowfall saved the church after her prayers.[20]

Before discussing some of Lynn's chapels and other religious institutions, a parish church just outside the borough is worth mentioning. This is All Saints, South Lynn, an ancient structure across the Millfleet, within easy walking distance of St Margaret's. The church is not mentioned in *The Book*, but it may well have drawn Margery since it had an image which is likely to have retained the miracle-working reputation it had in her girlhood, and it also had a long-established anchorhold attached to it (which has been reconstructed). These features helped to maintain the distinctiveness of the parish, which lacked the concentrations of wealth to be found in the overshadowing borough. The image was one of the Holy Trinity. Royal licence was granted to a group to found a fraternity (including women) in its honour in 1414, and John Gaysle, chaplain, was licensed to grant property in the parish to the fraternity in mortmain. Parishioners (John Clerk, 1431; Richard Game, 1432) left money to the altar of the Holy Trinity, and so did a former vicar, John Candeler, who had a special devotion to it and that of the Lady Chapel. His will of 1428 shows him to have been a notable benefactor of the church, bequeathing to it vestments and liturgical books.[21] The anchor-hold too might be a beneficiary. In 1408 Margaret widow of John Lok left 20s to the 'anchorite recluse' of All Saints. In 1417 Katherine Sampson, recluse there, a Cistercian nun, had recently died.[22] The anchor-hold was part of Lynn's strong eremitical culture; in 1406–7 Holy Trinity Gild gave alms to John and Thomas, hermits at St Margaret's, to John, hermit at St Nicholas's church, and the recluse at All Saints Church.[23] A young hermit attached to St Margaret's, Reynald, accompanied Margery and her daughter-in-law to Ipswich in 1433; he was upset when Margery failed to return with him, and only reluctantly accepted her proposal, after her return from the continent, to accompany her back to London and on to Lynn when she encountered him in the Brigettine church at Syon abbey.[24]

Lynn was served by two principal chapels besides St Margaret's church. In the mid-twelfth century episcopal sanction had been granted for the church to have two separate chapels; one dedicated to the seafaring St James, the other to St Nicholas, protector of sailors and wayfarers. St James's chapel was a short way inland, east of St Margaret's by way of Skinner Row. Only a small fragment remains of what was a substantial church, with large transepts.[25] St Nicholas is at the other end of town, to the north beyond Tuesday Market. Like the parish church, it was not far from the staithes, serving a populous area and convenient for seafarers. The chapel stands substantially as it was rebuilt by 1419, apart from the imposing thirteenth-century tower at the south-west corner. The new St Nicholas was rebuilt on a grand, swaggering scale, a manifesto for the standing of its leading worshippers and their ambitions for their church, whose state-of-the art design invited comparisons with the old, patched-up parish church. St Nicholas has an impressive two-storeyed porch, leading into the southern aisle of the nave, with parapet and adorned with a row of niches above the entrance. The church is of a piece in its design and proportions, carried through from the wide, aisled nave to the chancel. The timber roof vault with its flying angels is continued similarly. A notable feature is the amount of wall space taken up by the windows, especially the great east and west windows. Two fifteenth-century bench-ends (now in the Victoria and Albert Museum, London) have depicted on them 'cogs', trading ships, one riding at bay, the other under sail – a reminder of the connections of many of the congregation with maritime enterprise. The chapel was designed with the needs of the congregation to the fore and must have had a breath-taking display of the glazier's art.[26]

By the later fourteenth century permission had been granted for the two chapels in the parish to have their own burial grounds, which relieved pressure on the mother church's graveyard.[27] The communities of both St James and St Nicholas made attempts over a long period to acquire full parochial rights, but were opposed by Norwich cathedral priory (as rector), supported in 1379 by the mayor and community. In 1381 Margery's father appeared before papal judges delegate in St Margaret's as a witness for the prior and convent of Norwich in their successful attempt to oppose the renewal of a papal privilege permitting the holding of all the sacraments and exercise of all parochial rights at St Nicholas.[28] In 1426 a papal letter recited a petition asking that both chapels be granted the privilege of administering the sacraments of baptism, marriage and the purification of women. The petition asserted that the 'multitude and devotion' of parishioners had so increased that on Easter Day there were c. 1,600 communicants in the parish church, 1,400 in St Nicholas and 900 in St James. The pope (Martin V) commissioned the bishop of Ely (Philip Morgan) to enquire into the facts and, if the petition was accurate, to grant the requests, with the important proviso that the rights of the parish church and other parties should be safeguarded. Next year the prior and convent of Norwich appointed proctors to appear before the bishop and other papal judges.[29] However, the petitioners did not succeed. In 1432 another attempt was made on behalf of St Nicholas, backed by the full official weight of the urban community. The mayor (John Permonter) and Congregation wrote to the prior of Norwich in support of the ministration of baptism and purification in the chapel. The leading merchant John Waterden was a prime mover.[30]

This issue of public policy in Lynn is the only one on which a strong opinion was expressed in *The Book*. It related that all sacraments except christenings and purifications could be performed in the chapels, by sufferance of the prior of Lynn, but that some of their parishioners wanted them to have the same privileges as the parish church. In particular, those of the 'greater and fairer' chapel (presumably St Nicholas) were set on having a font (the area at the west end of the chapel intended for baptisms is especially spacious and impressively designed). Those who procured a bull at the papal court included 'rich men, worshipful merchants', enjoying 'great help of lordship'. There was great tension between them and their parson, the prior. Though poor, 'manfully he withstood them through the help of some of his parishioners who were his friends and loved the worship of their parish church'. Bishop Alnwick of Norwich laboured hard to effect a compromise agreement, one which St Margaret's supporters considered would undermine its status. However, the chapel's supporters, trusting in 'lordship and the process of law', rejected the bishop's compromise and had to accept the status quo. 'And so, blessed must be God, the parish church stood still in her worship and her degree as she had done two hundred years before and more.' *The Book*'s account of this episode provides an interesting commentary on the official documentation in its emphasis on the importance of money and maintenance in the prosecution of the case, and in its comments on the roles of the prior of Lynn and the bishop of Norwich. Over this matter, *The Book* was upholding the opinion of Margery's late father and other weighty members of the elite of the 1370s. It was an opinion that Margery shared not only with the monks of Lynn but with some secular clerks, such as her future amanuensis, who anxiously discussed the matter with her, and her confessor Robert Spryngolde, parish priest at St Margaret's, who in 1427 was appointed by the monks of Norwich as one of their proctors in the case.[31]

However, though a significant shift of opinion on the matter apparently occurred in Lynn between the 1370s and the 1430s in favour of the chapels' parishioners, they never acquired full parochial rights. Bishop Alnwick appears to have backed the cathedral priory and the clergy of St Margaret's. The papacy's sympathy with institutional reform proposed by laymen failed to move local entrenched ecclesiastical interests. It was not an issue over which the urban elite were prepared to jeopardise their delicate relationship with their episcopal lord, or their own laboriously reconstructed semblance of communal unity. Despite the recurrence of agitation, Margery's passionate feelings about it, and the unwonted display of partisanship in *The Book* over a controversial ecclesiastical issue, it did not generate sufficiently intense feelings to cause a serious split in the whole parochial community. Margery and other habitual worshippers in the parish church, it seems, had no objection to attending services in the chapels when it suited them. Some of them were in the crowds attracted to St James to hear a popular visiting friar preach; when Margery was banned from his sermons, she may have found herself attending services in St Margaret's abandoned by its congregation.[32] Some staunch worshippers in the chapels certainly retained a reverence for the mother church, such as the rich, well-connected widow Katherine Curson, parishioner of St Nicholas, who in her will of 1415 bequeathed equal amounts for the fabric of the mother church and the two chapels. The less well-to-do Joanne Blocke, who had willed in 1411 to be buried in the cemetery at St Nicholas, left 12d apiece to its altar and that of St Margaret's, and 40d for the chapel's fabric.[33] The burgess William Siliden, in his will of 1410, and John Cook, in his of 1447, both willed to be buried in St James, but also bequeathed worthwhile contributions to the fabric of St Margaret's as well as of the chapel.[34]

The monks dwelling in Lynn had an influence in the town disproportionate to their small number, as *The Book* bears witness, but it was the friars who were the most numerous and conspicuous of the religious in town. Typically of a booming thirteenth-century town, Lynn early on acquired houses of the four leading Orders of friars. The Franciscan house was in St James' End, a continuation of Skinners Row, on the way to the chapel dedicated to the saint. There remains the striking, tall octagonal tower, dating from the later fourteenth century, raised over the cross passage between the chancel and nave of the church. Stylish and rakish in appearance, now with an air of Strawberry Hill Gothic about it, the tower long remained a landmark on the Lynn horizon.[35] The Dominicans were to the north of the Franciscans, the other side of the Purfleet, at the end of Burghard's Lane, in which John Kempe (probably Margery's husband) for long had a tenement. No trace of the friary can be seen. The Augustinians were not far from St Nicholas and the hurly-burly of Tuesday Market; a solitary gateway is all that can be seen of what was probably the biggest friary in Lynn, with the best guesthouse and 'conference facilities'. It housed as many as thirty priests and sixteen brethren in minor orders in 1446.[36] It entertained distinguished guests. Bishop Arundel stayed there overnight in 1383; the future Henry V was accommodated there and so, on another occasion, were his brother, the Duke of Clarence and the duchess.[37] The Carmelite friary was in South Lynn, reached by crossing the Millfleet at Ladybridge, past All Saints Church, and situated damply at the town's edge near the confluence of the river Nar with the Ouse. On the night of 1 July 1363, when the brothers were at matins, atrocious lightning (*tam horribile*) set fire to the church and choir (as well as the town's Tolbooth). There were at least five brothers in the house in 1408, when their evidence was taken in Lynn in a case brought before the Court of Chivalry. They were apparently for the most part local men – the prior, Thomas of Lynn, Doctor of Divinity, the sub-prior, Peter of Lynn, Aleyn Gaywood, *lector* in divinity, Stephen Warram and William Lynn. The house had some local noble connections – as we have seen, Lord Bardolf of Wormegay (d. 1386) willed to be buried there. In 1408 a banner of the arms of Hastings had been in the house for over thirty years, and some of the friars had been acquainted with young Edward Hastings, scion of the Elsing branch of the family, for eight years. Of the friary there remains standing a humble, low entrance gateway of red brick with stone dressings, which has three niches for statues over the archway, the more elaborate central one above the apex probably intended for a statue of the Blessed Virgin. It dates from the fourteenth century.[38]

Princely patronage and the bequests of local folk testify to the continuing good reputation of the friaries of Lynn. Henry of Bolingbroke (later Henry IV) made a donation of 13s 4d to the Carmelites there in

1392 when he was preparing to go on crusade – the Order enjoyed the particular favour of his family. In 1413 Henry V established an obit for his parents and himself in the Augustinian church. Henry VI was so impressed with this house that on his visit in 1446 he granted John Capgrave's petition that he should be its patron.[39] In his will of 1429, the burgess Robert Salesbury, who wished to be buried among the Franciscans, had left sums to all four houses, as did John Cook (1447) and Theodoricus Slynghelant (1448). So did Stephen Guybon of North Lynn (1433) – an illustration of the connection of neighbouring villages with religious culture within the borough.[40] Its wider attraction is also reflected in the will of William Martenet, chaplain (1438), made at Lynn. He was the former vicar of Sporle (Norfolk); he made bequests to Lynn's churches, with a decided preference for St Nicholas, perhaps because it was a short walk from the Augustinians whom he particularly favoured among the Lynn friars. He wished to be buried in the chapel below their bell-tower, and their Provincial, William Wellys, was one of his executors. Another of their patrons was John Spycer, whom, P.J. Lucas has surmised, may be the same former mayor of that name. In his will of 1439, Spycer, then living in their house, made numerous bequests to them, including 3s 4d to the Provincial, William Wellys, and, as Lucas notes, 20d to Master Capgrave. Spycer too willed to be buried there. As his wife, Margaret, was first named among his executors, one wonders if the Spycers (like the Kempes) had taken vows of chastity.[41]

There is considerable literary evidence of intellectual activity among the Lynn friars in Margery's lifetime. Dr Antonia Gransden has identified brief annals by a Franciscan of Lynn, written on two folios of a fourteenth-century commonplace book. However, the author was not a good advertisement for standards of literacy in his house – he wrote 'bad Latin in a cramped charter hand'. The Franciscan, Nicholas Phillypp apparently presented the house with a volume of collected sermons in Latin, some of which he had preached, and some of which were preached by his *confrère* William Melton, a famous preacher, in 1431.[42] Henry IV's father, John of Gaunt, Duke of Lancaster (d. 1399) had patronised a Carmelite at Lynn famous for his mathematical and astronomical learning, who was respected for it by Geoffrey Chaucer. This was Nicholas of Lynn, who had dedicated his *Kalendarium* to Gaunt in 1386.[43] The Dominicans of Lynn were to produce an original and influential work of scholarship. In 1440 a Dominican recluse of their house, a certain Geoffrey, hailing from Norfolk, completed the first English-Latin dictionary, *Promptorium Parvulorum*, which was to become a standard text in England. He intended it to be used to help teach Latin grammar to schoolboys. This ambitious undertaking reflects a strong concern among the Lynn Dominicans for education, and their possession of a good library from which the recluse worked.[44] It may not be entirely coincidental that a schoolboys' gild (an unusual phenomenon) was in existence at Lynn in 1389.[45] The borough's patron, the Duke of Exeter (d. 1426) – another son of John of Gaunt – may have been impressed by the quality of education there. William Worcestre was to record that 'he had three or four children who died at Lyme [*sic*] with the friars'.[46]

The friar associated with Lynn best known for his literary works was John Capgrave, who was born there in 1393 and died there in 1464. He spent much of his life as a friar in the Lynn house, becoming its prior some time between November 1440 and April 1443, and Prior Provincial in 1453. There is no evidence of any contact between Capgrave and Margery, but there were resonances in some of their devotional interests. The English versions of saints' lives which he wrote were sometimes specifically done to meet a female devotional need for such works in the vernacular. The life of St Augustine was written, shortly before 1450, for a 'gentle woman', and the life of St Gilbert was written at the request of the Gilbertines of Sempringham (Lincs.) for 'the solitary women of our religion who cannot understand Latin'.[47] Margery certainly had some contacts in his house. *The Book* mentions a sermon on the Passion, preached by one of its brethren 'before a very large audience', which greatly moved her. The preacher told the congregation, dismayed by her noisy reaction to his words, to leave her alone.[48] Surprisingly, *The Book* does not mention any contacts between Margery and the Lynn Franciscans, though she went on pilgrimage to the shrine of St Francis – perhaps encouraged to do so by the friendly Franciscans she had met in the Holy Land. At Assisi an English friar expressed appreciation for God's 'homely dalliance' with her, 'wrought in her soul'.[49] Yet there is no suggestion in *The Book* that her visit to St Francis earned her merit and respect in the eyes of his brothers in Lynn, though she did make pious links with the Minoresses of Denney. Perhaps the Franciscans of Lynn did not have a brother so well versed in the meditative literature which provided validation for Margery's brand of devotion as clerics to be found among the other Orders and seculars there. However, *The Book*'s emphasis on her rapport with the friars of Mount Sion in Judea, and singling out of Assisi from the many continental shrines she probably visited, may in part reflect a desire to impress the local Franciscans. There is no mention of a visit to the shrine of St Dominic, though she passed through Bologna. If she did visit it, as seems probable, there was no need to refer to it in *The Book* in order to impress her Dominican friends as they would have doubtless been well versed in any particulars of it she was accustomed to relaying to her circle.

Within the religious Orders in Lynn, Margery received spiritual succour above all from some Dominicans and the Carmelites. It was when she was standing at her prayers in the Lady Chapel of a Dominican church (probably the one in Lynn) that she had an outstanding vision of the Blessed Virgin and Child.[50] Quite early on in her spiritual development, Margery received a great deal of apparently unswerving support from an unnamed anchorite attached to the friary. This anchorite was her principal confessor and understood the nature of her contemplation. He seems to have died before she returned from Jerusalem in 1415. The loss of such an influential and enthusiastic supporter may have been a blow to the establishment of her pious reputation.[51] However, she acquired a stout Carmelite admirer. Master Aleyn, Doctor of Divinity, investigated her escape from the fall of masonry and timber in St Margaret's (c. 1413), and pronounced it to be a miracle.[52] In 1417 he met her, at her request, across the Ouse at West Lynn, where her husband and her confessor Robert Spryngolde had come as well: she told them all about her recent ordeals in Leicester and Yorkshire.[53] Master Aleyn was probably the White Friar who, like some other Lynn clergy, interceded – in vain – with a visiting friar for her to be allowed to attend his sermons at St James.[54] Complaint was made to the Carmelite Prior Provincial (the distinguished writer Thomas Netter) about Master Aleyn's close association with her and the support he gave to her way of life. He was forbidden to speak to her and her confessor forbade her to visit his convent. It was a critical moment in her relations with the clergy: her confessor Master Robert (Spryngolde), she complained to Christ, scarcely dared speak to her. However, the prohibitions were withdrawn after Master Aleyn had a serious illness.[55] Meech and Allen identified him as the writer Alan of Lynn, a Cambridge Doctor of Divinity, born c. 1348, who died after 1423. Another possible identification is with Aleyn Gaywood, one of the Carmelites of Lynn who testified there for the Court of Chivalry in 1408. He may have been a former chaplain or, indeed, confessor of Bishop Despenser: he declared he had often heard the deceased bishop say that Edward Hastings was the nearest heir to the Earl of Pembroke who had died at Woodstock (in 1389). It is the sort of table talk that one might have expected of the aristocratic bishop. Gaywood's testimony points to a possible link between Margery and the bishop: it was a small, intimate world of intersecting elites.[56] As for Alan of Lynn, the sixteenth-century biographer and bibliophile John Bale named him as the author of a number of works, including indices 'In revelationes Brigittae', 'In prophetiae Brigittae' and 'In stimulum amoris'. Dom David Knowles described him as 'the prince of classifiers': he provided a table of contents for a vast French encyclopaedia of sermons.[57] If his identification with Master Aleyn is accepted, Margery had as one of her mentors one of the most diligent and learned scholars among the religious in England of his day, and one well versed in the contemplative and Brigettine devotion which were among her hallmarks. Carmelite piety certainly had a particular appeal to Margery. It was while she was walking up and down the Carmelite church in Lynn, shortly before the death of the 'old Prior' of Lynn (Thomas Hevenyngham), that she experienced a heavenly odour and Christ foretold to her the imminent succession of a new prior (John Derham, in 1422).[58]

Let us now consider Margery's mentors among the secular clergy. There were few beneficed in Lynn, though some former beneficed clerks, such as William Martenet, may have considered the town a good place to retire to, with congenial devotional and material amenities. It is likely that there were a considerable number of chaplains there, serving altars in St Margaret's, providing for the cure of souls in the two detached chapels, contracted to the Holy Trinity Gild, and being more casually hired by the large number of gilds to celebrate on feast days and at requiem masses and obits. It may have been to provide the chaplains of Lynn with unity of purpose and social coherence that, rather unusually, a clerks' gild was formed, honouring St John the Baptist in the parish church. Its statutes were ordained in 1369 and it was in existence twenty years later. In 1373 Bishop Despenser had issued a set of ordinances at Gaywood to enforce good conduct on the secular clergy of Lynn. There may have been a tendency for some of them to behave inappropriately; years later William Sawtre was to create scandal by preaching Lollard doctrines. Some of them were to take up with Margery, interesting themselves in her developed forms of devotion – such as her amanuensis and the priest who read devotional literature with her. Margery may have been discriminating about choosing confessors from what perhaps was a motley crowd of chaplains; she preferred her confessors to have standing as holy men, graduates and office-holders, men whose authoritative stamp would enhance her pious reputation. The secular clergy of Lynn certainly loom large in *The Book*. It does not give the impression that devotional life there was dominated by the friars. St Margaret's and its clergy, secular and monastic, remain central. Nor does it give any hint of antagonisms between the Orders, or between religious and seculars. Such material might have undermined its agenda. Nevertheless, the fact that its subject's devotion was infused and nourished by seculars, friars and monks at Lynn, and that they conferred and co-operated on how Margery's spirituality was to be handled, is impressive testimony to elements of religious harmony and unity among them.[59]

Margery's principal confessor among the seculars, Master Robert Spryngolde, was variously described in *The Book* as Bachelor of Law and as the parish priest of St Margaret's. Possibly in the 1410s, the mayor, burgesses and commons of Lynn wrote to the bishop of Norwich to defend Spryngolde (described as Bachelor in Decrees and parish priest of St Margaret's) against grievous accusations. He was, they said, to the best of their knowledge, very honest and discreet. He confessed Margery over a long period (with intervals during her absences from Lynn), from at least 1413 until the time when Book Two was written down (1438).[60] Spryngolde appears to have been on occasion harsh and critical of her, but he was fundamentally sympathetic to her characteristic spirituality and staunch in her defence against her critics. We catch glimpses of him taking leave of her when she set out for Jerusalem,[61] travelling to West Lynn to meet her on her return from Yorkshire,[62] and conferring with her and Prior Hevenyngham about the problems she caused during services.[63] When the Guildhall caught fire, he took the Blessed Sacrament in procession out of the church and towards the burning building – the clergy bringing spiritual aid to the stricken urban community.[64] In 1433, as Margery's daughter-in-law prepared to return to her native Prussia, Spryngolde was solicitously concerned about her being suitably accompanied. When Margery volunteered to go with her to Ipswich, he responded testily: 'How should you go with her? You but lately hurt your foot, and you are not yet fully cured, and also you are an old woman. You may not go.'[65] This is the authentic tone of discourse between aged, affectionate friends long exasperated with each other's foibles. Not surprisingly, he was indignant when she defiantly embarked at Ipswich with her daughter-in-law without telling him of her intention.[66] Nevertheless, her dialogues with Christ reveal how dependent she was on Spryngolde's support and how deep her respect and affection for him were.[67]

The other Lynn secular mentioned in *The Book* as important to Margery's spiritual life is the one who wrote out a revised copy of its first part and to whom she dictated the second part. He himself is on occasion a key character in *The Book*. He is shown having doubts about the validity of her spirituality in face of criticisms in the town. These doubts led him to defer his promise to copy out the text for up to four years. Yet he triumphantly overcame them so that his testimony in *The Book* to this struggle, reinforced by his labours in writing out Margery's 'feelings', bring weighty support of their truth. Apart from this, we learn little about this clerk. When he first started to write for Margery, he had problems with his eyesight, which worsened when he took to wearing spectacles. However, his sight improved and he was able to complete the work. He contributed a good deal to the detailed Proem to *The Book*, which, as we have seen, provided a fuller explanation of its purpose and the circumstances in which it was written than appeared in the existing brief preface. He wanted it to be made clear that he was a stickler for accuracy – he was concerned lest he had not spelt German place names accurately.[68] It is odd that he is never named. Though the use of proper names in *The Book* is erratic, anonymity in this case seems to be deliberate and is likely to have been an exercise in humility rather than the result of caution. Robert Spryngolde might be seen as a candidate for amanuensis, but he does not fit the bill: he is usually portrayed as authoritative, never as erratic and enfeebled – and as unswerving in his faith in Margery. Perhaps the amanuensis was a chaplain at St Margaret's who was subordinate to Spryngolde. He researched the phenomenon of her weeping, 'through the prompting of a worshipful clerk, a bachelor of divinity', which might be taken to imply that he held such an inferior position. He said, moreover, that there were 'many thriftier, richer priests in this church [St Margaret's] than I am'.[69] Moreover, unlike many of the clergy in *The Book*, he has no academic degree attributed to him. He spent a number of years in Lynn, not receiving promotion to a benefice elsewhere as some of Margery's earlier clerical friends had done in due course.[70] These straws in the wind suggest that he was relatively humble in status when he wrote out *The Book*. There was, indeed, the chance that it might not meet with favour, or even that it might prove suspect. The amanuensis's involvement with Margery probably put his prospects on the line. His undertaking was brave as well as arduous, though he frankly accused himself of cowardice in avoiding her company and hesitating for long before taking up the task.

There are a few other secular priests whom *The Book* mentions as Margery's supporters in the town – some of these references may be to identical priests. A chaplain in the Gysine chapel in St Margaret's confessed her on occasion, as we have seen. There was the chaplain at St James who was sympathetic to her problems, and the priest who came to Lynn (lodging with his mother) with whom Margery explored sacred and devotional literature.[71] When prevented from speaking to Master Aleyn, she had lamented the dearth of spiritual interlocutors. *The Book* names two sympathetic priests, Thomas Andrew and John Amy, who were unavailable because they had received benefices elsewhere; they are likely to have had prior employment in Lynn as parochial chaplains.[72] The Margery projected in *The Book* was lucky to have long-term confessors of the calibre of Master Aleyn and Robert Spryngolde – the impression given is of an eager penitent and clamorous visionary who would have been enormously demanding of time and patience. These two – and the amanuensis – are among the occasionally or scarcely serenaded heroes of *The Book.*

As we have seen, *The Book* is remarkably emollient in its references to the clergy of Lynn, projecting generally harmonious patterns in their relations with each other (whatever their order), in relations with Margery and, indeed, with the laity in general. Here one may, perhaps, detect guiding clerical tones, which the often strident heroine presumably saw the sense in meekly echoing. *The Book* does not attribute the alleged hostility in Lynn to Margery's religious personality specifically to the clergy; it is not clear that she provoked continuously bubbling clerical fury there, despite the serious repercussions of the complaint to Netter. That does not prove that there was an absence of clerical controversy about her: one of *The Book*'s intentions may have been to allay it. However, hostile reactions to her among townsfolk are in some part blamed on priests who were newcomers; a new monk at the priory, and the visiting friar who was a famous preacher, but in general such lay reactions are portrayed as instinctive and often impulsive. Lynn clergy mentioned are represented as on the whole caring and supportive of Margery, tolerant of her strange behaviour, if sometimes worried about its significance as, indeed, she was herself at times. As far as they are concerned, there is an absence in *The Book* of that hackneyed literary *topos*, anticlerical rhetoric. The religious and seculars encountered by Margery whom she regarded as malicious towards herself, or generally sinful, or too tolerant of the sins of those in their care, were mostly located elsewhere. Indeed, she did tell a striking anticlerical tale to Archbishop Bowet and she had a universal concern for the suffering of the souls of sinful clerics as well as layfolk. Yet the Margery of *The Book* signally fails to echo any strains of anticlericalism specifically emanating from the elite and populace of Lynn. Their clergy are not shown as dismissive of her or oppressive towards her but generally, it appears, keeping cool in face of the challenges to habit, custom and propriety which she presented. Rather, *The Book* show-cases clergy who fulfil the expectations of the laity, and laymen who work closely with the clergy to maintain parochial rights. It shows monks and friars who co-operate with secular clergy and layfolk in pursuit of the individual and the common good. Margery's thirst for good sermons is shared to a high degree by the townsfolk in general; clergy strive to fulfil these expectations. The friar renowned for his sermons is invited to preach in St James chapel, where he is a popular draw. Subsequently he preaches in the chapel's churchyard, 'where was much people and great audience, for he had an holy name and great favour of the people, in so much that some men, if they wist that he should preach in the country, they would go with him from town to town, so great delight they had to hear him and so, blessed might God be, he preached full holily and full devoutly'.[73] Master Aleyn, too, emerges as no mean preacher. Whilst praying in St Margaret's during Advent, Margery was seized by a desire to hear him preach and Christ assured her that he would preach a very holy sermon.[74]

One of the most remarkable institutional developments in the later medieval Church, often reflecting lay initiatives, was the proliferation of confraternities. They concentrated on honouring the divine and saintly, providing mutual help for suffering in Purgatory, promoting mutual amity and good conduct, and mitigating the temporal misfortunes of their brethren and sisters. Let us now consider the roles which confraternities played in religious life in Lynn. Our chief sources of knowledge about them are the surviving returns made by gilds in response to a royal commission in 1389. There are certificates from forty-five gilds within the borough, a very large number for a town of its size.[75] However, an account by the borough chamberlains of contributions made by gilds in 1371 for the repair of dykes lists as many as sixty-eight.[76] It may be that the 1389 survey was less thorough and that some certificates have perished – some of the remaining ones are in poor condition. The apparent disappearance of confraternities in the intervening period – and the foundation of new ones – may also in part reflect the rise and fall in the popularity of cults and the foundation of some on unsure bases, in terms of human and financial resources. It is striking that, of the twenty-six fraternities of 1371 for which there are no certain certificates in 1389, only five were among the twenty-five whose chattels were valued from £3 upwards, but twenty-one were among the forty-three with chattels valued at less.[77]

There were, indeed, great variations in the valuations of 1371, from the gild of the Ascension's £45 to a gild of St Katherine's 4s (the great gild of Holy Trinity not appearing among the assessed, presumably because of its special financial relationship with the government of the borough).[78] Such variations must to some extent have stemmed from distinctions in status and wealth between the memberships of the confraternities and have been a factor in determining continuity, besides rates of mortality, the efficacy of particular cults, and the attitudes towards them of the parish clergy.[79] Members of the gild of St Thomas the Martyr in St Nicholas chapel are likely to have been rich parishioners. According to its certificate, the entry fee was 5s (contrasting with 4d for St Peter's gild); the individual offering required towards Masses for a deceased member was a standard one ($\frac{1}{2}$d), but for an exceptionally large number of Masses (thirty).[80] Another gild of St Thomas probably consisted of poor folk, for its constitution laid down that no one should come to a gild feast barelegged or barefoot; the gilds of St Edmund and St Nicholas also made stipulations about respectable attire.[81]

Some gilds had a long lifespan. In 1389 the gild of the Ascension was said to have existed 'time without memory'[82] and Holy Trinity Gild was the ancient gild merchant. Only five gilds were categorised in 1389 as occupational – those of the clerks (St John the Baptist), the young scholars (St William of Norwich), the young merchants (Nativity of St John the Baptist), shipmen (Exaltation of the Holy Cross) and coifmakers (Decollation of St John the Baptist).[83] Some certificates give valuable information about the date, circumstances and rationale of the foundation. The earliest among the five gilds of St Thomas of Canterbury was probably one founded in 1272, with the purpose of maintaining a light before his image in the parish church, 'because of the honour which so many of the town bore towards him'.[84] Doubtless devotion to the saint was stirred by the relic in the church of St Edmund, North Lynn, just outside the borough – the staff which he took when travelling by sea (perhaps especially valued by seafarers).[85] A gild of St James had been founded in his chapel 'a long time before the great pestilence' and one of St Peter was founded there in 1329.[86] The number of gilds said to date from c. 1349–89 is as large as fifteen. During the great pestilence, 'in which the greater part of the people of the town died', three men (later joined by another thirteen) set up the Corpus Christi gild. They intended it to provide fittingly impressive lights to be carried in front of the Blessed Sacrament when it was taken to the sick.[87] Gilds were founded in honour of St Margaret (1354), St Nicholas (1359), the Decollation of St John the Baptist (1361), his Nativity (1362) and the Exaltation of Holy Cross (1368). The young merchants who honoured the Nativity of St John intended to do repairs to the parish church; in 1389 they aspired to build their own chapel as an extension to it.[88] St James chapel in 1367 acquired a gild of All Saints and the Purification of the Virgin at her altar there. In the following year the shipmen's and clerks' gilds were founded, the latter in the parish church.[89] In 1374 St James's acquired a Baptist's gild, and in 1376 St Nicholas chapel one of St Thomas of Canterbury.[90] The foundations in the two chapels suggest the vigour of their parochial life.

However, probably the most noteworthy foundation in 1376 in the parish church was the gild of St George, a saint closely associated with crusading in the Holy Land and with the Virgin Mary (as in another Lynn gild dedicated to both of them, which existed in 1389). His cult had been favoured by Edward III, ageing and debilitated in 1376. The 'Good Parliament' that year opened with dire warnings about how the French and their allies were planning to attack the realm. The inability of the king was exposed and his son, the Black Prince died during the session.[91] These worrying circumstances may have induced some burgesses to come together to honour and intercede with St George, giving expression to the conviction that, in obedience to the Virgin, he protected England.[92] The surviving Guildhall of St George, begun in 1406, testifies to the flourishing state of his cult in Lynn in the fifteenth century.[93]

In 1377 a gild was founded in honour of a saint of a very different stripe – a 'modern' saint whose cult was to flourish in England in the fifteenth century too. This was St Sitha (Zita of Lucca, d. 1272). She had been a maid in service and became the patron saint of female domestics. Her cult doubtless appealed to the many women in Lynn who served in households.[94] More conventionally, people living in Damgate founded a confraternity in St James chapel in 1378 in honour of Christ, the Blessed Virgin and All Saints.[95]

The pace of new foundations continued in the years shortly before 1389. The schoolboys started their gild in honour of St William in 1382, and shortly before 1389 six townsmen who had been on pilgrimage to Canterbury founded yet another gild especially in honour of St Thomas, with the object of maintaining a light at his shrine, for which one of their members was to go on pilgrimage to it each year.[96] St James's had recently acquired two more gilds – one of St Giles and another in honour of both St Giles and St Julian. St Giles looked after beggars and cripples, St Julian innkeepers and travellers, cults appropriate for a chapel which had an almshouse nearby and was on the outskirts of the town.[97]

The organisation of the gilds for the most part followed a set pattern: many of the certificates use identical phraseology in describing their organisation. It was considered preferable to copy tried and tested arrangements: one of the gilds of St Thomas was said to be constituted 'as the manner is'.[98] The ancient gild of the Ascension had a larger variety of officers than was usual – an alderman, a dean, clerk and steward.[99] The essential officers in most of the gilds were the alderman and the stewards (*custodes, scabini, skevyns*). They might be fined if they neglected their offices.[100] In the shipmen's gild there was concern that the alderman's authority over the brethren should be preserved and that he should settle disputes among them. Sailors were probably notable for rumbustiousness. The constitution of their gild illustrates well one of the purposes of gilds – to maintain harmony among groups of neighbours and fellow workers. The sailors were to pay fines in wax (common currency for gild fines) if they were rebellious or 'unbuxom' towards the alderman when the gild met to drink or for 'morrowspeech'. Those who wronged a brother were fined and had to make peace; fines were imposed for discussing gild counsel with 'any strange man or woman'. Was this drafted with gossips in taverns and girls in every port in mind? One is reminded of the animadversions on the sins of sailors, whose 'wickedness ... exceeds that of all other men' in a penitential manual for parish priests written in 1344, which W.A. Pantin cited: 'In all lands and regions they touch upon, they contract matrimony *de facto* with different women, believing that it is lawful for them'.[101] The number of *custodes* generally varied in the gilds from two to five: a gild's stock or cash was divided equally in their custody.[102] The schoolboys' gild had only one official, the custodian – in 1389 he was their master, John Goldsmyth. All their assets had been spent then on works in the parish church.[103] Some or all of the stock of other gilds may have consisted of ale; concerns were sometimes registered about unauthorised and clandestine ale-tapping. Most gilds are unlikely to have afforded dedicated premises; presumably these had formal meetings for drinking and feasting in a member's house and stored chattels there.[104]

The dedications in the certificates of 1389 are highly conventional. Six were made principally to feasts of the Godhead, eight wholly or in part to feasts of the Blessed Virgin.[105] Figures from the New Testament were St Anne, St Peter and St James – and, above all, as in 1371, St John the Baptist, prime patron of eremitical culture (a culture, as we have seen, well regarded in Lynn). In the Holy Land, Margery insisted on visiting the holy place associated with him on the Jordan.[106] Early male saints who had gilds were Antony, George, Julian, Lawrence, Leonard and Nicholas; the females were St Margaret and St Katherine. More modern saints were the eighth-century Giles and the thirteenth-century Sitha.[107] Two East Anglian saints were honoured, St Edmund and St William of Norwich, but St Thomas of Canterbury had more gilds dedicated to him in Lynn than anyone except the Virgin. The majority of certificates fail to state which church the confraternity was attached to. St Nicholas's chapel appears to be under-represented, with only four gilds,[108] St James had at least ten,[109] but it is probable that St Margaret's sample (fourteen) reflects the biggest concentration. They included the pre-eminent gilds of Holy Trinity and Corpus Christi, and three dedicated to feasts of St John the Baptist.[110]

The cults attributed to Margery in *The Book* to some extent replicate those popular in the confraternities when she was in her teens. Women as well as men were admitted to many of the Lynn gilds, but it is not clear whether young, unmarried women were. Besides saints from the Gospels particularly reverenced then, Margery was to place St Paul and St Jerome high in her canon – they were associated with the written word, which became so important in her devotion. However, she was a thoroughly conventional daughter of Lynn in her reverence for St Thomas. Other 'modern' saints who had been popular in Lynn were ignored in *The Book*. Sitha's omission is hardly surprising in view of the low view Margery expresses of her maidservants and her conviction that she knew best how to act the holy maid (in her contemplations).[111] Perhaps *The Book* reflects a shift or broadening of interests among the spiritual *cognoscenti* of Lynn, in its enthusiasm for St Bridget, St John of Bridlington and St William of York. Though *The Book* can be used to demonstrate how gild culture may have been a component in the formation of a young woman's piety in Lynn, it also shows how her pious interests were broadened by knowledge of books and by travel.

The importance of travel in the economy of Lynn may also have a bearing on why there was a marked enthusiasm there for confraternities. They were associations concerned with helping impoverished members and, in some cases, ensuring decent burials, as well as in assisting the passage of souls. Many Lynn men earned their living facing the hazards of travelling and trading, especially at sea. A practical reason for the foundation of the young scholars' gild was to give some assistance (perhaps with the costs of education) if any of their fathers suffered misfortunes: a boy was to be helped by his brethren if he suffered loss because of the sea or some other mishap.[112] A similar provision for alms was made by the gild of St Leonard.[113] As the patron saint of prisoners, he was probably popular among merchant venturers and sailors, vulnerable to this hazard from encounters with enemy shipping, pirates and foreign port authorities.

Another stimulus to the formation of gilds in Lynn was that, though a populous town, with well-defined status groups and distinctive areas, it had only one parish church. Attempts to establish new fully fledged parishes were frustrated. The formation of clusters of gilds may, to some degree, have been a substitute for the network of parochial communities found in towns of comparable size. It is tempting to argue that this gild culture acted as a barrier to the spread of heresy. However, one must not attribute a rock-like solidity to the traditional beliefs of brethren and sisters or assume that their highly public demonstrations of their cults had more than marginal effects on the spirituality of the generality of bystanders. It is, indeed, doubtful as to whether the majority of the inhabitants of Lynn were gild members. Some of the gilds started off, as we have seen, as small groups of friends or acquaintances. Not all may have wanted to alter the mix of the group by trying to attract larger numbers. Some confraternities were clearly ephemeral. The certificate for the gild of St Edmund includes what appears to be a membership list. There is a total of twenty-two names. Was this a moribund gild, perhaps founded by a group or individuals who had gone on pilgrimage to the saint's shrine and experienced his beneficence? The compiler seems to have been uncertain about the membership – two members were said to be dead and two had their names crossed through.[114]

We may know a good deal about gilds in later fourteenth-century Lynn, but we know very little about heretics there, apart from the episode of the chaplain at St Margaret's, William Sawtre, who was convicted of heretical beliefs in 1399.[115] As we have seen, there is a blank in the records as a result of the disappearance of many for the court of the peculiar in Lynn. We cannot assume that heresy was not a continuing problem there, smartly eradicated by Sawtre's retraction. However, only a few possible cases are known. In Congregation on 14 January 1429 the mayor reported that John Wythe, John Springwelle and Thomas Chevele had been arrested on suspicion of heresy under the authority of the bishop (Alnwick of Norwich), and asked what should be done with them. The matter was respited.[116] On 7 August Nicholas Drye of Lynn was examined before Bishop Alnwick at Norwich. He had asserted that confession was only licit when death was imminent. When he had been in Wymondham on Easter Day 1428, he said that he had not confessed for four years, and he failed to confess that day too. Drye promptly abjured and William Brystowe, shipwright of Lynn, went surety for him.[117]

The Book makes clear that Margery had been examined on suspicion of heresy in the diocese many years before it was written: 'when she was one time admonished to appear before certain officers of the Bishop to answer to certain articles which should be put against her by the stirring of envious people, the good Vicar [Richard Caister, of Norwich], prefering the love of God before any shame of the world, went with her to her examination and delivered her from the malice of her enemies. And then was it revealed to this creature that the good Vicar should live seven years after and then he should pass hence with great grace, and he did as she . . .' As Caister probably died on 19 March 1420, the examination may have taken place c. 1413.[118] In 1417 a friar told Archbishop Bowet that 'she should have been burnt at Lynn, had his order, that was Friar Preachers, not been'. It is not clear whether this accusation (if not false) referred to the same episode.[119] Perhaps the best evidence for continued fear about heresy arising in Lynn in the 1430s is *The Book* itself. It is an issue which recurs in it. Official examinations of heresy which had taken place twenty or so years before and which gave Margery the imprimatur of orthodoxy are recounted. So are ancient casual accusations flung at her, such at those made in the streets of Canterbury, and a remark by an irritable, well-dressed woman in Lambeth Palace.[120] Testimony to Margery's orthodoxy is always attributed to respected clerics; layfolk are not accorded any religious authority as they were among Lollards. One phenomenon laymen testify to is a fall of snow.[121] It is probable that *The Book* was composed partly in order to confound heretics and strengthen orthodox faith by firmly establishing its subject's orthodoxy, and by demonstrating beyond doubt that she was a holy woman of impeccable faith and life, through whom God's mercy flowed exceptionally, to help to save the people.

The largely favourable backdrop of ecclesiastical institutions and religious culture in Lynn which can be perceived in *The Book* receives some validation from record sources. Indeed, in these areas *The Book* was both discreet and slanted. However, there were factors in the ways in which the Church was constituted and had developed there which made it in the early fifteenth century a force which was on the whole socially bonding rather than divisive. A society which came to be factionalised by long-lasting secular issues needed this unifying culture in order to help avoid more extreme polarisation and to aid in the process of reconciliation. The Church in Lynn was well fitted for such a role. There was no ongoing jurisdictional struggle between the urban and monastic authorities such as the one which divided those of the city and cathedral priory at Norwich. There was not a large number of vicars and parsons in Lynn, concerned to limit the activities of friars on a host of small parochial patches. Despite attempts to redefine the role of the parish church, it remained the principal focus of worship. The writing of *The Book* and its tenor suggest that there were leading clergy in Lynn eager and well qualified to exploit their influential position in order to meet the devotional needs of the laity – and, indeed, to foster nourishing and challenging spiritual regimes.

The liveliness of some Lynn churchmen needs to be related to the expectations of a laity imbued not only with parochial patriotism but with cosmopolitan lore. The variety of Lynn's cults is likely to have been enriched not only by its regional economic and social links, but by its multifarious ties with a wider world. The visits of princes and nobles brought the piety of their households into contact with the town's.[122] The voyages of Lynn merchants and sailors, and the hosting of aliens there, vitally connected the town with the religious culture of Christendom, particularly across the North Sea. *The Book* bears striking witness to the variety of links with 'Dewchland', and also to cultural horizons which soared over the Pyrenees and the Alps and across the Mediterranean.

chapter 5

THE PIETY OF *THE BOOK OF MARGERY KEMPE*

An exposition of Margery's devotion is the rationale of *The Book*; this is the context in which it provides fullest information and a fulsome exposition. Its most valuable historical aspects are that it goes further in exploring and reconstituting the development of an individual's devotional life than any other text from England in the fifteenth century, and that it does so with a particular emphasis on social contexts not found in many devotional treatises. This emphasis gives us insights into religious attitudes and influences in Lynn, into the interaction of traditional and novel modes of pious behaviour, and the relationships between elite and popular forms of worship.

Margery's piety, as presented in *The Book*, cannot be assumed to be a series of snapshots accurately and fully depicting the development of a devout personality. The necessarily distorted and fragmentary image projected in the text is significant as a statement of what she considered to be acceptable, persuasive and edifying for readers and auditors in Lynn and elsewhere. We may be thankful that she felt that anecdotal verisimilitude (like that essayed by witnesses in judicial process), as well as searing soul dramas, would be appealing and convincing. For the historian, *The Book*'s admitted inattention to chronology is regrettable. This haphazardness makes it difficult to date the stages in Margery's spiritual odyssey. There is, indeed, a clear progression from an unregenerate state through stages of illumination. In this respect the scheme of *The Book* consciously tracks the traditional ones found in saints' written lives (*vitae*) and in treatises giving instruction in meditative methods. *The Book*'s focus is on states of mind. Incidents are often recalled out of sequence in order to develop or amplify a point. Margery's memories are likely to have often been confused and mistaken at many points. The recitative of humdrum terrestrial activity has faded; we are presented with carefully rehearsed and staged recordings of high and low spots, presented as spiritual arias. There is artfulness underlying the apparent artlessness of

The Book, evident particularly in the tight reconstruction of speeches and dialogue, human and divine, in accordance with the indulgent medieval convention of pious invention. The finished product is a vivid image of a devout *persona*, but one not constructed along conventional hagiographical lines.

Let us attempt to summarise the progress in religion of the 'Margery of *The Book*', the refining process by which she presented her mature pious personality as having been distilled. Then we will go on to consider some of the elements constituting the finished product, and some of their origins, traditional and novel. *The Book* starts by describing the circumstances of a breakdown, which may have occurred soon after her marriage and the birth of her first child, probably in the mid-1390s. Her attempts to allay the depression which led to the breakdown, by fasting and performing acts of charity, had been in vain. The illness lasted, with intermissions, for the best part of a year and ended after she had had a vision of Christ at her bedside.[1] Margery is then shown as reverting to a thoroughly worldly way of life, a phase which probably coincided in part with the years 1403–5.[2] However, she eventually grew dissatisfied with this worldliness. One night, as she lay next to her husband, she heard a heavenly melody and sprang out of bed. There followed two years of tranquillity during which she attended dutifully to her devotions. She engaged with a new intensity in conventional pious activities, some of which she later, as one who was further illuminated, came to disparage. She confessed as many as three times a day, she fasted, frequently attended church services and wore a hair shirt, made out of sacking which she procured from a malt-drying kiln. In the long run this did not prove to be an adequate spiritually nourishing regime. Margery had three years of temptations.[3] What finally transformed her way of life, triggering a liberating but painful rebirth as a resplendently garbed holy woman, was, we are told, a conversion experience, the sort of sudden illumination which has created or transformed Christians from St Paul onwards. Indeed, St Paul was one of the saints with whom she was particularly to relate, despite the fact that she suffered as a result of his strictures in the *First Epistle to the Corinthians* on women who preached. For Christ held him up as an example to her of the unworthy whom He had made worthy, and on occasion sent him to comfort her soul.[4]

Margery's critical experience occurred in Advent, when she was kneeling in St John's chapel in St Margaret's church, weeping and seeking mercy for her sins. Christ 'ravished her spirit'. He told her to give up wearing the hairshirt (for which St John the Baptist was the supreme exemplar) and also the eating of meat.[5] She was to receive the Sacrament every Sunday and was to cease frequent praying with beads, but was forthwith to 'think such thoughts as I will put in thy mind. I shall give thee leave to bide till six of the clock to say what thou will. Then shalt thou lie still and speak to me by thought, and I shall give to thee high meditation and true contemplation'. She was instructed to go afterwards to the anchorite at the Dominican friary, reveal Christ's words to him, and act according to his divinely inspired counsel.[6] This turning-point in her spiritual life occurred before she set off for Jerusalem in 1413. The visionary experiences described in the following chapters, concerned with the birth and infancy of the Blessed Virgin, and with the Nativity, appear to be the ones which she related to the vicar Richard Caister at Norwich 'long before' her visit to Archbishop Arundel in the same year and soon after the birth of her last child.[7] Since she had fourteen children, if she was married c. 1393 and gave birth less than once a year, the conversion cannot have occurred before 1408–9. It would seem that one or more of the clergy of Lynn read and expounded contemplative treatises to Margery and encouraged her to develop the meditative techniques which they advocated and set out. Speaking to Caister, she compared her experience of the workings of the love of God in her soul to those described in books she had heard being read; she specified 'Hilton's book . . . Bride's [St Bridget's] book . . . Stimulus Amoris . . . Incendium Amoris'.[8] These were among the devotional works that the priest who lodged with his mother in Lynn read to Margery for the best part of seven or eight years. He also read to her from the Bible and Biblical commentaries.

The Book does not imply that he was her principal instructor, but rather that she stimulated his devotion; it says that the reading broadened his knowledge and improved his spirituality, enhancing his career prospects. This relationship must have commenced after her return to England in 1415, for during it she was experiencing the full flood of weeping which had first occurred in Jerusalem.[9] The Dominican anchorite to whom Christ had sent her many years before is likely to have been among the earlier developers of her contemplative life. His reaction to her revelations had been to meditate on Christ as her spiritual mother. His words, as reported, succinctly laid down the central theme of The Book. He, 'with great reverence and weeping, thanking God, said, "Daughter, thou art sucking even on Christ's breast, and thou havest an earnest-penny of Heaven"'. He charged her to tell him her future revelations so that he could distinguish whether they came from the Holy Ghost or 'your enemy the Devil'. Margery's spiritual exaltation made her a prime and particularly vulnerable target for the Devil's illusionary wiles.[10] The spiritual direction and devotional schooling of Margery was a task in which various Lynn clerics are shown to have had parts over the years –

especially her confessors, the Carmelite Master Aleyn, who 'informed her in questions of Scripture when she would any ask him', and the secular priest Robert Spryngolde, who directed her in the technique of meditation.[11] Her ability to commune about Scripture 'she learned in sermons and by communing with clerks' – an impeccably orthodox approach.[12] The privilege which she received from Archbishop Arundel in 1413 to choose her own confessor doubtless gave her opportunities to broaden the range of her devotional experiences, though she appears to have been strongly attached to only a few confessors. Knowledge that she had been trained by learned clergymen from Lynn may account for the discerning reverence, or at least approval, with which she was apparently treated, as we shall see, by a remarkable number of archbishops and bishops – Repingdon, Arundel, Peverel, Wakeryng and Chichele.[13]

So Margery, according to *The Book*, was a hardened sinner who became a penitent, relying heavily on the strenuous performance of religious obligations, recitation of stock prayers and routine infliction of pain and discomfort. However, she was to be raised up from among the conventionally devout and received into the select band of the devotional elite, those to whose souls Christ, the Virgin Mary and some of the most revered saints spoke with intimate frankness and love. In this scenario, her words about the experiences of her soul's ears and eyes were worthy of being as gravely considered by the spiritual *cognoscenti* as, presumably, her aged father's pronouncements on public affairs had been received by his brethren of the Holy Trinity Gild. Margery had been inducted into a devout mode which was appropriate to the status of her family, which suited her temperament, and from which she was to derive psychological satisfaction. The practice of contemplation is shown as having given her life and her prospective afterlife new shape and meaning, of which she had had only dim and flickering intimations in what were presented as her unregenerate and unenlightened phases. She was empowered to overcome adversity and, indeed, seek it out through the zeal for Scripture and excitement about modern piety which, it can be surmised, gripped and was imparted to her by some of her local clergy. One wonders, however, whether her mentors viewed the emergence of her new spiritual *persona*, if as described, with a certain nervousness. Might they not originally have hoped that meditation would calm her down, not stir her up in new and alarming ways?

Margery's conversion either created or brought to a head a crisis in her marriage, as we have seen. She was unable to find a way to reconcile her intense devotional life with continued licit sexual activity. John Kempe eventually submitted to her will in this matter, enabling her to take a vow of chastity. She was able to fulfil Christ's commands that she should go on major pilgrimages abroad and wear white clothes.[14] These two commands appear puzzling. Vowesses may indeed have worn distinctive clothes. Many of them were widows, clad in their weeds, for whom black was the appropriate colour. They often boarded at convents – one does not have the impression that devout vowesses gadded about. The practice of contemplation was well suited to a quiet and stable way of life, like that of Margery's mentor Dame Julian at Norwich.[15] However, Margery is portrayed as seeking out distant shrines, noisily grabbing attention in public places, and buttonholing those she encountered in an unladylike way. She was notable as a contemplative determined to make her mark in the active life, traversing much of the known world and moulding people's lives not just through private prayer and the retailing of prophecies to individuals, but through utilitarian performance of often tough good works. She attended deathbeds and meditated at them. She cared for the sick. For the love of Jesus, she wished to embrace and kiss lepers whom, with other sick people, she could not abide to see in her days of worldly prosperity. Her visit to the grave from which Lazarus was raised from the dead at Bethany may have made a strong impression on her. She was emulating saints: Athanasius, Hugh Bishop of Lincoln and Francis notably kissed lepers. Her confessor forbade her to kiss male lepers, but she fulfilled her wish by kissing two sick women in a leperhouse on the lips and commiserating with them.[16] Perhaps she remembered that, when she was in her teens, her father had been officially involved with leprosy in Lynn. In 1389 John Brunham had been appointed by Congregation on a commission to enquire into the leperhouses outside the borough. There were five of them; some Lynn testators left sums to them in the fifteenth century.[17] Fear of leprosy is reflected in the story of how her son's master had discharged him when he developed facial eruptions. *The Book* associates these with the young man's fall into the sin of lechery – generally thought to be the cause of the disease.[18] *The Book*'s account of Margery's dramatic change of attitude towards those who supposedly suffered in this way as a result of lechery (a sin from which she had been redeemed) suggests that the disease was still a problem in Lynn.

Potentially more dangerous to Margery than the daring kissing of lepers was the habit attributed to her of making impromptu recitations of homilies to individuals and crowds, in startlingly convincing imitations of clerical discourse. This behaviour is represented as being as puzzling and disturbing to many as her desire to wear special raiment and her devout exhibitionism. It was to be expected that those well disposed to her were sometimes upset by elements in this hyperactive melange. *The Book*'s Margery Reformed seemingly proved at times as hard to control as Margery Unregenerate, who had aspired to attract admiring glances and to be a successful businesswoman. Some of the most conspicuous and controversial features of Margery's public devotional behaviour are winningly presented as becoming fully fledged in an impeccably orthodox and conservative context, that of her great pilgrimage. Before then, she had often wept devoutly, sometimes in public.[19] It was in Jerusalem that there occurred 'the first crying that she ever cried in any contemplation'.[20] This differed from earlier weeping in its volume of noise and the often extreme accompanying physical effects; it was to evoke repeated alarm and revulsion at Lynn and elsewhere.[21] These phenomena increased in intensity from c. 1423 after the disappearance of a pain in her right side which she had endured with difficulty for eight years after her return to England from the Jerusalem journey.[22] It is not clear whether contemplation accompanied by obstreperous crying continued during and after the period in which Book One was written down in its final form. The intensity of experience had certainly declined. For *The Book* focuses particularly on occasions of weeping recollected from earlier years. Describing, in the context of her stay in Rome, the physical sensation she had of the 'fire of love' in her breast and in her heart, it says that it had endured for about sixteen years, which implies that it had ceased at that level c. 1430.[23] A unique documentary reference to a contemporary Margery Kempe associated with Lynn records her admittance to the Holy Trinity Gild in 1437/8. If this was *The Book*'s Margery and the brethren had thought that she was likely to disrupt the solemnity of their processions and of the liturgies in their chapel in St Margaret's, it seems unlikely that they would have received her into the fraternity.[24]

Margery's contemplations were of two sorts. The more frequent one was an inner dialogue, principally with Christ, often with the Virgin Mary, or with both of them together, occasionally with God the Father, and with a variety of sacred beings and saints. The other sort of contemplation, also involving dialogue, was an inner vision of a sacred subject, notably key scenes from the lives of Christ and the Blessed Virgin. Margery's inner realisation of stupendous sequences from universal history are vibrant, in technicolor and stereo sound. The figures, so familiar in appearance to her from the plastic arts, hitherto frozen in a moment of time, start to move and speak. And they gesture and speak to her in the intimate recesses of her soul. In contemporary panel painting and manuscript illumination, patrons liked to have themselves, and sometimes their families, depicted in kneeling juxtaposition with sacred beings. With a similar lack of any sense of anachronism, Margery becomes a participant in some of the most solemn of humanity's encounters with the Deity, in the Christian version of history.[25]

Notable features of these visions are the scholarly precision and homely verisimilitude invested in their delineation. The circumstances and the manner in which Margery's spiritual experiences occurred are related in conversational vernacular, but with great circumspection. The intention was to enhance belief in their validity. Care was taken to position them within the conventions prescribed in both devout and contemplative literature. In conformity to the latter genre, a distinction was maintained between the bodily senses and those of the soul, a fundamental distinction for the mystic, which is made with a precision equal to that of such rigorous mystics as Hildegard of Bingen or Dame Julian. For instance, when Margery was present on one occasion in St Margaret's churchyard for the Palm Sunday procession, in the meditation which this stimulated she is said to have 'beheld him [Christ] in her ghostly [spiritual] sight as verily as if he had been before her in her bodily sight'.[26] She claimed to have had a bodily vision on only one occasion after her conversion: during Mass, the elevated Sacrament 'shook and fluttered to and fro as a dove flutters with its wings'. On the celebrant raising the chalice, it too moved violently. Since the dove is the symbol of the Holy Ghost, the vision embodied the intensity of her anticipation of the benefits which would flow from communion. Like many devout people in the period, she acquired the habit of taking it frequently.[27]

As regards the sound of voices as well as the appearance of objects, the emphasis is maintained on transfigurations within the soul. The key roles of the senses were vital but subordinate: they provided the information which triggered interior responses and they gave outward testimony to the seismic moments within the soul. Indeed, when Margery was imprisoned at Beverley in 1417, as she lay in bed at night in a state of trepidation, she heard 'with her bodily ears a loud voice calling "Margery"'. She awoke in fear. Such a manifestation was not part of her usual contemplative experience. Christ, 'everywhere present', soon spoke to her in her soul in a familiar comforting way.[28] However, it was acceptable in her circles to interpret the individual's particular experience of sounds which gave the impression of external reality as being connected with the interior life of the soul. They were regarded as having a physical actuality which was an important manifestation of divine beneficence, a separate circuit of reassuring evidence about the soul's true experiences. Margery heard melodious sounds with her bodily ears which she considered to have important spiritual meanings. These 'sounds and melodies' had been an almost daily occurrence for twenty-five years when *The Book* was written and they were so loud that they blocked out talk at a conversational level. In particular, she was taken aback by a sound like bellows blowing in her ear which, she was reassured, was the sound of the Holy

Ghost. But Christ fine-tuned the controls, turning the sound to that of a dove; 'since then he turned it into the voice of a little bird which is called a redbreast that sung full merrily often times in her right ear'. Yet the controlling voice which directs and rationalises her physical experiences and manifestations is the one within her soul. Lodged there, Christ has transformed and modified her being to receive His communications and others from the 'court' of Heaven.[29]

So most of the spiritual communications which she received occurred, in accordance with the mystical methods into which she had been inducted, through the ears and eyes of her soul. These heightened contemplations, which most commonly took the form of a crisp dialogue with Christ, might occur when she was lying still or kneeling in church – celebrations of the most holy days in the liturgical calendar acted regularly as triggers. The entities of the Godhead and other sacred beings conversed with her soul as clearly and plainly as one friend spoke to another.[30] Christ might speak unbidden and unexpectedly or in response to intense concentration on Him, or in answer to her spiritual anxieties.[31] He was 'a hidden God' in her.[32] Her soul was wide and spacious. The most intense scenes in the New Testament could unfold there, as well as her own spiritual dramas, notably her mystic marriage to the Godhead.[33] The Virgin Mary entered her soul and there suckled her Son. St Mary Magdalene came into it to welcome Him. Her soul could be palatial: there the Trinity sat down and the whole court of Heaven could be accommodated (just as the Augustinian friary at Lynn could accommodate princes and their companions). To welcome Christ, 'the chamber of her soul' had been arrayed 'with many fair flowers and with many sweet spices' – as the hall of her father's house may have been prepared for distinguished visitors.[34] Christ assured her that her soul was guarded by angels. She saw the Crucifixion 'verily and freshly' 'in the city of her soul'. Her imagination may have been stimulated by the transformation of Lynn and other cities and towns into simulacra of sacred environments for the principal religious processions, and the performance of plays associated with them in Lynn and other places.[35]

There is much concern in *The Book* about the characteristics of the involuntary physical transformations which first occurred, as we have seen, on her visit to Jerusalem, and also about their spiritual significance and the reactions they evoked. She is described, one Candlemas at Lynn, when taking her candle to the priest, as 'wavering on each side as it had been a drunken woman', and weeping and sobbing so intensely that she could hardly stand. The cause was 'the fervour of love and devotion that God put in her soul through contemplation'.[36] When she received communion in the prior's chapel in St Margaret's, she was held up by two men until her crying ceased.[37] She experienced different sorts of weeping: 'with profound tears, sighings and sobbings, and sometimes with great violent cryings . . . and sometimes with soft and secret tears without any violence'.[38] There could be notable physical effects. As the sensations developed, she struggled to suppress them until she went leaden in colour.[39] At Mount Calvary, she fell down and 'wallowed and wrestled with her body, spreading her arms out wide, and cried with a loud voice as if her heart should have burst asunder'.[40] Sometimes violent crying made her perspire all over. As she fought the urge to cry, it laboured increasingly in her mind until it burst out. Then her body, exhausted with spiritual labour, was 'overcome with the unspeakable love that wrought so fervently in the soul, then fell she down and cried wondrously loud. And the more that she would labour to keep it in or to put it away, much the more should she cry and the more louder she fell down and cried astonishingly loud'.[41] Though she resisted these occurrences, she came to regard their outcome as an integral and necessary part of her mystical experiences. She felt deprived if she did not experience one for more than a day and a half. For they arose from 'the fervour of love and devotion that God put in her soul through high contemplation'.[42] Christ often told her that 'thinking, weeping and high contemplation is the best life on earth'.[43] She associated the gift of tears with the presence of Christ in her soul: He sometimes withdrew her tears and devotion, in part 'so that thou shouldest verily know what pain it is for to be without me, and how sweet it is for to feel me'.[44]

Thus these transformations are presented as a precious gift from Christ and as an expression and token of His closeness to her. It is a prize which utterly outweighs physical discomforts and adverse reactions among witnesses. Such behaviour was, indeed, a puzzle to some 'great clerks', who could not find warrant for it in Scripture or saints' lives.[45] Alternative explanations put forward were that Margery on these occasions was being tormented by a wicked spirit, that she was physically ill, a charlatan, or drunk – a sly accusation if she was indeed a vintner's daughter.[46] Margery herself sometimes feared that she was the victim of diabolical possession. Probably echoing the queries of her confessors, she was concerned lest her inner 'voices' and visions were illusions of the Devil.[47] In order for *The Book* to have authority and carry conviction, it was essential that all these dark explanations should be raised and demonstrated to be false through an exposition of her holiness and through accounts of the recognition of that holiness by the learned and spiritually discerning.

The Book's basic explanation of the significance of violent weeping was both reactive and proactive. From the earlier, more conventional manifestations onwards, they were presented as expressions of her sense of her sinfulness and as tokens of her repentance. In their mature form they also demonstrated the intensity of her meditations. The development of her contemplative life enabled her and her confessors to discern vital meanings and purposes in her public weepings and in a variety of her other physical symptoms. In fifteenth-century society every individual, however much temperamentally uninclined to develop a sophisticated religious personality or drawn to agnosticism, felt the pressure to make provision for his or her soul and for the souls of kinsfolk, alive and dead, in order to help the living avoid the pains of Hell and to minimise sufferings, present and anticipated, in Purgatory. People sought reassurance through the recitation of conventional prayers, by fulfilling the terms of indulgences and by arranging for the saying of soul-masses and other prayers for the dead. As we have seen, when Margery was a girl, there was a remarkable variety of voluntary corporate provision for souls in Lynn.[48]

Not surprisingly, Margery was deeply concerned for the future welfare of her soul and the souls of her kinsfolk – the torments of Hell and Purgatory were to the forefront of her mind. She was highly conscious, too, of the fragility of life and the threats constantly posed to it by famine, pestilence, war and natural disasters.[49] A familiarity with dying underlines the concern expressed in *The Book*, perhaps particularly appropriate in an older person, with the physical pain associated with the process. Margery was often consulted about the fate of the sick, the dying and the deceased.[50] Yet the text does not exude a morbid pessimism about either living or dying. In recollection, Margery is credited with a resigned chirpiness in the face of past adversities. Something or somebody turns up to get her out of scrapes, as it did for the heroes of chivalrous romances, or for Buonaccorso Pitti, the Florentine diarist who in old age colourfully recalled the adventures of his youth. Some, on meeting Margery for the first time, may have been fazed by the hair-raising insouciance of what became her habitual greeting: 'It is full merry in heaven.' They grumbled that she had no more been there than they had. Merriness was a quality with which people desperately tried to invest their uncertain world, this 'merry England', rather than that distant and wavering ethereal goal.[51] England was peculiarly blest, according to its natives, because it was the Virgin's dower, defended by her knight, St George.[52] Yet there was a lot to be despondent about in a land menaced by pestilence, uncertain weather, heretics, and the habitual malice of foreigners who sought, allegedly, to destroy the use of the English tongue. The idea propagated by *The Book*, that, the merriness of heaven was present in Lynn in the soul of a homely neighbour whose pious antics were tokens from God, was, surely, startling and, if accepted,

MARGERY KEMPE

exhilarating. *The Book* is testimony to the revitalising rather than the autumn of the Middle Ages. The good news it conveys outweighs the stern warnings to repent.

For Margery is presented as having gained a remarkable assurance of salvation through her contemplations, assurance which the generality of mankind quakingly sought by conventional means.[53] However, in this regard *The Book* probably gives a slanted view of the piety of the 'real' Margery, emphasising the exceptional rather than the humdrum elements in it. She did, after all, in later life probably join a gild, and a prime purpose of gilds was to provide soul-masses. However, if in real life she had wholly rejected the common way to heaven in favour of her own fast track, that course, surely, would not only have been extraordinarily rash in spiritual terms but might have brought down upon her more persistent accusations of heresy. Also, such singularity would have cut her off from the communal devotion and social involvement which she was loath to relinquish, above all because they were crucial for her brand of contemplation and provided opportunities for the experience of rejection and for the performance of good works, sometimes deliberately of a harrowing and socially demeaning kind. It is of a piece with the argument of *The Book* that, in its surviving copy, there are no supplications for prayers for its subject. The fact that her name is mentioned so rarely in it (only once in full) suggests that, at least in this context, such pious soliciting was far from the intention.

In some of her dialogues with Christ, Margery expressed what to the man or woman in a Lynn street might have appeared as a terrifying and inexplicable hope: that her death might be imminent. This is to be contrasted with the recollection of her terror when she thought that she might drown during a storm in the North Sea (surely an inherited fear among the folk of Lynn). Nevertheless, the 'Margery of *The Book*' rationally anticipated her demise with pleasure (though concerned about the manner of it) because she had had repeated assurances from Christ and the Virgin Mary that the rejections and humiliations she suffered on earth would cancel out the penance which she might have been due to endure in Purgatory.[54] The divine intention was that she should go straight to Heaven, to the high place assigned for her in the hierarchy – that was, in the *familia* of the Holy Family, among the celestial equivalents of Lynn's *potenciores*. Her extreme tears were among the main instruments of her salvation. Not only did they illuminate the Passion and fuel her love of Christ, but through them for His sake she endured a repeated purgatory of public shame and rejection. Thus she constructed a means of steadfast assurance of salvation which was psychologically uplifting and replaced inner turmoil by deep serenity. *The Book* poses a highly individual solution to a central problem in the piety of the period: how to avoid the expiatory time in a Purgatory which appeared as a pale imitation of Hell, a casualty ward of bleeding spirits rather than as a spartan waiting-room for Heaven. The resolution presented in *The Book* provided an edifying narrative, but there was no suggestion that it was easy to imitate. Margery's way required regular doses of dramatic social rejection and a readiness to go into hierarchical free-fall completely at odds with the spirit of what Professor Robin Du Boulay has perceptively labelled 'an age of ambition'.[55] Margery is described as behaving in public in ways which were shown in the text to be antisocial and disruptive. The men at the top of English urban elites, such as the *potenciores* of Lynn from whom she was sprung, were supposed in public and in their households to set examples of 'wise' and 'sad' behaviour; in religious observance, social relations and business affairs, their ideals were to cultivate and demonstrate a sense of the common good and of collegiality. Their womenfolk were expected to act conformably.[56] As we have seen, *The Book* attributes behaviour to her as a younger married woman which flouted these codes – a love of flaunting herself by wearing finery, an inclination in one instance to commit adultery under cover of going to church, and greed for business profits. How then did it justify her outrageous behaviour, after her conversion, albeit of a very different kind, in terms of the common good?

To start with, let us accept that, as *The Book* insists, the bouts of weeping in public were involuntary adjuncts of her meditations and that they became a crucial part of her contemplative life. However, the spiritual rewards which she received from them seem to have been made at the expense of conformity and collegiality with her fellow townsfolk. This clash in values reflected a characteristic tension in urban society in which there was a continuous struggle to balance the competitive needs of erntrepreneurial activity with those of social solidarity. *The Book* proposed that Margery's histrionic exhibitions were not just for her gain but for that of humanity. They were demonstration of the divine essence in action, which ought to have moved the spectators to piety, if they were not blinded by their secular preoccupations or the misguidance of diabolically manipulated clerics. The elitist Margery exudes a sad tolerance (characteristically elitist?) for the frailties of many fellow townsfolk, though she recognises the 'goodness' and 'worthiness' of individuals among them, high and low. The generality of townsfolk had to work hard to earn a living and were less well placed than the daughter of a late alderman of Holy Trinity Gild to develop the luxury of a complex and eruditely based spiritual life. Indeed, she too had failed to do so when she was bearing children and when preoccupied with running businesses.

Did the 'milk women' who were officially enjoined to sell only good and sweet milk and cream and butter of similar quality 'as it comes from home new made' have time to haunt St Margaret's and to seek out sermons?[57] Were they likely to have had sacred texts and devotional treatises expounded to them privately by priests, or to have received permission to take communion in the choir and the prior's chapel and to enter the prior's cloister as Margery did? In *The Book* it is implied that Margery used her spiritually privileged status to redress the inequalities of devotional opportunity endured by the likes of milk women – not just to save her own soul. Christ's assurance was that her sufferings and humiliations were gaining salvation for others too, in their thousands. Her tears were pleas to Christ for mercy for the sins of mankind as well as for her own. The more that people reviled her for her devout manifestations and the more she suffered, the greater the general benefits flowing to them from that suffering.

Let us now consider some particular aspects of the religious personality projected in *The Book*, some analogues to the text, and some of the cultural strands which influenced and moulded it. A detailed knowledge and understanding of the New Testament and Christian doctrine is attributed to Margery, which, it is stated or implied, derived from sermons, homilies and readings from legends about the life of Christ, such as pseudo-Bonaventure's *Meditationes Vitae Christi*, a treatise written c. 1335 by an Italian Franciscan, which had become an old favourite in England.[58] Margery is shown as having a precise and deep understanding of the orthodox interpretation of the New Testament and an ability to cite Scripture in her defence. Indications of her reverence for the Vulgate were that, when she was in Rome, she visited St Jerome's tomb and that, on that occasion, he spoke directly to her soul.[59] So Margery's stance was firmly differentiated from that of the Lollards; it was clearly demonstrated that her religious beliefs and practices were rooted in the orthodox version of Scripture, not the Lollard Bible, and in the traditional teaching of the Church, as expounded by learned, respected clerics – an orthodoxy for which *The Book* paraded impressive testimonials from some of the highest ecclesiastical authorities in England.[60]

The Book's religious mode links it up with the genres of writings about the spiritual experiences of illuminated women which had developed on the continent since the eleventh century, though it is differentiated from many of these texts by its somewhat chaotic form. They were commonly written down, or translated from the vernacular into Latin, by a cleric who was often mentor and confessor of the visionary as well as her amanuensis. They reflected on or recorded ecstatic, sometimes poetic visions of the sort which flowered in the early Middle Ages. Some of these works were well known in English ecclesiastical circles and provided validation for both Margery's spiritual experiences and her urge to have them written up. Let us briefly examine an example of the genre – the revelations of Mechthild of Magdeburg (1210–97). Unlike Margery, she received greetings from the Holy Spirit when she was a girl, and she was able to preserve her virginity. When aged twenty-three, she went to Magdeburg and became a beguine in a sisterhood attached to the Dominicans. Mechthild emphasised the humanity of Christ: 'I saw with the eyes of my soul the beautiful manhood of Jesus Christ.' The theme of Christ's physical beauty, a projection of His love, was a frequent one in her meditations.[61] It is paralleled in *The Book*. Margery had 'great pain' whenever she met a 'semly' [seemly] man in Rome, in case it was Christ, and wept sorely for his manhood as she went round the streets. Such bitter-sweet feelings (rather than any sexual impulse) underlay her description of a Saracen as 'welfaryng' (comely), and of an interrogator who menaced her chastity as 'semly'.[62]

Mechthild, like Dame Julian and Margery, had a spiritual awakening or intensification after a severe illness. Her enhanced sensation of the love of God led her over the next fifteen years to write down her revelations in the vernacular, encouraged by her Dominican confessor, Heinrich of Halle, who was to rearrange them in a Latin version. Mechthild's writings got her into trouble which, like Margery, she embraced. 'Now the time is come when some, who appear to be spiritual, torment God's children in body and persecute them in soul, because He wills that they should be like His Son, who was tormented in body and soul.' Mechthild's revelations, poetic in form and language, are a series of dialogues with the persons of the Trinity. Their imagery, borrowed from the poetry of courtly love, is passionate. Her soul is mystically married to Christ and experiences the agonies of His Passion.[63]

Parallels have been drawn between the devout *persona* projected in *The Book* and those found in the *vitae* of Flemish and German holy women, some of which may have contributed to *The Book*'s brand of piety, though only two continental hagiographies are cited in it, to support a particular point.[64] There is an echo of one controversial feature of Margery's behaviour in the sacred life of the Castilian mystic, Mother Juana de la Cruz (1481–1534), which has been studied by Professor Ronald Surtz. From an early age Juana experienced visions; when aged fifteen, in order to avoid marriage, she fled in male attire to the Franciscan convent of Sta Maria de la Cruz at Cubas, between Madrid and Toledo. Over a period of thirteen years, she delivered sermons which God put in her mouth. They retold Gospel stories and described the celebration of major feasts in Heaven. They provided salvatory interpretations. The sermons were printed as *El libro del conorte* (The Book of Consolation), in sequence with the liturgical year 1508–9. In Castilian society, pre-occupied with judaising, such a striking female appropriation of a clerical role does not appear to have aroused such suspicions as the evidence of *The Book* suggests it did in Lancastrian England, threatened by heresy raised within the bosom of orthodoxy. Juana was widely reverenced and visited by Cardinal Cisneros and the Emperor Charles V.[65]

It would be as rash to argue that Mechthild of Magdeburg's writings influenced the piety of *The Book* as to argue that *The Book* influenced that of Juan de la Cruz. The striking parallels in their spirituality arose from possession of a shared cultural background – as do many such parallels in works presenting the particular devotion of individual mystics. There was a historic strand in clerical discourse and instruction – particularly evident in the Orders of friars – which encouraged forms of intense Christocentric devotion, including gendered modes of response. These forms of piety did, indeed, rely heavily on literary articulation and validation, as reflected in the research undertaken by Margery's priestly amanuensis, encouraged by a Bachelor of Divinity, in order to find precedents for weeping among the *vitae* of holy women and in devotional treatises. His research implies that an impressively eclectic selection of such works was available to a cleric in Lynn who appears to have lacked high status. He cited approved examples of holy weeping from the life of the Brabantine mystic, Mary of Oignies (d. 1213), the pseudo-Bonaventuran *Stimulis Amoris*, Richard Rolle's *Incendium Amoris*, and the life of St Elisabeth of Hungary (d. 1231), a royal saint of Franciscan piety, whose cult was popular in Germany and who, like Margery, had had a special compassion for lepers.[66]

However, the four treatises, which, as we have seen, were listed twice as central in Margery's instruction and devotion, strongly position the piety of *The Book* in the mainstream of later medieval English contemplative interests. Rolle's *Incendium Amoris* and Hilton's *Scala Perfectionis* were among the most popular devotional texts. Richard Rolle (c. 1300–49), a Yorkshireman, rejected academic life and became a wandering hermit. In his later years, he occupied an anchorage associated with the Cistercian convent of Hampole (Yorks.). He wrote the treatise in the vernacular, 'for the simple and unlearned'.[67] Part of its general appeal, and its appeal for Margery, was its emphasis that God could be known through what we do and how we love, rather than through the abstruse debates of theologians. However, Margery did not share Rolle's contempt for academics and for the rich and powerful. *The Book* carefully records the academic qualifications of many of the priests whom she encountered, and often mentions the patronage and favour shown to her by highly placed and 'worthy' individuals, echoing (in contrast to Rolle) the values of clergy who were beneficed, hoped for benefices, or had standing within their Order, as well as those of the *haute bourgeoisie* of Lynn. Nevertheless, Rolle's work is central to the piety of *The Book*. The account of Margery's spiritual progress reflects the influence of its eremitical emphasis on rejection of conventional comforts and consolations, and concentration on kindling the 'fire of love' for Christ in one's heart. Penances are insufficient to attain this holy state: there must be as well 'conversion' to a spiritual mode of life which only few can attain. In particular, the concept of 'the fire of love', an old mystical concept into which Rolle breathed intense life, was one which, as has been seen, Margery found especially valuable.[68]

Walter Hilton (d. 1395) was an Augustinian canon at Thurgarton priory, near Southwell (Notts.). *The Ladder of Perfection* was written for the guidance of an anchoress who lacked knowledge of Latin. The treatise, whose writer was academically trained, had the advantage over Rolle's work that it presented a clear and rigorous scheme for progress in meditation, with the goal of obtaining release from carnal affections, and illumination with a soft and sweet love of God. When the soul was visited by grace, an ecstatic level of perfection could be reached, a mystical marriage with God which was a foretaste of Heaven. Hilton gave warnings about visions in bodily form which might be diabolical in inspiration. One of the attractions of Hilton's work as a manual of instruction for Margery's mentors was its authoritative assurance that 'simple, unlearned' persons could progress in contemplation. Hilton buttressed this argument by citing St Paul and by the example of St Mary Magdalene.[69] However, he made a key distinction, which may have posed problems in Margery's devout circles, between the active and contemplative life. He said that the active Christian life was appropriate to rich and powerful people: they needed to concentrate on performing good works and on chastising the body.[70] 'The contemplative life consists in perfect love and charity inwardly expressed through the spiritual virtues, and in true knowledge and perception of God and spiritual things. This life belongs especially to those who for the love of God forsake all worldly riches, honours and outward affairs, and devote themselves body and soul to the service of God in spiritual occupation.'[71] For Hilton, the contemplative life was especially appropriate to those who, like the anchoress to whom he addressed the work, were enclosed. Indeed, the distinction between the two ways in Christian life is important too in *The Book*. Margery is shown to have struggled to free herself from worldly entanglements so that she could concentrate on developing her inward relationship with God. *The Book* gives notable testimony as to how Margery was able to maintain and revert to the contemplative life at an exalted level, despite the fact that she was not *reclusa* like Dame Julian, and even when she was strenuously engaged in muscular good works. Margery's mentors may have cited examples of the beguines in the Low Countries, who strove to lead lives that were both active and prayerful. They formed communities of working women, chaste and devout, but not living enclosed under a monastic rule. However, a key factor in convincing those who instructed Margery in Hilton's scheme that it could be modified in her case (and, perhaps, for other layfolk) was, it may be surmised, the rise in England of the cult of St Bridget (Birgitta).

St Bridget is singled out in *The Book* as Margery's modern exemplar. In *The Book*, many of her attitudes and experiences are replicated by Margery. In Rome Margery is shown seeking out reminiscences about the saint from those whom had known her and visiting the chamber in which she died (which one can still see, in the Brigettine convent in the Piazza Farnese). The accounts which Margery received about the saint probably influenced her own demeanour and her emphasis on heavenly merriment. Archbishop Bowet's steward was to be affronted by Margery's laughter and sociability, saying to her 'Holy folk should not laugh'. However, she had the warranty of the saint's maid, who told her (through an interpreter) that Bridget had 'a laughing cheer', and of her host in Rome, who recalled that Bridget 'was ever homely and goodly to all creatures that would speak with her'.[72] *The Book* also compares the privileges which each of them received in their contemplations. Christ said that the truth of Bridget's book would be recognised through Margery – which suggests that one purpose of her book was to spread Brigettine piety. *The Book* provided a more homely and accessible model of it in action within a familiar environment.[73] The English centre of the cult is highlighted. When in London in 1434, after a gruelling journey across the Holy Roman Empire, Margery made a point of visiting the Brigettine convent of Syon in Middlesex. She wished to gain the indulgence on offer, but it may have been in her mind that she had failed, when in Danzig, to cross to Sweden to seek out St Bridget's tomb and shrine in the monastery which the saint had founded at Vadstena – though, indeed, she had had pressing spiritual and secular reasons for sailing to Stralsund instead.[74] Margery was well aware that her circumstances and devotional history differed markedly in important respects from those of St Bridget. *The Book*, perforce, did not present a generally slavish imitation of the saint but a distinctive model, the product of other individual circumstances and of a different environment. What were the similarities and differences, as women singled out by God, between the Bridget of the *Revelations* and the Margery of *The Book*?

We are, indeed, much better informed about Bridget because of the survival not only of her spiritual writings but of some of her correspondence and two well-informed *vitae*. Birgitta (1302/3–1373) was born near Uppsala. Her father, Birger, like Margery's, was a man of authority, governor of the province of Uppland. Whereas Margery's childhood, according to the little said about it in *The Book*, was spiritually undistinguished, Bridget – like some other notable holy women – had early intimations of a special spirituality. She started to have visions from the age of seven, including a vividly realised one of the Passion, after she had heard a sermon on the subject. Such visions (and there were many of them) reduced her to tears. At the age of thirteen, she was married to a nobleman, Ulf Gudmarson (d. 1344). She continued to live in a prayerful and ascetic way and, after the birth of her eighth child, persuaded her husband that they should live in chastity. A few days after Ulf's death, Christ told Bridget that He had chosen her as his bride. She developed an intense religious life. When she was living in the monastery of Alvastra, Christ told her to go to Rome. At His bidding in 1372 she went to Jerusalem. However, the pilgrimage debilitated her and she died soon after her return to Rome. Bridget was canonised in 1391 and this was confirmed by the anti-pope John XXIII in 1414 – Margery was in Bologna in 1413/14 when he was there, and before going to Rome in 1414 she went to Assisi, the resting place of St Francis, who had been St Bridget's favourite saint.[75]

The *Revelations* which Bridget dictated in the vernacular were focused in form, in contrast to the scattered and fragmented nature of those in *The Book*, but in important respects some of them did provide a model for the latter. Margery, too, has interior dialogues with the Divinity and with the Virgin Mary, and visions of key episodes in the Gospels. However, Bridget did not boldly project herself into these scenes, as *The Book* was to project Margery, implying her greater intimacy and privilege. The saint wrote more about the pains of Hell and Purgatory; she did not flaunt the luxury of assured salvation which Margery derived from repeated rejection in the world. Generally, indeed, Bridget had been treated with great respect. In 1370 Pope Urban V showed her quite exceptional favour by approving her foundation of a new monastic Order. Though drawn to the enclosed life, Bridget had been compelled to stay in the world by her family responsibilities, and then by Christ's commands that she undertake long journeys. She provided a valuable model, for Margery's devout coterie, of sanctity in action in secular society, in the attainment of a contemplative way of life which was also active. Indeed, these aspects of Bridget's piety may help to account for the remarkable rise of her cult in England, which lacked the traditional culture of the beguines established on the continent. Yet in one respect Margery was projected less boldly and stridently than Bridget. As has been seen, Margery's admonitory gaze was generally averted from the misdeeds of great men, individual and collective. By contrast, Christ commanded Bridget to denounce the king of Sweden, Magnus Erikson, and his court, the deficiencies of bishops, abbots and monks and, on occasion, to write accusingly to Urban V. For instance, when he decided to abandon Rome in 1370, she had campaigned vigorously for the return of the papacy thither from Avignon.[76] Bridget's strictures on the great were often painfully *ad hominem*; Margery's more occasional ones were generally vague. Indeed, Margery may have recognised that her lower hierarchical status gave her more restricted scope and licence to make criticisms than Bridget. Nevertheless, she echoed the saint in denouncing wickedness, clerical as well as lay, sometimes specifically at Christ's request. Individuals denounced in *The Book* were seldom named, and the bishops whom she is shown as reproving to their faces were none of them bishops of Norwich and were all safely long since deceased when it was completed. *The Book* conspicuously fails to expand on her dealings with Archbishop Chichele: he was still alive when it was written.[77] However, the descriptions of Margery squaring up to bishops may have been hyped partly to present her as in Bridget's mould. In the edgy society of Lancastrian Lynn (and generally in the realm), a woman's noisy weeping was more defensible than any sharp-tongued political comment.

The cult of St Bridget received royal patronage in England in the early years of Lancastrian rule, in part coincidentally with the course of Margery's conversion. Kings sought the saint's aid in lightening their spiritual burdens. Henry IV showed an interest in founding a house of the Brigettine Order in part expiation for the execution in 1405 of Richard Scrope, Archbishop of York. Next year he was in Lynn when a devout Yorkshire landowner, Henry Lord FitzHugh, was among those who departed in the entourage of his daughter, Philippa on her voyage; FitzHugh was to sound out the Order about having a house founded in England. The lady who was appointed Philippa's chief lady-in-waiting as queen of Denmark and Norway was a grand-daughter of St Bridget; Philippa was to become a lay sister associated with the saint's foundation at Vadstena, which she was to visit frequently – she became closely involved in the affairs of Sweden, whence she received her dowry income. FitzHugh commenced negotiations with the community at Vadstena for the foundation of a house in England. This was achieved in 1415 by Henry V, originally on a site across the River Thames from his palace at Sheen in Surrey (later known as Richmond Palace). In 1431 the convent moved to a more convenient site, known as Syon abbey (on the site where Syon House now stands). In 1434 Margery may have been curious to see the newly built monastery (a rarity in England), more easily reached from London in her decrepit state than was Sheen.[78]

Prestigious patronage helped to ensure that the cult of St Bridget flourished in England. Lynn's close royal connections, notably with Thomas Beaufort, may have been a factor in focusing the attention of clergy there on the cult, with which, as we have seen, his niece Queen Philippa continued to be closely involved. She died in 1430 and was buried in the monastery of Vadstena.[79] Interest in her (and perhaps in the cult which she zealously promoted) may have been stimulated in Lynn through Norfolk merchants' activities in Bergen and the problems there which brought them into contact with Eric IX's court.[80] John Capgrave, Augustinian friar of Lynn, and witness to her departure thence as a girl, noted that 'those who know her say that she so increased in wisdom that, during the continual infirmities which oppressed the king, all the causes of the kingdom were laid before her, and that by her prudent counsel she brought everything to a propitious issue'.[81] In 1479 William Worcestre, a literary-minded layman living in retirement out-side Norwich, received a good deal of information about the Scandinavian kingdoms and neighbouring regions from a hermit living at Elsing (Norfolk). The hermit said that he had stayed with Philippa for the eleven years before her death. She had, he asserted, instituted the Sound dues paid by every ship passing between Helsingør and Hälsingborg and had been killed by her husband in Copenhagen because she had resisted a proposal to retreat in face of the attack from the people of Pomerania and Holstein. Reacting to her death, the nobles drove the king out. Much of this was garbled stuff. Philippa did, indeed, play an important part as regent, supporting her husband's efforts in wars with Pomerania and the Hanseatic League. She died apparently of natural causes at Vadstena, in the king's absence. The remarks of the Lynn friar and the Elsing hermit suggest that there was a continuing interest in Scandinavian affairs in the shire. This interest may have helped to sustain the Brigettine cult there; it may not be just due to the accidents of survival that two rare representations of the saint in England are to be found on screens in East Anglian churches.[82]

The instruction which Margery received about St Bridget provided her with a model with which she could most easily relate, the model of a married noblewoman, long sexually active, who eventually was able to live in chastity, who performed good works, upbraided sinfulness, went on pilgrimages and, above all, was privileged to have Christ reveal Himself in her soul. Margery could relate to Bridget as a modern saint about whom she heard reminiscences – the only near contemporary devout woman with whose spirituality *The Book* compares Margery's and on whom it was modelled in various general aspects, and in particular instances. Let us take a couple of examples of happenings in the temporal world. When Bridget was passing through a street in Stockholm, a resentful knight threw the contents of his dirty washbasin down on her head; she responded: 'It is right and just that I endure such things! But may God spare him and not repay this to him in the age to come.' In similar circumstances Margery's response was meek to: 'And at one time a reckless man, little caring for his own shame, with will and with purpose cast a bowlful of water on her head coming in the street. She, nothing moved therewith, said, "God make you a good man", highly thanking God thereof . . .' The story of Margery's relations with her deceased son, a reformed delinquent, may be highlighted as a response to Bridget's concern over the fate of her son, Karl's soul and the adequacy of the penitence of this former lover of the Queen of Naples.[83]

Margery's clerical mentors presumably helped her to meld this new contemplative cult with English devotional traditions, as reflected in the works of pseudo-Bonaventure and the vernacular manuals. One wonders whether they tailored Brigettine piety to suit other laywomen (and laymen). In English society generally the works of St Bridget were easily assimilated with existing devout modes, and refreshed pious strands of behaviour, components of that great surge of Christocentric and Marian devotion which had been gathering pace from the twelfth century onwards. Thus *The Book* is closely attuned to literary exemplars which are, indeed, part of its imprimatur, relating it to well-established and approved meditational genres, which had a wide appeal to particular pious mentalities among layfolk as well as clergy. By casting Margery as disciple of this mystic way, *The Book* was intended to explain and justify aspects of her pious behaviour which puzzled or affronted those less familiar with this devotional genre. Focus was maintained on the soul's flight towards God and the company of Heaven, powered by the growth of its ability to love God and the reciprocal extension of divine grace. This was combined with a continuous martyrdom of rejection and vilification. The promise of salvation which this scheme offered crowded out the more conventional fears of the pains of Hell and sufferings in Purgatory. The performance of canonical duties and pious acts are mentioned mainly because they relate to the Incarnation and Passion, central to the meditational thrust.

The text does, however, hint that in major respects its subject was more conventionally religious – which would have been reassuring for the conventionally devout reader. Thus it provides a vision of the consecrated Host. Margery appears to have been a devotee of the popular cult of the Holy Blood. Long before she went on pilgrimage to the Holy Blood of Wilsnack, in 1417, after her voyage from Spain to Bristol, she had gone, probably on her way home, to see the phial of Holy Blood at Hailes abbey (near Winchcombe in Gloucestershire). An elaborate architectural setting had been created at the east end of the abbey church to house the shrine – a bay had been built behind the high altar, with an ambulatory from which five chapels radiated. It may be indicative of how the cult generally gained in popularity in the period that in 1431 Pope Eugenius IV provided lavish indulgences for those who honoured it at Hailes. The most famous cult centre of the Holy Blood was Bruges, where the relic was carried in procession on the feast day of the Invention of the Holy Cross (3 May). There, by the early fifteenth century, as Dr Andrew Brown has described, the festivities had become costly and elaborate. The feast inaugurated the fifteen days of the May Fair: Margery's general interest in the Holy Blood may be evidence that the cult at Bruges had spread along the commercial networks to Lynn.[84]

Margery was eager to gain indulgences. It is only incidentally that *The Book* reveals that she went on pilgrimage to St John of Bridlington, St Thomas of Canterbury and St William of York. Her vexation at the loss of a relic, recorded over two decades later, suggests that she was a collector of pilgrim souvenirs, though the one incidentally mentioned, a cutting from Moses' rod, may have had a special significance for her as regards her weeping. St Bridget, in her *Revelations*, interpreted the holy deeds performed through the rod: 'Lastly, the rock gave out water by means of that staff. The rock is the hard parts of the people, for if they are struck with the fear of God and love, remorse and tears of repentance flow out. No one is so unworthy, no one is so evil that his tears do not flow from his eyes and all his limbs are quickened towards virtue if he turns to me [Christ] interiorly, considers my suffering, realises my power and thinks of the goodness which lets earth and trees bear fruit.'[85]

Margery was also typical of the conscientiously devout (not necessarily contemplatively informed) in her concern to confess and take Communion frequently and in her enthusiasm for the great religious processions such as Corpus Christi, for sermons, and visual representations of the divine. The saints who were named in her meditations, with few exceptions, such as St Mary the Egyptian, were among the most familiar from the New Testament and the *Legenda Aurea*, the standard collection of saints' lives compiled by the thirteenth-century Dominican, James de Voragine. The central role Margery accorded to St Mary Magdalene, the prime female repentant and lover of Christ, renowned for her healing powers, would have struck a popular chord.[86] One must not make too sharp a distinction between standard and popular pious practices, and the devotionally sophisticated, literary-minded exercises of contemplatives. The two were intimately connected and fed into each other.

One important strand in *The Book* which intertwines popular and contemplative devotion is the theme of martyrdom. It is clear from *The Book* that Margery empathised with the lives and martyrdoms of early female saints: 'She thought she would be slain for God's love, but dreaded the point of death, and therefore she imagined herself the most soft death, as she thought for dread of impatience, that she was to be bound head and foot to a stock and her head to be smitten off with a sharp axe for God's love.'[87] St Katherine of Alexandria was the archetypal female martyr most prominent in *The Book*; here again, Margery was following fashion in Norfolk, and generally in England. Dr Duffy has noted that statues of St Katherine and St Margaret flanked the shrine image of Our Lady of Walsingham. These saints were, it appears, depicted more frequently in stained-glass windows in Norfolk than any other early female martyrs.[88] Along with the Virgin Mary, St Peter and St Paul, St Katherine was one of the saints whom Margery said instructed her soul in how to love and please Christ.[89] St Margaret and St Katherine (together with the twelve Apostles and St Mary Magdalene) were the only saints whom Christ specified would attend Margery's deathbed.[90] Christ promised that if anyone who believed that God loved Margery asked her for a boon, it should be granted – a privilege said to be enjoyed by St Katherine, St Margaret and St Barbara.[91]

One reason why Margery reacted so strongly to the legends of these early martyrs was that in their public sufferings there might be found parallels to and validation of the humiliations and denunciations which she endured. Dr Katherine Lewis, in her examination of the role of St Katherine in *The Book*, has perceptively drawn attention to this theme. For instance, the account of Margery's examination by Archbishop Bowet might have recalled Katherine's defiance of Maxentius. *The Book* positions Margery with these heroic figures, if on a minor scale, by highlighting the threats and denunciations she endured when summoned to appear before Bowet and the callous treatment and imprisonment inflicted on her by secular officers in Leicester and by agents acting on behalf of the Crown in the North, among other episodes.[92] The theme of martyrdom was exploited by Margery to sustain and justify the busy quotidian thrust of her piety into the social world. The mimicking of martyrs distinguished her role from that of anchoresses and conventional vowesses. Hers was a painful, heroic one, a mission to give strident testimony both by the staithes and markets of her native town and along the far-flung highways and byways of Christendom.

It was not just St Katherine's popularity that led Margery to prefer her over her own name-saint or St Barbara, whose cult was often to be found alongside theirs. St Margaret and St Barbara were less apposite to Margery's case because they preserved their virginity, unlike St Katherine. They were also unsuitable because they were persecuted by their fathers, whereas Margery wished to present a conventionally reverential image of her feelings for hers. For Margery, the Beaufort family's connection with St Katherine may have added to the cult's cachet. Katherine Duchess of Lancaster (d. 1403), mother of Thomas and Joan Beaufort (the former personally connected with the Lynn elite, the latter with Margery), adopted the Katherine Wheel as her badge. Margery may well have seen it adorning the splendid sets of vestments which the Duchess Katherine gave to Lincoln cathedral.[93] The saint is among those invoked and depicted in the 'Beaufort Book of Hours', commissioned by Katherine's son, John Beaufort, Earl of Somerset (d. 1410) and his countess.[94] However, Dr Lewis has distilled the essence of St Katherine's appeal to Margery in her analysis, showing how the legend provided a universally hallowed exemplar for her chaste living, her homiletic role and the persecutions she suffered as a consequence of her successful teaching. To many of *The Book*'s readers and auditors (however humble), the Alexandrine references would have been easily recognisable and telling, underlined by the 'wicked' mayor of Leicester's disparaging comparison of Margery with the saint; although a mayor of Leicester's unfavourable judgement is unlikely to have carried weight with Lynn folk.[95] St Katherine provided heavyweight support for some of the controversial aspects of Margery's devotion.

Margery's book demonstrated how an ordinary sinful, unlearned woman (albeit one of high status) might attain an illuminated interior life, though in this case one whose exterior manifestations needed a detailed explanation. *The Book*'s exposition was, above all, accessible, with its homely language and imagery and its referential background of canonical obligations and popular cults. It grasped attention through its accounts of the toils and troubles of its subject and of her riveting encounters with the divine. *The Book* could surely have been understood and enjoyed if read out to even the most ill-informed and poverty-stricken inhabitants of the borough. Indeed, *The Book* insisted that Margery had attained entry into the supreme spiritual elite through knowledge of contemplation, but it did not posit such a liberty as open to the toiling multitude any more than the *potenciores* considered that burgess-ship should be. Rather, it demonstrated how a distinguished alderman's daughter used her spiritual benefits for the common profit, contrary to the opinions of many.

The common folk, by implication, are often present in *The Book* as witnesses – part of the crowd at services, sermons and processions, spectators of Margery's agonies, auditors of her homilies, beneficiaries of her prayers, prophecies and ministrations. As such they are part of the mix of her piety; their reactions are integral to its unfolding and presumably were as articulate and vigorous as those expressed to Robert Brunham by the riotous congregation in St Margaret's on 30 September 1415. In *The Book*, religion in Lynn is presented as being monocultural as well as multi-faceted. The view presumably approved by Margery's clerical coterie was that religious opinion about her in Lynn did not divide according to its precisely defined secular hierarchy. They were, on this assumption, likely to have been concerned that she should avoid the overt presentation of politically contentious views. Rather, they wanted her, I surmise, to explain the joyous spiritual relevance to all of a contentious religious phenomenon. Seen in this light, *The Book*'s aim was to stir devotion within all status groups. In its ultimate form, it was not just an *apologia pro vita sua* or the commemoration of the crowning achievement of the Brunham family, but an attempt to reveal the workings of meditation in the soul of an ostensibly unlettered but privileged neighbour, much of it set within a familiar social setting and written up accessibly in a gossipy and sometimes racy way. It was a tract for conversion and reformation: towards the end of Book One it was reported that Christ had said to Margery: 'Daughter, by this book many a man shall be turned to me and believe therein.'[96] It was for the benefit of mankind, for the reformation particularly of men, giving examples of how she could reform them in the flesh, as Christ now asserted she could do through her recorded words. Thus *The Book* shows how her husband curbed his sexual impulses and lived meekly in (presumed) chastity. Her son gives up his wild ways and settles down to a respectable and repentant married way of life. The well-to-do and well-educated layman Thomas Marchale 'was so moved by the good words that God put in her to say of contrition and compunction, of sweetness and devotion that he was all moved as [if] he had been a new man with tears of contrition and compunction, both days and nights, as our Lord would visit his heart with grace, that sometimes when he was in the fields he wept so sore for his sins and his trespass that he fell down and might not bear it and told the forsaid creature [Margery] that he had been a full reckless man and misgoverned, and that sore rued he, thanked be God. And then he blessed the time that he knew this creature and purposed him fully to be a good man'.[97]

We do not know whether *The Book* had the hoped-for impact. That would have depended on how persuasive its interpretation of her controversial behaviour was, how relevant its messages seemed and whether its approach appealed. To modern readers, used to reading more socially circumspect or detached medieval religious tracts, Margery's self-imaging may appear to have been too singular and eccentric to facilitate a widespread influence. It would be easy to dismiss *The Book* as an idiosyncratic one-off, not easily assimilable in the canon of popular devotional works. Yet it does provide testimony that oral digests had on occasion stirred individuals to devotion, in its delineation of the effects a variety of them had on her piety. It is perhaps too facile to dismiss the 'Margery of the Book' as a wholly unrepresentative figure, incapable of being imitated, since she is presented as exceptionally blest, on a highly individual trajectory. As regards 'her meditations and the grace that God wrought in her soul', at one point *The Book* appears to present a contrary assumption. William Sowthfeld, Carmelite of Norwich, seemingly recognises her symptoms as a known devotional virus: 'Thank him [God] highly of his goodness, for we all be bound to thank him for you, that now in our days will inspire his grace in you to the help and comfort of us all which are supported by your prayers and *by such others as ye be*. And we are preserved from many mischiefs and diseases which we should suffer and worthily for our trespass *if there were not such good creatures among us* [my italics].'[98]

Others who caught the meditational bug may have reshaped their *personae* in excitingly individualistic ways – and sometimes in ways which led them to behave in uncomfortably non-conformist fashions. We have a brief written schedule, dating from the early fifteenth century, laying down a pious daily regimen for an unnamed gentleman from Oxford.[99] The intention of the confessor who drew it up was certainly not to induce antisocial behaviour. The spiritual conventions with which it was suggested that he clothe his active life were, on the whole, unobtrusive. The discreet, inward-looking aspects of devotion are suggested by the form of a reliquary, of silvergilt enamel, thought to be of early fifteenth-century English provenance (*Musée de Louvre*). When opened out, it forms a triptych, the Crucifixion being flanked by pictures of St George and St Katherine. Being smaller that a matchbox, it could be worn inconspicuously about the person. However, there were aspects of the Oxford regimen which might have encouraged bizarre and alarming behaviour. Passers-by might have been alarmed if they had seen the *dévot* coming out of his door with tears streaming down his face and uttering a groan, or welcoming a bite from a dog on his way to church and there throwing himself down, in imitation of St Mary Magdalene, before the figure of Christ. By the later fifteenth and early sixteenth centuries the overt shaping of lay devotional behaviour according to the canons of meditational treatises may have been more widespread and acceptable than in Margery's day, as their authority and (especially after the invention of printing) their circulation grew. It is in this period, as we have seen, that there is evidence of a *frisson* of interest in *The Book*. Certainly, some great ladies then shaped their behaviour in conspicuously devout ways, sometimes influenced by the kind of literature which Margery favoured. One example was her patroness Countess Joan's daughter, Cecily Neville, Duchess of York (d. 1493), who in old age (c. 1485) ordered her day in a semi-monastic way. During dinner, she had 'a reading of holy matter, either Hilton of contemplative and active life, Bonaventura's De Infancia, the Salvatoria Legenda Aurea, St Matilda, St Katherine of Siena, or the Revelations of St Bridget'.[100] Another aged devotee was Margaret Beaufort (d. 1509), great-niece of Countess Joan and the mother of Henry VII. In his funeral oration on her, John Fisher praised her for her austerities, including the wearing of 'sharp clothes' such as 'shirts and girdles of hair', for the vow of chastity which she took in her husband's lifetime, and for her holy weeping.[101]

We must not forget the likely importance in promoting meditational piety of the shadowy army of anchorites, anchoresses and hermits. They pop up frequently in *The Book*, generally sympathetic to meditation, sometimes charismatic and influential figures. Recent research, some of it on East Anglia, has shown how lively and prevalent eremitical culture was in England in Margery's day.[102] One must not assume too readily that Dame Julian was the only one whose spiritual experiences were recorded or that, if any others were, they were recorded in her mode, without any flashes of the sparkling and individual social cabaret of *The Book*. We have only occasional vignettes fitfully bringing these figures to life – in *The Book* there are, notably, besides Julian, the excitable Dominican anchorite of Lynn, the harshly judgemental anchoress of York and the petulant hermit Reynald. In William Worcestre's notes, there is the gossipy, sensationalist hermit of Elsing. If more was known about their religious culture, we might have a fuller setting for the piety of *The Book*.

chapter 6

ENGLISH TRAVELS AND
CONTEXTS

*T*he Book gives us, in a desultory way, one of the first extensive accounts of travels in England, though of travels mostly recalled about two decades after they had taken place. The recollections were selected and coloured by the need to explain and illustrate important stages in the development of Margery's spiritual *persona* and to satisfy a very English need – the vindication of her orthodoxy, in case of any alarms or doubts experienced by the readers and auditors of her, at times, spectacular revelations. In the process, *The Book* is uniquely informative about some of the prelates whom she met, along with many other (usually unnamed) individuals. It outlines experiences in being dealt with by ecclesiastical and secular officials – an unusual sort of testimony for this period. It distils something of the diverse flavours of religious culture in urban and other settings, and a mode of their acculturation, in the evidence of the influences they sometimes exercised on Margery's pious amalgam.

The journeys in England to which *The Book* alludes were purportedly undertaken by Margery for her spiritual health. Occasionally, she went a long way from Lynn; she visited the principal English cities – London, York, Norwich and Bristol. Most of the incidents described were located in towns or associated with visits to them. In the countryside, Margery went to monasteries in order to worship at shrines and have devout conversations, and to bishops' residences to petition for licences to sanction her way of life or in answer to an episcopal summons. There were two visits – probably in 1413 and 1417 – to the Augustinian priory at Bridlington on the coast of the East Riding of Yorkshire, where there was the splendid shrine of Prior John Thwenge, who died in 1379 and was canonised in 1404. Earlier in 1417, when Margery had returned from Santiago to Bristol, she had visited the Cistercian abbey at Hailes in Gloucestershire and the Augustinian abbey at Leicester. At both these houses she was apparently received with considerable sympathy; this was remarkable in the case of Leicester as the abbot, Richard Rothley, and some of the canons had recently been among those who had examined her on suspicion of heresy. However, the fact that she had been received favourably a few years before by Philip Repingdon, Bishop of Lincoln, who had been the previous abbot of Leicester, may have helped her cause there.[1] In her later years, Margery, according to *The Book*, was a frequent and welcome visitor among the nuns of Denney abbey (Cambridgeshire), of the Order of Minoresses.[2] In 1434, whilst staying in London on the way back from the continent to Lynn, she made a pilgrimage to the Brigettine house, Syon abbey in Middlesex.[3]

The Book dwells, often in minute detail, on Margery's interaction with some members of the episcopate.[4] There are mentions of audiences she was granted by Bishop Repingdon (d. 1424), Thomas Arundel, Archbishop of Canterbury (d. 1414), Thomas Peverel, Bishop of Worcester (d. 1419) and Henry Bowet, Archbishop of York (d. 1426). John and Margery visited Repingdon in 1413, hoping to take public vows of chastity and for Margery to receive permission to wear white raiment. They went to him because the see of Norwich remained vacant from the death of Alexander Tottington (before 13 April) until the consecration of Richard Courtenay on 13 September. The meeting probably took place in the fine episcopal castle at Sleaford in Lincolnshire, where Repingdon had arrived by 6 August, after making his way northwards from London in July.[5]

Philip Repingdon, an Augustinian canon, had when young been a prominent supporter at Oxford of John Wycliffe, but when Repingdon convicted of heresy in 1382, he was abjured. His election as Abbot of Leicester in 1393 was either the cause or the consequence of his patronage by the House of Lancaster. In 1400 he was appointed Chancellor of the University of Oxford and in 1404, at the request of Henry IV, he was provided by the pope to the see of Lincoln.[6] The editor of Repingdon's Register, Dr Margaret Archer, has concluded that he was a hard-working and fair-minded bishop, whose main interest was in achieving 'an efficient administration and a higher standard of religious life' in his diocese.[7] *The Book*'s account of him, though not entirely sympathetic, bears out this judgement. After arriving at his residence, he quickly gave the Kempes an audience on being told that they had been waiting for him for three weeks. He greeted Margery warmly and reacted positively to her account of her meditations. John publicly avowed to him their intention to live in chastity. Margery was moved at viewing Repingdon's daily practice of giving charitably to the poor before he sat down to eat. He took in good part her stinging reproof of his refusal to give her the mantle and ring, symbols of her new way of life, or to agree to her singular request to wear white clothes without archiepiscopal consent.[8]

The Kempes seem to have had no difficulty in getting an audience with Archbishop Arundel, who in 1413 was administering the vacancy business of the see of Norwich, at Lambeth Palace. He speedily granted Margery's requests to choose her own confessor and receive communion every Sunday, waiving all fees for the issue of the appropriate documents. Like Repingdon, he listened sympathetically to her exposition of her piety. Arundel, too, according to *The Book*, received a reproof from her in good part.[9] Thomas Arundel was the younger son of Richard Earl of Arundel (d. 1376) and a close kinsman of royalty. He was one of the leading political figures of his day, an architect of Henry of Bolingbroke's usurpation in 1399.[10] In the new reign he showed particular zeal in opposing Lollards and in suppressing their heresies.[11] When Margery met him he was Chancellor of the Realm, an office he had first held in 1386. The account of the meeting throws an unexpected light on a highly born prelate, whose life had been deeply immersed in secular administration, and stormily so in court politics. Yet the pastoral concern which he showed to the Kempes – well, one might think, beyond the call of duty – was of a piece with the conscientiousness he had shown in the discharge of his office as bishop of Ely in the 1380s, which Dr Margaret Aston has demonstrated.[12] A sympathy with some aspects of Margery's piety might be adduced from the sanction which he had given c. 1410 to the Carthusian Nicholas Love's translation of the pseudo-Bonaventuran *Meditationes Vitae Christi*. It was submitted for Arundel's approval and he authorised its issue 'to the edification of the faithful and the confutation of heretics'. His favourable reception of Margery may have been partly the result of recognition that her piety was heavily influenced by this work.[13]

The third bishop with whom *The Book* recorded a meeting was Thomas Peverel of Worcester, whose diocese bordered on Bristol. He asked Margery to visit him whilst she was waiting there for a berth to sail to Santiago.[14] Perhaps he was in part responding to the suspicions voiced about her by a wealthy citizen of Bristol. The largest contingent in the Lollard rebellion of 1414 had come from the city.[15] Despite the discourteous reply which *The Book* attributed to Margery, the bishop insisted on her making the visit and treated her with warmth, even humility. He accommodated her in his household, confessed her, asked for her prayers, and gave her money in aid of her pilgrimage. The bishop told her: 'I know well enough that you are John of Brunham's daughter of Lynn.'[16] The knowledge he displayed about her, which suggests another motive for his particular interest in her, was gained at the start of his career, in 1377, when he had been a brother in the Carmelite friary at Lynn. He had earned Richard II's favour, being provided to Irish and Welsh bishoprics in the 1390s, and managed to get Henry IV's benevolence too, receiving the see of Worcester in 1404. In 1409 Peverel had condemned as an incorrigible heretic John Badby, tailor of Evesham, who was one of the two men executed as such in Henry IV's reign. A contemporary adjudged Peverel 'a man of evil life and unseemly conversation who spent his life in the company of lords and ladies'.[17] His household servants aroused Margery's wrath because they wore clothes 'very fashionably slashed and cut into points'.[18] However, her portrait of the bishop is a sympathetic one of a man who sensed that his life was nearing its end and who wished to 'die in charity'.

The one bishop to whom Margery showed downright hostility was Archbishop Bowet of York, whom she accused to his face of being reputed 'a wicked man'. 'And, if you are as wicked as men say, you shall never come into Heaven unless that you make amends whilst you are here.'[19] Late in 1417, after his return from taking part in a campaign against the Scots, he examined her faith and activities in the chapel of his favourite residence at Cawood on the Ouse, ten miles south of York; the fine remaining gatehouse dates from later in the century. Clerics as well as laymen of his household are likely to have taken up arms: having warded off the external enemies of the realm, it would not have been surprising if, pumped up with success, they had reviled (in the manner *The Book* suggests) one whom they suspected of being the enemy within. It was in this chapel that Bowet had examined the orthodoxy of William Cooke of Blyth, tailor, in 1410.[20] Bowet personally tested Margery's faith once more in the chapter-house of Beverley Minster (Yorks.), possibly within a few days of 27 February 1418, when he held a chapter at Beverley.[21] He appears in *The Book* as exasperated, brusque and intimidating, but possessed of a certain fair-mindedness and a grudging appreciation of some of Margery's pious attributes. Bowet was even more advanced in years than Peverel and Arundel. He had been a commoner at the University of Cambridge as long ago as 1363 and had entered royal service by 1372. He was a distinguished canon lawyer, with a fine working library. He held chief offices in the duchy of Aquitaine, at a time when John of Gaunt, Duke of Lancaster (father of Henry IV) was, at least nominally, Duke of Aquitaine. In 1399 Bowet risked this long and distinguished administrative career – and possibly his life – by supporting Henry's invasion of England and challenge to Richard II's rule. In 1407 he was translated from the see of Bath and Wells to that of York, then a particularly sensitive and demanding office, for which the Lancastrian government rightly judged this ageing lawyer, though not the first choice, to have a safe pair of hands.[22]

His predecessor, Richard Scrope, scion of a distinguished Yorkshire baronial family, had in 1405 headed a protest movement against Henry

IV's government. Captured and convicted of treason, he had been speedily executed outside York. The citizens were punished by the suspension of their liberties. From his tomb in the Minster, Scrope continued to play an embarrassing political role by performing miracles and attracting the devotion of the common people. Attempts were made to frustrate pilgrims by partitioning off his tomb – though the cult was to be permitted to flourish under Henry V. The archbishop is depicted, with the invocation 'Sancte ricarde scrope ora pro nobis' in the Book of Hours which is thought to have been written for John Bolton (d. 1445), mercer of York.[23] Maybe the adverse opinion Margery had heard about Bowet, who appears to have been a conscientious bishop of blameless life, reflected a local opinion that he was a stooge of the man who bore the main responsibility for Scrope's execution – the king. However, the bequests which Bowet made in his will of 1421 to the Minster and its clergy show that he regarded them with considerable benevolence. The tomb which he had made for himself, much mutilated and restored (as is its fine stone canopy), adjoins the south-east end of the Lady Chapel.[24] He donated a window which is in the north choir aisle. This has side lights dedicated to the lives of Saints Peter and Paul, and a centre light with an Annunciation. Bowet is shown praying before an altar. So Margery shared devout interests with her alleged persecutor – a special devotion to both St Peter and St Paul. Moreover (though there is no hint of this in *The Book*), it is likely that Bowet, who had unusually close knowledge of Brigettine piety, recognised the saint's influence on Margery's behaviour, which helped to account for its exasperating character but also reinforced her orthodoxy. Bowet had headed the escort for Princess Philippa when in 1405 she had left King's Lynn for Denmark, where, as we have seen, she was speedily immersed in the cult of St Bridget.[25]

The interviews with these four bishops were highlighted in *The Book*. Shaped perhaps all too vividly and dramatically in Margery's memory, they were important to her and to the authority of the text because they provided validation of one sort or another for her religious way of life. The fraught confrontations with Bowet formed a key episode in her *via dolorosa*, the suffering she endured in this world for her sins and the sins of others, which, in her devotional scheme, would anticipate and replace suffering in Purgatory. If the accounts of these interviews can be taken at face value (or even if one regards them as heavily cosmeticised), they give unique and credible insights into the discharge of episcopal duties by four notable and mature members of the bench, all of whom were, or had been, preoccupied for much of their working lives with the affairs of the king and realm. The interest of Repingdon (who allegedly had long wished to meet her) and Arundel in her meditations is noteworthy.

Peverel too was keen to learn about her spirituality. So there was enthusiasm in the highest ecclesiastical echelon in the 1410s for the contemplative way, and interest in the unlearned laity's engagement with it.

In a period when orthodox pieties were under vigorous radical attack, those who had the harsh and sometimes harrowing burden of maintaining the Church's defences against heretics may have been especially eager to hear about and encourage contemplative devotion, whose revelations vividly and reassuringly soothed them and reinforced the inner meaning of the cults and rituals they were defending. Margery appears to have been attuned to religious trends at the highest levels of the Lancastrian eccleciastical establishment in the first decades of the fifteenth century.

To what extent did Margery have contacts with and countenance from the bishops' secular counterparts, princes and nobles? There is one intriguing piece of evidence. During her examination by Bowet at Beverley (c. 1418), his Dominican suffragan alleged that she had recently been at Lady Westmorland's. This may have been the Dominican called John, who was titular metropolitan of Soltaniyeh in Persia, one of Bowet's suffragans who was active in carrying out ordinations at Cawood in 1417–18. *The Book*'s suffragan may too have been identical with Dr John Paris, who with his fellow Dominican, William Helmeslay, had been among those commissioned by Bowet to deal with Lollards in his diocese in 1411. According to the words attributed to the suffragan of *The Book*, 'My lady herself was well pleased with you and liked your words but you counselled my Lady Greystoke to leave her husband, that is a baron's wife and daughter to my Lady of Westmorland'.[26] Margery replied that she had not seen the countess recently, as was claimed, but had been sent for by her before setting out for Jerusalem. Joan Beaufort, Countess of Westmorland (1379–1440) was Henry V's aunt, the daughter of John of Gaunt and his mistress Katherine Swynford, whom he married as his third wife in 1396. One of the countess's brothers was Henry Beaufort, Bishop of Winchester, for whose soul (with two others) Bowet wanted prayers especially to be said at the chantry which he had set up in York Minster in 1413. The countess was married to Ralph Neville, Earl of Westmorland (d. 1425), who was one of the mainstays of Henry IV's rule in the North. He had commanded the army opposing the rebellion in which Archbishop Scrope participated, and had induced the archbishop to abandon the revolt. In 1417 he took part with Bowet in the campaign against the Scots. Joan bore fourteen children – the same number as Margery, according to *The Book*. The countess was also a forceful lady, as correspondence surviving from her widowhood reveals.[27] She may have summoned Margery to one of the Neville residences in Yorkshire, either at Sheriff Hutton or Middleham, when the Kempes were on pilgrimage in the shire in 1413. Sheriff Hutton castle is a few miles north of York, not a great diversion from the way thence to Bridlington.

The countess's son-in-law, John Lord Greystoke, entered into his inheritance in 1418, becoming head of a leading family in Cumberland and Northumberland. He had been contracted to marry Elizabeth, Joan's daughter by her first marriage, to Sir Robert Ferrers, in 1407. At the time of Margery's earlier visit to Yorkshire, Greystoke was aged about twenty-three and his wife about twenty. Their eldest surviving son, Ralph may have been born in that or the following year; four more surviving children were to follow. In view of their supposed marital problem some time in the 1410s, perhaps it is significant that Elizabeth Greystoke apparently did not choose to be buried with her spouse (despite having had no other) in his family's collegiate church at Greystoke (Cumberland), where he was laid to rest in 1436 – an unusual if not unique separation in death. She had been buried two years previously at the Dominican friary in York.[28]

How did Countess Joan and her apparently troubled daughter hear about Margery? It may have been from her brother, Bishop Beaufort (who was long to be involved in dealings with Lynn on behalf of the Crown), but her most likely source of information was her other surviving brother, Thomas Duke of Exeter, through his close and very personal association with the affairs of Lynn and relationships with its elite. An affection for his sister and a shared interest in romance is suggested by his bequest to her of a book called 'Tristram'.[29] He probably shared devotional interests with her too. He was well known for his charity and the strict moral code he imposed on his household; 'he would have no swearers nor liars nor tale-bearers'.[30] Margery, who reproved Archbishop Arundel's household servants (and many other men) for their swearing and loose talk, would have been edified by this. Like the duke, she had a devotion to St John of Bridlington; he was on pilgrimage to the shrine in 1417 when he was diverted to take part, with Bowet and the Earl of Westmorland, in dealing with the Scots. A copy of the pseudo-Bonaventuran life of Christ may have belonged to the duke's wife, Margaret.[31] So it seems that some of Margery's devotional modes were closely attuned to those to be found at the Lancastrian court, and that her piety was becoming known and respected in princely circles in the early 1410s. Her emulation of St Bridget may have made her an object of particular interest there.

However, Margery was not to become a pious adjunct of great households. Her devotional modes became suspect in royal circles by 1418; she was not a religious *politique*, quick to adapt to changing moods and fashions. She probably felt uncomfortable in the worldly atmosphere of nobles' households; she was prone to confrontations with their domestic servants. On one occasion she refused an offer of hospitality from a worthy lady because she did not approve of the ways members of her household dressed and behaved.[32] Where Margery was most at home, not surprisingly, was in urban environments, especially in bigger towns where ways of doing things were most like those she had grown up with. In such surroundings, pilgrims and other travellers were familiar and welcome; catering for their needs was good business. Lynn merchants and merchants with Lynn connections might be encountered. Such ties, as we have seen, were especially strong with London and help to account for the succour which Margery and her husband found there.[33] She made connections in Canterbury and Bristol, though both cities were off Lynn's commercial networks. The fact that the Kempes lodged in Canterbury with a 'Dewchmann' may be significant in view of the strong trading and personal ties between Lynn and Hanseatic ports. In Bristol, Thomas Marchale, a well-to-do penitent from Newcastle, invited her in for meals in order to hear her devout conversation. It is not clear that he was from Newcastle-upon-Tyne (rather than Newcastle-under-Lyme), but a man from the city might well have had links with Lynn resulting from the ports' vigorous mutual trade.[34] There was probably not the same closeness between Lynn and the Yorkshire ports.[35] However, strangers made Margery welcome in York: for some years, at least, the city and the East Riding had strong attractions for her.[36]

Travel within England, and contact with distinctive regional elements in piety, were germane to the development of Margery's religious personality. Her experiences in Yorkshire made particular impressions. In 1413 she and her husband went to York and then on to Bridlington: 'And also to many other places, and spoke with God's servants, both anchorites and recluses, and many others of our Lord's lovers, with many worthy clerics, doctors of divinity and bachelors of divinity also, in many different places.'[37] In 1417 she returned to York, saying when examined in the Minster chapter-house that she had come to offer at St William's shrine (the principal shrine in the Minster).[38] She had previously asserted that her original intention had been to stay there for a fortnight but that she had decided to prolong her stay – in all, a much longer one than was necessary simply to visit St William. She seems to have spent a good deal of her time in the Minster, attending the services or button-holing passers-by. Perhaps she was bursting to tell her old friends and mentors in the city and region about her great pilgrimages abroad and the effects they had wrought in her soul.[39] Soon after arriving in the city, she had visited an anchoress whom she already knew (presumably from the 1413 visit) in order to hear about her spiritual progress and to fast with her – but the anchoress repudiated her because of the evil rumours she had heard.[40] After Margery's first examination by Bowet, at Cawood, despite his vehement wish to have her escorted out of his diocese, she went to Bridlington and sojourned there to commune with the confessor she had met on a previous visit. He had also been the canonised prior's confessor there. She 'spoke with him and many other good men who had cheered her at previous times, and done much for her'.[41]

What attracted Margery to the particular Yorkshire cults which she mentions? St William (d. 1154) was the Archbishop of York who, after ten years of enforced exile from his see, was able to occupy it for only a few weeks before dying at the High Altar of the Minster on Trinity Sunday. His cult was principally a regional one: the canonisation took place in 1227. The tomb was originally in the nave and the shrine, erected for the translation of the saint in 1284, was at the west end of the choir, behind the wooden screen which backed on to the High Altar.[42] The saint is represented in various windows in the Minster. The miracle most frequently reproduced is his triumphant re-entry into the city, being greeted on the Ouse bridge by the civic dignitaries, when the bridge collapsed, but without causing any fatalities.[43] The cult was one which glorified the city – and emphasised its connection with the Crown, since St William had been of royal blood. Its character may have given it special importance in the aftermath of the 1405 rebellion as an antidote to the Scrope cult and as a means of reasserting the dignity of the city, whose citizens had had to humble themselves publicly in vile array in the king's presence after the rebellion. Leading promoters of St William may have been the two royal servants who were successive deans – John Prophete (1406) and Thomas Polton (1416). Janice Smith suggests that the dean and chapter promoted the cult in order to raise money for the ambitious building programme at the Minster. Ms Smith reinforces arguments that the magnificent St William window was put up, c. 1415, in the north choir transept (originally flanking the High Altar) and that it was donated by a great Yorkshire lady, Beatrice Lady Roos. Five of its panels depict members of the Roos family of Helmsley. This window, with its total of 105 panels, was the definitive iconographical statement about the saint's life and works.[44] Margery, as a devotee, would have been eager to study the new window, but it is not clear why she was one – the cult seems to have had hardly any resonance in Norfolk. She may have come to attribute her recovery from a fall of masonry and timber in St Margaret's, Lynn, prior to her 1413 visit to York, partly to the saint's protection. It was for her 'ghostly health', in the light of her cure, that she set out soon afterwards to visit York and other places.[45] Two of

the miracles depicted in the St William window in the Minster concern
escapes from a falling stone. One of them occurred in the Minster during
his translation. Two panels show a man hit by a stone whilst asleep during
the ceremony, and unharmed after the accident. A sequence of three
panels has a man putting up a tapestry, being knocked down by a falling
stone, and carrying it before the saint's shrine.[46] The theme of suffering
in exile would have had resonances for Margery. Her second known visit
to the shrine may have been made in fulfilment of a vow made before
or during her recent, often perilous, wanderings abroad. The simplest
explanation for her feeling for St William is that she was reflecting a
current enthusiasm in York.

Margery was modish too in her devotion to the recently canonised
and translated John of Bridlington. It is not clear what his general
and widespread attraction was. No writings have been attributed to him,
neither was he a spectacular miracle worker, nor extravagantly ascetic.
He was reputed to have been a scrupulous observer of his Rule, holy in
character, and a benefactor of the poor. Miracles were attributed to him
in his lifetime. A monk-chronicler of St Albans praised vaguely 'his most
holy life, his excellent behaviour'.[47] In particular, local enthusiasm and
her friendship with the saint's confessor may have stirred Margery's
devotion. Her strong empathy with local religious feeling is reflected in
her reference, apropos her visit to York in 1417, to her friendship with
the priest 'who sang by the Bishop's grave'. Since Margery (a stickler for
giving correct titles) always refers to the canonised archbishop as 'saint',
a reference to a bishop's tomb and chantry which assumed recognition
must surely be to those of Richard Scrope. Margery is likely to have been
well informed about Scrope's martyrdom before her 1413 visit, since
Lord Bardolf, also opposed to Henry IV in 1405, had had his residence
at Wormegay near Lynn, and the town's noble patron, Thomas Beaufort
(the new owner of Wormegay) had taken part in Scrope's condemnation.[48]

Yorkshire's strong eremitical traditions and culture doubtless drew
Margery to the city and shire. Dr Warren has calculated that over half
the anchorholds known to have existed in England in the fifteenth
century were in London and three other shires, of which Yorkshire was
one. York had the biggest concentration of anchorholds in the shire,
which the bequests of the merchant community helped to maintain.[49]
The author of one of Margery's favourite meditative exemplars, the
Yorkshireman Rolle, had, as we have seen, ended his days in 1349 as an
anchorite in a cell attached to the Dominican convent at Hampole near
Doncaster.[50] Margaret Kirkeby, a nun and recluse who had gone there
in 1380 and who was alive in the early years of the fifteenth century, had
been prepared for the eremitical life by Rolle. He had written epistles to

her on the subject.[51] Rolle's works and those of some other meditative writers which became dear to Margery were appreciated by members of York's clerical elites in the early fifteenth century. John de Neuton, treasurer of the Minster, provided chapter headings for a surviving copy of the *Incendium Amoris*.[52] Neuton was a notable bibliophile, who bequeathed forty books to the Minster Library, including a copy of the *Incendium*, bound up with Walter Hilton's *Scala Perfectionis*, another key text for Margery.[53] In 1415 Stephen Scrope, a nephew of the executed archbishop, was bequeathed by his brother Henry a copy of St Bridget's *Revelations*, which he had purchased at Beverley.[54] In 1432 Robert Semer (appointed sub-treasurer of York Minster in 1418) left a book called 'Brigidia' and a volume containing works by 'Richard the hermit'.[55] Margery may have met well-informed citizens of York who admired her Brigettine inclinations. The 'Bolton Book of Hours' has, among its illuminations of a large and eclectic number of saints invoked, one of St Bridget. Clad as a nun, she sits with a scroll in her left hand, inscribed with the words 'Ecce sponsa xpi [christi]' (to which the Hand of God points) and, in her right hand, a quill with which to pen her 'revelations'. The illumination encapsulates some of the appeal of the saint to the likes of Margery.[56]

York had plenty of attractions for the piously minded besides its particular cults, its eremitical traditions and meditative sympathies. It had a rich liturgical life and dazzling iconographical culture, maintained in its diversity in forty-one parish churches and numerous religious houses, besides the Minster. The outstanding works of the gild of glass painters, patronised by clergy, nobles and merchants, provided scenes and sequences from the Bible and saints' lives, scattered through the city. The apotheosis was the great east window of the Minster, which was donated by Walter Skirlaw, Bishop of Durham, and designed by John Thornton of Coventry: it had been completed in 1408. This enormously ambitious undertaking had as its subjects the beginning and end of the world. The principal themes are taken from the Old Testament and, realised with imaginative power and terrifying vivacity, from the Apocalypse. The window, one of the largest in England, surely soon must have been one of the most famous, a draw for the devout.[57] Other major attractions were the city's Corpus Christi procession and the renowned cycle of related mystery plays.[58]

However, York was not the main civic focus of Margery's devotional interest in England. That, not surprisingly, was Norwich, an easy journey from Lynn: the two were closely connected by ecclesiastical, religious, economic and social ties. Outranked probably only by London and York among English cities in its concentration of wealth and size of population,

Norwich, with its forty or so parishes, probably had more secular clergy than Lynn, despite the latter's phenomenal number of gilds.[59] Norwich had a larger number of religious houses. The city offered a wide variety of religious experiences. Indulgences were available to those who visited the cathedral on certain days. The cathedral's most famous shrine was that of St William, the little boy about whose death the first medieval antisemitic accusation of the ritual killing of a Christian child had been concocted in the twelfth century.[60] In 1389, as we have seen, there had been a gild of schoolboys in Lynn dedicated to St William.[61] Margery expressed conventional feeling about the Jews' supposed treatment of Christ and prayed that their 'blindness', together with that of Saracens and other 'false heretics', should be cured. However, *The Book* reveals no interest in St William's cult.[62]

More particularly, the city is likely to have attracted Margery because of its traditional benevolence towards 'holy women'. A remarkable number of anchorholds were maintained there in the fifteenth century, some for women. The Carmelite friary had several for its brethren; Carrow convent had five or six holds for women. Dr Norman Tanner's research has shown Norwich to have contained communities of chaste women with some apparent similarities to those of the beguines which flourished in Flanders in the thirteenth century – so far it is only one of two English towns where these have been identified. In the Low Countries and Rhineland, in the regions more strongly urbanised than anywhere in England, beguinages continued to fulfil social and spiritual needs, though in the fifteenth century they were under strict ecclesiastical supervision. Here we have one Flemish socio-cultural tradition which, unlike so many others, did not flow easily into the English environment, though it provided opportunities for a way of life which appealed to many temperaments. Evidence about one group in Norwich dates from after 1450. The other one, variously described as sisters living together or dedicated to chastity, stayed c. 1427–44 in a tenement belonging to John Pellet (or Pylett), in St Swithin's parish.[63] The existence of this group suggests that a devout woman, even one apparently so troubled and troublesome as Margery, might have been received with more sympathy in Norwich than in some towns. And so does the reverence shown there to the anchoress whose profound and moving meditative writings ensure her reputation as the best-known and best-loved English female writer of the Middle Ages. The anchoress, who lived from 1343 until at least 1416, is known as Dame Julian, perhaps because she was enclosed in a cell attached to the parish church of St Julian, Conisford in the city.[64] An unmarried laywoman, in 1373 she experienced sixteen revelations. They were to form the basis of the two versions which she made of her treatise known as 'Revelations of Divine Love', generally regarded as the culminating achievement of the distinctive medieval English mystical tradition. Dame Julian's reputation for sanctity in her own lifetime is reflected in local testamentary bequests to her.[65]

So there was much in the religious culture of Norwich to attract Margery and to provide incentives for her visits. She communed on spiritual matters there with the aged Dame Julian, whom, according to *The Book*, she found sympathetic to her meditations and, indeed, inspirational; on one visit, she says, she spent many days with the anchoress.[66] *The Book* does not suggest that Margery moderated the more controversial aspects of her pious behaviour when she was in the city. It refers to hostile reactions to her and mentions an interview she had with a monk-anchorite which turned sour.[67] However, no big scenes of rejection and persecution are set in Norwich. Rather, it was a place for spiritual renewal and nourishment for Margery, especially from her long-standing attachment to Richard Caister, vicar of St Stephen's church. Her description of her first meeting with him, in the church, suggests his good humour, humanity and open-mindedness.[68] Dr Tanner has emphasised that Caister was a cleric of austerity and highly individual devotion, whose reputation was to make his tomb a cult centre.[69] He was steadfast as Margery's staunch supporter and comforter; he confessed her whenever she came to Norwich. Another sympathetic Norwich priest was the Carmelite, William Sowthfeld.[70] It is likely that she also found lay patrons there. On her return from pilgrimage abroad in 1415, staying in the city on her way back to Lynn, she was provided with a new set of white clothes by a 'worshipful' man.[71] It was probably there that she had the garments made up and first wore the controversial raiment in England. On this visit she made an offering 'in the worship of the Trinity', in thanks for her safe return from pilgrimage; she had made a corresponding offering on her way out (c. 1413) to seek passage at Great Yarmouth.[72] In 1433 she once again passed through Norwich, accompanying her daughter-in-law, who was to embark for her homeland at Ipswich. On this occasion Margery had a favourable reception in Norwich from a Franciscan who had heard about her way of living and 'feeling'.[73] We may conclude that Norwich was, among English cities and towns, the place where Margery felt most comfortable – less conspicuous than in Lynn, more tolerated as an acceptable example of devotion, and familiar (as she was not in York) as hailing from the same 'country'.

Besides her visits to these principal cities and their environs, Margery also went to or passed through Beverley, Canterbury, Hull, Leicester, Lincoln – and Calais. 'Calice', as it appears in contemporary English vernacular, can be accounted an English town in the period, since it was governed as a lieutenancy of the English Crown. It was economically closely connected to London and Kent and was thronged by residents of English origin, and merchants, factors and soldiers who were their fellow countrymen. *The Book*'s accounts of Margery's visits to or passage through these and other towns and places vary in length and character. Some contain elaborate setpieces; others are perfunctory or slight. The extended comments are principally about Margery's behaviour in public places – in churches, at the sight of especially sacred objects, and during acts of worship or in streets bedecked and transformed for the ritual celebration of holidays. These accounts cast some light on religious mentalities. Her distressing public bouts which, as we have seen, developed in their mature form during her visit to Jerusalem in 1414, were a recurrent cause of concern among her companions and among bystanders, provoking both compassionate and hostile reactions. *The Book* mentions her outbursts at Bristol during Sunday communion services and during a Corpus Christi procession (10 June 1417),[74] at the sight of the Holy Blood at Hailes abbey,[75] and in front of a vividly realised Crucifixion in a Leicester church.[76] *The Book* refers to her 'sobbing full boisterously and weeping full plenteously' in London in 1433/4.[77] However, her behaviour is sometimes described in more extreme words than these. At Bristol and Hailes there were 'loud cryings'; in Bristol there were 'shrill shriekings' too, with her plentiful weeping and boisterous sobbing at Sunday Mass. She became extremely debilitated during the Corpus Christi procession there in 1417 – she was carried into a house, where she appeared to be dying, and 'roared' astonishingly.[78] However, *The Book* does not always highlight this dissonance and debility as the significant aspects of her behaviour as a traveller in England. In the prolonged description of her visit to Yorkshire in 1417–18, she is generally represented with a somewhat different emphasis, as an articulate expounder of religious truths, a precise and outwardly calm homilist persecuted for her words.

Common reactions to Margery's hysterical behaviour were astonishment, puzzlement and revulsion. People 'wonder at' it and decry it in Bristol, and many years later, at Syon abbey, a young man politely asks her for an explanation.[79] There were others sympathetically concerned, such as those who lifted her indoors at Bristol, the Cistercians of Hailes, and canons of Leicester abbey. However, *The Book* emphasises hostile reactions – public vilification, in imitation of the Passion, was, as has been seen, an integral part of the text's devotional scheme. In London in 1433/4 she had to shift from one parish church to another as successive curates and priests debarred her from services.[80] Maybe angry reactions stemmed not just from revulsion at her repellent physical symptoms or

Plate 2   Bench end from St. Nicholas' Chapel, King's Lynn, with
carvings of fifteenth-century ships.
© V&A Picture Library

Plate 3   St Nicholas' Chapel, King's Lynn, Norfolk.
Used by kind permission of The Churches Conservation Trust/Christopher Dalton

Plate 4 Thomas Arundel, Archbishop of Canterbury.
The Bodleian Library, University of Oxford, MS Laud Misc. 165 fol. 5

Plate 5 Entrance to the Chapter House, York Minster. Margery Kempe describes how she was examined by clerics on her way of life and her faith in the Chapter House.

Plate 6 Supplicant asks the executed Richard Scrope, Archbishop of York, for his prayers. From The Bolton Book of Hours, *circa* 1420–30.

© Dean and Chapter of York: reproduced by kind permission

Plate 7 Figure of pilgrim who was devoted to Santiago de
Compostela, formerly in St Saviour's church, York, now in former
St Mary's Church (*YORK STORY*).

Plate 8   Gentile Bellini (*circa* 1429–1507) Procession in St Mark's Square, 1496 (oil on canvas), Galleria dell' Accademia, Venice, Italy/Bridgeman Art Library.

Plate 9 Jan van Scorel (1495–1562) Members of the Jerusalem Guild of Utrecht, *circa* 1535.
© Centraal Museum Utrecht

the disruption they caused to private devotions, sermons or business transactions, but from the threat they posed to concentration by layfolk on public ritual. There may, indeed, have been fears that the efficacy of the ritual might be damaged by alarming and unaccustomed individual behaviour: some may have been angered because they considered that Margery was threatening a break in the current of spiritual benefits flowing to themselves and their community from uninterrupted performance of liturgies. The accounts of hostile reactions certainly suggest that, in these respects, Margery's public behaviour was untypical of the especially devout. It came as an unwelcome surprise to bystanders. In a period when there was general nervousness about heresy, ostentatiously eccentric religious behaviour quickly aroused suspicions.

Margery's public religious manifestations of various kinds on her travels in England before she departed for Jerusalem, and after her return from Santiago in 1417, were among the factors which led to repeated accusations of heresy against her, arrests, and formal examinations on the articles of faith. Before her defining Jerusalem experience, it was her highly self-controlled scriptural and homiletic presumption in Canterbury Cathedral, more fitting in a priest, which incensed people (presumably in the main fellow pilgrims to St Thomas, as well as monks) even more than her weeping. Some followed her out of the cathedral precinct shouting, 'You shall be burnt, you false Lollard. Here is a cartful of thorns ready for you, and a tun to burn you with'.[81] She fled out of the city gates, pursued by threats. In Lambeth Palace she again behaved like a cleric, her reproof of swearing provoking a woman to curse her and exclaim, 'I would you were in Smithfield and I would bring a faggot to burn you with – it is a pity that you live'.[82] Such remarks alluded to the burning in Smithfield of William Sawtre (formerly chaplain at St Margaret's, Lynn) and Badby.

After Margery's return from Jerusalem, her enhanced spiritual *persona* brought further trouble. The public rhapsody in Leicester led to her being questioned by the mayor, who, among other things, called her a 'false Lollard', and to her imprisonment and examination of her faith.[83] Her wearing of white clothes was puzzling, indeed disturbing, in a society in which attire was minutely regulated as an expression of status and avocation. In York Minster, shortly before her first examination, a cleric took hold of her by the collar of her gown (no way to treat a respectable lady) and said, 'You wolf, what is this cloth that you have on?' Some passing choristers piped up brightly, 'Sir, it is wool'.[84] Whilst she waited in attendance on Archbishop Bowet in the chapel at Cawood, members of his household upbraided her as a Lollard and a heretic, and swore that she would be burnt. The first questions Bowet asked her were, 'Why do you go round in white? Are you a maiden?' – for whom white raiment would have been appropriate.[85] Even though Bowet found her faith to be orthodox, her behaviour, or the reputation for bizarre behaviour which preceded her, led to more accusations of heresy. Two yeomen of Henry V's brother, the Duke of Bedford, arrested her after she had crossed the ferry across the Humber at Hessle. They told her that the duke had sent for her and that she was accounted a leading Lollard. When they took her back to Hessle, men called her a Lollard and women ran out of their houses holding their distaffs, shouting to the people, 'Burn this false heretic'.[86]

As Professor John Thomson has remarked, *The Book* provides evidence of popular hostility to Lollardy, and official concern about it.[87] Since 1382 ecclesiastical authorities had been taking firm measures to suppress the spread of John Wycliffe's unorthodox doctrines by his followers. In the years 1407–11 Archbishop Arundel introduced tight restrictions to control teaching at Oxford and Cambridge, and preaching generally.[88] The support which secular authorities gave to the Church in suppressing heresy had been augmented by the statute *De heretico comburendo* (1401), which obliged royal officials to assist in tracking down and arresting suspected heretics and to search them out on their own initiative. The statute prescribed that relapsed heretics should be handed over to the secular authorities and burnt to death.[89] The first person to be executed under the provisions of the statute, in 1401, was Sawtre. On 30 April 1399 he had been examined by Bishop Despenser of Norwich at the bishop's residence in South Elmham (Norfolk). Sawtre declared himself to be opposed to the doctrine of free will, the cult of images, and the practice of pilgrimage; his views on the Blessed Sacrament were un-orthodox too. Sawtre retracted his views and submitted to correction. On 25 May he abjured publicly at Lynn. The formidable Despenser treated him lightly; he was free to go. He resurfaced in London, where he courageously resumed the preaching of heresy. This led to his down-fall and martyrdom in 1401: examined in Convocation by Archbishop Arundel, Sawtre was condemned as a relapsed heretic.[90] In 1413, the year in which Arundel apparently examined Margery's beliefs and medita-tions with such patience and sensitivity, he had to deal with a grave, politically difficult case of heresy – that of Sir John Oldcastle of Cooling castle (Kent). Oldcastle was in Henry V's service and highly rated by him as a soldier. Evidence incriminating Oldcastle as a heretic first came to light during the Convocation which met in March.[91]

In view of the mounting concern about the spread of heresy in Henry IV's reign, reaching a crescendo at the end of it and at the start of his son's, Margery's public homilies, special raiment and vigorous ecstasies seem to have been, to say the least, imprudent, if they were indeed projected as described in *The Book*. So does her apparent failure to carry in her bag any episcopal or spousal letters justifying her way of life.[92] However, her well-advertised devotion to the Real Presence in the Sacrament, to the Blessed Virgin and the saints ran clean counter to characteristic Lollard beliefs. The Sawtre episode (the like of which had presumably never been known in Lynn) should have made her better informed about Lollards than those seemingly bewildered men and women in the street, whose immediate, unthinking reaction to her was, we are told, a cry of heresy. Yet in one crucial respect her behaviour was startlingly like what was popularly anticipated in heretics. Lollard women as well as laymen had long been denounced for expounding Scripture, as Dr Margaret Aston has shown.[93] Moreover, Margery's strictures echoed those of Lollard preachers (and, indeed, those of many perfectly orthodox ones) in their castigation of unworthy clerics, blasphemy, luxurious attire and worldly behaviour in general. No wonder she alarmed clerical as well as secular watchdogs.

Margery's public behaviour was even more imprudent in the circumstances of 1417. Maybe she was lulled into a false sense of security by the archiepiscopal approval she had received (perhaps less comprehensive than she imagined) for the devout way of life she had constructed, and maybe she was further buoyed up in her conviction by her transcending spiritual experiences in Jerusalem and Rome, and the ways in which Christ had protected her in the manifold hazards and fraught situations she had experienced abroad. During her absence from England, Oldcastle's arrest and its aftermath had made the issue of Lollardy even more prominent and politically critical. On 19 October 1413, now excommunicated but obdurate, he had escaped from the Tower of London. The following January armed contingents of his followers from different regions linked up outside the city, with the intention of seizing Henry V and his brothers, staunch defenders of orthodoxy. This feeble attempt at rebellion, of which the king received warning, was a dismal failure.[94] In the wake of its easy suppression, in the parliament summoned to meet at Leicester at the end of April 1414, a statute was made obliging royal and urban officers to take an oath to assist bishops and their officers in arresting Lollards. Suspected heretics were to be handed over to the diocesan within ten days.[95]

Margery was stepping into a minefield when she exhibited her uncommon devotion whilst passing through Leicester, probably flushed with the success of her pilgrimage to Santiago, in 1417. The town had been one of the first urban centres of Lollardy in the 1380s, and traditions of religious dissidence persisted there. In 1413 some members of its Corpus Christi gild had been suspected of Lollardy; Leicester men took part in the 1414 rising.[96] By contrast, the borough was appurtenant to the Crown as a possession of the dukes of Lancaster; it was the ducal 'capital' in southern England, where, in the collegiate church in The Newarke, Henry V's mother was buried along with some of his most illustrious Lancastrian forbears. Leicester castle was the administrative centre of the duchy's honour of Leicester, presided over by its steward. In view of all these circumstances, it is not surprising that the mayor reacted to reports of Margery's behaviour so jumpily and that the steward was also keen to interrogate her. These secular officials, according to *The Book*'s account, treated her in a brusque and intimidating manner. The steward was said to have been particularly brutal – and lecherous in his behaviour, perhaps with the intention of exposing a devil in her.[97] The duchy steward in 1417 was Robert Babthorpe (d. 1436), former esquire of Henry IV and executor and administrator of his will. His brother, William was then acting as deputy steward and it was probably he who, if *The Book* is to be believed, terrorised Margery.[98] Apparently she antagonised a powerful family at the heart of the Lancastrian establishment.

In the summer of 1417 that establishment was particularly exercised over the dangers of subversion and invasion, and the possibilities of their conjunction or interaction. On 25 July Henry V appointed the Duke of Bedford as lieutenant of the realm, and five days later set sail from Southampton for his second, decisive invasion of France.[99] Yet the dangerous Oldcastle was still at large; rumours about his clandestine movements and malignant machinations loomed large for the chronicler at St Albans abbey. Before the king left, in Capgrave's version, Oldcastle had 'caused his emissaries to scatter many writings in the ways and places of public resort, setting forth the increase and glory of the realm as their object, but really intended to stir up the hearts of the people'. The Lollards were alleged to be plotting with the Scots, inciting them to invade the realm. They were suspected of being particularly active in Yorkshire.[100] A flashpoint was the siege laid to the English garrison in Roxburgh castle by the Scots. In letters dated at Cawood on 18 and 27 July, Bowet said that news of the siege had been sent to him by the Earl of Northumberland, Warden of the East March; in response, Bowet ordered arrays of the clergy. Royal letters of Privy Seal were issued, dated 14 and 24 August, ordering men to join Bedford in arms at Leicester, where he had arrived by 20 September. However, Bedford's army was not needed; the Scots decamped after the prompt deployment of the forces mustered earlier in the North, including the archbishop's. He had dated a letter at Ripon on 2 August, the day before the muster of the clergy there which he had ordered; thence they were to proceed to join the muster of the Marchmen at Newcastle. On 12 September Bowet dated a letter at Northallerton, presumably on his journey back from the Borders; from 7 October, through the winter, he dated letters at Cawood. Bedford, whilst returning southwards, conducted a reign of terror against suspected Lollards, having arrests carried out vigorously. By the end of November Oldcastle had been captured; on 14 December, in Bedford's presence, he was both hanged as a traitor and burnt as a heretic.[101]

In view of these dramatic events, Margery's decision to go to York appears to have been the height of folly. It is not clear why she went (or in which month). On her return from Spain to Bristol, she presumably set out for home. However, she had to make a diversion because, when the mayor of Leicester released her (but not her bag), it was on condition that she got Bishop Repingdon to write him a letter discharging him of his responsibility in the case. This made it necessary for her to seek out the bishop.[102] After such unexpected, additional ordeals and inconveniences, why did she not just go home, as originally planned? Perhaps, as in 1413, she decided to seek out the Yorkshire saints to give thanks for deliverance from her recent peril. However, in the hectic, febrile political atmosphere of the later months of 1417, it made sense for the careful and thorough Bedford to detail two yeomen to go to Yorkshire in order to arrest a woman who had been acting suspiciously and bring her to speak to him. With what sounds like grimly triumphant relish, they told her that she was 'held to be the greatest Lollard in all this part of the country, or around London either'. Perhaps one of the Babthorpes or the mayor of Leicester had written to the duke, denouncing her. In Bowet's presence at Beverley the ducal claque accused her of being 'Cobham's daughter' – Oldcastle held the barony of Cobham (Kent) – and of being a letter-carrier for him. They were excited by the thought that they had bagged the leading female Lollard. Bowet made plain his dilemma: he did not wish to offend the duke, but he had already found her faith to be orthodox. *The Book* records how he stood firm to his principles.[103] It presents in this Yorkshire sequence and in the account of earlier events at Leicester vivid and credible vignettes of the panic among secular officials and clamour among some sections of the clergy and populace in the crisis of 1417. The impression one gains from the account in *The Book* is that what saved Margery from being the victim of general hysteria were the cool, rational heads and courageous firmness of influential ecclesiastics. Once more, Bowet expelled her from his diocese, a mild prescription, though he insisted that she and her husband seek further written authorisation from the Archbishop of Canterbury for her way of life before she returned home. Margery passed through Lincoln, incorrigible as ever, confounding the clergy with her knowledge, and was dutifully met by her husband at West Lynn. They proceeded to London and obtained licence from Archbishop Chichele without difficulty. There was one last scare, overcome simply by production of the document. Just south of Ely, they were arrested by a pursuing (and literate) horseman, who exasperatedly released them immediately on sight of Chichele's letter.[104] Perhaps Margery had created a stir passing through Cambridge and the university or town authorities were alerted to take action under their statutory obligation to seek out heretics.

The Book does not mention any further persecutions of this colourfully remembered kind. Why not? Chichele's authorisation was clearly important. It does not appear that Margery modified her characteristic behaviour because of these troubles. However, *The Book* notes only local trips afterwards, apart from her journeys on the way to and from the continent in 1433. Perhaps the terrifying experiences of 1417–18 deterred Margery from travelling to parts of England where her piety might appear more questionable because she was a stranger, preceded perhaps by wicked rumour. On the other hand, further travels to visit shrines and like-minded devout persons outside Norfolk may not have been included in *The Book* because they went off quietly: they did not merit mention simply because they did not involve persecution. The fact that she had emerged unscathed after terrible accusations, imprisonments and intimidating examinations perhaps helped to establish a grudging acceptance of her orthodoxy, despite the continuing climate of fear about heresy. In 1428 there was a concerted drive by the authorities against Lollards.[105] Suspects in Norfolk continued to be arrested, examined and convicted, as the records of Bishop Alnwick of Norwich's prosecutions between September 1428 and March 1431 show.[106] At various times a few Lynn men are known to have come under suspicion.[107] General concern about heretics was raised by an anticlerical revolt with Lollard overtones which occurred in 1431. It was a feeble echo of the 1414 rising, but the Protector of the Realm, Henry VI's uncle Humfrey Duke of Gloucester, made a big show of suppressing it.[108] A few years later, at a great feast in London, Margery heard her reputation being picked over. When she revealed her identity, she was treated apologetically and with respect. Present at the banquet were some 'from the Cardinal's house'.[109] The cardinal was Henry Beaufort, Bishop of Winchester, the Countess of Westmorland's brother, Duke Humfrey's uncle, and a staunch opponent of the Czech Hussite heretics, whose clutches Margery had recently evaded. The cardinal had a long acquaintance with Lynn's personalities and political affairs. Whereas Margery had once been denounced as a dangerous heretic, she was now just laughed at in table-talk as a hypocrite.

However, *The Book*'s accounts of Margery's reception away from home in England are not as negative as this summary of them has suggested. The support and appreciation which her distinctive spirituality received in towns and other places, within elites and commonalty, is emphasised in it too. As we have seen, *The Book* casts Thomas Marchale into the role of faithful disciple. Moreover, when she left Leicester, 'many good folk . . . came to cheer her, thanking God that had preserved her and given her victory over her enemies, and went forth out of the town's end, and made her right good cheer, promising her that if she ever came again she should have better cheer among them than ever she had before'.[110] Staying in London, probably in 1418, she 'had right good cheer of many worthy men'; her acquittals in the teeth of wrath may have helped to impress them.[111] When she had gone to York in 1417, according to *The Book*, 'many good men and women prayed her to meat and made her right good cheer and were right glad to hear her dalliance, having great marvel of her speech for it was fruitful'.[112] The contrasts between, on the one hand, sympathy and approval, and, on the other, revulsion and denunciation suggest that, even on a brief visit to a town, Margery had the capacity to stir up division and dissension. At Canterbury (if the report is not exaggerated) she caused a near-riot. At Leicester storms of thunder and lightning which broke out after her arrest with fellow pilgrims made 'all the people in the town . . . so afraid that they did not know what to do'. They believed that they were being punished for the arrest of pilgrims.[113] The mayor expressed the fear that her persuasiveness would cause a fundamental disruption of borough society: 'I believe thou art come hither to have away our wives from us and lead them with thee.'[114] Indeed, his fears about her impact may have been compounded by the fact that she was, as she had made plain to him, a lady from Lynn with a distinguished social background; the pride characteristic of Lynn *potenciores* did not play well with a mayor of Leicester. Her eminent urban provenance was one of the factors which made her a potentially formidable influence, combined with her abilities.

An anecdote about her imprisonment at Beverley illustrates one of *The Book*'s themes – her ability to sway individuals and groups by her eloquence. In this instance she had a casual and potentially hostile audience: 'Then stood she looking out at a window, telling many good tales to them that would hear her, in so much so that women wept sore and said with great heaviness of their hearts, "Alas, woman, why shalt thou be burnt?".'[115] Years later in London, despite her detractors, 'much of the common people magnified God in her, having good trust that it was the goodness of God which wrought that high grace in her soul her'.[116] In York some of the clergy had been worried about the effects of her rhetorical power, especially in view of the anticlerical content of some of her homilies. When she made clear to one cleric that she intended to prolong her visit beyond a fortnight, he promptly ordered her to appear for examination in the chapter-house of the Minster.[117] At Cawood, clerics told Bowet: 'We will not suffer her to dwell among us, for the people hath great faith in her dalliance, and peradventure she might pervert some of them'.[118] Bowet may have trodden carefully because she had her supporters in York, including some noteworthy clerics. After her first examination, by clergy in the Minster chapter-house, 'secular people' opposed her imprisonment, going surety for her appearance at Cawood and undertaking to accompany her there.[119] After Bowet dismissed her from Cawood, on her return to the city she 'was received by many people, and by very worthy clerks', who rejoiced in her acquittal. It was, surely, above all her charismatic power which gave her the reputation of being able to stir up and disturb people from the highest to the lowest, from Henry IV's niece Lady Greystoke to the commons thronging cathedral or street; this made Bowet and some of his leading clergy anxious to get her out of a diocese in which the stability of society had been shaken by political and spiritual tremors. Scrope's remains, noted a chronicler of St Albans, had been the object of frequent pilgrimage by common folk (*plebanorum*). Besides, at a time when the Scots were on the offensive, the encouragement of a possible family rift between the Lancastrian House of Westmorland and the young Greystoke who, it was anticipated, would soon become one of the principal regional landowners, might have hampered co-operation in Border defence.[120]

Let us turn to consider briefly the information which *The Book* contains about travel in England. Travellers such as Margery (who had a keen interest in mileages) found it easy to move round much of the realm. Royal itineraries show the speed with which kings could reach most parts from their residences in the vicinity of London and reflect the complexity of the road network and the adequacy of many of the tracks. The Gough Map (c. 1360) has been described by Dr Paul Hindle as demonstrating the existence of 'a national road system radiating from London', despite the fact that several major towns, including Lynn, were not connected up with the network on the map. However, Lynn had an outstanding network of riverine communications. The Gough Map depicts as much as 2,940 miles of road or track.[121] *The Book* certainly gives the impression that travel between major towns was comfortable, especially when compared to Margery's expectations of travel abroad and some of her experiences of it. Indeed, when she was about to set out from Lynn for Santiago in 1417, it was said that there were 'many thieves by the way'; she feared that she might be robbed of the gold which she was carrying.[122] Assuming that the section of the route from Lynn to Bristol rather than from La Coruña to Santiago was intended, the unsafe conditions alluded to may have resulted from the exceptional movements of soldiers converging on the embarkation port of Southampton for Henry V's expedition to Normandy. Otherwise, no concern is expressed about highwaymen in England.

However, *The Book* makes it clear that a woman on her travels needed to be accompanied by a man, preferably her husband.[123] John Kempe frequently travelled with his wife, but he was not always available, and it is unclear in some instances as to who was with her. In 1417 she went from Bristol to Leicester with Thomas Marchale and at least one other man, a certain Patryk, who, like Marchale, had been on pilgrimage with her to Santiago. She arranged at Leicester to travel with Patryk to Lincoln and back, and then hired him to go with her to York.[124] Archbishop Bowet hired 'a good, sad man' of his household to escort her out of his diocese.[125] Whether she was normally accompanied too by a maid is uncertain. Nor is it certain whether she customarily travelled in England on horseback, by waggon, or on foot. Patryk led her on his horse from Leicester to his house at Melton Mowbray, a few miles' journey. Patryk is represented as steadfastly doing errands for Margery and Marchale when she was detained at Leicester, though grumbling to her about his ordeal at the hands of the mayor of Leicester, endured because of her. Dr Jane Laughton has plausibly identified Patryk as a member of the Paterike family, who appear to have moved to Melton Mowbray in the late fourteenth or early fifteenth century and stayed there for some fifty years. The town's port moot rolls mention an affray which John Patryk committed on William Holand during time of market in 1411, and an affray which his servant, Robert committed on Michael, the servant of John Goldsmith (?1415). In 1416 Patryk seems to have had property in Kirkelane.[126] If this Patryk was Margery's fellow pilgrim, put-upon gofer and hired travelling companion, his low status relative to hers (and, presumably, Marchale's) would explain his humbler role in *The Book* and his entitlement simply by his surname, which is unusual in it.

On Margery's return from the continent in 1433, when she was old and slow in movement, she hired a horse near Canterbury.[127] Her visit to Denney abbey suggests that Lynn folk may have habitually travelled long distances by their riverine communications.[128] Good lodgings – by which Margery set considerable store – do not seem to have been hard to come by in major towns. On arrival at Leicester, Marchale and Margery soon found lodgings, where a meal was provided for them and an upper chamber for her.[129] She recollected that the upper chamber in a private house in which she was imprisoned in Beverley was fair, with an 'honest' bed and all the necessary facilities, though there was no access to adequate drink as her keeper had locked her in and was unavailable.[130] By contrast, when practically destitute in 1433, she was unable to find suitable lodging for the night on the way between Dover and Canterbury.[131]

The Book gives an impression of a society in which strangers were made welcome, especially in larger towns, as long as they behaved conformably. They were not catered for just for the sake of gain or solely as objects of pious charity. They were valued too if they brought news of the wider world, providing political and business information, and if they retailed entertaining and edifying anecdotes. In some of these respects, Margery is likely to have been a disappointing visitor – her knowledge of current worldly affairs seems to have been gravely, even recklessly, defective and her much stressed merriness was purely of the evangelical kind that we associate with those who have found joy in the Lord. Indeed, she told good homilies well, and we may well believe she had an encyclopaedic knowledge of exotic shrines; using a cord, she could demonstrate the dimensions of Christ's tomb.[132] She had news value in herself as a phenomenon which could be joyously or darkly interpreted. Gossip about Margery apparently blew far and wide through the realm and across the continent. When she was in Rome, an English priest – apparently one of a company of newly arrived pilgrims – sought her out since 'while he was in England he heard tell of such a woman who was in Rome'.[133] The Bishop of Worcester knew about her and about her arrival in Bristol, as we have seen. At Leicester a man from Boston (Lincs.) remarked to her gaoler's wife that she was accounted to be a holy woman in his town.[134] On the other hand, the York anchoress who had greatly loved her before she went on pilgrimages abroad would not receive her afterwards, 'for she had heard tell so much evil told of her'.[135] It is alleged in *The Book* that a saying had long been widely attributed to her, implying that she was a religious hypocrite who, despite her pretensions to austerity, indulged in delicate foods – 'False flesh, you shall eat no herring.' This was the anecdote which was a subject of mirth among the well-to-do group in London in 1433/4.[136]

The allusions in *The Book* to travels in England pertain particularly to journeys which Margery apparently undertook in the years 1413 and 1417–18, journeys which had special significance in her spiritual development and in justification of her way of life. So what *The Book* tells us about them is highly selective. Moreover, we do not know whether she traversed the realm on other occasions and for different purposes. We can place some reliance on the fragmentary reminiscences which we have because they do not contradict our knowledge from other sources about personalities and circumstances. *The Book* enhances our knowledge of the Lancastrian ecclesiastical and political scene, especially in the 1410s, in convincing and sometimes surprising ways. There are insights about the personal characters and households of bishops, the devotional interests of well-educated clerics and well-to-do layfolk, the varieties of reactions to heresy, religious opinions among the commons and elitist concerns about them. The ruling 'establishment' had been deeply apprehensive about the spread of heresy since the 1380s and had been politically fractured by Henry of Bolingbroke's usurpation in 1399. Dissenters of various stripes were encouraged by the apparent vulnerability of Henry IV's rule. *The Book*'s evidence about Margery's experiences in 1417–18 valuably shows how nervous government was then; Henry V's expedition to Normandy might provide a window of opportunity for the regime's opponents. At this juncture, despite the victory of Agincourt, Lancastrian rule appeared to some to be as threatened as under his father. By contrast, the tranquillity of Margery's journeys in England in 1433/4 may have reflected Henry V's success in laying secure foundations for the stability of the dynasty.

The Book reinforces the view that, by contemporary standards, travelling conditions were remarkably easy and convenient through much of lowland England. Both as a person of high status and as a pilgrim, Margery was a privileged traveller. Yet as a woman of eccentric habits, she was a vulnerable one, especially when unaccompanied by her husband. But *The Book* does not record that she was robbed or molested, nor that she returned home debilitated and sick, as she did after her more extensive travels abroad. The ease of travel and the expectation of friendly reception were factors which promoted a unitary sense of community in England. Devotional travel to a large extent tracked and fed off commercial networks, but it also acquired its own momentum and rhythms, promoting acculturation between different regions. Pious trends in York as well as in Norwich were important in the development of *The Book*'s spirituality. It may be significant that London does not play a similar part, in a period when, much other evidence suggests, it was exerting an increasing commercial and cultural influence in the regions. According to *The Book*, Margery's visits to London were for the purpose of conducting ecclesiastical business or as a short-stay traveller, passing through, enjoying the hospitality and making use of the credit facilities available. Margery was enthusiastic about visiting its great variety of parish churches, but overall it appears in *The Book* as a business rather than as a devotional centre. Refreshingly, *The Book* provides us with a provincial view of fifteenth-century England and an insight into some sorts of the mentalities which near and distant urban communities shared, and the ties which bound them together.

chapter 7

A WIDER WORLD

The *Book of Margery Kempe* provides important evidence about international pilgrimage in the early fifteenth century – the motivations behind it, its mechanics, and the hazards and problems which pilgrims faced. It also casts light on the behaviour of the English abroad, the ways in which they interacted with foreigners, and the question of how far the development of a sense of nationality in England was coming to overshadow affective adherence to the concept of Christendom.

The Book alludes to three trips which Margery made abroad. The first two, in the period 1413–17, were intended as pilgrimages to the principal Christian shrines; the third, in 1433, not originally intended as a pilgrimage, ended up as one to a modern cult. The latter, at Bad Wilsnack in Brandenburg, was an example of the sorts of cults which mushroomed locally, such as the one which was recorded as existing on the outskirts of Lynn in 1389. It was reported that crowds flocked to the parish church of South Lynn, congregating before an image of the Trinity, since miracles and cures had often taken place there. A parish gild had been founded in 1377 in order to maintain a light before the image.[1] Considering the availability of such local centres of exceptional numinous power, why did people opt to go to faraway shrines? Most were, indeed, probably content to rely on local or regional images and relics. Some such cults had the disadvantages that they lacked episcopal sanction and that their power and popularity waxed and waned. Ecclesiastical authorities promoted the advantages of visiting the great historic cult centres, and chief among those advantages, in an age when the doctrine of Purgatory was deeply and vividly implanted in people's minds, were the large number of indulgences available there and the generosity of some of their terms. Guidebooks for pilgrims intending to go to Jerusalem or Rome, written in the vernacular, advertised the indulgences to be gained at each altar and sacred site. The strength of 'pilgrim culture' in Lynn in the later fourteenth century is suggested by the ordinance which the Holy Cross

gild had in 1389 that 'if any brother or sister be in pilgrimage, he shall
have a gallon of ale to his drink'.[2] Local cults stimulated fervour to visit
related ones, more prestigious and far away. Bold undertakings to set
out for the latter helped to sustain the former, for one sought out first
familiar numinous sites for approval and protection. The culture of
pilgrimage was unitary and unifying: respect in Lynn for it in the 1430s
is reflected in a homily in *The Book*. A messenger from God could be
plausibly described as a 'seemly aged man like to a palmer or a pilgrim'.[3]

Pilgrimages abroad were legally protected but hazardous undertakings.
Canon law prescribed excommunication for those who robbed pilgrims.
The provision of safe conduct for them was sometimes the subject of
clauses in treaties between princes. The safe passage of pilgrims between
England and Flanders was confirmed in treaties between Henry IV and
John the Fearless, Duke of Burgundy.[4] It made sense for pilgrims to
advertise their status in hope of garnering the charity which they ought
to have received, as well as the promised (though not always forthcoming) security. Individual pilgrims found it convenient and comfortable
to bond with others; small groups had to muck in as parts of larger and
more amorphous ones, at least on sea voyages, and on the highly restricted
and regulated tours of the Holy Land.

Pilgrimages to major shrines abroad were certainly popular among
English folk in Margery's day. *The Book* recounts her frequent encounters
abroad with compatriots also on pilgrimage, as well as some on ecclesiastical or mercantile business, and others who seem to have been drifters on
the margins of society. The royal licences by letters patent which shipowners or captains had to procure in this period to take pilgrims abroad,
stating the destination and the number of pilgrims to be embarked,
show that the trade could be big business. In 1434 royal licences were
issued for six Bristol ships to take pilgrims to Santiago, two of them with
a capacity to take eighty pilgrims each.[5] We have some detailed information about the pilgrimages of great men, notably that of Henry Earl of
Derby (the future Henry IV) to the Holy Land in 1392–3, an expedition
for which his household accounts fortunately survive. We have no such
documentary evidence, or much else, about the pilgrimages abroad of
the middling sort, such as Margery, or of peasants and other common
folk, such as Agneys Snelle of Knowsthorpe, near Leeds (Yorks.), a *neif*
(villein) of the duke of Lancaster, who in 1380 successfully petitioned
him for discharge from her office of bailiff whilst she was on pilgrimage
to Rome and elsewhere. She undertook to pray for the soul of the duke
and the souls of other benefactors.[6]

The denunciations of the homilist William Langland in his lastingly
popular poem *Piers the Ploughman*, and of Lollard preachers and writers,

the powerful satire of Chaucer and strictures of Erasmus have created unfavourable and cynically viewed stereotypes of later medieval English pilgrims. Their critics, medieval and modern, have variously characterised them as tending to be worldly in their behaviour, credulous in their beliefs, and mechanistic in their piety. Besides, there were professional beggars and idle spongers who abused the status. Indeed, *The Book* bears witness to popular cynicism about motivation, reporting that the Kempes, after taking their vows of chastity, were rumoured to go on pilgrimage really to seek out 'woods, groves or valleys to use the lust of their bodies' in secrecy.[7] Its account of the group with which Margery set out for Jerusalem strongly suggests that they conducted themselves as they would normally when travelling about on business or for recreation. In perhaps similar vein, Sir Bernard Brocas had intended to take greyhounds with him when he went to the shrine of Our Lady of Walsingham; in 1380 the Duke of Lancaster licensed him to hunt with them in his warren at Methwold (Norfolk) on the way there and back.[8] Dr Duffy has more sympathetically discussed the religious and secular motives which impelled later medieval English pilgrims. He declares that Margery 'undertook her many pilgrimages very largely to gain the indulgences available at shrines'. Yet *The Book* makes only fleeting, almost muttered references to indulgences, one of the most explicit apropos her visit to Assisi, when there was 'great pardon of plenary remission', with which she purchased grace, mercy and forgiveness for herself, her friends, enemies and all souls in Purgatory.[9]

Indulgences were not central to the themes of *The Book*; long before it was written, the 'Margery of The Book' had received Christ's assurances of her instant admission to Heaven. In accordance with the meditative theme of *The Book*, the probable importance of gaining indulgences in her original motivation seems to have been marginalised. The explicit reasons given for her journey to the Holy Land were that she had gained a desire to see the places associated with Christ's ministry, and that He had 'bidden her in her soul' to go to Jerusalem, as well as Rome and Compostela.[10] Christ assured her in Jerusalem that she had not needed to come (or to go to the two other cities) for absolution, which she had received from her confessor, but for the increase of her 'meed and merit'.[11] This frame of mind contrasted with the one attributed to her son after he had repented his sins: 'He went on many pilgrimages to Rome and to many other holy places to purchase pardon for himself.'[12] It is dangerous to generalise about the motives which lay behind individuals' decisions to go, even when straightforward ones of gain, spiritual or financial, are clear, for many pilgrimages were undertaken for a fee as a substitute, as the terms of some wills show. For instance, in his will of

1388 Sir John Multon left 50s for the expenses of John Belle, a friar, in going to Rome for him, and five marks (£3 6s 8d) for the expenses of a man going to Jerusalem for Multon's soul. In 1408 Sir John de Copildik made provision for a man to go to Jerusalem for his soul and forgiveness of his sins if he was unable to go himself.[13] Such surrogates may, indeed, have been ardent pilgrims casting about for finance, rather than hardened professionals; Margery probably acted as such. Moreover, one must not discount the potential for spiritual awakening of the experience of pilgrimage, however much it was embarked upon in secular moods of drudgery or adventure.

Reactions, even among the routinely devout, the unreflective and the ignorantly superstitious, were surely conditioned by the complexities of their cultural and social milieux. Margery's England had an imagined Middle Eastern landscape repetitively powdered over it, more familiar to English folk in gilt and shimmering appearance than the totality of their own damp and mysterious land, and peopled gloriously by Prophets, the Holy Family and the Disciples, and by a multitude of spiritual beings. For in the decorative schemes of churches, in glazing, panel-painting and sculpture, and in tableaux and plays on the great feast days, the Holy Landscape was endlessly recreated, a background to the eternal dramas. Walsingham, a few miles from Lynn, through which many pilgrims passed to and from it, was one of England's principal shrines. Margery doubtless knew the venerable, miraculously realised replica of the Holy House of Nazareth, where the Annunciation had taken place, which stood adjacent to Walsingham priory church. Near the altar of the replica was the venerated wooden statue of Our Lady of Walsingham, and in the priory church was a reliquary containing her milk. A number of representations in the West of sites in the Holy Land may have been based on models brought back by pilgrims.[14]

In respect of motivation and context, the narratives of Felix Fabri, Dominican friar of Ulm, are relevant. He wrote painstakingly detailed but vivid accounts of his two pilgrimages to the Holy Land in the 1480s. He was careful to explain his reasons for leaving his brethren and setting off to act as a chaplain to a group of nobles. Some of his reasoning is relevant to his clerical status and may apply more generally to the particularly large number of clergy who went. Fabri cited St Jerome on how going to the Holy Land helped one to understand the Scriptures. He wanted to be able to hold his own in discussion against 'unlearned men (who) return theologians from the holy places'.[15] Despite terrible privations on the voyages between Venice and Jaffa, he went back a second time because he felt that his first visit had been too hurried; he had not seen all that he wanted, and he could not remember well what he had seen.[16] He wanted to fix clear images in his mind; his dense descriptiveness was one means of helping him to do so. In Margery's *Book*, her interior visualisation in situ of scenes from the life of Christ and His Passion are realised with the intensity of film. In their very different ways, Margery's passionate imaginings and Fabri's restrained photographic recordings both flow from the later medieval focus on the humanity and sufferings of Christ. These themes were given affective force in the writings cherished by contemplatives and, for the generality of humanity, in the startling literalism of contemporary paintings and sculpture. It may be that the pervasive presence of such images of the holy landscapes was a powerful inducement for the devout to set off with the intention of immersing themselves in the environment of Christ's sufferings.

As an account of medieval pilgrimage abroad, and of travel on the continent and in the Near East, *The Book* is at once disappointing and tantalising. Fittingly for its purpose, its accounts of places, conditions and incidents are generally patchy, though sometimes surprisingly informative. Information given about the routes Margery took is sketchy and the stages of her pilgrimages are difficult to date. She set out on the Jerusalem journey probably in 1413, sailing in a group of pilgrims from Great Yarmouth to Zierikzee in Zeeland. Thence they travelled to Constance (soon to be the venue of the General Council of the Church). After overcoming the Alps (presumably via the St Bernard or the Splügen Pass), Margery and the group she had formerly been with did not cross Lombardy directly to go to Venice, the customary embarkation port for the Holy Land. Instead, they went separately to Bologna (presumably through Milan and along the Via Emilia) and travelled from Bologna to Venice.

The route which the pilgrims took from England to Venice is in some parts puzzling. The choice of a port in the Low Countries was probably determined by the availability of shipping in East Anglian ports, consequent on close economic ties, and by the desirability of avoiding routes through France. There, tensions between the factions competing for control of government, headed respectively by John the Fearless, Duke of Burgundy, and the Duke of Orleans, threatened to precipitate another outbreak of civil war.[17] But why Zierikzee? In a paper addressing this question, Harry Schnitker has noted its close East Anglian trading connections. Zierikzee imported wool and coal from England; the bulk of its exports consisted of the herring caught by its large fishing fleet. Schnitker notes that its advantage as a port for English travellers was its position 'as a nodal point for the inland waterways of the Low Countries . . . from there she and the company . . . could have found a ship sailing up the river Rhine to Constance'. It is not clear that the company travelled through the Holy Roman Empire by boat, but riverine travel was familiar to Margery and people from her 'country'. Alternatively, the pilgrims may have taken the land route through Cologne, Mainz, Strasbourg and Basel. Zierikzee was not itself without attractions for a pilgrim company: the impressive church of St Lieven, with its forty-nine altars, was a spiritual powerhouse where the apprehensive traveller could petition for divine support. It was in this church that Margery probably received communion on Sundays, with copious tears.[18] There could have been both positive and negative reasons for the diversion to Bologna. The company may have been persuaded to go there by the English friar, a papal legate, whom they met in Constance. There may have been anxiety about the warfare between the Venetian Republic and Sigismund, King of the Romans, though a truce was made between them that year.[19] Moreover, Pope John XXIII and the papal court were in Bologna; the pope had fled to this papal lordship as a consequence of King Ladislas of Naples' seizure of Rome.[20] The pilgrims perhaps sought a papal blessing for their hazardous enterprise – Margery for her way of life as well. The silence of *The Book* about this putative episode is understandable in the light of John XXIII's subsequent deposition by the Council of Constance and his categorisation as an antipope. If Margery had enough time to do the pious rounds of Bologna, she would have found plenty of things to stir her devotion, both in relics and in sculptures and paintings, including in profusion those of the local schools, such as Simone de Bologna's traditional and moving depictions of Christ on the Cross. In view of Margery's relations with the Dominicans of Lynn, the tomb of St Dominic and his head reliquary in the friary church would have been of prime concern to her: the beautiful sculptures by Nicola Pisano on the Arca di San Domenico vividly recalled the saint's life and miracles. Another draw, in anticipation of Jerusalem, would have been the complex of churches and associated structures centred on the church of San Stefano, which were said to replicate features of the Holy Places in and around Jerusalem. The adjacent tomb of San Petronio, bishop of Bologna c. 432–50, and its patron saint, was allegedly modelled by his own measurements on the edicule in the Church of the Holy Sepulchre. The courtyard outside, known as the *cortile di pilato*, recalled the place where Christ was judged, and in its centre is a huge ancient bowl, known as the *catino di Pilato*, thought in Margery's time to be the very one in which Pilate washed his hands.[21] Moreover, Margery could hardly have ignored the massive new church of San Petronio, whose west front faced the Piazza Maggiore – one of the most ambitious modern churches in Christendom, in the process of being decorated expensively and impressively as an expression of the commune's piety and pride.

On Margery's return from the Holy Land to Venice, she first went to Assisi, then Rome, where she stayed probably from October 1414 until after the following Easter, which was on 31 March. *The Book* has little to say about the return journey from Rome until the company reached Middelburg, a flourishing port in Zeeland (not far from Zierikzee), where they embarked for England. The reason they did not go to Zierikzee may have been that much of the town had been burnt down in a fire the previous year.[22] There was a more pressing reason than in 1413 for a company of English travellers to take a route through the Empire, skirting France: from early on in 1415 preparations were being made in England for Henry V's invasion of France, which resulted in the capture of Harfleur and the battle of Agincourt.

It is probable that Margery had been out of England for eighteen months or even longer, which was an unusual length of time for the pilgrimages she had undertaken. William Wey, canon of Eton, going solely to the Holy Land in 1458, took thirty-nine weeks on the round trip and, on his second visit in 1462, just over thirty-seven weeks.[23] Margery's journey to Santiago was a much shorter pilgrimage. Most of her time on this pilgrimage in 1417 was taken up by an enforced stay at Bristol, awaiting shipping. The focus of the account was on events in Bristol and its neighbourhood; it is succinct about Santiago, saying that she spent fourteen days in that country, where she was comfortable and spiritually uplifted, and that the voyage back took five days.[24] There is no mention of specific divine reassurance for a safe return journey being received at the shrine, though before she set out she and her fellow pilgrims had been concerned about the perils of the crossing. In 1406 four Lynn ships in an English mercantile convoy heading for Bordeaux had all foundered in unfamiliar waters off Spain.[25] At the cathedral of Compostela, since it was a jubilee year, Margery was probably able to view the relics kept in the sacristy, as well as the great wooden shrine on the high altar, the saint's staff fixed to the altar, and the chain with which he was bound. Some well-travelled foreign visitors later in the century were not overly impressed.[26] For Margery, her pilgrimage to St James was rewarding but necessarily on a lower plane than her dizzying experiences in Rome and Jerusalem. It provided valuable indulgences and was well suited to enhance her 'street cred' with readers of *The Book* and with Lynn folk in 1417, especially since she succeeded in getting a berth in a year when there were apparently no sailings there by English ships.[27]

Margery underbook her third visit abroad, in 1433 (which did not start out as a pilgrimage), when she was aged about sixty. It turned out to be the least structured and the most hazardous: the narrative concentrates on escapes from dangers, not devotional experiences. She accompanied her widowed daughter-in-law, returning to her native Prussia, on the journey from Lynn to her embarkation port, Ipswich. Margery 'was ever commended in her heart to go over the sea with her daughter' and embarked, to the latter's understandable consternation.[28] Margery lacked warm clothing for the voyage. The weather was terrible. The ship was blown haplessly across the North Sea, making landfall on the Norwegian coast, but was soon able to set sail again, reaching its destination, Danzig, safely. There it was suggested to Margery that she might like to go on pilgrimage to the Holy Blood in the parish church at Wilsnack. Since the land route was unsafe, she had to take a boat westwards from Danzig to Stralsund in Pomerania, and travel inland south-west from there.[29] Quite apart from the perils of the sea voyage, she put herself in grave danger by going to Danzig in 1433. She appears to have been there in April and May: towards the end of April a formidable army of Hussite Bohemians, allied to Vladyslav II of Poland and Duke Bohuslav of Pomerania, invaded Neumark, part of the territory of the Teutonic Knights. After successes in Neumark, the Hussites turned eastwards and invaded Pomerelia, where they were held up besieging the Knights' great fortress of Konitz (Chojnice). Danzig was now a feasible objective: the Hussites did, indeed, briefly besiege the city late that summer, after Margery had left it. A Bristol man related how about 17 June monks from a monastery near Danzig (probably Oliva) took refuge there.[30] The suggestion to Margery that she should go by a circuitous route to Wilsnack was probably made to try to get her out of harm's way. She adamantly refused to take the voyage back by sea and probably hankered to leave Danzig and travel by land, as her son and daughter-in-law had done a few years before, when stormy weather on their voyage to England had driven them back to port. Margery 'could not easily travel back by land, as there was war in the country that she should pass by'.[31] The pilgrimage provided a compromise solution to the problem, taking her away from the likely main route of the Hussite army. Her resumption of pilgrim status gave her a modicum of protection from the Bohemians' Catholic allies.

So Margery did make most of the return journey – unscathed – overland, traversing much of the Holy Roman Empire. *The Book* is extremely hazy about her route, but highlights Aachen as an important stage because of its sacred connotations. A later visitor remarked on 'the great absolution' flowing from the relics in the cathedral, which included notable personal items associated with Christ and the Virgin Mary.[32] Margery was particularly eager to benefit from the Marienschrein, the reliquary containing the Blessed Virgin's cloak, and stayed for over a week until 'Our Lady's smock' and other relics were exhibited on 20 July.[33] Various other towns along the way are mentioned but not named. Illness and distressing circumstances may have reinforced lapses of memory; this part of the narrative was strongly focused on Margery's sufferings. Her destination was Calais, which she approached wearily for two days, presumably along the Flemish coast, through 'deep sands, hills and valleys'.[34] Notions about her probable route on this section of her travels can be gained from the itinerary of Isabel of Portugal, Duchess of Burgundy, travelling from Bruges to the Boulonnais in 1451 (passing through Ostend, Nieuwpoort, Dunkirk and Gravelines), and Wey's itinerary from Calais to Aachen in 1458.[35]

In her choice of pilgrimage destinations abroad in the 1410s, Margery was thoroughly conventional.[36] For Westerners, Jerusalem and Rome were the principal Christian holy cities. Her original group was ambitious in tackling both. The notable popularity of Santiago in England was enhanced because, though the journey might hold terrors, he was the Apostle whose major shrine was most accessible from England.[37] Margery may have been familiar with the church of St Saviour's, York, a parish in and near which anchorites were concentrated in the later fourteenth century.[38] In one of its windows (c. 1380) there was strikingly depicted an archetypal figure of the male pilgrim to Santiago, garbed and accoutred in a way which marked out his status. He wears a white hat adorned with a scallop; the scallop commemorated the saint's rescue of a drowning man who had emerged from the sea covered with shells. That miracle may have been especially appealing to folk like Margery from a seafaring environment. The figure has a pilgrim staff in his right hand, a book in the left, and a bag at his waist with its strap over his shoulder.[39] The finest remaining memorial to the English medieval cult of St James is to be found at Compostela. It is a retable of Nottingham alabaster, presented at the shrine, c. 1462, by John Goodyear, an Englishman. This vigorous and splendid altarpiece has five panels depicting the saint's life, passion and translation, the central one showing him preaching.[40] In Lynn, Margery's awareness from an early age of the cult doubtless stemmed from its vigorous maintenance there.[41]

By contrast, the cult of the Holy Blood of Wilsnack seems to have been little known in England; hence, perhaps, *The Book*'s implication that the cult there had a strong international following in 1438.[42] In 1417 Sir Richard Arundel had willed that his executors should make haste after his death to find a man to go, for the good of his soul, to the papal court in Rome, to the Holy Sepulchre, and to 'holy blood' in Germany.[43] Dr Tanner has identified a reference to the cult in the will of Edmund Brown of Norwich (1446): he instructed his executors to hire a man to go on pilgrimage there on his behalf, as well as one to go to St Thomas of Canterbury, and one to Santiago during the next year of grace.[44] The cult was well known in the Low Countries: in a cross-section of evidence about penitential destinations taken from urban records, it appears 44 times among 'near' destinations, surpassed only by 'far away' Santiago (75), Rome (59) and Rocamadour (52).[45] Wilsnack was characteristic of many new cults in the period in its sacramental focus; it mushroomed unofficially as a result of a Host miracle. Dr Sumption has outlined the origins and development of the cult. When the parish church burned down in 1383, according to the parish priest three consecrated Hosts were found intact, marked with drops of blood. Pilgrims flocked there, to the alarm of the ecclesiastical authorities, who were concerned about the hysterical atmosphere surrounding the cult and the possibility that fraudulent miracles were being performed. Despite official condemnations, it continued to flourish.[46] Perhaps it was one of the shrines to which Margery's son went. One can see why she might have been attracted by the sort of reports she is likely to have heard about the cult and why she decided to perform the pilgrimage, though it necessitated taking to the sea again and then passing through a region disturbed by warfare. Margery's pilgrimage to Wilsnack illustrates the importance of travellers in nourishing and spreading cults. Those who went abroad – especially sailors and their passengers – were great haunters and seekers-out of shrines, before they set out, en route, and when they had reached their destination. Presumably Margery, fresh from divine deliverance from the perils of the North Sea, heard about the Holy Blood from English merchants or sailors who made the hazardous Danzig run, and their German colleagues and friends, some of whom may have performed the pilgrimage or sent offerings there in connection with travel.

In *The Book*'s recitation of Margery's tribulations, travels abroad do not in fact present human threats of such terror as encountered on her travels in England. *The Book* bears witness to her survival unharmed and without being robbed when far from home, whereas in her own country she reportedly endured abusiveness, imprisonment and death threats. *The Book* provides some good evidence about English attitudes to travel to the continent and experiences of staying there. Its unique value in these areas (as in others) is that it projects the perspectives and reactions of a woman. Margery, from a seafaring environment, was deeply conscious of the hazards of the sea, as we have seen, though she is unlikely to have felt the bewilderment and apprehension in the shipboard environment expressed in a vernacular poem by an English pilgrim who embarked for Spain.[47] The first voyages mentioned in *The Book* – from Great Yarmouth to Zierikzee, and out from Venice to Jaffa and back – were apparently blessedly uneventful. On the return journey to England, passage could be found only on a small boat: the passengers grew fearful as they sailed into dark and stormy weather, but it became calm.[48] At Bristol the pilgrims going to Santiago are said to have threatened to throw Margery into the sea if a storm blew up; fortunately, the weather on the crossing was fair.[49] Perhaps her mostly reassuring experiences of sea voyages in the years 1413–17 lulled her in old age into impulsively braving the long and hazardous voyage to Danzig. This, as we have seen, turned out to be a dreadful ordeal; the storms in the North Sea had so upset Margery that during a calm trip in a small ship along the Baltic coast she angered the others on board by keeping her head lowered so that she could not see the waves. To get home, that only left the short but often bumpy voyage from Calais to Dover. On this her fellow pilgrims were seasick; Margery, seasoned sailor by now, was not, to her relief.[50]

The Book makes little reference to the privations and discomforts of travel as regards the early pilgrimages abroad but reflects a preoccupation with them on Margery's later travels. The contrast stems from her physical robustness when young and enfeeblement in old age. Discomfort and hazard were accepted as inevitable on such large undertakings and were appropriate to the penitential nature of pilgrimage. However, the cleric Adam Usk, on his way to Rome in 1402 (not as a pilgrim), recorded his terror of the Alps. Crossing the St Gotthard Pass, he tells how he arrived at the hermitage at the summit, 'where I was carried in an oxcart, almost frozen to death from the snow, and blindfolded to stop me seeing the perils of the journey'.[51] By contrast, *The Book* projects a stoical Margery by failing to allude to the terrors of the Alps, which one might have expected to have strongly affected someone hailing (unlike the Welshman Usk) from one of the most low-lying and flat parts of Britain. Rather, Margery recollected the fear of assault of her companion William Wever as he guided her from Constance to Italy: 'I am afraid you will be taken from me and I will be beaten because of you and lose my coat.'[52] Pilgrim apparel did not guarantee benevolent treatment; besides their own money for expenses, pilgrims sometimes carried valuable trinkets belonging to others which they had undertaken to get blessed. The eccentric white raiment in which Margery was sometimes garbed is unlikely to have enhanced her security. *The Book* bears ample witness that pilgrims, among other travellers from England, were in constant fear of assault and robbery. On the way from Zierikzee to Constance, Margery's companions were warned of troubles ahead, though these did not materialise.[53] A priest in another pilgrim band, leaving Rome for England, said to her a little way outside the city, 'Mother, I dread being dead, slain by enemies'.[54] This conversation and that with Wever are intended to illustrate how Margery received Christ's reassurances and how a priest and a layman had come to rely and depend on her holiness to fortify their resolve. *The Book* mentions only one robbery of a group – a company of English pilgrims whom Margery met in 1433 somewhere between Aachen and Calais, on their way back from Rome. They were travelling fast to eke out their slender remaining resources.[55] Perhaps most remarkable had been the survival of Margery and her German male companion unscathed on the potentially troublesome journey from Stralsund to Wilsnack. On that, she seems to have had a pious certainty of her safety, borne of her previous escapades as a pilgrim. The relative jumpiness of her companion was apparent when, as she vividly recalled, 'there came a man out of a wood, a tall man with good weapons, and well arrayed, as it seemed to them'. The warrior sensibly went about his own business.[56]

Pilgrims and other travellers preferred to travel in groups; Margery's narrative suggests that these groups could be partly fluid in composition, with leavers and joiners at different stages having a variety of purposes and destinations. Groups of English folk might be particularly well equipped to defend themselves because of the native skill in archery. The company with which Margery set out from England for Jerusalem had bows and arrows.[57] On his journey to Rome in 1402, Adam Usk had had a guard of archers.[58] At Assisi, after her return from the Holy Land, and no longer with her group, Margery was relieved to be able to attach herself for the journey to Rome to a company of pilgrims headed by a Roman lady, Dame Florentyne, which included some knights of the crusading Order of St John.[59] She and her companion were admitted in 1433 to a company of merchants in Germany, on the way to Aachen; later on the journey, when she was alone, in extremis, she was glad to be with some lice-infested beggars.[60] She was to attempt desperately, and in vain, to join a London widow's company at Aachen, and at a later stage.[61] Travelling with solitary males abroad, even if they were honest, and especially if they were decrepit, like Wever and Richard the Irishman, was foolhardy as their reactions to Margery's proposals show. It provided insufficient protection against robbery and rape. Nearing Calais in 1433, accompanied only by an English friar, Margery had to spend a night in an outhouse, lying on bracken. At this painful stage in her journey, fear of ravishment gave her sleepless nights, alleviated by the availability of maidens prepared to sleep beside her.[62] However, according to *The Book*, Margery was for the most part treated respectfully by foreigners and received cordially, both when she had money to spend and when, becoming indigent, she was an object of charity.

Such benevolent attitudes seem to have been more prevalent along leading pilgrimage routes. The good repute and, indeed, profits of those who catered for pilgrims at their customary halts were at stake.[63] In Rome, Venice and the Holy Land many inhabitants had, in some respects, a cosmopolitan outlook: they were used to foreigners in their midst and to their sometimes outlandish behaviour. On Margery's journey from Constance and through northern Italy, people were friendly and hospitable: they 'met with many jolly men. And they said no evil word to this creature [Margery] but gave her and her man meat and drink.' In many places good wives gave up their beds for her 'for God's love'.[64] As we shall see, nuns in Venice and denizens of the Holy Land treated her kindly, and she was helped by charitable people, notably women, on her travels in Italy, after her return from Venice, and when she was indigent in Rome. On the way to Wilsnack, when she was sick and disabled, she was placed in a wagon. Local women were compassionate, upbraiding her companion John for his insensitive behaviour towards her.[65] She was not always so well received in Germany and adjacent parts of the Empire, partly, perhaps, because she was clad poorly, not according to her status, presumably in order to avoid being robbed. The fact that she had come from Wilsnack may not necessarily have won her respect among the well-to-do because of the cult's ambivalent reputation in some quarters. However, she was made welcome in Calais, where people were used to coping with a variety of travellers.[66]

Margery's recollections throw considerable light on the mechanics of pilgrimages. The question of finance was fundamental. It apparently took two years for her to raise the money for the Jerusalem journey; she relied heavily on donations from friends in different parts of the realm. Going around English shrines was one way of raising money to go on major pilgrimages abroad.[67] A deterrent to going was the necessity of first settling one's debts; a priest asked in the pulpit at Lynn for any creditors of her husband as well as herself to make contact.[68] One source of finance, as we have seen, was the money given to the aspirant pilgrim to pray and make offerings at shrines for passive donors – sponsorship which was a form of spiritual investment. In this way the pilgrim culture was kept afloat by the populace in general; anxiety to hear news of the pilgrim's fate – and whether he or she conducted themselves properly – reflected a desire to check up on one's investments and helps account for the interest in England in Margery's doings when she was abroad in 1413–15. Later, folk in Lynn gave money to her to pray for them at Santiago. She received further donations on the way to Bristol; Thomas Marchale paid for her sea passage, and Bishop Peverel gave her gold.[69] Archbishop Bowet was to express surprise at the amount of money she had to support her travels round the country; she explained that good men gave it to her to pray for them.[70] Her journeys to Jerusalem and Rome may have given her prestige as a pilgrim in the eyes of many.

When Margery had set out for Jerusalem, she had been well provided for – about £36 was being held for her by one of the company when they reached Constance, about £20 of which was returned when she was expelled from the company.[71] Margery the merchant's daughter then had to arrange her own money exchange (which an English friar undertook for her), hire a male companion and, when she reached Venice, book a berth.[72] Margery's funds certainly compared favourably with the amount Sir John Multon bequeathed to Brother John Belle in 1388. However, friars were expected to live frugally and receive charity along the way; Multon probably envisaged that Belle would undertake other suffrages. By contrast, Margery's funds approached the amount (£40) which was considered a sufficient annual income for a knight.

Why Margery did not rely on a bill of exchange? In the 1420s Lynn friars were making use of them, including some in the Dominican house, where she was well known. For instance, in 1423 Umberto di Bardi, of the Albertini Company in London, acknowledged a debt of 100s. to John de Byntre, Dominican of Lynn.[73] A pilgrim company might arrange a collective bill of exchange. In March 1392, Daffydd ap Jeuan and other Welshmen, going to the Holy Sepulchre, received a bill of exchange in London from Gualtieri Portinari (whose surname suggests that he was a Florentine merchant): this was recorded in the protocols of a Venetian notary, Giacomello Girardo (26 April 1393).[74] So the Welsh company's finance for the most expensive payment on their pilgrimage (the contract with the galley captain) was awaiting them safely in Venice. If Margery's company was carrying similar amounts in specie, it helps to explain the nervousness they displayed after disembarking in Zeeland. Maybe they were not a close-knit group and lacked the mutual confidence to make a collective bill; on the other hand, Margery may have joined them too late to enter into a contract.

In Rome Margery took the bold step of transforming herself from a well-to-do pilgrim into a poor one, giving away the money she had left, including the recent loan from the Irish beggar, Richard, and begging her way from door to door. This shocked the English priest who befriended her then: she was allowed to eat with his party and he gave her enough money to return to England.[75] There her purse was empty, but some pilgrims gave her three halfpence because she had told them 'good tales'.[76] Her experience in Rome may have emboldened her to set out underfunded for the journey to Santiago, confident of securing donations along the way. In 1433 Margery seems to have had adequate funds for most of the journey back from Danzig – perhaps she received a loan from a Lynn merchant there or from her German kinsfolk by marriage. She agreed to pay her fellow pilgrim, John's expenses to accompany her from Wilsnack to the English coast; she entrusted him with her money and goods.[77] After he had repaid and abandoned her and she had passed through Aachen, she met the English friar with whom she made a bargain to pay his expenses if he accompanied her to Calais. There she paid him as agreed.[78] The penury to which she was then reduced was probably relieved by a loan she hoped to receive when she reached London, possibly from a merchant she knew with Lynn connections. In London she was certainly once more moving with ease in polite circles.[79]

It would be rash to generalise about the size, composition or behaviour of pilgrim groups. *The Book* offers interesting evidence about behaviour. It was important for any group, however small, to act in concert and adhere to agreed norms. One must not take the group with which Margery set out for the Holy Land as stereotypical. Their distaste for her good tales was not shared by all the pilgrims mentioned. Since they embarked at Great Yarmouth, the presumption is that they were Norfolk folk and knew beforehand about Margery's dubious reputation as a wife.[80] They are likely to have been of similar status to Margery; they seem to have willingly borne the financial loss which was surely a consequence of changing shipping arrangements at Venice.[81] It is likely that Margery and her maidservant were the only women in the group, since the maid cooked and washed for all of them (except her mistress) in Venice. According to *The Book*, they had the reputation of being 'right good men'.[82] It is not clear whether the group had a leader entrusted with secular responsibilities, such as keeping a common purse, working out a route and organising billets and messes. *The Book* emphasises the collective nature of decisions about the terms on which Margery was either allowed to remain in the company or expelled from it, and about arrangements made in Venice for their voyage. However, this emphasis can be seen as part of the text's running themes about her isolation from and victimisation by the secular-minded crowd, like that which had bayed for the Crucifixion. Reflecting *The Book*'s theme about clerical shortcomings, there was a hostile priest in the company who acted as her confessor and who clearly had considerable influence over the others. He was displeased with her because she did not stick to his instruction to eat meat.[83] This seems to have been the same priest who denounced her at the English Hospice in Rome and who remained angry with her in Rome over her refusal to obey his command that she give up wearing white clothes.[84] *The Book* implies that the English priest whom she first met there, belonging to another group, had considerable influence over his fellow pilgrims, since he got her accepted as one of them. The dynamics of this group seem to have been different from those of her original company; *The Book* does not mention any problems arising with them.

Possibly this was a group of well-educated priests from Norfolk; they may have been able to converse in Latin and, after returning to England, apparently went with Margery to see Richard Caister in Norwich.[85] On occasion, those who had forged close bonds during pilgrimage were reluctant to part. Margery had her reunion in Bristol with Richard the Irishman, whom she had first met, wearing his patched clothes, in Venice.[86] After the return from Santiago, she and other pilgrims travelled companionably through the Midlands.[87]

By contrast, Margery's original Jerusalem company, and their relations with her, are put in a dismal light. From early on, we are told, her rejection of her confessor's commands – notably about her inappropriate clothing – antagonised her companions. So did her devout weeping and her pious conversation, especially at meal times.[88] The group seem to have felt that it was important for their coherence and harmony to adhere to conventions of everyday discourse. Margery's behaviour was a threat. They may have been worried that it would adversely affect the ways in which they were perceived and treated by foreigners. The solution which they are said to have essayed – before expelling her – was to marginalise her, inflicting dishonour on her by denying the privileges, in attire and at table, appropriate to her status. Allegedly, on the way to Constance they adapted her clothing so that it included inferior material that a burgess's wife would not wear in public and produced overall a bizarre effect. They cut her gown short so that it did not come much below her knee and made her wear 'a white canvass garment, so that she would be considered a fool and be held in small repute'. At meals they placed her at the bottom end of the table.[89] These attempts to degrade her status may have been intended, however humiliating for her, for her protection as well as theirs, according to their lights. They may have considered that in strange and potentially menacing environments it would redound to their credit if they signalled their recognition that one of their company did not conform to the discreet norm which they were presumably attempting to project. Images of the 'holy fool' were internationally recognised and acceptable. To brand Margery as such was a gentler judgement than at various times others made on her, that she was a heretic, a hypocrite, a witch, possessed by the Devil. The company's ambivalent attitude towards her, their wondering whether she was exceptionally holy (despite her confessor's hostility), was demonstrated in Venice. After she had changed her choice of ship, 'because our Lord warned her in her mind', they allegedly did not dare do otherwise but follow her example.[90] Nevertheless, they found her company as intolerable as ever. Some of the other pilgrims and travellers she subsequently met on her wanderings were also apprehensive about being in her company or deserted her because of her devout conversation and weeping.

On Margery's great pilgrimage, *The Book* represents the reception she received from foreigners as for the most part in marked contrast to the ways in which the compatriots with whom she had set off treated her. This was notably the case in Italy and the Holy Land. Indeed, in Rome there were divisions of opinion about her reminiscent of those which she provoked in English towns and cities (probably in part generated among the English in Rome). However, according to *The Book*, it was in Rome that she demonstrated an ability to live and be accepted as a 'holy woman' more successfully than in her home town or in any other English town. What were the reasons for these contrasts? Perhaps self-delusion bolstered *The Book*'s assertions that her holy persona had flourished in this way, accepted as genuine and praiseworthy in the holiest city in western Christendom, and before that, necessarily more briefly and fitfully, in the Holy Land. However, there was an important distinction which facilitated her acceptance by foreigners; most of them could understand only a few words she said. The religious *lingua franca* of international pilgrims consisted of a limited vocabulary of pious buzzwords and gestures.[91] Foreigners could not be shocked and offended, as many English people were, by what they considered preaching by a woman, especially when anticlerical in content. One trademark of Margery's devout public behaviour was, at its most intense, its sheer physicality. In Mediterranean lands, Muslims as well as Christians seem to have accepted more readily her loud weeping and piercing crying. The friars of Mount Sion reacted with kindness and sympathy, whilst her English company were doing their best to distance themselves from her.[92] From the start of the pilgrimage the latter are likely to have been worried that her behaviour was diabolically inspired and that it might contaminate the benefits flowing from their pilgrimage. No doubt the possibility of such possession occurred to foreigners, but perforce they based their conclusions on gesture and conduct, not discourse. They observed Margery's intense interaction with cult images and objects and, in Rome, her charitable activities.[93] They concluded that she was possessed by the divine spirit. In Rome and Jerusalem people were probably more used to esoteric religious behaviour than at English shrines. Hysterical reactions may have been intensified in the presence of the holiest relics, and at sacred places and those where there had been recent numinous manifestations in this period because of the intense contemporary christocentric focus. However, people living in an environment in which spiritual manifestations were frequent and ambiguous – seismic promises of punishment or beneficence – were often wary about the significance of Margery's behaviour patterns when they were not familiar and easy to categorise. Margery was a challenge to complacency and often to peace of mind. If *The Book*'s account is to be believed, she was, indeed, a bad member of one pilgrim company, since her singularity was disruptive of the group dynamic which needed to be created and maintained. Margery became for a time a drop-out (as must have many others, for various reasons). *The Book* triumphantly rationalises and justifies her failure and, in the process, provides insights into the contrasting behaviour of pilgrimage groups which were intended to be plausible and acceptable to Lynn audiences, some of whom, it can be assumed, were just as well travelled as her.

One of the notable features of *The Book* is that it describes, however sketchily, the experiences of an Englishwoman travelling abroad – it is the first such description, and it is particularly valuable because the travels occurred during a period when the concept of an 'English nation' seems to have been gaining a stronger and more widespread affective force, fuelling discontent against aliens in England and spewing out popular discourse which disparaged foreigners in comparison with the English. Do the accounts of pilgrimages and travelling abroad in *The Book* suggest that they enhanced a sense of nationality or that they sustained the sense of being part of Christendom? An English chronicler, recounting a conversation which Archbishop Arundel allegedly had with Henry IV in 1404, attributed to the former (who had travelled extensively in Italy a few years before) the view that there, 'where people are seen to be most inclined to slanders (*criminosissima*), and especially in Lombardy', they showed the greatest reverence to the Sacrament.[94] The inexperienced pilgrim, reliant on such bewilderingly contradictory stereotyping and on travellers' tall tales, is likely to have been apprehensive about how far he or she would be suspect as a stranger or welcome as a fellow Christian and so, probably, highly receptive to the impact of actual experience. Margery's original company bound for Jerusalem, the pilgrims armed, doubtless shared her concerns about being robbed or poorly lodged. To hear the English tongue was a relief: differences in dialect paled amidst alien babble. The company were glad to meet other English travellers; Margery, in difficult straits, relied on a Devonian, whose language she did not understand, and an English-speaking Irishman. Language was either barrier or gateway; Fabri's accounts of his pilgrimages suggest that the coherence of a pilgrim company depended on their being of the same nationality. A priest who was a fellow countryman was an invaluable companion, to hear confessions and to converse in Latin with foreign priests. However, the need of fifteenth-century town-dwellers and travellers in England to understand speech in a multitude of dialects may have made them adept at grasping foreign languages. *The Book* gives the impression that though after her return from the Holy Land Margery could not understand Italian dialects, during her stay in Rome she mastered enough of the vernacular to function in secular society. She is shown understanding Roman wives when they ask her whether 'malendrynes' had robbed her (*malandrino* – highwayman).[95]

However, the impressions of many pilgrims abroad were narrowed by a tendency to cling to people of similar tongue, and curtailed by the short time they often spent at the shrine. Probably like other English pilgrims to Santiago, Margery spent almost as much time on the ship with her compatriots as in Spain, and on land she was probably cocooned in a large packaged group of them since, as the result of the shortage of English shipping, considerable numbers were doubtless waiting for a berth at Bristol. Discomforts abroad and the slights of foreigners are likely to have been vividly recalled. Fabri remembered in detail the hazards of journeys between Venice and Jaffa on his first visit, but little about the Holy Land itself.

Margery's experience of Rome was entirely different because of her long stay there. Having lost her packaged status as a member of a probably well-heeled national group, she became dependent to an exceptional degree on the kindness of strangers, principally Romans and, to some extent, the German community in Rome. A German priest came to her rescue when she was abandoned by her compatriots, and became her confessor. *The Book* mentions few instances of hostility being shown to her on her travels because she was English. In 1433 she had difficulty in getting leave from a Teutonic Knight to travel from Danzig to Stralsund since 'she was an Englishwoman'; a merchant of Lynn procured a licence for her.[96] The problem she encountered related to the long-standing tensions with the Hanseatic League over English merchants' attempts to enlarge their share of North Sea and Baltic trade. The issues had been intensified by the conditions attached to the parliamentary grant of tunnage and poundage for two years in 1431. Hanseatic merchants at the Steelyard, their base in London, were obliged to provide sureties for payment of the additional dues imposed on aliens' goods. There were also problems of piracy.[97] The only recorded specific vilification of Margery on account of her nationality was when, during her travels through Germany, some priests called her 'English tail'.[98] They seem to have been scandalised that she was travelling without female company. The jibe that the English had tails was widely used on the continent; they were supposed to have been marked with the appendage as punishment for the murder of St Thomas of Canterbury.

The worst incident of hostility against Margery (when she was in company with an English friar) occurred in a town two days' journey

from Calais in 1433. The atmosphere was so menacing that the pair took
the extraordinary step of leaving the shelter of a town shortly before
nightfall. This was a frontier region, much ravaged by warfare; 'there
were few towns by the way that they went and full feeble lodgings'.[99]
The count of Flanders – Philip the Good, Duke of Burgundy – was
nominally in the allegiance of Henry VI as King of France, but Anglo-
Burgundian relations were highly strained – in 1435 Duke Philip was to
withdraw from Henry's allegiance and recognise Charles VII as King of
France. The following year the Flemings enthusiastically attacked Calais.
Commercial relations constituted a major flashpoint. In 1427–30 the
royal council had passed the Bullion and Partition Ordinances, which
had probably been devised with the Company of the Staple. This was a
London-dominated merchant cartel monopolising the sale of most English
wool exported by native merchants through the Staple port of Calais.
Among other provisions, the ordinances required them to increase the
sale price and sell only for cash in hand; the method of apportioning
receipts helped to make the ordinances more easily enforceable for it had
the effect, as Professor J.H. Munro has shown, of driving lesser merchants
out of the business and putting control of native wool exports at Calais
into the hands of twenty or thirty rich Staplers. The effects of the ordinances on the duke's cloth-making subjects and drapery merchants in
Flanders, Brabant and Holland have been described as disastrous, with
Flanders being hit hardest. The ordinances were supposed to lapse in
1433, but in July they were renewed for an indefinite period and parliament strengthened the monopoly powers of the Staplers.[100] This background of manufacturing distress and economic tension explains the
hostile reception which the two English travellers had on the way to
Calais – another instance of Margery rashly clumping into a delicate
political situation.

These episodes of foreign hostility do not amount to much; Margery
may have been phlegmatic in her dealings with foreigners and seems to
have had a generally good rapport with them. Lynn's historic trading
ties with the Low Countries and the Hanseatic ports induced familiarity
and stimulated acculturation. Merchants and sailors from across the North
Sea were to be seen on the staithes and streets of Lynn, some 'hosted' in
merchants' houses. There was a sprinkling of alien residents. Professor
Sylvia Thrupp's analysis of the royal survey of aliens residing in England
in 1440 gave a total of 245 men and women in Norfolk; of the ninety
whose origin was stated, or can be inferred from personal names, sixty-
six were 'Duche'.[101] The aliens dwelling in Bishop's Lynn and South
Lynn totalled fifty-seven. Some were craftsmen, others servants. Four
were styled 'Duchemen', including two shoemakers. There was Isabella

Duchewoman living in Hobbehorslane. Theodoricus Slynghelant of Lynn, who made his will in 1448, sounds as though he was Dutch or German by birth, but his will suggests that he was well settled in the town and well connected in Great Yarmouth and Norwich, from where his executors were drawn, as well as from Lynn. He had a wife and son; though he wished to be buried in Yarmouth, his will echoes other Lynn wills in its provision to the altar of St Margaret's for unpaid tithes and its bequests to the priests who served in the church and to the friars of the four Orders in the town.[102] The office-holding elite in Lynn is likely to have disapproved of hostility to alien artificers and servants, an excuse for disruptive behaviour. In 1424 John Draper appeared before Congregation, charged with asserting that at his suit all shoemakers of the German tongue living in the town would be outlawed. He confessed to having said so and promised to give up the suit he had commenced in London.[103]

The Book probably reflects the elite's tolerant frame of mind. It also bears testimony to the continuing cultural exchange between Lynn and North Germany, culminating in Margery's visits to Danzig and Wilsnack. It is, indeed, a monument to that exchange, since the original version was written in a mixture of English and 'Duche', apparently a sort of North Sea *lingua franca* stemming from commercial practice. Margery probably had a smattering of Plat Deutsch. If so, this would explain her eventual ability to communicate with her German confessor in Rome. Her former pilgrim companions accused her of not being truly confessed, since she and her confessor could not understand one another. When the English priest who favoured her invited the confessor to a meal with his group, neither could they – but he and Margery could miraculously now do so. Maybe the confessor spoke Hoch Deutsch and it took time for the pair to identify a common basic vocabulary, eked out with Latin tags and quotations.[104]

So Margery's Lynn provenance is likely to have given her the mental resources to cope with living among foreigners when she became isolated from her fellow countrymen. The cosmopolitan element in her background probably helped to calm her fears of the hazards of travelling abroad and to prompt her into setting about finding a niche, even a living, among strangers. There are, in fact, more criticisms in *The Book* of English folk than of foreigners. Its lack of animosity to the latter makes a marked contrast to the denunciations and insults to be found in some of the vernacular literature of the period. The best-known example is the poem *The Libelle of Englyshe Polycye* (c. 1436), with its violent and scurrilous polemic against Flemings and most other nations trading with Flanders and England. The poem, a call for the seas to be well guarded, and for an aggressive blockade of Flanders, seems to have been a reflection of the anger and discontent of London overseas traders, especially the London Staplers: they were suffering because of the war with Duke Philip of Burgundy and the consequent embargoes on wool exports to the Low Countries.[105] A great deal of the surviving fifteenth-century vernacular historical literature ('the chronicles of London') was compiled either for or by citizens of London and expresses generally hostile views of foreigners, reflecting commercial rivalries. As we have seen,[106] Lynn folk had a long history of fraught relations with the Hanseatic League and there were hostilities in the town towards alien residents. However, *The Book*, expressing views current in a distinctive regional society and written from a particular religious perspective, advances a more favourable view of foreigners – one which must have been recognisable and acceptable to the influential men and women who were among those whom it was probably intended to edify and please.

It is arguable, at the risk of gender stereotyping, that, uniquely, it projects too a female perspective on foreign travel. Because Margery was not educated to fight with weapons or to 'adventure' cloth overseas, but was schooled in a feminised devotional mode which made her socially vulnerable, she was strongly inclined to judge everyone at their face value. In the context of her spirituality, what mattered to her was not their tongue or their provenance but their emotional reaction to her behaviour as a *devot*. In this context, Christendom emerges in *The Book* as a reality made up of spirit and flesh and blood, realised intensely in its great pilgrimage centres. England is an integral part of the one body, but in *The Book* the beneficence of the saintly English dead often seems pallid beside the malevolence of some of the living. Only Christ can prevail over that, and Christ commands Margery to become better acquainted with His wider domain. *The Book* suggests that, among members of one provincial urban elite (an elite with strong overseas links), the concept of Christendom, conspicuously absent from much secular writing in English by or for laymen, still had great vigour and import.[107] International pilgrimage appears in *The Book* as a force sustaining and refreshing Christendom in a period in which the rise of incipient notions of nationality has been much stressed by modern historians. *The Book* casts light on the reasons why people were still strongly drawn to undertake often arduous and hazardous pilgrimages. The emphasis is on their curative powers for the soul, not the body – Margery suffers debilitating physical effects during and after major pilgrimages.[108] There was a general wish to gain indulgences, but this text suggests that there may have been impulses to travel springing from the sacramental, christocentric, Marian and contemplative strands in contemporary religion. They pushed the

Margery projected in *The Book* into seeking out the principal relics and places associated with Christ and His Mother. Visits to the shrines of modern saints appear more as incidentals in the text; these saints do not speak as individuals to her soul but may be subjects of reminiscence and anecdote by those who knew them. *The Book* noted that she received the great indulgence associated with St Francis of Assisi, but it is the relic of the Virgin Mary in his church which is mentioned; both the saint and St Clare remained silent, and, as we have seen, unnamed.[109] *The Book* relates the pilgrimages it highlights to its subject's mystical devotion.

Margery's *Book* provides important evidence as to how pilgrimages were organised and as to the sorts of problems which pilgrims faced. It reveals group dynamics at work and how they were coloured by social composition and cultural conditioning; there does not seem to have been one stereotypical English group model. It shows how an English-woman, rich or poor (for Margery was protean in this respect), might travel around Europe without having harm done to her and might have notable successes in fitting in with local society. This was especially the case south of the Alps; to the north, in societies more like her own, Margery encountered tensions arising from economic rivalries and political hostilities. In *The Book*, Mediterranean society and culture are viewed sympathetically: the cracks are internal ones in northern society. However, there too international pilgrimage sustained habits of accultura-tion. Long before East Anglian society was shaken by Reformation im-pulses from across the North Sea, emanating originally from Wittenberg, there were clerics and layfolk in Lynn excited by Christ's revelation in a village not far from Wittenberg.

chapter 8

GREAT CITIES AND SACRED SOIL

*T*he *Book*'s image is of a woman making the supreme Christian journeys to the holiest of sites – Jerusalem, the Holy Land and Rome, and, in between visits to them, passing through Venice, unique as a Christian city in its combination of awesome cults and worldly splendour. True to its nature and purpose, in these sublime contexts *The Book* focuses on its subject's feelings, in contrast to some other fifteenth-century narratives, whose fuller observations about places, peoples and customs can be used to counterpoint its more haphazard evidence, underscoring the accuracy of its cursory references and expanding on their significance. Indeed, these feelings are particularly valuable, in that they provide unusual evidence; the reactions of a woman to the great pilgrimages and to Venetian gorgeousness, and their impact on her pious mentality. Moreover, in order to sustain her credibility, the impressions her amanuensis recorded had to accord with the stereotypes embraced by the clerical and secular elites of Lynn. We have in *The Book* striking fragments of evidence for established views in a northern European port about cities and places in the Mediterranean whose profiles were among the highest in Western Christendom.

Venice

In the later Middle Ages the usual starting-point for the voyage of western pilgrims across the eastern Mediterranean to the Holy Land was Venice. In the fifteenth century two or three great galleys customarily sailed each year, usually casting off soon after the celebration of Corpus Christi, when pilgrims joined in the great procession around Piazza San Marco.[1] Henry of Bolingbroke was exceptional (and exceptionally rash) in setting off unseasonably just before Christmas 1392.[2] If, as is possible, Margery sailed after Corpus Christi 1414 (7 June), she arrived in Venice in March, since *The Book* says that she stayed in the city for thirteen weeks.[3] This was an unusual length of time; pilgrims were generally keen to minimise their stay as good lodgings were dear in the city and they were nervously agog to see the Holy Land and return safely. If this calculation is correct, her company must have been ill-informed about the time the journey to Venice was likely to take or about normal sailing schedules. In 1462 William Wey would arrive in Venice on 22 April, just in time for the celebrations for the feast of St Mark, leaving for the Holy Land on 26 May.[4]

The Book has little to say about Margery's experiences, spiritual or otherwise, during her prolonged visit. She broke her agreement not to speak about holy things when at table with her companions and ate alone in her chamber for six weeks. Her maid avoided her and cooked for the company and washed their clothes. Margery felt deathly ill, but was suddenly restored to health.[5] One might have thought that in these distressing circumstances Christ would have spoken reassuringly to her in Venice, but He only told her on which ship it would be advisable for her to book her passage. Margery took communion every Sunday at 'a great house of nuns'.[6] It is tempting to identify this with the Benedictine convent of San Zaccaria. Margery might have had an interest in the saint, since in one of her meditations, when she was acting as the Blessed Virgin's maidservant, she was present at the birth of his son, St John the Baptist, and she was praised by his wife, St Elisabeth for her service to the Virgin.[7] Felix Fabri says in the narrative of his 1483 pilgrimage that he attended a Sunday Mass there: 'I was astonished at the wealth of this church in relics.' These included three early martyrs, three other notable saints (including St Sabina, virgin and martyr) and above all, the entire body of St Zacharias, 'with his mouth open', as Fabri notes with his eye for picturesque detail. Fabri was unimpressed by the nuns – 'rich and noble, and . . . very lax in their rule'.[8] Another pilgrim, Pietro Casola, canon of Milan, who visited the house in 1494, was disquieted by the nuns – 'they do not trouble much about being seen'.[9] Their church was splendidly rebuilt after the time of Margery's pilgrimage, but the early fifteenth-century presbytery remains (now the Capella d'Oro), giving an impression of magnificence, with its bright fourteenth-century altar paintings and wooden statues of San Zaccaria and another saint. However, the identification of this church as the one which Margery attended is unsafe, since Venice had other great houses of nuns.

The fact that Margery attended Sunday Mass in a convent does not help in speculating as to which parish she lodged in. There was no visible English community in Venice; if there had been, Dr Richard Mackenney points out, the Signoria would have obliged them to form a *scuola*. In contrast, the English community in Rome was large and well organised;

The Book dwells on interaction between English residents and pilgrims there. In Rome Margery seems to have made contacts in German circles. This made sense for a merchant's daughter of Lynn, possessing a lifetime's familiarity with Hanseatic merchants. Their premises in Lynn, dating from the late fifteenth century, still stand. Considering the East Anglian starting-point of their voyage, Margery's companions were probably acquainted too with the Hanseatic merchants who traded in the region's ports: she and they may have agreed on one thing – that it was prudent to seek hospitality in Venice among the Germans. There, the Fondaco dei Tedeschi, on the Grand Canal just by the Rialto Bridge, was the German merchants' great southern European outpost. In 1497, the German pilgrim, Arnold von Harff saw in the Fondaco 'daily much traffic in spices, silks and other merchandise packed and dispatched to all the trading towns, since each merchant has his counting-house there'.[10] Richer merchants of the German community lived there or in the vicinity; poorer Germans (e.g. clothworkers) were scattered around the city, clustering for instance in the parish of San Moise and near Santa Maria Gloriosa dei Frari.[11] The inn of St George, where Fabri and his company stayed in 1483, had a German landlord and landlady, and German servants. The big, black guard dog greeted them in a friendly manner, 'showing how pleased he was by wagging his tail'. This dog was similarly tolerant of beggars and dogs of its own nationality, but attacked Italians and other nationalities, human and canine, driving away Italian beggars: 'I have often rescued poor men from this dog's teeth.'[12] The inn was near the Fondaco, in the parish of San Bartolemeo, whose church is a stone's throw from the Rialto Bridge. A servant of nobles, Fabri regarded it as a boon that he was assigned a chamber by himself. Margery too had had her own chamber, and she had no complaints about her lodgings, a matter on which she was fastidious. If she and her company did lodge at a German inn, it is likely to have been in this part of the city, so convenient for making arrangements for the voyage, which necessitated visits to the environs of Piazza San Marco.

Venice was second only to Rome in Western Christendom in the magnificence of its churches and the size and importance of its relic collection, above all accumulated in the basilica of San Marco. 'I have not found in any city so many beautiful and ornate churches as there are in Venice,' Casola wrote.[13] 'The relics at Venice cannot be numbered,' wrote an English pilgrim of 1506.[14] In these respects, Venice was a fitting waiting-room for Jerusalem, as pilgrims appreciated. In 1392 Henry of Bolingbroke went frequently with Doge Antonio Venier to San Marco and he gave offerings to other churches.[15] When Fabri's group realised that they would have to wait there for a month, they readily accepted his proposal that they should behave like pilgrims, gain in virtue and acquire indulgences by visiting relics in a different church every day. The arguments he put forward for this were in part practical; there were no gardens, there was no country life for them to enjoy, and it would not befit their religious status for them to attend dances and tournaments. The day before the group was due to leave, they went on a lightning, wide-ranging tour of churches whose patron saints (Raphael, Michael, Christopher and Martha) were experts in helping to overcome difficulties which pilgrims might encounter.[16] Casola too thought it meritorious for waiting pilgrims to 'seek out the churches and monasteries and go and see the relics', but he was more interested in describing the mouth-watering abundance of foodstuffs on sale than any relic. He was enthusiastic about the splendour of secular as well as sacred buildings and fascinated by distinctive Venetian attire – the old-fashioned black robe favoured by men and the black clothes in which most women swathed themselves in public, with the riveting exception of those who wore extravagant and immodest fashions. Casola was minutely particular when cataloguing these – the platform shoes, hair brushed forward veiling the eyes, the hair pieces. The pretty ones in particular 'try as much as possible in public to show their chests'. The canon noted the jewels adorning collars, the expensive rings, the lavish application of make-up to decolletage as well as features.[17] How would the Margery characterised in *The Book* have reacted to Venetian attire? In other contexts, she lamented that in her younger days she had dressed on occasion to attract men's attention and described how, reformed, she boldly reproved men who wore fashionable clothes. It is likely that she would have regarded the appearance of some Venetians with mixed feelings.

In view of the behaviour of the other pilgrims we have discussed, and Margery's devotional preoccupations, it does seem likely that when she was well enough she visited Venetian churches to see relics and gain indulgences. She surely responded to the city's intense devotion to the cults of the Virgin Mary. Let us hazard some guesses about what might have particularly moved her. She may have been drawn, for instance, to the Frari, to Santa Maria Formosa founded as a result of a vision of the Blessed Virgin and to the church of the Madonna del' Orto, housing a miracle-performing statue of the Virgin and Child. As a disciple of Carmelites and Dominicans, Margery may have wished to worship in Santa Maria del Carmelo, or at one of the three Dominican convents, such as the magnificently reconstructed Santi Giovanni e Paolo. If Margery had heard about Venice's holiest relic, a fragment of the True Cross, her devotion to the Passion would have made her want to contemplate it. The Scuola di San Giovanni Evangelista acquired the relic in 1369, and its procession was to be the subject of startlingly vivid paintings by Giovanni Mansueti and Gentile Bellini. Margery would have missed the Scuola's procession on their saint's feast day (27 December).[18] If in Venice, and well, she was probably present on the feast of the Ascension (17 May) among the crowds watching the procession winding from the church of San Marco through the piazza to embark for the ceremony in which Doge Tomaso Mocenigo performed the annual rite of reaffirming Venice's marriage to the sea, by casting a gold ring into it.[19] Anywhere in Venice that day, one could not have avoided hearing the bells of all the churches ringing, the cannon firing, the shouting and singing. As a devotee of Corpus Christi, if she was still in Venice on the feast day (7 June), she may have been in the main procession or seen one of the others. Commenting on the former, around Piazza San Marco, Fabri was to write: 'Never had we seen such magnificence on that day as at Venice. The procession was marvellous . . . we saw there so much gold and silver, so many precious stones and costly raiments, that no man could reckon their value.' However, he condemned 'vanities' in the crowd at the Dominicans' procession later in the day on the Grand Canal – the 'extravagant dress of women, and the dissolute behaviour of laymen, and disorderly conduct of both regular and secular clergy'.[20]

Surely Margery would have been impressed by the awesome relics in Venice, its great churches, the solemnity, splendour and scale of its processions. The Corpus Christi celebrations at York, which she had probably witnessed, could not have held a candle to this. Why, then, was Christ so taciturn in Venice, apart from His advice about how to get out of it? Was He rendered speechless by the sort of vanities which Fabri deplored, and which embarrassed Casola? At other times Christ intimated to her that He was about to mete out punishment in this world to the wicked. Yet the spectacle of hectic commercial activity on a scale she had never witnessed before is unlikely to have shocked Margery: she had a bourgeois appreciation of English townsfolk's need to earn a living.[21] She approved her Venetian nuns because they gave her good cheer, and marvelled at the great devotion and plentiful tears which Christ sent her.[22] We may not conclude from the lack of Christ's recorded messages that she considered Venice to be a wicked city, only that it may have been too bold and brassy to fit easily into the devotional scheme of *The Book*. The Venice that practically silenced the loquacious Margery was at the height of its wealth and power.

Was the negative depiction of Venice influenced by stereotypes? Evidence about contemporary English views of the city is hard to come by. The bas relief known as the 'Mowbray Stone' may reflect an appreciative princely view, corresponding with the impression which the city's jousts made on Petrarch. Chivalrous values were upheld by the Doge and nobles. Apparently, the sculpture was originally set into a wall of the Doge's Palace. In style and composition, it is similar to the heraldic reliefs which generations of Venetian nobles have placed over the main entrance or on the display facades of their palazzi. It is rectangular, but in its present form (in the entrance hall of Corby castle, Cumbria) is reduced in size and has been recut and brightly repainted. The sculpture is not a heraldic achievement, but comprises an awkward compositional melange. The central figure is of a swan, with a great helm clamped over its head and neck. This represents the Swan Knight, whose legend had crusading overtones and was claimed as a family origin by some leading European noble dynasties, including the Bohun earls of Hereford. The figure is adorned by the livery badge of linked esses used by John of Gaunt, Duke of Lancaster, and his son Bolingbroke. The swan is connected up to symbols of allegiance to realm and king (a standard of England and France Ancient; Richard II's badge of the White Hart). The mount on which the Swan Knight stands, its standard pole, and the chains symbolically binding the knight recall in character and juxtaposition the allegorical devices and legends which adorned the lavish ephemera of princely tournaments, and rehearsed their chivalrous meaning in the later Middle Ages. The stone has been identified as symbolising the noble qualities and achievements of Henry of Bolingbroke (whose mother was Mary de Bohun) and as being connected with his visits to Venice, on his way to the Holy Land in 1392, and on his way back in 1393, when sums were granted officially for his entertainment.[23] It is likely that the sculpture was commissioned by the Doge or Henry to commemorate his visits.

There is nothing in the financial accounts of Bolingbroke's stay in Venice to suggest that he participated in a tournament there, but it may be of a piece with perceptions of Venice as one of Christendom's prestigious lordships that a monument to him was placed in the city's most awesome and extravagantly decorated secular setting, and that he considered it appropriate to be remembered there as a great figure in the chivalrous canon, not as a humble pilgrim. An English or French view of Venice as an ideal city, glittering in its splendour, is projected in the frontispiece to a manuscript, dating from c. 1400, of *Li Livres du Graunt Caam* (based on Marco Polo). This gives a view of Piazza San Marco, looking downwards from a point the other side of the Bacino San Marco, from behind the church of San Giorgo Maggiore (on whose island Bolingbroke and his entourage stayed). The illumination is clearly informed by a witness: some of the monuments and buildings in and around the Piazza are identifiable.[24] What is being celebrated in this illumination is the secular as well as the religious splendour of Venice. However, the wealth of the Venetians, so conspicuously on display in the goods piled high for sale in the square of the Rialto and the streets leading off it (where Margery may have stayed), could be viewed as based on corrupting and dishonest trade. This was a view some of their envious English rivals took, reflected in the polemical poem *The Libelle of Englyshe Polycye*, in which Venetian and Florentine merchants who traded in northern waters were pilloried:

> *The great galleys of Venice and Florence*
> *Be well laden with things of complacence,*
> *All spicery and of grocer's ware,*
> *With sweet wines, all manner of chaffer,*
> *Apes, and japes, and marmosettes tailed,*
> *Nifles, trifles, that little have availed,*
> *And things with which they cleverly blear our eye,*
> *With things not enduring that we buy;*
> *For much of this chaffer that is wastable*
> *Might be forborne for dear and deceivable.*[25]

Margery may have come to Venice with some of these mixed preconceptions, none of which promised great religious experiences. Once there, she is likely to have been distracted by the astonishing secular magnificence, the prominence of worldly vanities and the pressure of the diversely composed crowds. The population was greater and more dense than Margery had experienced; she had never stayed in a city with anything like the 100,000 or so inhabitants – and tightly packed inhabitants. Pilgrims were, indeed, well catered for, and their rights and interests were carefully and efficiently protected by the Signoria (perhaps more so than by any other government). However, although pilgrims were recognised by the Venetians as a significant presence and one to be cherished, they were fleeting, marginal folk, perhaps, if mighty, of diplomatic importance, but a small and in some respects specialised segment of business. Even on board dedicated galleys, they had to pick their way over and round stacks of merchandise and sometimes bed down with ordinary travellers, who might not even be Christians. What contrasts Jerusalem and Rome were to provide! In the Holy City they were made to feel welcome and special by the sometimes heroically embattled resident Latin clergy, who valued them as one of their lifelines to the West, were anxious to shepherd them out of trouble with the Mamluks, and keen to milk the drama of the Holy Places there and elsewhere until no eye was dry. In Rome pilgrims were big business. Romans became wonderfully sympathetic to Margery's devoutness. Awed by Rome's aura, she may have come to feel comfortable and homely there because of the conspicuous poverty (and perhaps the seediness). Such cracks in the social facade might have produced a frisson of superiority in a bourgeoise from tidy-minded Lynn, whose style (and that of other English cities and leading towns) appeared wan by comparison with Venice. The 'real' Margery may well have been more stirred to devotion there than appears in *The Book*. However, devout pilgrims may often have contained their ardour, in anticipation of intensity in the Holy Land. Venice's spiritual riches may have come as a surprising embarrassment to some, though they recognised their utility for the holy insurance they needed for the voyage. In any case, for *The Book*'s maximum impact, Jerusalem and Rome had to be the settings for Margery's spiritual crescendoes. To highlight those visits (however they turned out) was to respond properly to the generally accepted images of these holiest of cities. Nevertheless, *The Book*'s reticence about the pious side of her stay in Venice – including what seemed like her near-death in Venice – suggests that she was responding, in what she decided to leave out of *The Book*, to English stereotypes of the city.

The Book does reflect concerns which must have preoccupied pilgrims whilst they were in Venice – the negotiation of a berth to and from Jaffa, and the organisation of the practical side of the voyage. Margery's company arranged for passage in a ship and procured containers for their wine, and bedding. She had to go to the same trader to procure her own bedding. Unexpectedly, she decided to embark in a galley, not the ship they had chosen. This isolation might have added to her hazards, if they had not joined her and she had failed to find other companions to bond with. The company's decision to travel with her in the galley reflected their deep anxieties about the voyage. It necessitated the sale of their wine vessels, presumably because the patron of the galley regarded these as excess baggage and refused to take them in a galley's hold, more restricted in size, and taken up with accommodation for pilgrims.[26]

Passage from Venice to Jaffa and back was cheaper by sailing ship than by galley since the ships sailed directly. But it was less hazardous and healthier to go by galley because, though galleys sailed under canvas, they had rowers who could get them out of trouble and station them offshore more easily. So their passengers could on occasion stretch their legs on land, have a good night's sleep there, and lay in fresh produce, though Wey warned the English that they would eat the local fruit at grave peril.[27] Fabri's company in 1483 stipulated in their contract that the captain should provide them with a boat and crew to put them into ports which he did not intend to visit, for their own reasonable purposes.[28] The role of the Signoria in regulating pilgrim traffic was crucial. Fabri says that they appointed nobles who owned galleys to carry the pilgrims. Each 'patron' set up a shaft bearing a red-cross banner outside the basilica of San Marco. There, their servants would vie for custom; they obsequiously received on board in person rich prospective clients such as Fabri's nobles.[29] Fabri recounts the tense process of negotiating a contract. It was settled that the patron was to provide his company with two meals a day on shipboard and was to guide them and pay their major fees in the Holy Land. Wey said that the meals should include hot meat, good wine, water and biscuits; the contract should stipulate the route to be followed, the havens into which the galley should put (he specifies six ports) and the stocking of fresh provisions. The patron was to promise to cause no delays and to bring no inconvenient merchandise on board. Wey emphasised the necessity of binding the patron before the Signoria in a large surety to fulfil the contract, and Fabri records how his group's contract was copied into an official register by a notary in the Doge's Palace.[30] The Signoria thus guaranteed that the terms of pilgrim contracts were legally binding.

The charge for the voyage and stay in the Holy Land varied according to the quality of the accommodation and services provided, but it was very high for all. Wey, the rich Fellow of Eton writing for his peers, gave the price for a good berth and fare as forty ducats.[31] Francesco Quirini's account for the voyage of the galley he captained in 1414 shows that he charged from forty to fifty ducats for well-to-do passengers. Others, who received modest amounts of food and drink, paid between twenty-four and thirty-two ducats. At one rate of exchange received by Bolingbroke's expedition in the early 1390s (one ducat is twice given the rate of 3s 2d at Venice), twenty-four ducats would have equalled £3 16s.[32]

The galleys, Fabri wrote, were 'as like one another as a swallow's nest'.[33] The evolution in the fifteenth century of the great Venetian trading galley was traced by F.C. Lane. They had capacious holds, which could load as much as around 250 tons below deck.[34] Casola says that his galley took on 170 pilgrims – men and women, friars, priests and hermits.[35] The well-to-do (like Bolingbroke) had superior quarters in the poop; the majority slept in the big cabin between deck and hold, which ran forward of the poop. There they had their beds in two rows, cheek by jowl, heads to the ship's sides, with a central gangway which might be stacked with goods. Margery and her company were probably in such a cabin. Their quarters were certainly in close proximity. *The Book* describes how, when it was time to make their beds and lock up the bedclothes, a priest took away a sheet from her and said it was his. A heated dispute arose, probably a common occurrence in such unfamiliar, cramped and uncomfortable conditions.[36] They probably locked their bedclothes in the sort of sea chest which Wey advised the pilgrim to take on board to contain medical supplies, food delicacies and supplementary cooking kit.[37] Conditions in the cabin were always fetid because of the 'most loathsome smell' (Fabri) coming from the bilge well. So pilgrims spent as much time as they could on deck; there they ate, heard Mass and socialised at the 'market place' in the areas near the mast, all in the central gangway between the benches occupied by the rowers and crossbowmen.[38]

Quirini's account book throws some light on the circumstances of a pilgrim voyage by galley in the year in which Margery went. He took on board a good deal of merchandise – Casola was to remark on the goods not just in the hold and cabin but stacked on deck and on the rails which projected along the galley's sides. The rowers were avid traders, exempt from the payment of customs.[39] The trading aspect of Quirini's enterprise is reflected in an uninspiring port of call for a pilgrim company – Beirut. Passengers who were not pilgrims, including a Jew, were embarked at Venice and picked up en route. Journeys were being made from Rhodes to Jaffa, from Jaffa to Rhodes. Among the passengers for Venice who came on board at Rhodes were its bishop, with six companions, and Rodolfo Riskemer, said to be an Englishman. He may have been a member of the knightly Reskymer family, of Mawgan-in-Meneage (Cornwall).[40] Passengers were listed individually (some with unnamed servants); many were priests and friars. There was a pilgrim from Milan, and one from Piedmont; there were several Germans (some from Ulm) and Hungarians. A merchant from Ulm who was at the Fondaco dei Tedeschi sent three Germans as pilgrims. There were Frenchmen, and there was Giovanni Martini from Flanders. Apart from Riskemer, the only passengers listed as from the British Isles were David Polo, Englishman, and Robert Moffat, from Scotland. This may have been the Robert Moffat, born 1380 or before, who was nephew of Bishop Matthew de Glendonwyn of Glasgow. He was a beneficed priest who had studied at Avignon and who at least a few years before 1414 may have been studying law on the continent.[41]

The account shows how the pilgrimage trade fitted into the general pattern of Venetian commerce in the eastern Mediterranean. It also suggests possible reasons why Margery did not contract to go on this galley, which arrived back from Jaffa, according to the *Chronicle* of Antonio Morosini, on 15 August, just over a fortnight after the time when she was at Assisi.[42] One likely deterrent to Margery's contracting with Quirini was that he apparently had no women aboard. Besides, the probable presence of a Scotsman of distinguished birth, if she knew about it, would have been a deterrent too. Conflict at sea was a cause of antagonism between Scots and the men of Lynn, but what was more important was that Scots were schismatics in English eyes. The Scotsman, Moffat was probably a chaplain of the anti-pope, Benedict XIII. It is likely that the galley which Margery sailed in carried as cosmopolitan collection of passengers as did Quirini's galley. Among her fellow pilgrims were probably two Germans, one of them a priest, and three other foreigners, a woman and two Franciscans.[43]

I have not been able to identify Margery's galley. Morosini does not note any sailings in 1414; Lorenzo Priuli's galley, according to a senatorial register, set off for Jaffa only on 4 September.[44] Margery is likely to have had only a limited choice of shipping, but she chose her vessel shrewdly and organised her berth efficiently herself. Her seafaring background was doubtless a help to her in sizing things up. She was to be proud of having judged a problematic shipping situation well in Bristol in 1417. Besides, the solicitous Venetians had routines for looking after pilgrims smoothly. Wey described how, near San Marco, one could buy a featherbed, mattress, two pillows, two pairs of sheets and a quilt for three ducats, and sell them back at half price to the vendor, even in a poor condition, on return.[45] Nevertheless, one wonders whether Margery, when bereft of her company's support, found an adviser and interpreter in Venice, her relationship with whom concerned practical not spiritual matters, and who was consequently left out of *The Book*, like many other helpful folk undoubtedly were. It is not clear how she had managed when she was ill in her lodgings, apparently shunned by her companions. Perhaps kindly German hosts both nursed her and advised her on how to arrange her voyage.

Jerusalem and the Holy Land

The Book devotes two separate chapters and part of a third to Margery's experiences in the Holy Land. This does not amount to much in total, but *The Book* projects her stay there as having a crucial role in the development of her spirituality. Some of her contemplations in other parts of the text may owe their vividness to the intensity of emotion which she experienced at sacred sites in the Holy Land, skated over or omitted in chapters dealing specifically with her experiences there.[46] These chapters have a particular character. They are the parts of *The Book* that most resemble the pilgrim guides and individual accounts of pilgrimages circulating in the period in their focus on supremely holy places, in contrast to *The Book*'s more haphazard mention of shrines elsewhere, even in Rome. For potential readers, Rome itself had less resonance than Jerusalem, the centre of Creation. Pilgrims to the Holy

Land, if they were not rushed around like Felix Fabri's company was on his first visit (a stay of only nine days), may have had as much opportunity to experience the numinous treasures of the Holy Land as those of Rome, since touring was more rigorously organised in the former, and the latter was particularly insecure in the 1410s.

However, as regards the Holy Land, *The Book* displays its characteristic authorial indifference to the physical environment. It can only be glimpsed through the prism of Margery's recorded behaviour. The searchlight is maintained on her 'feelings' and their repercussions in her soul, on her bodily manifestations, and the reactions she provoked. Rigid and somewhat arbitrary selectivity is applied in singling out sites and relics from among the plethora listed in the guidebooks, many of which she presumably saw and reverenced. *The Book* mentions some of the most important places connected with the Gospels, particularly those redolent of the Passion and Resurrection and associated with the Virgin Mary and St Mary Magdalene. The Mount of Olives is omitted, though it is mentioned in one of Margery's later contemplations of the Passion.[47] Old Testament sites, lengthily recorded in guidebooks and pilgrim narratives, are excluded. The selection was doubtless calculated to appeal to the prime religious interests of the pious circles in which Margery moved. The holy places are referred to in a reverential but familiar and almost dismissive manner. The wonders and marvels *The Book* is intent on describing lie in the effects they produce in Margery's soul. This oblique stance may in fact have enhanced her credibility in the face of her detractors, such as the Duke of Bedford's yeomen, who denied that she had actually been there (or on other pilgrimages).[48] The bookishly inclined readers and auditors of *The Book* could easily relate to Margery's Holy Land: there was no troubling 'otherness' about it. *The Book* thus firmly distances Margery from the sort of false pilgrims whom Fabri was to denounce, peddlers of fabulous stories about the Holy Land, intent on deceiving the credulous. The one piece of factual information which *The Book* shows Margery relaying was exact and prosaic, a demonstration of the size of Christ's tomb.[49]

To return home intact to northern Europe from the Jerusalem journey was a remarkable achievement. A number of distinguished Englishmen (able to afford the easiest travelling conditions) had died in the attempt in preceding decades. In 1385 the Earl of Stafford had died on the way back on the island of Rhodes. Sir William Neville and Sir John Clanvowe perished on the way there in Galata (Pera), the Latin suburb of Constantinople, possibly of plague contracted in Greece, in the Morea. Their tombstone has been identified. Sir Lewis Clifford died in Rhodes the same year, John Lord Roos on the way out in Cyprus in 1393, and Sir

John de Seton at Jerusalem in 1396. The exiled Duke of Norfolk died of plague in Venice on his way back from the Holy Land in 1399. A knight from Norfolk, Richard Carbonell, a member of the household of Lynn's patron, the Duke of Exeter, was to die on the way. It was sensible to make a will before setting out to Jerusalem, as Roger Wode, gentleman, of East Barsham (Norfolk) did in 1520. He stipulated: 'My body to be beryd in such holy place on that side of the see or beyone the see wher it shall please al mighty god to take me to his mercy.'[50]

An anecdote current about a company of English pilgrims, lost in a desert in 1403, illustrated some of the more colourful imagined hazards. They took refuge from wild beasts one night by climbing trees and managed to drive off predatory bears with their weapons. In their wanderings they came upon a hermit's hut in a well-watered place. The aged inhabitant welcomed them in and fed them, and when he knew that they were English pilgrims, exhorted them to give thanks to God that they had escaped not only the beasts but the terrible fighting that was about to break out in their country. Not long afterwards, an English chronicler noted, the battle of Shrewsbury took place.[51] The story certainly conjured up the perils of pilgrimage, somewhat in the vein of chivalrous romance, but it did provide some reassurance. A friendly holy man might be miraculously encountered who would succour distressed pilgrims – one, moreover, who had heard of England and was well disposed towards its inhabitants. Besides, staying apparently snugly at home was not always the prudent option. Death struck suddenly there too, often in less spiritually propitious circumstances.

English folk who had made the Jerusalem journey are likely to have been rare, and viewed with some awe. The survival of guides written by Englishmen, and Chaucer's fancy that his Wife of Bath went there three times, perhaps give a false impression that it was a common undertaking. Oblique but more solid evidence about typical numbers of pilgrims who went from north-west European towns comparable to Lynn may be found in paintings by Jan van Scorel (1495–1562) and Anthonie Mor van Dashorst (1519–1567/77) of members of the Jerusalem Gilds of Haarlem (founded c. 1506) and Utrecht. The Haarlem panel, by van Scorel, depicts twelve male pilgrims (including the painter, who went in 1520), each bearing a palm in procession – the first bears two palms, indicating that he had been twice. The figures (head and bust) face towards a framed picture being held up of the edicule, which van Scorel presumably drew in Jerusalem and presented to the gild. Each of the highly individualised members has below his portrait a parchment giving his name and the year of his pilgrimage. The set of three panels painted by van Scorel for the Utrecht gild has an almost identical formula. They depict thirty-five pilgrims, including seven clerics and one young woman named as Dirck Euerts' daughter. Like the other pilgrims of Haarlem and Utrecht, she is austerely but well clad; she wears a white wimple and chemise and black gown. All the pilgrims from both towns have their coats of arms depicted. The absence of heraldry is the main difference in the panel painted for the Utrecht gild by Anthonie Mor of five male pilgrims who went to Jerusalem in 1541, presumably as a group. A priest, Jan van Dam, 'vicarius', is followed by a pair of two mature laymen; two youthful-looking laymen respectfully walk behind. However, the Haarlem panel depicts twelve pilgrims who went over several decades, and the Utrecht set's thirty-five went over the years 1525–37.[52]

The daunting nature of the undertaking led to postponements and delegations, as we have seen reflected in wills. Fabri bears eloquent and repeated testimony to the hazards and miseries endured by pilgrims on their travels in the Eastern Mediterranean and the Holy Land. When, on his first pilgrimage, the company returned to the coast from Jerusalem, he says that 'we were all weak from our labours, worn out with the heat, the night-watching, and the hardships which we had endured'. Their galley 'became like a hospital full of wretched invalids'. Fabri's heartfelt delineation of the pilgrim's miseries highlights the courage behind Margery's undertaking.[53] As we have seen, she was commanded in her soul to go, and eagerly sought out indulgences.[54] We do not know what role models she had in local and middling society, but in that society the often edifyingly fatal and well-publicised pilgrimages undertaken by English nobles to Jerusalem in Margery's youth were probably recalled – none more so than that accomplished by the future Henry IV in 1392–3. Two nobles familiar with the Lynn elite in the early fifteenth century had participated, William Lord Willoughby of Eresby (Lincs.) and the Norfolk knight Thomas Erpingham.[55] In 1408 a pillar of the Lancastrian establishment, the young and doughty knight, Richard Beauchamp, Earl of Warwick, set off on travels abroad which lasted for two years, including pilgrimages to Rome and Jerusalem and the performance of feats of arms. He spent ten days in the Holy Land. Memories of his achievements on his travels were cherished in his family circle in the later fifteenth century.[56] Margery's journey in the footsteps of the great, the good and chivalrous was a heroic way of demonstrating the truth of her conversion to those in Lynn who doubted it. Bishop Repingdon had urged her to wear special raiment only after she had proved her devotion and had it recognised by fulfilling her resolution to go to Jerusalem.[57] It may be that the resolution had been strengthened by the need to stifle accusations of heresy.[58] However, above all, for Margery, the most holy places provided the apposite settings for the consummation of her devout way of life. There, dizzily, she was to experience sublime Gospel scenes, unreeling in her inner sight in settings which were at once intensely familiar and disorientatingly exotic. In her later recollection, the tourist high spots were replayed and enhanced, and cut and coloured in the light of English mystical devotion.[59]

The itinerary evident in *The Book* was a standard one, though, unlike some companies, hers did not venture as far as Mount Sinai and St Catherine's Monastery. Nevertheless, a stay of three weeks in the Holy Land was a lengthy one (thus increasing the hazards).[60] It enabled the company to see and absorb a good deal. Their activities, like those of other such groups, were rigidly channelled and scheduled. Centuries of custom hallowed what pilgrims should see and how they should behave; the conventions operated within the rigid but in some respects remarkably tolerant rules upheld under the authority of the sultan of Egypt (then al Mu'ayyad Shaykh) by the Mamluk officials residing in Jerusalem. The father guardian of the Franciscans of Mount Sion was the papally appointed protector of pilgrims, as of other Latin Christians; his position was recognised by the Mamluk governors. The Franciscans instructed pilgrims on how to behave, preached to them and accompanied them on some of their journeys.[61] *The Book* emphasises the compassion shown by the friars to Margery, their concern for her weeping and sympathetic reactions to her revelations.[62] They were, presumably, used to calming eccentric modes of behaviour among pilgrims. Fabri describes the wide variety of agitated responses after a friar announced to his group that they were actually standing in the forecourt of the Church of the Holy Sepulchre. 'Above all our companions and sisters, the women pilgrims shrieked as though in labour, cried aloud and wept.'[63] The tolerance shown to Margery's pious exhibitions in the Holy Land, particularly by the friars, may have strengthened her confidence in replicating them subsequently. There Christ had spoken to her with the clarity and intensity of the sun which irradiated the stark, white hills and buildings of Judea, and she obeyed without demur.[64]

A principal Franciscan aim, strongly reflected in Fabri's memoirs, was to keep the pilgrims out of trouble with the Mamluks which might lead to punishments, possibly to curtailment of the privileges generally accorded to groups of Western pilgrims, and disfavour for the Order. The Mamluks were prepared to let in only a limited number of pilgrim companies, conveyed in Venetian ships. Their captains formally assumed a large degree of responsibility for the conduct of the pilgrimage on land and for their group's relations with the authorities. Some of the arrangements are reflected in the contract which Fabri's company and their captain made in Venice on his second pilgrimage. The captain agreed to take them unhurriedly to the customary shrines and to pay all dues and other expenses. Not surprisingly, he was anxious to get his pilgrims re-embarked without a major incident or additional expenses which would eat into his profits. There were the dangers that they might give offence, unintentionally or not, to Islam, or respond with violence to the street baiting, petty extortion and theft with which, according to Fabri, they were continually assailed, or that they might request trips which the captain did not consider to be part of the contracted package.[65]

In Jerusalem, secular pilgrims lodged in the Hospital of St John, part of the complex of buildings attached to the Church of the Holy Sepulchre. In the country, they spent nights in the open or in ruined churches or unmanned shelters for travellers.[66] The English pilgrim of 1506 described how Christians of Eastern sects sold victuals to his company at Ramle and Jerusalem.[67] Other Eastern Christians hawked supposed relics.[68] Those specially prized by pilgrims were supplied by the friars of Mount Sion, who gave Margery 'many great relics'. In 1506, after an English company had had a 'right honest dinner' with them in their cloister, the guardian took a basin, from which he distributed to them relics wrapped in paper.[69] Margery may have acquired from the friars her prized staff made from Moses' rod, which she brought from Jerusalem and which was confiscated from her at Leicester.[70] Arnold von Harff's narrative throws possible light on its provenance. He was shown the bush from which the branch supposedly came with which Moses parted the Red Sea; he and his companions cut sticks from it.[71] Margery, after her return to Italy from the Holy Land, met a foreign woman who had also been there (possibly in the same galley). This woman travelled with an ass which bore an image of Christ (probably as an infant), in a chest (her sea-chest?) – a practical as well as a symbolic ensemble. The image was probably also a souvenir of pilgrimage, one whose cumbersomeness highlights Margery's practicality in procuring a stout staff.[72]

The indigenous inhabitants with whom pilgrims had the closest and most crucial group and individual relationships, fraught with possible tensions, were in fact Muslim. There was the Mamluk (the dragoman) officially appointed as the group's guide and protector. Then there were the muleteers hired by the galley captain. Fabri's account exemplifies the mutual ambivalence in the attitude of muleteers and their charges. Pilgrims soon came to resent being under the control of infidels of low social standing and apparently capricious temper. Yet their services were essential: Fabri remarks that if people had had to walk to Jerusalem, few would have survived because of the dust and heat. In addition, they would have been easy prey to the Bedouin who tracked and circled the bewildered pilgrims as they made their painful way up from the coast.[73]

In *The Book*, Margery is portrayed as an ideal Jerusalem pilgrim, whose meekness and lachrymose devotion impressed not only the local Franciscans but even the Muslims, who 'made much of her'. She is shown, therefore, as bearing witness to Christ among the unbelievers, as some of the great female saints had done. There is no hint of Arab hostility. As Fabri instances, some Muslims might show flashes of sympathy with the earnestly devout.[74] Perhaps some of them recognised her as an authentic holy woman and were confirmed in this opinion by the tenderness of the friars towards her and even, perhaps, by the hostility which, according to *The Book*, her compatriots continued to exhibit towards her. Kindness to Margery may have been a way of baiting a particularly stiff-necked tribe of Franks.

In other respects, too, Margery emerges as the ideal pilgrim, transcending harsh circumstances far from home and familiarity, achieving recognition in the holy places as one nourished and sustained in Christ's embrace. Fabri bears eloquent testimony to some of the awful privations which were the common lot of pilgrims in the Holy Land. *The Book* in general amply shows how Margery – also used to a comfortable bourgeois environment – was upset by difficult travelling conditions, poor lodgings and fare, and verminous infestations. Yet apart from comments about physical difficulties experienced at the Jordan and Mount Temptation, there are no hints of afflictions she endured in the Holy Land. Maybe, in her exceptionally ecstatic state, her usual fastidiousness and any unpleasant physical reactions to the environment were anaesthetised. She may have considered that harping on her physical suffering in the places where Christ's ministry and Passion had taken place would have detracted from the image of her piety which she was trying to present. The omissions added to the impact of the account: the well-informed reader or auditor of *The Book* is likely to have known about the hidden layer of cruel experience born lovingly, like a hair shirt, for Christ's sake.

What variety of experiences is Margery likely to have had in the Holy Land, and which did *The Book* pick out as significant? It is probable that her company, on landing at Jaffa, was penned, as other companies were to be too, in the unwholesome caves known as St Peter's Cellars – not the sort of place for 'rest and rehab' after a debilitating sea voyage.[75] They would have soon been launched into a hostile, unfamiliar environment, through the sand and scrub of the coastal plain, bent, we may imagine, under the oppression of the hot wind rising from the desert. Not far inland they would have passed through Ramle, whose inhabitants, Fabri says, were especially hostile.[76] Thence their asses plodded towards the Judean hills, stumbling upwards along ravines to the bleak tablelands. The first incident which *The Book* notes in the Holy Land is the ecstasy

Margery experienced on glimpsing Jerusalem, a moment of intense communal rejoicing for Fabri's company.[77] However, in *The Book* it is Margery's individual behaviour which is singled out, misinterpreted by her companions and, to modern secular-minded readers, of a Monty Pythonesque turn. She nearly fell off her ass. Two German pilgrims held her in place and fussed over her. They thought she was ill. Where were her English companions? Perhaps they were warily keeping their distance, having gloomily deduced the correct reason for a well-to-do English-woman's humiliating inability to keep her seat on a by no means mettle-some beast.[78]

In Jerusalem, after lodgings had been secured, the complex of holy sites enclosed within and juxtaposed with the Church of the Holy Sepulchre was the first as well as the principal destination. It is not far from the Jaffa Gate, through which Western pilgrims usually entered the city under the eyes of the Mamluks. As was customary, Margery's company was locked into the church overnight to prepare for their pro-cession around its shrines. They entered at Vespers, staying in vigil till Evensong the next day. Then Franciscans led the company, candles in hand, around the holy places. They climbed up the steps of Mount Calvary (in the south transept of the choir) to the chapel at its summit, where there is the socket hole of the Cross. At Mount Calvary Margery had the first of the momentous holy seizures, high points of devotion, which she was to experience for many years. There she heard with her bodily ears, and saw with her spiritual sight, the mourning of Our Lady, St John and St Mary Magdalene at the foot of the Cross. Her group processed to the edicule (the Chapel of the Holy Sepulchre), in the western part of the church, to worship at the tomb where Christ was laid to rest when He was taken down from the Cross. On seeing it, Margery fell down, with her candle in her hand. She received communion in the chapel.[79]

The Book thus deftly picks out the two most sacred sites in the church complex, focusing on Margery's reactions to them. The *via dolorosa* also gets summary treatment, though processing along the Stations of the Cross was a highlight for pilgrims. The fourth Station is singled out, the place where Christ met His Mother – this reflects Margery's pre-occupation with their relationship. The episode was to provide the basis of one of Margery's most poignantly visualised contemplations after her pilgrimage. *The Book* recounts how the group went along the *via dolorosa* (presumably with Franciscans as their guides) early one morning before they headed for Mount Sion (rising to the south of the city) in the 'great hills' – a rare topographical reference in *The Book*, faintly evoking vistas of the high tableland of Judea, with the surrounding ranges glimpsed in the clear light and cool air after dawn.[80] The English pilgrim of 1506 was moved by the eminent situation of Jerusalem: it 'is in a fair eminent place, for it standeth upon such a ground that from whence soever a man cometh thither he must needs ascend. From thence a man may see all Arabia and the mount of Abaryn and Nebo, and Phasga, the plains of Jordan and Jericho, and the Dead Sea, unto the stone of desert. I saw never city nor other place have so fair prospect'.[81] On Mount Sion the Franciscan convent was the focus of pilgrimage. *The Book* mentions the company's visits to the places where Christ washed the Disciples' feet and where the Last Supper was held. They are both marked by altars in the choir, the former on the south side, the latter (where Margery received communion) by the high altar. She also visited the room where the Holy Ghost descended (a chamber to the east of the choir). From Mount Sion the company made their way back, doubtless through the Valley of Kidron, which separates the city from the Mount of Olives. Margery visited a church in the valley, the Church of the Tomb of the Virgin. There, whilst she heard two Masses, Christ and the Virgin spoke to her soul.[82]

Margery subsequently went with her company to Bethlehem, a relatively easy ride of about three hours, descending into a valley teeming with numinous sites and abundant in grapes, figs and olives. She visited the Church of St Mary of the Nativity and the grotto beneath it where Christ was born. Her 'feelings' are not detailed, but her companions' decisive rejection of her there was noted. They refused to eat with her, but the Franciscans took pity on her, allowing her to share their meals.[83] Probably the most gruelling visit Margery undertook was one eastwards from Jerusalem, descending through deep gorges and sometimes along narrow ledges to the green but stifling haven of the Jordan valley, and on to face the rigorous challenge of the Mount of Temptation, where Christ spent forty days in the wilderness – known to her as Mount Quarantine. Her compatriots opposed her resolution to go with them on this pilgrimage. They are likely to have been forewarned about its perils – the precipitous track through the hills, the debilitating heat of the Jordan valley, and the dangerous climb up the Mount. In the light of these hazards, they may have feared that Margery would become a physical liability for whom they would be considered responsible. She was adamant, presumably determined, like generations of pilgrims, to gain the indulgences on offer, and to bathe and dip cloths in the healing waters of the Jordan.[84] Also she probably wanted to track St Mary the Egyptian, whose legend she found particularly consoling. According to the *Legenda Aurea*, this Alexandrine prostitute paid her sea fare on pilgrimage to the Holy Sepulchre by offering her services to the sailors.

There, through prayer to 'Our Lady, she received pardon on condition that she renounced the world and lived chastely. For forty-seven years she then lived as a solitary in the desert across the Jordan.[85]

Pilgrims foregathered near the river's point of entry to the Dead Sea, at the place where St John the Baptist was said to have baptised Christ. This, as we have seen, was the only journey in the Holy Land on which *The Book* alludes to physical privations – they seem to have blotted out revelation. At the river the weather was so hot that Margery thought that her feet would burn, presumably when she bared them to bathe. She may have recalled how an aged priest had spied the reformed Egyptian, 'when she was walking naked thereabouts, the body blackened and burned by the fiery sun', and had run after her as fast as he could. The pursuit ended in a decorous and edifying encounter.[86] Margery's company crossed the Plain of Jericho – typically, the site of the city went unmentioned, since Jericho pertained to the Old Testament. Through the plain lay the way to Mount Quarantine. Other pilgrim narratives amply testify to the Mount's perils. Von Harff climbed by stony paths to the chapel built into the rock where Christ fasted for forty days and nights, and upwards 'in great fear' to the summit where He had been taken and tempted by the Devil. This and other accounts underline Margery's intrepidity. She, too, found the going hard. Her companions, toiling themselves, would not help her, so she enterprisingly hired a 'Saracen' to do so. During the ascent she suffered great thirst; her companions were unsympathetic, but the Franciscans again proved compassionate.[87]

With her usual physical resilience and tough-mindedness, Margery recovered from these ordeals. One more journey is mentioned, a short, relatively easy one, to Bethany, past the Mount of Olives, to go to the house of Mary Magdalene and Martha ('where Christ often lodged' – von Harff) and the tomb of Lazarus nearby, which, according to other pilgrim sources, was in a ruined church. As was usual with pilgrims, Margery was drawn back to the Church of the Holy Sepulchre. *The Book* singles out her visits in the church to the place where the risen Christ had appeared to His Mother (the Chapel of the Apparition) and, close by it, the place marked by two circles of marble stones where Christ and Mary Magdalene stood when she mistook Him for a gardener, an episode which was to figure in her future contemplation on the Passion.[88] At the end of Margery's pilgrimage, on the way back from Jerusalem through Ramle to re-embark at Jaffa, she wished she could return to the city, partly because of the devotional experiences which she had had there. These may not have been uncommon feelings among serious-minded pilgrims who arrived back at the coast in a reasonable physical state, especially those from the very different environments of northern Europe. They may have felt that they were returning for ever to a humdrum, grey scene after living intensely, uncomfortable but exhilarated, in a strange world, punishing, humiliating, but uniquely stimulating.[89]

Rome

Margery arrived in Rome probably in August 1414 and stayed there at a time of high political instability and armed confrontations. The control which the Crown of Naples had gained over the city had slipped away as a result of the death of King Ladislas on 6 August 1414. A month or so later, an attempt was made by his captains to secure the city for his sister and heir, Queen Joanna, but this failed. Pope John XXIII, now committed to attending the General Council of the Church, summoned to Constance to attempt to end the schism, did not proceed from Bologna to Rome but appointed Cardinal Jacopo Isolani as his spiritual and temporal vicar there. There was a revolt in the city against the restoration of papal rule on 16 October, which petered out when Isolani made his entry a few days later. Dr John Law has pointed out how politically fractured Roman society was in this period, a situation which helped to frustrate efforts to maintain the pretensions of the commune against papal authority. However, forces flying the Neapolitan flag were holed up in Castel San Angelo, an encouragement to Queen Joanna's sympathisers in the city to plot and agitate. Isolani's forces were still besieging the castle when Margery left Rome.[90]

Margery stayed in Rome longer than she did anywhere else abroad, not leaving until after Easter 1415. As we have seen, the attractions which Rome offered to the devout were excelled only by those of the Holy Land. Besides the principal shrines of St Peter and St Paul and the other shrines associated with them, there were the tombs and relics of thousands of early martyrs, and the traditional places of martyrdom of many of them. Rome had been a magnet for relics, especially ones allegedly from the Holy Land and ones associated with Christ's ministry and Passion. Pilgrim-guides gave information and advice about how pilgrims might discriminatingly pick their way through this unparalleled treasure-house of holy objects. They categorised the essentials as the 'Stations of Rome'. A fifteenth-century rhymed guide in English lists the relics to be found and the indulgences available in thirty-nine churches, including the seven major basilicas. Rome was the indulgence capital of Christendom.[91]

Margery intended to visit the Stations, and certainly did go to some of them, but she says that on one occasion, when she was lying in bed in her lodgings with the intention of setting out for them, Christ warned

her not to because of the storm He was sending. There was a sequence
of feast days on which the Stations were to be visited in Lent, which
John Capgrave was to set out in *The Solace of Pilgrimes*. Margery may
have been attempting to follow this sequence.[92] She does not mention
visiting St Peter's, but it would be surprising if she failed to do so,
despite the nearby presence of the papal soldiery besieging Castel San
Angelo. St Peter's one hundred altars, one might think, would have drawn
her moth-like. St Peter was one of the select group of saints who customarily spoke to her in her mind, and Christ had cited the church to
her as the safest possible place to be.[93] Would she not have ardently
wished to be present at the Ostentation of the *sudarium* (16 January)?
This was the cloth with which St Veronica was said to have wiped Christ's
face on the way to Calvary, and which retained the imprint regarded
as His most authentic representation. The 'vernicle' was well known in
England.[94] Margery had seen the place where this was supposed to have
happened, the sixth Station of the Cross on the *via dolorosa*, outside the
house of Veronica.

However, *The Book* mentions only five churches which Margery visited
in the context either of her revelations or of the problems which she
encountered as a pilgrim. No attempt is made to sketch out a pilgrim
narrative, as was the case with the Holy Land. The image of Rome was
probably more familiar, less exciting and esoteric, in England, even though
it did not have a 'package tour' character for English folk like Santiago
– where Margery, as we have said, was to have no revelations worth
recording at all.

Nevertheless, the revelations which Margery received in certain Roman
churches were crucial in the development of her spiritual personality.
The particular sacred character of these churches, and of the relics they
housed, may provide samples of the stimuli which helped to launch her
spiritual leaps. San Giovanni in Laterano, Rome's cathedral and its first
basilica, built by the Emperor Constantine, contained the heads of
St Peter and St Paul. It had a miraculously painted portrait of Christ.
Other relics belonging to the church were the table and tablecloth from
the Last Supper, loaves and fishes left over from the feeding of the five
thousand, Christ's swaddling clothes, His foreskin, and blood and water
from His side.[95] According to *The Book*, when Margery was at Mass in
the church, she was impressed by the demeanour of the officiating priest,
the German Wenslawe, who was to become her confessor, rescuing her
from the ignominy into which she had fallen among her compatriots
and encouraging the development of her singular spirituality.[96] The other
major basilica mentioned in *The Book* is Santa Maria Maggiore; there
she probably saw the remarkable thirteenth-century mosaics in the apse

depicting scenes from the life of the Blessed Virgin. Relics in the basilica listed in the pilgrims' guide, the *stacions of Rome*, were the bodies of St Matthew and St Jerome, the cloth on which Christ was laid when He was born, and the hay on which He lay before the ass. Others there were a portrait of the Virgin painted by St Luke, and notable relics of St Thomas of Canterbury.[97] In *The Book*, Margery referred to the miraculous translation thither of St Jerome, whose cell and original place of burial she had presumably seen on her visit to Bethlehem. In this instance, and in others, she was probably concerned with connecting what she had experienced in the Holy Land with relics in Rome. In Santa Maria Maggiore, St Jerome appeared to her inward sight and spoke to her soul, reassuring her about the spiritual significance of her weeping.[98]

Three other churches in which Margery had special experiences may have been frequented by her because they were within reasonable reach of where she lived. After she was rejected at the English Hospice of St Thomas, she went with the Irishman Richard to a church opposite the Hospice, where he persuaded the priest to give her communion. There, apparently, she confessed in her soul to St John the Evangelist, and was consoled by Christ.[99] The Hospice was not far from the Campo de' Fiori, within the bend of the Tiber where the bulk of Rome's population was densely concentrated, conveniently placed to fetch water. By then, only one of the ancient aqueducts still functioned.[100] However, another church she visited, Santi Apostoli, is a considerable walk from the Campo de' Fiori. It is at the foot of the Quirinal Hill, on the opposite side of the Via del Corso, medieval Rome's main thoroughfare. In this church Margery had one of her most important meditations, in which she was mystically married to the Godhead.[101] In the Corso is the church of San Marcello, where she lay worried about having given away her money, and was reassured by Christ, who pointed out that she was not yet as poor as He had been when He hung on the Cross for love of her.[102] The church possesses a highly expressive wooden crucifix dating from the fourteenth century, which acquired a miracle-working reputation.

Margery prolonged her stay (as apparently did her original companions) probably in order to visit the Stations in their sequence up to Easter 1415, gaining the indulgences, which reached their maximum in the more solemn half of the liturgical year. Rome was renowned for the splendour of its papal ceremonial in the celebration of the liturgies. Adam Usk, the Welsh clerk who arrived at the papal court in 1402, considered them worthy of description in his chronicle. Something of their splendour is caught in Vittore Carpaccio's painting of pilgrims encountering an early pope in procession near the Castel San Angelo (see cover).[103] However, with John XXIII absent at the Council of Constance, and the confused political circumstances in Rome, Margery is likely to have missed out on much of this. Dr Sumption cites a canon of St Peter's, who wrote that in 1414 there had not been enough money to light the candles in the basilica on the feast of the Apostles, and that at Corpus Christi, 'we celebrated mass in great poverty on account of the war and the tribulations of St Peter's. We carried the Eucharist on foot in a small crystal tabernacle . . . lighting our way with six torches . . . for the canons could not afford the oil'.[104]

Some visitors to Rome in the later Middle Ages, with images of ancient splendour in mind, were taken aback by the city's decay. Their views have been echoed by modern historians, but some aspects of them have been questioned by Dr John Law, who emphasises the city's economic buoyancy.[105] Adam Usk, who lodged in the Borgo Leonino, across the river from the English Hospice, was typical of literary-minded medieval visitors in his lament for the condition of Rome. At night he observed the watchdogs barking at the doors, and their confrontations with marauding wolves. 'Oh God,' he wrote, 'how pitiful Rome is! Once it was teeming with princes and their palaces; now it is abandoned and full of slums, thieves, wolves and vermin, reduced to misery by the notorious internecine feuding of the Romans themselves.'[106] In size of population, Rome was certainly not one of the leading European cities. It stood around only 17,000 at the end of the fourteenth century, and rose to about 35,000 by the mid-fifteenth century, probably considerably smaller than the population of London, the one big city with which Margery was well acquainted. Rome, however, had a completely different ambience from that of London; it lacked the orderliness characteristic of English urban landscapes. The family towers of the nobility were a prominent feature. The inhabitants clustered between areas of overgrown ruins and patches of cultivation and pasturage – stock-raising was an important Roman occupation. 'The Roman Forum was known as Campo Vaccino, because it served as a cow pasture, the Tarpeian Rock on the Capitoline was called Monte Caprino, for there the goats foraged, and the Castrum of the Praetorian Guard near the Baths of Diocletian was, around 1500, made into a hunting preserve.'[107] A remark in *The Book* makes Rome sound like part of a peasant economy. On one occasion, when Margery was in St Bridget's chapel, just round the corner from the English Hospice, storms arose in this main centre of population. Those 'who were in the fields', as well as others working in the open air, hurried indoors.[108] Provision and processing of foodstuffs for the households of the pope and cardinals was an important part of the Roman economy – their absence in 1414–15 is likely to have caused impoverishment.

Margery was lodged when she arrived in Rome at the Hospice of St Thomas the Martyr, whose function was to provide succour to English pilgrims. She received communion there every Sunday and was confessed there, and she considered that she was 'highly beloved' by the master and all his brethren. However, her reception was soon blighted; she was banned from the premises after being denounced by the priest in her former company of pilgrims.[109] If the rules the Hospice laid down in the later fifteenth century were in force in 1414, she could have looked forward when she arrived to board and lodging for eight days, the maximum for commoners (three days for nobles).[110] After she had gained a local reputation for holiness, the master and brethren apologised to her for the ban and rescinded it. She discovered that her maid, who had deserted her, was acting as butler at the Hospice. Margery looked to her for handouts of food, drink and small change.[111] According to an inventory of 1445, the Hospice had sixty-three beds – twelve of them were in the noblemen's chamber, twenty in the *camera pauperum*, and five in the women's chamber.[112] It is unclear how many slept to a bed. Surviving lists of the names of the pilgrims accommodated, the earliest of which dates from 1479, show that the total in non-jubilee years was about 200.[113] The Hospice relied partly on gifts and bequests from pilgrims past and present, English clerics with business at the curia, and English residents of Rome; sums were raised from individuals and parishes in England.[114] Income was derived from property acquired in Rome, which was accumulating in this period. For instance, a certain William Richardson gave a house to the Hospice in 1407, Stephen Warner one in 1412; reference was made in 1408 to a house bought from Richard Rogerson.[115] By 1406 the Hospice possessed twenty-three houses in the city, besides other properties.[116] It was rising in repute and status, in Rome as well as in England. The guardian (*custos*) and chamberlains (*camerarii*) were elected annually by those members of its confraternity present in the city. The offices of both a clerical and a lay chamberlain are first documented in 1391.[117] In 1414–15 John Thomassen *alias* Palmer was probably guardian, and Philip Newton probably clerical chamberlain.[118] English residents who were *confratres* may have been among 'the brethren' to whom *The Book* refers, influential in making decisions about how Margery ought to be treated.[119]

Her German confessor, Wenslawe, who, *The Book* implied, was the holder of high ecclesiastical office, articulated her eventual acceptance into both well-to-do and poor sections of Roman society. *The Book* says that she went to sermons where Germans, among others, preached, but it is not clear whether she was received into a German community, or whether, indeed, there was a single, identifiable German community in Rome.

Nicholas Schofield, archivist of the Venerabile Collegio Inglese, argues that, if she did attend a church with close German associations, it is most likely to have been Santi Sergi Palatii Caruli. Its origins went back to the gift by Pope Leo III (c. 781) to Charlemagne of a piece of land next to St Peter's. Charlemagne built a palace and church there. A cemetery developed which in the fifteenth century had wolves prowling about it. Schofield surmises that Margery may have visited the church of Santa Maria dell' Anima near the Piazza Navone, easily accessible from the area of the Hospice of St Thomas. Its foundation dates to 1400, and the building was completed in 1514. Today it is the church of the German nation.[120]

It is to Wenslawe that we owe some of *The Book*'s glimpses of a society far removed in hierarchical terms from the world of well-to-do, status-conscious English pilgrims. Before Christmas 1414 he had ordered Margery to act as servant to a poor old woman, a very challenging and testing request to make to the daughter of an alderman of the Holy Trinity Gild at Lynn, accustomed to fine sheets and tableware and choice wines, to whom it was natural to order around her own servants (such as her unresponsive maid). Margery dutifully left her lodgings to live in squalid conditions for six weeks: 'She served her as she would have done our Lady. And she had no bed to lie in, nor any bedclothes to be covered with save her own mantle. And then was she full of vermin and suffered great pain therewith. Also she fetched home water [from the Tiber?] and sticks on her neck for the poor woman, and begged both meat and wine for her. And when the poor woman's wine was sour, this creature herself drank that sour wine, and gave the poor woman good wine that she had bought for her own self.'[121] These hard experiences gave Margery the courage to embrace mendicancy. In the New Year she gave away all her money which Richard the beggar had lent her. She subsisted on meals and doles which well-to-do patrons gave her (possibly on the recommendation of Wenslawe or the Hospice?), supplemented by begging door to door. She gained a reputation for holiness; the histrionic aspects of her behaviour now seem to have been accepted as holy baggage. When *The Book* has Margery noting that she saw much poverty among the people in Rome, it was reflecting heartfelt personal experiences.[122] Perhaps degradation was greater in scale and depth than what she was accustomed to seeing in Lynn and other English towns. The vividly remembered experience of extreme deprivation probably gave her new insight into the life of the poor and an empathy with such wretches likely to have been rare in persons of her status, who generally had a ritualised commitment to alms-giving. *The Book* at this point (and briefly at some others, such as when she was part of a vermin-infested company in Germany) gives the authentic feel and aroma of poverty.

It was to be expected that the greatest centre of pilgrimage in Western Christendom should have had a large and floating population on the margins of society. In the later fourteenth century there were English folk in Rome in trades in demand among pilgrims – rosary selling, cobbling and tailoring.[123] Margery's former maid found employment serving pilgrims. The apparently remarkably well-heeled beggar, Richard, who spoke Italian, was in Rome (and flush) some of the time that Margery was there.[124] Poor folk probably crowded within the Aurelian Walls for security, especially in time of war. The reputation of the Campagna as bleak and barren, a region 'of marsh, pasture and abandoned villages', seems overdrawn, but it could be insecure. Margery shared her new companions' apprehensions about warnings, as they prepared to leave Rome, that there were many thieves along the way who would rob and perhaps kill them.[125] Though Margery accepted the charity of this pilgrim company, she does not seem to have targeted her begging in Rome at fellow pilgrims. She aimed to establish a niche in the urban society of the hallowed city as a holy woman following Christ's instructions about poverty to the letter. Despite the doubts she had experienced about plunging into this course, which came to a head in the basilica of San Marcello, her remarkable success in it suggests that there was surplus wealth available in the higher echelons of Roman society and that Romans were piously inclined to invest it in sustaining holy and largely incomprehensible foreign beggars. It is notable that *The Book* does not mention any apprehensions Margery felt about dangers in Rome, or the occurrence of any mishaps to her there, though she probably covered considerable distances within the city, for instance to visit Santa Maria Maggiore and San Giovanni in Laterano. The only concerns expressed were about foul weather. Her adoption of the practice of mendicancy may have given her some security; so may have an eccentric air of holiness. If she lived and moved around mostly within the cocoon of those densely packed and, presumably, mutually protective communities which clustered between the Tiber and the Corso, that may have helped to preserve her too. The glimpses that *The Book* gives of Margery's time in Rome – a time of political upheavals – are a tribute to the calm and stable elements in the life of the city, in notable contrast to the desolate and menacing aspects highlighted in some other contemporary accounts.

Thus *The Book* gives us strongly contrasting glimpses of Margery's sojourns in Venice, the Holy Land and Rome. As regards Venice, its focus is mainly on the practicalities of her relations with her pilgrim group and of arrangements for the voyage to Palestine. Despite the length of Margery's stay in Venice, there is scant reflection of the city's character as one of Christendom's great devotional centres. In Jerusalem Margery is presented as at her most ecstatic as a pilgrim, interacting vigorously with holy sites, enriching her subsequent contemplative life. *The Book*, like conventional guidebooks, gives no sense that Jerusalem, in terms of population and culture, and of the great rebuilding since the overthrow of the crusader kingdom, was overwhelmingly a Muslim city. The earliest figures from the Ottoman archives, for 1525–6, show that there were then in the city 616 Muslim households, 199 Jewish ones and 119 Christian ones. It had long been a place of pilgrimage to rival the two holy cities of the Hijaz, and was often visited by pilgrims going to or from Mecca. There was a large and culturally vigorous Mamluk society in Jerusalem – not just the governor and his staff, but the many Mamluks who had retired there or had been banished from Egypt, and their free sons and daughters. They gave endowments not only to mosques but to foundations supporting Islamic learning and students, and providing charity for the poor. There were also many Sufi brotherhoods established in the city.[126]

Jerusalem's restored and newly built mosques and its pious Islamic foundations far outshone the sites of Latin churches and crusader foundations, shabby, ruinous, razed. The pious, rich Muslim elite and the crowds of the Faithful put in the shade the native Christians, the beleaguered monks and the trickle of Latin pilgrims. Glimmers of this imbalance are conveyed in the accounts of the clear-eyed Fabri and von Harff, but for the majority of pilgrim writers, it was too unpalatable a truth to be told. Perhaps for some of the great nobles who went (such as Henry of Bolingbroke), these shocking aspects of their experience provided an incentive which reinforced their ambition to help free the Holy City. For deeply devout pilgrims such as Margery, the spiritually overwhelming complex of the Holy Sepulchre may have provided a comforting laager. To them, the other patched-up, encroached on and defiled locations – such a contrast with the magnificent churches and monasteries back home – may have reinforced a sense of the poverty and homely environment of the Holy Family and Disciples. There were no grand architectural images; the exterior of the edicule, as painted by van Scorel, is dull and blank. Later medieval pilgrimage is likely to have had powerful effects on Western religious imagination, underlining the simple human character and settings of the Incarnation and Passion. *The Book* shows the transforming effects of the Holy Land on Margery. Soon after her visit she became a beggar. She elaborated a portable Holy Land of the imagination.

It was in Rome that, according to *The Book*, Margery first reflected upon and refined feelings relating to her experiences in the Holy Land.

In a devotional sense, Rome was the ideal place to unwind after the supreme pilgrimage, though it is not clear that that was the reason for the order in which her group visited it. Rome had such a stunning concentration of relics relating to the Holy Family and Disciples, which could be reverenced at leisure and without restriction, in more congenial and sympathetic physical and social conditions. Rome was the only place on Margery's travels abroad where we are told that she entered into a complexity of social relations – with English pilgrims and residents, possibly with Germans, and certainly with Roman society at various levels. *The Book* gives some fascinating glimpses of the variety of communities in Rome and the ability of its society to harbour them and individual strangers, which perhaps relates to its inability to develop a strong communal identity, and to economic imperatives. Could the sympathetic view of Rome in *The Book* have been a response to attitudes and expectations in Lynn? Perhaps it was viewed as a city whose religious aura was beneficent. There, in the midst of spiritual riches, pilgrims could connect with fellow countrymen and women, and with hospitable Romans. In this setting, conspicuous poverty and stark pagan ruins may have been acceptable, whereas the wealth of pushy Venetians, with their painted women, and of silky Mamluks in their slippered ease was, to say the least, distracting. Perhaps we may conclude that Rome unrestored, with the papacy challenged and eclipsed, kept its hold on religious devotion in Lynn. The will of John Scotte (1429), citizen and bowyer of York, suggests a similar awe of 'great Rome'. His executors were to give four marks (£2 13s 4d) to a 'guide trewman' going on pilgrimage there, half of the sum for his labours, half for masses at a discriminating selection of altars – at the *sudarium*, *scala coeli*, St Fabian and St Sebastian, and at the Stations ('seyrkyll') of Rome.[127] One wonders whether a Rome more comparable in worldly magnificence to other great cities of Christendom, the Rome of the Renaissance, had the same affective grip on townsfolk in the distant North.

chapter 9

CONCLUSION

Let us now come to conclusions about *The Book of Margery Kempe* –
about the significance of the personality and life constructed in it
for Margery, and about *The Book*'s historical worth and import in general.

The significance of the presentation of Margery's life remains the central
puzzle. Within the context of medieval devotional writing, the treatise
stands out not only for the thoroughness and intensity with which it
analyses the development and character of a devotional life, but for the
scale on which the subject's interactions with society is investigated.
Indeed, the presentations of personality and spirituality are clearly influenced strongly by stereotypes of gender and piety. The accounts of experiences and episodes in society were probably often shaped through the
imitative and inventive conventions of hagiography. In any case, they are
occasional and carefully posed snapshots of a life. We must *prima facie*
be sceptical about the factual basis of lifelike snatches of dialogue and
colourful touches of detail, as adjuncts of a true record of events which
had in many cases occurred years before, and which are recalled to enhance
a complex and focused agenda. Their assured value is the insight they
give into the modes in which the author wished to be represented –
modes which reflected current mores. However, one must not be too
dismissive of the factual basis: the prevalence of oral learning and the
relative paucity of written *aide-mémoires* led to the training of memory
to a much higher level than in today's society, pampered by the availability
of text. Moreover, if *The Book* was to be persuasive to those who knew
or had seen Margery, or had heard gossip about her, it had to present a
figure and anecdotal adornment which were plausible. We can incline to
accept a good deal of incidental information as accurate recall or credible
reconstruction. Though we have no specific information about Margery's
travels to back up what is said in *The Book*, general information about
pilgrimages in the later Middle Ages reinforces its accounts of hers at
many points.

We can surely regard the assumptions made in *The Book* about matters both eternal and mundane as important evidence about facets of Margery's personality and about the culture of Lynn. In one instance, there is a little evidence possibly bearing on a point in her narrative of a sequence of events which had occurred well over ten years before. This tends to support the accuracy of her memory. According to *The Book*, when she was examined by Archbishop Bowet at Cawood (probably in the autumn of 1417), she told him a homily, which she had already told a Doctor of Divinity. Bowet commended it – therefore it is likely that she had often repeated it since. It is, indeed, extremely well honed. The homily centres on a vivid allegory concerning the digestive habits of 'a bear, great and boisterous, ugly to behold'. On 2 July 1416, the mayor of Lynn, Thomas Hunte, had written to the sheriff of Norfolk, John Spenser, saying 'we send to yow be the bringer of this lettre a litill yonge hee beer'. A chamberlain's account for the mayoral year ending the following September accounts for 5s 11d for the carriage of a little bear to London, sent by the Mayor to Spenser.[1] Could it be that there was a well-known family of bears being kept in Lynn in 1416 (when Margery was apparently at home) and that their messy habits had made a particular impression on her? Perhaps a preacher had used their example to construct a homily. Dirt and muck, as is amply borne out elsewhere in *The Book*, were particularly offensive to Margery. Her record of the homily may have preserved a genuine memory of her feelings in 1417. The accuracy of her memories about what happened on her travels that year is of special interest because this is the one part of *The Book* that contains important evidence bearing on national affairs – on the challenges to Bedford's rule posed by the plots of opponents of the Lancastrian regime, and the reactions of secular and ecclesiastical government to them.

The information we may be able to glean from *The Book* about public moods in that tense period is incidental to its purposes: central to those is the presentation of a devout personality, both in its origins and as fully fledged. As a construct, that personality is of itself of intense interest, but does it present a rounded view of her piety? Its focus is on particular forms of Christological and Marian devotion which, it is argued, in this case gave its subject deep insight into the nature of the Divinity, regular foretastes of heavenly bliss, and Christ's reiterated promises of instant admission to Heaven. Implicitly, these promises obviate the need, generally felt so keenly in the period, for the procuring of indulgences. Some other aspects of common pious culture are ignored or downgraded in importance. In Margery's contemplations, the huge range of contemporary saints' cults is excluded – only the Trinity, sacred persons associated with the New Testament, and angels constitute the *dramatis personae*.

Early on in the reconstruction of her piety, Christ is dismissive about her wearing of a hair shirt and heavy telling of beads.[2] Yet this is not the whole story: her developed devotion, so notably marked out by the unusual wearing of special clothes, had strands which placed her in the supermarkets of holiness along with the bargain-hunting hoi-polloi, as well as in the bespoke outfitters of tailor-made spirituality. The references to her keen acquisition of indulgences on her pilgrimages of 1413–15 suggest that, though she may have set off because of Christ's command in her soul, she had as well quite commonplace motives for going. One focus of the text – the persecutions which she endured – reveals incidentally that she followed the cults of some of the fashionable saints of the day.[3] So the devout personality presented by *The Book* is not a fully integrated one: there are contradictions. Beneath the flaunting of a transcendent devotional robe there are glimpses of a quite ordinary piety. This was, probably, reassuring for the folk on the staithes of Lynn. The contradictions may be reassuring for the reader in search of the 'real' Margery's piety. They can be read as indications that *The Book* does give us unintended insights about her spiritual dilemmas and hesitations, a revelation of untidy clutter in her soul which might have taken the neat housewife in her aback but which gives *The Book* a particular value which the more polished works of some other holy women fail to.

I have argued that the historical value and significance of *The Book* lie in the insights it gives not only into the construction of an individual pious mentality but into a broad spectrum of characteristic outlooks and opinions in Lynn in the 1430s. Arguably *The Book* could have been intended for the edification of a few devout friends or members of a religious community, such as the allegedly receptive nuns of Denney. That was to be the fate of the copy which fetched up at Mount Grace priory. However, the attention lavished on events and opinions in Lynn suggest that it was, rather, intended to win over detractors and establish there the transcendent nature of her devotion. *The Book* set out to refute the damaging folklore about her which, it appears, had accumulated over several generations. To fulfil this aim, it had to engage public opinion in ways which were both persuasive and reflective, so enabling us to use it, in a speculative way, as in some respects a barometer of opinion. It is pro-urban, not written in the genre of denunciation of cities, echoing Old Testament prophecies, or paralleling classical praise of country living. Christ castigates the sins of mankind in general. Lynn is a place where the performance of the liturgies, the public celebration of feast days and the state in which holy places are maintained are stimulants to meditation. The inhabitants are notable for their charity. Let us take a couple of instances which may reflect ways in which *The Book* was moulded to suit opinion in Lynn in the 1430s. Take the way in which it treats prelates who interviewed Margery. I would judge that Bowet gets the booby prize, Repingdon scores equivocally, Peverel is runner-up and Arundel the winner. One reason for this ordering may be that the first two had had little or no connection with the town and were not remembered there, whereas Peverel's memory was probably honoured (and perhaps commemorated) by the Carmelites, and Arundel's more widely honoured for his strenuous efforts as chancellor to resolve the town's internal conflicts in 1410–11. A notable aspect of *The Book's* treatment of the four is that members of their households, clerical and/or lay, are regarded critically, and sometimes appear as being overtly criticised by Margery – Peverel's men make amends and treat her well, which would have pleased the Carmelites. Perhaps the critical attitude to episcopal *familiae* relates to townsmen's occasionally edgy relations with those of the bishops of Norwich when they came to Gaywood or Lynn priory. As we have seen, townsmen shot them up in 1377, and we may deduce from one of Bishop Despenser's later letters that on one occasion he was intending to ride defiantly into town with them when opinions were running high against him.[4] Presumably there were personal links between episcopal officials at the Tolbooth (who sometimes got into disputes with the urban authority) and clerks, esquires and yeomen in the *familia*.

I have argued that the approach and content of *The Book*, though distinctively Margery's, were heavily influenced by particular clergymen in Lynn, or by a coterie of them. This would help to account for the generally emollient view of the town's clergy and positive treatment of their relations with the laity. Unlike so many of the clergy in the literature of the period, and in the records of church courts, these are not inappropriately attired, fornicators, gluttons, wine-bibbers or men of violence. The harmonious and edifying picture projected in *The Book* strains credibility. Indeed, tensions among the clergy about the phenomenon of Margery herself are to be inferred. It is likely that the town's Franciscans (unmentioned) and the Augustinians (briefly mentioned) were unenthusiastic, and that there was one time when she caused controversy among the Dominicans and another time among the Benedictines. A striking exception to *The Book's* blandness of approach to the internal politics of the Church in Lynn is its partisan and triumphalist treatment of the long-standing issue of parochial rights. This appears to be a surprising lapse of discretion, especially in view of the fact that opinion among the laity seems to have been moving in favour of a dilution of the mother church's rights, in contrast to Margery's traditionalist stance. Here she was upholding the views of the Benedictines and the vicar of St Margaret's. Presumably, her views on the matter were so well known that their repetition was unlikely to cause offence. The fact that she aired them with unaccustomed vehemence, dragging in an ecclesiastical controversy, is, perhaps, paradoxically a tribute to the degree of unity in matters of ecclesiastical jurisdiction and worship which existed among the clergy and laity of Lynn. The controversy was not tearing the place apart.

The Book's engagement with this issue contrasts with its silence about the controversies in secular affairs for which Lynn became notorious when Margery was in her thirties. Indeed, the silence accorded with opinion in the town in the 1430s. However, might not the accounts of the culminating crisis in Margery's marriage and of the circumstances of her spiritual rebirth in part be related to this blanked-out destabilising background? Could it be that, mortified and outraged by the dishonour heaped on her aged father's associates, and by her husband's inability to participate in defending them, she found it congenial to turn to intro-spection and flight? It is notable that John Kempe is not mentioned among the many whom we know to have been involved in the process of constitutional compromise and debate in the early 1410s. Moreover, Magery's emergence as a vociferous vowess (especially if she made shrill remarks too about secular affairs) may have become a clog and an embarrassment to the *potenciores*, denigrated by their critics as an example of their antisocial behaviour, as she flouted the stately and demure behavioural code appropriate to ladies. According to the proem to *The Book*, her kindred and friends deserted her. Perhaps dignified exile seemed attractive in these circumstances, despite the fraught and gruelling journeys which pilgrimages to Jerusalem and Rome entailed. Margery spent much longer abroad than pilgrims going there normally did, in a period when the conflict in Lynn was at a height. At a time when folk of her rank at home were heavily engaged in politicking, she became accepted as a holy inhabitant of the Eternal City. It may be that *The Book* reflects how the conflict in Lynn had repercussions on one prominent family and how it intensified but eventually helped to resolve their more personal problems.

This issue of Margery and the politics of Lynn is one among many which can be pursued in the hope of illuminating the attitudes projected in and underlying *The Book* and their roots in a provincial society. Admittedly, on some issues the light that can be cast is flickering and uncertain. Nevertheless, let us rehearse some others which have been discussed or touched on. What light does *The Book* throw on attitudes to royal government and to the nobility? It contains no criticism of kings and princes to parallel St Bridget's. The favour which Henry IV's half-sister, the Countess of Westmorland, is said to have shown to Margery parallels that which her brother Thomas Beaufort showed to Lynn, though the episode demonstrated that it could be dangerous for someone of lower status to become closely involved in the family affairs of great personages. Some of their – and the Crown's – agents (the Duke of Bedford's yeomen and the steward of Leicester) are handled critically. Perhaps this attitude accorded with bad memories in Lynn of the intrusion of royal agents to override its liberties when he was guardian of the realm during Henry V's absences in France.[5] *The Book's* accounts of Margery's 'persecutions' as a suspected heretic in 1417 at the hands of such agents and of a mayor and clerics give a powerful impression of how effectively government policy might be implemented, though in the case of Lancastrian measures against heresy, it was a policy strongly approved in the elites and (as episodes in *The Book* suggest) among the populace at large.

Assumptions made about English society in general and its relationships with the rest of the world are instructive. Journeys between towns in the lowland parts of England are shown as generally safe and comfortable for pilgrims and other travellers of high social status. Though Margery sometimes encountered hostility in the many cities and towns which she went to or passed through, their inhabitants are not treated as hostile by nature. At Leicester the people commiserate on the treatment which she has received at the hands of the secular authorities there. Favourable notices of English townsfolk accord with the men of Lynn's co-operation with them in internal and coastal trade. Lynn was notable in 1389 in having a well-established gild of young merchants which had come to attract young merchants from other towns.[6] Another possible reason for the favourable views of other towns and regions in *The Book* is the likely hope that it might attract a wide readership, for instance in Norwich and York. *The Book* provides valuable testimony too of attitudes in Lynn to aliens and to foreign parts. It reveals the complexity of relations in particular with 'Duchemen' and 'Dewchland' – Margery had cause to be grateful to 'Duchemen' in Canterbury, the Holy Land and Rome. It reveals modes of acculturation along trade and pilgrimage routes. It gives a variety of illustrations of how international pilgrimage helped to sustain Christendom as a functioning concept. *The Book* provides remarkable insights into the various types of English pilgrims and pilgrim groups, and the sorts of motives which prompted them.

Let us conclude by discussing the significance of *The Book* as evidence in the context of religious history. In it there is inventively constructed a holy figure which is both traditional and original. In some respects, it is an 'Identikit' figure, which projects opinions strongly held by stern moralists, for instance on the nature of women and the correct ways of marital behaviour. Margery's contempt for the extravagant headgear which she formerly flaunted echoes a particular theme in the denunciation of female folly.[7] Her reproval of swearing relates to a trend of pious revulsion reflected in representation and vernacular verse. These puritanical reactions expressed the view that injury was inflicted on Christ by the blasphemous invocation of various parts of God's body. A vivid representation of it, dating from c. 1400, is to be found in a wall-painting in Broughton church (Bucks.). This depicts the Virgin Mary with Christ lying across her lap. In Dr Christopher Woodforde's words: 'The figure of Christ has the right leg ending at the ankle and the right arm at the elbow. In all the limbs the bones show through the flesh, Around this central group are placed fashionably dressed young men. The first holds an arm, the second a head, the third a heart, the fourth bones, the fifth two large bones, the sixth bones and a wafer, the seventh a bone in his left hand and a foot in his right hand. In the lower part of the picture there are two youths at a gaming-table. One, who holds a dagger, is being struck on the head by the other with a sword.'[8] Margery would have thoroughly approved of the moral!

If we did not have *The Book*, we would not have such rich and startling detail about the vibrancy of a particular urban religious culture and its resonances of such pious trends. There was, the evidence of *The Book* shows, a buzz in Lynn among some clergy and laity about contemplative devotion, and about some unexpected as well as familiar cults. Margery is proclaimed as a spiritual athlete in meditative discipline of international stature. She is portrayed as exceptional, but presumably this was not meant to discourage others from aspiring to develop this sort of devotional muscle – indeed, she is represented as helping a priest to do so. The prayers at the end, concentrated on the focuses of her devotion, at any rate relate it to the needs and concerns of the spiritual couch potato who did not have her sort of hot line to Christ and the Blessed Virgin Mary. The messages that came down it sometimes contradicted the precepts of Margery's confessors and the conventions of behaviour prescribed by the Church and society. Should one therefore see her as paradigmatic of a certain lay mentality which was to stimulate and embrace the Reformation, struggling to reconcile conventional religion with an individual response to the New Testament? I think not. Her problem in this respect was inherent in the way of mysticism, as may well have been understood by her tolerant spiritual mentors. Moreover, they may have understood, too, that her defiances were partly inspired by impeccably orthodox, dog-eared sources – the *Legenda Aurea* and its derivatives. The pious invention of Margery as slapped down by clerics and reviled by the crowd had origins in the tribulations of martyrs (who were like her trying to savour the Passion).

Versions of their lives in the vernacular were popular in East Anglia, catered for notably by John Capgrave and Osbern Bokenham.[9] We know, from *The Book* and from other sources, that there were anchorites, anchoresses and vowesses around with more time than the typical merchant venturer or housewife to study such hagiographies and the literature of contemplation. Why, then, do we not have a multitude of treatises in the vernacular from the period about others illuminated in ways similar to Margery? According to *The Book*, Bishop Repingdon and other great clerks were eager for Margery to have her feelings written down. If so, surely she was not solitary in receiving such encouragement. Perhaps an inhibiting factor for aspiring quills was fear of being pounced on as unorthodox. One of the defining characters of the 'English heresy' was that it promoted and fed off devotional writings in the vernacular. Margery manifestly had a boldness of character likely to take her crashing through any such barrier, but even she hesitated for long before having her feelings written down – and a good deal of *The Book* was taken up with parading her orthodox credentials. Moreover, she had a particular reason for providing a definitive account of her piety, besides defending her orthodoxy, promoting the cause of her holiness and stimulating individual reformation. Her supposedly notorious physical transformations (sometimes with similarities to diabolical possession) needed a rational analysis and explanation. If others who were illuminated had felt equal compulsions to write, they might have augmented the influence of tried and tested meditative manuals in reinforcing and deepening the inner meanings of communal rituals and cults for pious individuals. The mechanistic use of them and concerns about the accretion of legends around them were among the elements which were to worry rational and better-informed disciples of the New Testament in the later part of the fifteenth century.

If the effects of Lollardy and its persecutions were to stifle a proliferation of new exemplars for patterns of holy living in the autobiographical genre, they may have limited the influence of an eremitically influenced culture which encouraged the individual's exploration of religiosity within the traditional liturgical and ritual framework. If so, Lollardy can be accounted a powerful force which unwittingly helped to keep a crucial spiritual field fallow, ready for the scattering of Reformation doctrines. So *The Book of Margery Kempe* stands out as singular, not as an example of an accepted English genre, as Wynkyn de Worde's practical publisher's decision to gut it implies.

NOTES

Chapter 1

1. *B.M.K.*, Introduction.
2. Ib., xxxiii.
3. Ib., xxxii.
4. For these and other annotations, ib., xxxv ff.
5. Ker, N.R. (1941) *Medieval Libraries of Great Britain*, London: Royal Historical Society, 73, 220; Knowles, D. (1955) *The Religious Orders in England*, ii, Cambridge: U.P., 222–6. For asceticism at Mount Grace in this period, and mystical treatises written by its monks Richard Methley (1452–1528) and Prior John Norton (d. 1521/2), Dickens, A.G. (1989) *The English Reformation*, London: Collins, 33–6.
6. Gasquet, F.A. (1906) *Henry VIII and the English Monasteries*, London: George Bell and Sons, 355.
7. Ker, 98, 102–3.
8. *B.M.K.*, xlvi–xlvii.
9. Ib., xlvii–xlviii.
10. *The Book of Margery Kempe 1436*, London: Jonathan Cape; *B.M.K.*, 9, 109, 111, 243.
11. References to the text in the following pages are given to both this edition and Dr Windeatt's.
12. *The Book of Margery Kempe* and a dramatisation based on it featured on BBC Radio 4's *Woman's Hour* in September 2000. I owe thanks to Mrs Monica Angold for alerting me to this. For a new translation, see Staley, L. (ed.) (2001) *The Book of Margery Kempe*, New York: W.W. Norton & Co. Inc.
13. I have been told that K.B. McFarlane on one occasion expressed considerable irritation with Margery Kempe. He used *The Book* minimally in his published works, and it was not on the agenda when I was privileged as an undergraduate to be tutored by him in fifteenth-century English history.
14. Le Roy Ladurie, E. (1978) *Montaillou: Cathars in a French village, 1294–1324*, London: Scolar Press.
15. For some Lynn wills from the fifteenth century, see below, 59–60, 84, 86.
16. For example, Atkinson, C.W. (1983) *Mystic and Pilgrim: The Book and the World of Margery Kempe*, Cornell U.P.; Hirsch, J.C. (1989) *The Revelations of Margery Kempe. Paramystical Practices in Late Medieval England*, Leiden: E.J. Brill; Lochrie, K. (1991) *Margery Kempe and Translations of the Flesh*, Philadelphia: Pennsylvania U.P.; Staley, L. (1994) *Margery Kempe's*

Dissenting Fictions, University Park, Pennsylvania: Pennsylvania State University Press. For a good introduction to Margery and her background, finely illustrated, see Gallyon, M. (1995) *Margery Kempe of Lynn and Medieval England*, Norwich: The Canterbury Press. For an interpretative essay on the historiography of *The Book*, see Kettle, A.J. (forthcoming), 'Kempe, Margery (c. 1373 [–] c. 1439)' in Loades, D. (ed.), *Reader's Guide to British History*, London: Fitzroy Dearborn. I owe thanks to Ms Kettle for allowing me to refer to this article.

17. *The Tablet*, clxviii, no. 5033 (24 October 1936), 570–1; *The Month*, no. 869 (November 1936), 446–56; cf. Allen in *B.M.K.*, lxv.

18. The couch is rejected for the surgery by Stork, N.P. (1997) 'Did Margery Kempe suffer from Tourette's syndrome?', *Medieval Studies*, lix, 261–300. This article helpfully classifies the terms used in *The Book* to describe Margery's physical symptoms during her contemplations. I owe thanks for this reference to Professor Michael Angold.

19. *B.M.K.*, 6; Windeatt, 38. For Margery's devotion to the cult of St Mary Magdalene, see below, 107, 121, 240, n 86.

20. *B.M.K.*, 5–6; Windeatt, 38.

21. *B.M.K.*, 1–5; Windeatt, 33–7.

22. *B.M.K.*, 4; Windeatt, 36.

23. *B.M.K.*, 221; Windeatt, 265; Voragine, Jacobus de, trans. Ryan, W.G. (1993) *The Golden Legend*, Princeton: U.P., 249–50.

24. *B.M.K.*, 221; Windeatt, 265.

25. *B.M.K.*, 248–54; Windeatt, 292–7.

26. *B.M.K.*, 3; Windeatt, 35.

27. *B.M.K.*, 45; Windeatt, 80–1.

28. *B.M.K.*, 111; Windeatt, 148–9.

29. Aston, M. (1984) 'Devotional literacy' in *Lollards and Reformers*, London: Hambledon, 101–33.

30. *B.M.K.*, 141–4; Windeatt, 181–2.

31. *B.M.K.*, 112–13; Windeatt, 150. Margery is described as 'not lettered' (*B.M.K.*, 128; Windeatt, 167).

32. Owen, 138. Erl and Brunham had been among those appointed in 1389 to enquire into lepers at Lynn (ib., 215).

33. *B.M.K.*, 88; Windeatt, 124. This was part of the chant proclaimed by the multitudes who went before Christ on His entry to Jerusalem (*Matthew*, xxi, 9). It will have been especially familiar to Margery through its use in the common preface before the canon of the Mass.

34. *B.M.K.*, 121; Windeatt, 159.

35. *B.M.K.*, 235–6; Windeatt, 279–80.

36. See below, 170.

37. For evidence about girls being taught to read, see Orme, N. (1999) 'Children and literature in medieval England', *Medium Aevum*, lxviii, 225, 232–3, 240. St Anne was often represented as teaching children to read; see also Lewis, K.J. (1998) 'The life of St Margaret of Antioch in late medieval

England: a gendered reading' in Swanson, R.N. (ed.), *Gender and Christian religion. Studies in church history*, 34, Woodbridge, Suffolk and Rochester, New York: Ecclesiastical History Society/Boydell, 135. *The Book*'s account of St Anne does not show her in this role (*B.M.K.*, 18; Windeatt, 52–3). The Bolton Book of Hours, which may have been produced for a citizen of York, depicts St Bridget penning her Revelations (see below, 137), one respect in which Margery conspicuously failed to follow her exemplar.

38. *B.M.K.*, 142, 168–9; Windeatt, 181, 208.

39. Aston, M. (1980) 'Lollard women priests?', *J.E.H.*, xxxi, 441–61, reprinted in *Lollards and Reformers*, 49–70.

40. *B.M.K.*, 4, 6; Windeatt, 35, 38.

41. *B.M.K.*, vii–viii. Meech and Allen were sceptical of this theory.

42. Ib., 4; Windeatt, 35–6.

43. *B.M.K.*, 4–5; Windeatt, 36–7.

44. See below, 90–1.

45. Most of Chapter 62 is taken up with a presentation of his literary research for parallels to her extreme weeping, and of how these in their early stages converted him from rejection of Margery (*B.M.K.*, 152–4; Windeatt, 191–3). Chapter 75 is an account of how a woman became insane and had to be put under restraint after childbirth, and of how she was calmed by Margery's ministrations and cured after her prayers. It concludes with the amanuensis's reactions: he accounted the recovery 'a right great miracle', having never seen anyone so out of reason restored to normalcy (*B.M.K.*, 177–9; Windeatt, 216–19). Sometimes, when writing out *The Book*, he could not refrain from weeping, apparently stimulated by Margery's like behaviour as he wrote – a personal testimony to involuntary devout tears (*B.M.K.*, 219; Windeatt, 260). Cf. also below, 114, 239, n 66.

46. *B.M.K.*, 221, 234; Windeatt, 265, 278.

47. *B.M.K.*, 247; Windeatt, 292.

48. For an abbreviated translation of the *Vita Caroli*, Jarrett, B. (1935) *The Emperor Charles IV*, London: Eyre & Spottiswoode, 33–68. For earlier examples of medieval autobiography and the subject in general, see Morris, C. (1972) *The Discovery of the Individual 1050–1200*, London: The Society for Promoting Christian Knowledge; Clanchy, M.T. (1997) *Abelard. A Medieval Life*, Oxford: Clarendon Press, 122–4.

49. Taylor, F. and Roskell, J.S. (1975) *Gesta Henrici Quinti*, Oxford: Clarendon Press, 76–99.

50. Morris, especially Chapter 4; Clanchy, 122–4.

51. Lancaster, Henry of, (ed.) Arnould, E.J. (1940) *Le Livre de Seyntz Medicines*, Oxford: Blackwell; Fowler, K. (1969) *The King's Lieutenant. Henry of Grosmont, First Duke of Lancaster 1310–1361*, London: Elek, 193–6.

52. Clanchy, 124.

53. See below, 112–13.

54. Fowler, 193.

NOTES

Chapter 2

1. Roskell, J.S. *et al.* (1992) *The History of Parliament. The House of Commons 1386–1421*, 4 vols, Stroud: Alan Sutton for History of Parliament Trust, i, 513; Twemlow, J.A. (ed.) (1906) *Calendar of Entries in the Papal Registers Relating to Great Britain and Ireland. Papal Letters*, vii, 1417–31, London: Stationery Office, 441–2. The poll tax of 1377 indicates that the tax-paying population was then 3,217 and that Lynn ranked seventh in wealth among provincial towns (Parker, V. (1971) *The Making of King's Lynn*, Chichester: Phillimore, 4). I owe thanks to Mrs Katherine Parker for commenting on the sections of this chapter on government and politics in Lynn.
2. Cameron, H.K. (1979) 'The fourteenth-century Flemish brasses at King's Lynn', *Archaeological Journal*, cxxxvi, 152–66; *B.M.K.*, 9; Windeatt, 43–4. The brass of Adam de Walsokne (d. 1349) and his wife Margaret, also in St Margaret's church, is similar in provenance and general character to that of the Braunches.
3. For the topography and development of Lynn, I have relied heavily on Owen, op. cit. Chapter 1 of Parker, *The Making of King's Lynn*, provides an excellent introduction to topography and trade.
4. Owen, 5–12.
5. Ib., 16. For the origins and evolution of Holy Trinity Gild, ib., 61.
6. Ib., 21–2; Parker, *The Making of King's Lynn*, 137–40; Richards, P. (1997) *King's Lynn*, Chichester: Phillimore, 8.
7. Parker, Chapter 3, quotation, 56; Owen, 22–6; Richards, xiv.
8. Owen, 41–51.
9. Ib., 49–50; Aston, M. (1967) *Thomas Arundel*, Oxford: U.P., 229, 265, 267.
10. *Derby's Expeditions*, xlvii, 151–3, 155–62, 270.
11. K.L.R.O., KL/C38/7 (Holy Trinity Gild account).
12. KL/C38/8 (Holy Trinity Gild account).
13. *B.M.K.*, 202–3; Windeatt, 243–4.
14. In 1412, for instance, William Oliver, citizen and grocer of London, appointed John Cross, burgess of Lynn, and John Warren, citizen and grocer of London, as his attorneys (Asshebourne, no. 19).
15. Owen, 138. For Wesenham's high poll tax assessment in 1379, see below, 21.
16. *S.A.C.*, 103; Capgrave, John, Hingeston, F.C. (ed.) (1858) *The Chronicle of England*, London: Rolls series, 316.
17. For licences for a Newcastle merchant to load ox hides in the port and ship them either to London or Lynn, *C.P.R., 1374–1377*, 210, 250, 254.
18. Owen, 47–9.
19. Asshebourne, no. 83.
20. Owen, 331, 335–6.
21. Carus-Wilson, E.M. (1954) *Medieval Merchant Venturers*, London: Methuen, 102–25.
22. Asshebourne, nos 211–12.
23. Ingleby, f200.

24. Owen, 331–3. For Kempe's losses, see below; for Brunham's losses, see below.
25. KL/C7/231–2. For Margery's son, see below, 67.
26. Owen, 54.
27. Cf. for a study of succession rates among London citizens: Thrupp, S.L. (1948) *The Merchant Class of Medieval London 1300–1500*, London: Michigan U.P., 198–203.
28. Gransden, A. (1957) 'A fourteenth-century chronicle from the Grey Friars at Lynn', *E.H.R.*, lxxii, 275; Gottfried, R.S. (1978) *Epidemic Disease in Fifteenth Century England*, Leicester U.P., 2, 143–4. The Franciscan annalist noted that in 1369 there was a great plague among nobles (*magnatum*) and boys (ib., 277; for this chronicle, see below, 86). Lynn was one of the first ports of entry for the Black Death. The brethren of the gild of St James recalled in 1389 that a majority of their brethren had died in the great pestilence (Westlake, H.F. (1919) *The Parish Gilds of Mediaeval England*, London: Society for Promoting Christian Knowledge, 194). For plague and the gilds, see also below, 94.
29. *B.M.K.*, 17; Windeatt, 51. Margery considered storms, lightning, thunder, rain and earthquakes to be tokens from Christ, in some cases not to people in general, but especially to her (*B.M.K.*, 48, 95, 101, 103–4, 182–3, 185–6, 202, 229–30; Windeatt, 84, 132, 138, 141, 222–3, 226, 243, 273–4).
30. Owen, 57–9.
31. Cf. ib., on the possible identification of craft gilds and associations of craftsmen. For the poll tax returns, ib., 221–32.
32. Ib., 39–40.
33. Ib., 40.
34. Ib., 34.
35. Asshebourne, nos 73–4.
36. Owen, 36–7; *C.C.R.*, *1402–1405*, 30–1. I owe thanks to Mrs Parker for the last reference, and for information as to the probable location of the Tolbooth. For the Black Prince's share in the Tolbooth, *Register of the Black Prince*, iv, 1351–65 (1933), London: Stationery Office, 267–8, 396, 432, 531–2, 550. He leased it to John de Sustede of Lynn in 1358 and to Thomas Clerc of Ely in 1362.
37. Asshebourne, no. 75. Tenants of the share of the Tolbooth attached to Castle Rising in Richard II's reign, when it was in the Crown's hands in the absence of a king's son, were John, Duke of Brittany (1378) and Richard II's uncle, Edmund of Langley, Duke of York (1396) (Jones, M. (1970) *Ducal Brittany 1364–1399*, Oxford U.P., 175–83; *H.M.C.*, *Lynn*, 245, citing chamberlain's account for 22 Ric. II, dated 20 September 1398). In 1378 it was leased to a wealthy burgess of Lynn, Geoffrey de Tolbothe, for 40 m (£26 13s 4d) (*C.I.M.*, *1377–88*, no. 76). In 1397 the farm was valued at only half that amount – which may have been a deliberate undervaluation rather than a reflection of a decline in trade (*C.I.M.*, *1392–1399*, no. 265).

38. Ormrod, W.M. (1990) *The Reign of Edward III*, London: Guild Publishing, 56, 221–2.

39. Thompson, E.M. (ed.) (1874) *Chronicon Angliae*, London: Rolls series, 139–40. Henry Despenser had apparently stayed at the priory in Lynn in the mayoral year 1375–6; the mayor and jurats had sent him wine there (Harrod, 83).

40. *C.P.R., 1374–1377*, 502. The rioters included a tailor, a mercer, two glovers and a skinner.

41. Harrod, 84, citing chamberlain's account for 50 Ed. III–1 Ric. II.

42. 'Grey Friars Chronicle', 278.

43. *R.R.*, ii, 132.

44. Harrod, 84, citing chamberlain's account, 50 Ed. III–1 Ric. II. The community offered a wax candle in Norwich cathedral, weighing 21lb and costing 13s 5d, to end its discord with the bishop.

45. Capgrave, *The Chronicle of England*, 138; Powell, E. (1896) *The Rising in East Anglia in 1381*, Cambridge: U.P., 28, 35–6, 134–5; *C.P.R., 1374–1377*, 502. For the 1379 poll tax, Coventry paid, above the minimum, 6d, and Whetewong paid the minimum, 4d (Owen, 221, 230).

46. *H.M.C., Lynn*, 223. The chamberlain's account for 1384–5 recorded costs of the community's presents to the bishop, and that for 1388–9 the cost of the mayor's entertainment of him to dinner in 1388.

47. Alexander, J. and Binski, P. (1987) *Age of Chivalry. Art in Plantagenet England 1200–1400*, London: Royal Academy of Arts and Weidenfeld and Nicolson, 516–17.

48. *Derby's Expeditions*, 273, 278; *C.P.R., 1399–1401*, 291; Riley, H.T. (ed.) (1866) *Johannis de Trokelowe . . . Chronica et Annales*, London: Rolls series, 332–3; Wylie, J.H. (1884) *History of England under Henry the Fourth*, i, London: Longmans, Green, 132. A ship called the *Holigost* of Lynn took part in transporting Henry V's expedition to France in 1415 (*C.P.R., 1413–1416*, 382). For the authorship of the *Annales* and other historical works of the period produced at St Albans abbey, see Clark, J.G. (forthcoming), 'Thomas Walsingham Reconsidered: Books and Learning at Late Medieval St Albans', *Speculum*.

49. Hingeston, F.C. (1860) *Royal Letters, Henry IV*, i, London: Stationery Office, Rolls series, 40–3.

50. Given-Wilson, C. (1993) *Chronicles of the Revolution 1397–1400*, Manchester: U.P., 34–5, 50, 120, 250; Kirby, J.L. (1970) *Henry IV of England*, London: Constable, 89–90. There may have been an attempt to rally support for Richard in Lynn. Asshebourne recorded a mandate from the sheriff of Norfolk (William Rees), ordering a proclamation to summon all knights, esquires and others defensibly arrayed in the shire to meet the Duke of York at Oxford. This was dated St Albans, 10 July (Asshebourne, no. 87). The royal council at St Albans was trying to raise forces for the Regent, York, to oppose Bolingbroke. York's tenure of the Tolbooth gave him a link with Lynn (see 216, n 37 and 219, n 70). In a letter which Dr

Owen dated as c. 1400 from the mayor, he referred to the royal share of the Tolbooth as 'est avoir tres redoute sire le prince monsieur de Lancastre' (Owen, 103–4). Could this curious statement, with its odd way of referring presumably to Bolingbroke, have been written in August or September 1399, when Richard was in his hands but as yet undeposed? If so, it would show the mayor, Edmund Belleyetere (former apprentice of Margery's putative father), trying to be circumspect in uncertain times.

51. *C.P.R., 1401–1405*, 67. For the location of the bishop's staithe, Owen, 18.
52. *C.P.R., 1401–1405*, 274. The Percies had acquired a potential power base in East Anglia through their appointment by Henry IV in November 1399 as principal administrators of the Mortimer estates, including the honour of Clare. The Earl of Northumberland less than a fortnight afterwards secured the appointment of a knight from Northumberland, Thomas Swinburne, as steward of the honour. Two days after the battle of Shrewsbury he was deprived of the office. Erpingham was granted the keeping of the honour in November 1403 (Dunn, A.J. (2000) 'The endowment and disendowment of lay magnates in England and the Welsh marches, 1396–1408', Oxford D.Phil., 252–5).
53. Legge, M.D. (1941) *Anglo-Norman Letters and Petitions*, Oxford: Blackwell, 46–7, 368–9.
54. Ib., 370–1.
55. Ib., 50, 112, 370–1; *C.C.R., 1402–1405*, 30–1. For past tenure of the king's share of the Tolbooth, see above, 216, n 37.
56. Ib., 45–6.
57. Ib., 92. For Northumberland's loss of control of the honour of Clare, see above, n 52. For a writ of *supersedeas* in the bishop's case, addressed to the justices of assize at Norwich, and mandate to the sheriff not to execute judgement, see a letter dated 5 August 1404 (*C.C.R., 1402–1405*, 384). Judgement in the case, brought by the bishop against Mayor John Wyntworth, Thomas Drewe, Thomas Brygges, John Kenynghale and the whole community of Lynn, which concerned a messuage, 100 acres of land and 20 of pasture, had been given in the plaintiff's favour at Norwich on the previous day. Henry IV acted swiftly to bring the parties into his presence to effect a settlement (KL/C10/2, f19v; Asshebourne, no. 54).
58. *Anglo-Norman Letters and Petitions*, no. 103.
59. Asshebourne, no. 103.
60. Ib., no. 94.
61. Ingleby, f37–8. Wakeryng died on 9 April 1425.
62. Asshebourne, no. 294.
63. For Courtenay, Taylor and Roskell, *Gesta Henrici Quinti*, 44–5 and 44, n. 2 and Catto, J. (1985) 'Religious change under Henry V', in Harriss, G.L. (ed.), *Henry V. The Practice of Kingship*, Oxford: U.P., 57–8. For Bishop Wakeryng's co-operation over water courses, see below, 48.
64. Ingleby, f67.
65. Ib., f67–8.

66. *B.M.K.*, 167; Windeatt, 207.
67. Jones, *Ducal Brittany*, 175–83. For the favour to Brunham, see below.
68. *Register of Edward the Black Prince*, iv, 531–2. Cf. above, 216, n 37.
69. Harrod, 3. The community of Lynn gave to the king £66 13s 4d in gold, six falcons and £23 6s 8d; they gave the queen (Ann of Bohemia) two gilt cups. The total cost of the visit was the large sum of £161 18s 5d. The information was derived by Harrod from an antiquary's summary of a lost chamberlain's account. There is no reason to doubt it – it fits in with what is known of the royal itinerary in East Anglia and the East Midlands that month (see Saul, N. (1997) *Richard II*, New Haven and London: Yale U.P., 470).
70. Aston, *Arundel*, 84–5, 385. Gifts to the Duke and Duchess of York, and to their son Edward, recently created Duke of Aumale, were recorded in the chamberlain's account for 1398–9 (K.L.R.O., KL/C39/42). For York's lease of the Tolbooth, see above, 216, n 37. The grant to Aumale by the Crown of the custody of the Mortimer properties in the honour of Clare gave him fleetingly in 1398–9 an important power base in East Anglia (Dunn, 251).
71. K.L.R.O., KL/C39/47. For Willoughby, *C.P.*, xii, part ii, 261–3; below, 188. For the Roos family and their devotion to St William of York, see below, 135.
72. K.L.R.O., KL/C38/11; *C.P.*, iv, 150–1. Warr held prebends in York Minster and Lincoln cathedral.
73. Ib., i, 419–20; *C.P.R., 1399–1401*, 214. I owe thanks for information about Wormegay castle to Mrs Katherine Parker.
74. *The Chronicle of England*, 272; id., ed. Hingeston, F.C. (1858) *Liber de Illustribus Henricis*, London: Rolls series, 117; Wylie, *Henry IV*, ii, 420, 451; Kirby, J.L. (1970), *Henry IV of England*, London: Constable, 202.
75. Harrod, 86.
76. Ib., 104.
77. Ib., 106; Allmand, C. (1992), *Henry V*, London: Methuen, 160.
78. Ingleby, f78. Beaufort had been appointed Chancellor on 16 July. In Congregation on 27 July it was agreed that the chamberlains should pay the expenses of his men and household during his stay (ib., f79r). On his way to Walsingham in 1428, Beaufort reached Lynn by 1 October (Harriss, G.L. (1988), *Cardinal Beaufort. A Study in Lancastrian Ascendancy and Decline*, Oxford: Clarendon Press, 178).
79. Capgrave, *Liber de Illustribus Henricis*, 137–9; Wolffe, B. (1981) *Henry VI*, London: Eyre Methuen, 25–6.
80. *C.P.*, v, 201–3; Goodman, A. (1992) *John of Gaunt*, London: Longman, 365–6.
81. Ingleby, f84–5.
82. *C.P.R., 1405–1408*, 443; *C.P.*, v, 201; Asshebourne, nos 293, 294, 297.
83. KL/C10/2, f54v–r; Asshebourne no. 163; cf. below, 36–7. Beaufort's fellow commissioners included Sir Thomas Erpingham and Edmund Oldhall.

84. Ib., f57v–59 and no. 232.
85. *C.P.R., 1416–1422*, 456. Beaufort may have been omitted from the 1422 commission because he was heavily involved in the war in France.
86. Asshebourne, no. 61.
87. Ib., no. 149.
88. Ingleby, f90.
89. Ib., f47.
90. K.L.R.O., KL/C39/47.
91. Asshebourne, no. 79.
92. Ingleby, f78 (17 July). At the previous Congregation (1 July), it had been determined how the duke was to be greeted. The mayor and his associates, clad in scarlet robes, were to go on foot, and the jurats and their followers were to go with the rest of the burgesses of the Common Council (ib., f75r).
93. Ib., f78.
94. Jacob, E.F. (ed.) (1938–47) *The Register of Henry Chichele: Archbishop of Canterbury, 1414–1443*, 4 vols, Oxford: Clarendon Press, ii, 355–64. For Beaufort's possible connection with Lynn friars, see below, 87.
95. Worcestre, William (1969) Harvey, J.H. (ed.), *Itineraries*, Oxford: U.P., 354–7; *History of Parliament. House of Commons 1386–1421*, iv, 617–18.
96. See below, 132–3.
97. Cf. below, 46–7.
98. *H.M.C., Lynn*, 191–2, citing memorandum drawn up between parties.
99. Strachey, J. *et al.* (ed.) (1783) *Rotuli Parliamentorum*, London: Record Commission, iii, 565 (under parliament held at Coventry in the autumn of 1404); Kirby, J.L. (ed.) (1978) *Calendar of Signet Letters of Henry IV and Henry V*, London: Stationery Office, no. 557; cf. above, 34. For their trades, P.R.O., KB27/580, Rex, m 5r. I owe thanks for this reference to Dr Philip Morgan. Cole was probably the William Colles styled *mediocris* in 1411–12, when he was party to an attempt to end the current disputes, and the William Cole, tailor, indicted in 1416 for riotous behaviour (Owen, 392–3; KB9/188, m 9–11).
100. K.B. 27/580, Rex, m 5; *C.P.R., 1405–1408*, 248. The sureties named on the King's Bench roll were Henry Welles, clerk, of Norfolk, John Colman of London and John Hauberk of Lincoln.
101. Owen, 392–3, 404–5.
102. For the summonses before Beaufort, see above, 34; for the summons of Petypas, Asshebourne, no. 46.
103. *H.M.C., Lynn*, 191–4; Asshebourne, nos 31, 146; Owen, 392–3; *B.M.K.*, 22, 368; Windeatt, 57. Brekeropp was elected mayor in 1432. He was the alderman of Holy Trinity Gild when, under the year 1438, a Margery Kempe was mentioned in the account roll of one of its *scabini* (*B.M.K.*, 358). Brekeropp had a tenement in that year in Mercerrowe (KL/C50/233) [Be 237, 236]; cf. KL/C50/236 [Be 243]). I owe thanks for the last references to Ms Susan Maddock.

104. *B.M.K.*, 372.
105. KL/C10/2, f34v–35r; *H.M.C., Lynn*, 191–4.
106. *History of Parliament. House of Commons 1386–1421*, ii, 175–6.
107. *H.M.C., Lynn*, 193–4.
108. *C.I.M.*, vii, *1399–1422*, no. 517; Owen, 392 (Bilney, 1411). For the lawyer Tilney's connection with Beaufort, see above, 34. In August 1412 John Tilney delivered a letter to the mayor (Roger Galyon) from Bishop Tottington, who excused himself from coming to Lynn to discuss the troubles, on the grounds that he had been summoned to the king's presence in London. The bishop sounded concerned; tensions were probably rising because of the imminent mayoral election (KL/C10/2, 12r–v; Asshebourne, no. 33).
109. *C.I.M., 1399–1422*, no. 517.
110. Ib.; Asshebourne, no. 213. The glazier, John Warden, was among those indicted in 1416 for riotous behaviour (KB 9/188, m 9–11). Edmund Oldhall esquire was the Duchy of Lancaster receiver in Norfolk and Suffolk, j.p. in Norfolk, and had represented Norfolk three times in parliament. He was an executor of Bishop Tottington of Norwich (Somerville, R. (1953) *History of the Duchy of Lancaster*, i, London: Chancellor and Council of the Duchy of Lancaster, 596).
111. *C.C.R., 1413–1419*, 148. Tilney's other surety was Nicholas Lymnour of Norwich.
112. *C.I.M., 1399–1422*, no. 517; Owen, 393–4.
113. Asshebourne. nos 213–14.
114. *C.P.R., 1413–16*, 545.
115. Owen, 394–5.
116. *C.I.M., 1399–1422*, no. 517; *C.P.R., 1413–1416*, 345. The commissioners were Oliver Groos, John Glenham, John Norwich and Richard Lound.
117. See above, 39–40.
118. Asshebourne, no. 232. KB 9/188, m 9 refers to the disturbances surrounding the 1415 election.
119. Ib., 396. Mrs Katherine Parker informs me that, as alderman of Holy Trinity Gild, Brunham would have automatically deputised if need be for the mayor.
120. Asshebourne's narrative (f105v–109) is printed by Owen, 396–400. For Littlebury's career in royal service, Given-Wilson, C. (1986) *The Royal Household and the King's Affinity. Service, Politics and Finance in England 1360–1413*, New Haven: Yale U.P., 195–6; Somerville, 575.
121. *C.P.R., 1413–19*, 409.
122. Owen, 401; text of Asshebourne's narrative.
123. *C.P.R., 1413–19*, 232.
124. Ib., 411. The other commissioners were Thomas Derham, Richard Peverel, Oliver Groos and the sheriff. Peverel was a servant of the Duke of Exeter (Asshebourne, no. 328). Perhaps he was related to the Bishop of Worcester with the same surname who summoned Margery in 1417 (see below, 129).

125. *C.C.R., 1413–19*, 236; Owen, 392–3 (1411–12 declaration). Sherman was said to be a shearman in the 1416 indictment (KB 9/188).

126. Ib., m 10; Powell, E. (1989) *Kingship, Law, and Society. Criminal Justice in the Reign of Henry V*, Oxford: U.P., 245 and 245 n. The jurors were Thomas Brygge (*potencioris*), William Hunderpound (*p.*), Andrew Swanton (*p.*), Ralph Badyngham (*p.*), Thomas Botesham, John Drew (*mediocris*), William Badyngham (*m.*), Henry Drew (*m.*), Robert Hadle, John Castelacre, Henry Erl (*m.*) and John Sidesteree (cf. Owen, 392–3). Eleven tailors were indicted, five goldsmiths, four shearmen, three skinners, three souters, two fletchers, two glaziers, two mercers, a baxter, a locksmith, a fisher, an hostler, a barber, a brasier, a fuller, a smith, a hosier and a leadbeater. Dr Powell cites for the fines KB 27/621, fines section, m 1d.

127. *C.P.R., 1416–22*, 3.

128. Owen, 404–5, printing copy of letter from Asshebourne, f101v.

129. Asshebourne, no. 281.

130. Ib., no. 100.

131. Owen, 401–4, printing Asshebourne, f114v.

132. K.L.R.O., KL/C4/11.

133. *H.M.C. Lynn*, 245–6.

134. Myers, M.D. (1996) 'Well-nigh ruined?: Violence in King's Lynn 1380–1420', Notre Dame, Indiana Ph.D. Exports of raw wool, running at nearly 2,000 sacks towards the end of the fourteenth century, fell to below 100 sacks in the mid 1400s, but picked up to over 1,000 sacks, 1409–10, 1413–14, 1414–15. The total again fell below 100 sacks in 1419–20, and remained at that low into the 1440s. Exports of cloth fell from over 3,000 cloths to well below 2,000 in 1409–10, but into the 1420s there was some recovery, with the number of cloths exported steadying up towards 2,000 (Carus-Wilson, E.M. and Coleman, O. (1963), *England's Export Trade 1275–1547*, Oxford: U.P., 134, 152). In her paper, 'Lordship or liberty? Counting the cost in Lynn: 1399–1406', Mrs Parker, in discussing the causes of the town's internal discontents, lays stress on the problems of maintaining consensus about the upholding of the borough liberties in the changed political climate of Henry IV's reign. I owe thanks to Mrs Parker for allowing me to cite her paper.

135. Owen, 392–3; Harrod, 139. Permonter played a mediatory role in the tense situation in Guildhall in 1415 (see above, 43).

136. KL/C7/2, 53; translated passages from Ingleby, f53. Lynn priory was a cell of Norwich cathedral priory: see below, 78–9.

137. *B.M.K.*, 359.

138. John de Brunham was vice-dean of the deanery of Lynn in 1315 (Owen, 130–1). The Black Prince had had clerics called Brunham in his service. Robert de Brunham was prior of Lynn in 1402 (Owen, 123). The Leet and Hustings Roll for 1403–4 mentions Edmund Brunham (K.L.R.O., KL/07/14) and the one dated 28 October 1404 mentions William Brunham (KL/C17/15). Dr C. Scott Stokes surmises that the Isabelle de

Brunham mentioned in the codicil of a Lynn will in 1410 was Margery's mother ('Margery Kempe: her life and the early history of her book' (1999) *Mystics Quarterly*, xxv, nos 1 and 2, 21). I owe thanks for this reference to Ms Susan Maddock. For Isabelle Brunham who had a 'ducheman Taylour' staying in her tenement, possibly in 1425, KL/C7/2, 119. On 14 November 1438 Nicholas Martyn was acting as executor for Juette Brunham, who had bequeathed a large sum (£18 6s 8d) to pay tax for numbers of men (KL/C7/2, 231).

139. *B.M.K.*, 359. Ralph de Brunham was listed as a jurat in 1348–9 but his name was cancelled. A Ralph de Brunham had witnessed a grant of plots of land in South Lynn in 1280/90 (Owen, 153).

140. *R.R.*, ii, 173; text of John Brunham's admission in *B.M.K.*, 359. The vintner Edmund Belleyetere was his apprentice when admitted to the liberty, 13 March 1364 (*R.R.*, ii, 78). For John Brunham's involvement in shipping wine, see below, 65.

141. *B.M.K.*, 359–60.

142. *C.P.R.*, 1385–9, 81. Brunham had been appointed on the commission of array for Lynn and its suburbs dated 29 April 1377, in anticipation of the renewal of war with the French and Castilian Crowns (*C.P.R.*, 1374–7, 500).

143. *B.M.K.*, 360.

144. *C.P.R.*, 1381–5, 291. Though Brunham received the exemption on 8 July 1383, he was appointed j.p. on 20 November (ib., 349). He had been appointed j.p. for Norfolk in 1371 and 1373 (*C.P.R.*, 1370–4, 106, 305).

145. *B.M.K.*, 360–1; P.R.O., E101/93/31. John Brunham was first named among the mayors' councillors in 1399–1401 (KL/C6/2, Hall Rolls, m 1–4). In the Lynn customs accounts, there are few entries for any John Brunham in the 1380s and 1390s, and none for 1400–21 (Myers, 181). For grain shipped by a John Brunham, see Lynn controller of customs' account for 1392–3, printed in Gras, N.S.B. (1918) *The Early English Customs System*, Cambridge, Mass.: Harvard U.P., 549–50.

146. *B.M.K.*, 361. For Herford, see above, 38.

147. Ib.; Owen, 197. Among Herford's three fellow grantees, all burgesses of Lynn, Richard Denby had been classified as *potencioris* and John Mawpas as *mediocris* in 1411–12. The named witnesses were Thomas Brygge and John Brandon, former mayors and leading *potenciores*, Richard Lechour and John Berewyk, *mediocres*, John Goche (draper, *inferioris*), Adam Whyte and Thomas Cumethe (?) (cf. ib., 392–3). The witness list appears to reflect a 'politically correct' intent to include representation from each status group. Brunham's property in Briggate is mentioned in a chamberlain's account for 1401–2 (KL/C39/43). In 1379 John Brunham (probably the father) and Thomas Botekesham, Richard Houton, Henry Betele, Geoffrey Fransham and John Titelyshale, burgesses of Lynn, had leased a messuage in Burghard's Lane and a quay with buildings opposite it to John Bolt, Roger Charleypoynt, vicar of Methwold, and Richard Faukes (KL/C50/203 [Be 395]). I owe thanks for this reference to Ms Susan

Maddock. In 1391–2 John Brunham held property in Stonegate, leased from the borough (Owen, 185). A number of chamberlains' accounts show him leasing it thereafter, e.g. in 1411–12 (KL/C39/48).

148. *B.M.K.*, 361. A John Brunham, hosier, is mentioned in the borough chamberlains' accounts for 1412–13 (Stokes, 19).

149. *B.M.K.*, 366. For the Corpus Christi Gild, see below, 94.

150. A John Brunham appears as one of the twelve electors of the Gild of St Giles and and St Julian on 7 July 1410 and was elected as one of its *scabini* on six occasions between 6 July 1422 and 1431 (ib., 362).

151. Westlake, *Parish Gilds*, 194; cf. below, 97.

152. For a biography of Robert Brunham, see *History of Parliament. The House of Commons 1386–1421*, ii, 395–6.

153. Ingleby, f62.

154. *B.M.K.*, 171–2; Windeatt, 211–12.

155. See below, 116ff.

156. *B.M.K.*, 32–3; Windeatt, 68.

157. *B.M.K.*, 105–6; Windeatt, 142–3.

158. *B.M.K.*, 54, 57–8, 151, 202; Windeatt, 89, 91, 190, 243. For Wyrham, see above, 38, 44.

159. *B.M.K.*, 34–5; Windeatt, 70. In Rome, a 'worshipful lady', Dame Florentyn, 'set her at her own table above herself and laid her meat with her own hands' (*B.M.K.*, 93; Windeatt, 130); for Dame Florentyn[e], cf. below, 163.

160. Furnivall, F.J. (ed.) (1868) John Russell's 'Book of nurture', in *Manners and Meals In Olden Time*, London: E.E.T.S., 185–7.

161. *B.M.K.*, 25–6; Windeatt, 61.

162. *B.M.K.*, 17, 160–2; Windeatt, 53, 200–1.

163. *B.M.K.*, 86; Windeatt, 122.

164. *B.M.K.*, 93; Windeatt, 130.

165. *B.M.K.*, 137; Windeatt, 176. An account submitted by the *scabini* of Holy Trinity Gild for 1392–3 mentions fourteen spoons formerly belonging to Isabel Waterden (*H.M.C., Lynn*, 231). In Congregation on 15 February 1425, two tax collectors pledged three silver spoons as part surety for a debt of 4s 9d (Ingleby, f34).

166. *B.M.K.*, 94; Windeatt, 131.

167. *B.M.K.*, 85–6, 237; Windeatt, 122, 281.

168. See below, 167.

169. *B.M.K.*, 242; Windeatt, 286.

170. *B.M.K.*, 243; Windeatt, 287.

171. See below, 149–50, 163–4.

172. *B.M.K.*, 210–11; Windeatt, 251–2.

173. *B.M.K.*, 11–12; Windeatt, 46.

174. *B.M.K.*, 172; Windeatt, 212.

175. Stone, B. (ed. and trans.) (1959) *Sir Gawain and the Green Knight*, Harmondsworth: Penguin, 897–8.

176. *B.M.K.*, 93; Windeatt, 130.

NOTES

Chapter 3

1. For women's property rights, see Kettle, A.J. (1984) 'My wife shall have it: marriage and property in the wills and testaments of later medieval England', in Craik, E.M. (ed.), *Marriage and Property*, Aberdeen: U.P., 89–103. I owe thanks to Ms Kettle for her comments on this chapter.
2. Sheehan, M.M. (1996), 'Marriage, family and law in medieval Europe', in Farge, J.K. (ed.), *Collected Studies*, Cardiff: U.P., 192.
3. Borthwick Institute, York, Register 17, Register of Henry Bowet, Archbishop of York 1407–23, f291 v. For examples of a bishop dealing with marital problems among humbler folk, Aston, *Arundel*, 39–41.
4. Kettle, 94–6.
5. See above, 105.
6. *B.M.K.*, 212; Windeatt, 253. In the Proem Margery's rejection by her 'kindred' is asserted (*B.M.K.*, 2; Windeatt, 33–4).
7. For what follows, see Leyser, H. (1995) *A Social History of Women in England 450–1500*, London: Orion Books, Chapter 6; Brundage, J.A. (1993) *Sex, Law and Marriage in the Middle Ages*, Aldershot: Variorum, 375–85. For a well-balanced view of medieval marriage, which brings out the positive sides of the Church's contributions to its development as a sacred and stable institution, Brooke, C. (1989) *The Medieval Idea of Marriage*, Oxford: Clarendon Press.
8. Ib., 365.
9. *B.M.K.*, 38–40; Windeatt, 74.
10. Kettle, 90–9.
11. Sheehan, 191–2; Leyser, 161–3.
12. *Chichele Reg.*, iii, 404–6, 410–12. The concern among townsmen of Lynn to balance provision for members of their family and the investment of wealth in the health of their own souls, when deceased, is reflected in Gilbert Watson of Lynn's will of 1479, in which he bequeathed a tenement and curtilage to his daughter Katerine, and a tenement to his daughter Agnes, but only for their lives. The residue of his goods was to be sold for the repose of his soul, under the daughters' direction (K.L.R.O., KL/C12/12).
13. K.L.R.O., KL/C12/11 (Salesbury); N.R.O., 86 Doke (Roper); ib., 83 Wylbey (Cook); 139 Wylbey (Mechyll); KL/C12/9 (Silisden); N.R.O., 121 Doke (Spicer); ib., N.P. 2 Aleyn (Slynghelant). For widows as executors, Kettle, 100.
14. *Chichele Reg.*, iii, 404–6.
15. Ib., 404–6.
16. See above, 45.
17. KL/C7/2, 177–8. Scarlett was adjudged in Congregation to have broken the liberty of the borough and was fined 6s 8d.
18. KL/C7/2, 207. For Draper's case, see below, 172.
19. See above, 45.

20. Toulmin Smith, J. and Toulmin Smith, L.T.S. (ed.) (1870) *English Gilds*, London: E.E.T.S., 94–6; cf. above, 96.
21. See below, 132.
22. Accusation by the mayor of Leicester; cf. below, 141.
23. See above, 53–5.
24. Orme, N. (1994) 'Children and the Church in medieval England', *J.E.H.*, 564ff.
25. Ib., 573–4.
26. Ib., 585.
27. Orme, N. (1995) 'The culture of children in medieval England', *Past and Present*, cxlviii, 51–73; *B.M.K.*, 77–8; Windeatt, 113. Orme, op. cit., 56–8 puts this episode in Italy in context.
28. *B.M.K.*, 31; Windeatt, 66.
29. *B.M.K.*, 31; Windeatt, 67. Despite Margery's well-advertised reverence for her father, her reproach to her husband that he was not of the right status to have married her might be taken to imply resentment at John Brunham's choice of spouse for her (*B.M.K.*, 9; Windeatt, 44).
30. *H.M.C. Lynn*, 223. In 1445 a Nativity play was performed before the mayor of Lynn (Harrod, 88). For a discussion of the problem of Margery's literacy, see above, 7–8.
31. *B.M.K.*, 13; Windeatt, 48.
32. *B.M.K.*, 181; Windeatt, 221.
33. *B.M.K.*, 14–15; Windeatt, 49–50.
34. *B.M.K.*, 144–5; Windeatt, 183–4.
35. For Margery and her confessors, see below, 88ff.
36. *B.M.K.*, 184; Windeatt, 224.
37. See above, 25.
38. *B.M.K.*, 8–9; Windeatt, 42–3.
39. *B.M.K.*, 18–19; Windeatt, 52–3. For her troubles with maidservants on pilgrimages, *B.M.K.*, 33; Windeatt, 68, and below, 166, 199.
40. Owen, 221–32; *B.M.K.*, 19, 195; Windeatt, 53–4, 236.
41. *R.R.*, ii, 171; *B.M.K.*, 363. Margery's husband is said to have been 'a man in great age passing threescore years' when he had a serious accident (*B.M.K.*, 179; Windeatt, 219).
42. Owen, 331–3.
43. Perroy, E. (ed.) (1933) *The Diplomatic Correspondence of Richard II*, London: Royal Historical Society, Camden third ser., xlviii, nos 104–5; P.R.O., E101/93/31 (Particulars of Customs Account); Gras, *The Early English Customs System*, 545–6, 549; *B.M.K.*, 364–5. Mr Harry Schnitker informs me that Osterdam is a drowned village south of Zierekzee, and that 'Kampe' is the modern Camtveer in Holland.
44. *B.M.K.*, 365–6.
45. *R.R.*, ii, 5; *B.M.K.*, 262–3.
46. *R.R.*, ii, 9–10, 15; *B.M.K.*, 363–4.
47. Notably, John does not appear among the long list of sureties pledging in 1411 to abide by the decisions to be made by the Eighteen (cf. above,

38). Might not Margery have been disappointed at his inability to take a part in standing up for the interests of her father and the other *potenciores*?
48. In Dr Myers' tabulation of the entries in the Lynn customs accounts, under the name of John Kempe there were two entries for the period 1388–9, twelve for 1390–9, but none for 1400–9 and 1410–21 ('Well-nigh ruined? Violence in King's Lynn, 1380–1420', 179).
49. *B.M.K.*, 367–8.
50. Ib., 368.
51. *B.M.K.*, 6; Windeatt, 41. The evidence analysed by Dr Jeremy Goldberg suggests that 'teenage marriage, though certainly a real phenomenon, was probably not the norm in post-plague society below the level of the aristocracy'; he cites the evidence about Margery's age at marriage (Goldberg, P.J.P. (1992) *Women, Work, and Life Cycle in a Medieval Economy. Women in York and Yorkshire c. 1300–1520*, Oxford: Clarendon Press, 225–232, esp. 231).
52. *B.M.K.*, 366–7.
53. Ib., 115; Windeatt, 153.
54. *B.M.K.*, 6–9; Windeatt, 41–3.
55. *B.M.K.*, 38–9; Windeatt, 73–5.
56. See above, 20.
57. *B.M.K.*, 48; Windeatt, 84.
58. See above, 19–20.
59. *B.M.K.*, 221–5; Windeatt, 265–9.
60. *B.M.K.*, 31; Windeatt, 66–7.
61. *B.M.K.*, 90; Windeatt, 126.
62. *B.M.K.*, 11–16; Windeatt, 46–50.
63. *B.M.K.*, 21; Windeatt, 56.
64. *B.M.K.*, 23–5; Windeatt, 58–60.
65. See below, 128.
66. *B.M.K.*, 36–7; Windeatt, 72–3.
67. *B.M.K.*, 27–9; Windeatt, 62–3.
68. *B.M.K.*, 179–81; Windeatt, 219–21.
69. *B.M.K.*, 9; Windeatt, 43–4. Cf. Dr Leyser's remarks about Margery's financial independence (op. cit., 164–5). One cannot be confident that her father made a substantial bequest to her, especially if, as seems likely, she had a brother or half-brother. Maybe her father considered that his obligation to her had been discharged by the provision of a dowry to her husband (probably substantial by Lynn standards, as befitted the father's status). When he made his will, his main concern is likely to have been provision for his soul and those of his wife or wives. If, as I have assumed, he was the John Brunham who died in 1413, his daughter had long ceased to be his responsibility, having been married for about twenty years.
70. *B.M.K.*, 9–11; Windeatt, 44–5. According to the Proem, 'her worldly goods, which were plentiful and abundant at that day [when she recovered from her breakdown] in little while after were full barren and bare' (*B.M.K.*, 2; Windeatt, 33–4).

71. Cf. above, 59–60.
72. *B.M.K.*, 24; Windeatt, 60.
73. *B.M.K.*, 32, 60; Windeatt, 67, 96.
74. *B.M.K.*, 106; Windeatt, 144. After her return from Rome, 'then it drew in towards winter, and she had so much cold that she wist not what she might do, for she was poor and had no money, and also she was in great debt'. She was in the same indigent situation in 1417, partly, according to her friends, because she had given away her money and other people's. She relied on donations to finance her pilgrimage to Santiago (*B.M.K.*, 104–6; Windeatt, 142–3; cf. below, 164).
75. *B.M.K.*, 180–1; Windeatt, 220–1.
76. *B.M.K.*, 9; Windeatt, 43–4.
77. See Thomson, E.P. (1972), ' "Rough music": le charivari anglais', *Annales E.S.C.*, xxvii, 285–312; Ingrams, M. (1984) 'Risings, rough music and the "reform of popular culture" in early modern England', *Past and Present*, cv, 105, 113.
78. Cullum, P.H. (1996) 'Vowesses and female lay piety in the province of York, 1300–1530', *Northern History*, xxxii, 21–41.
79. *B.M.K.*, 27; Windeatt, 63.
80. Leyser, 206–21.
81. *B.M.K.*, 8; Windeatt, 43.
82. *B.M.K.*, 32; Windeatt, 68.
83. Chapter 83 of *The Book* mentions a pilgrimage to an isolated country church two miles from where Margery lived. Two priests had asked her to accompany them there; 'a child or two' went with them. The church has been identified as St Michael's, Mintlyn (*B.M.K.*, 200, 336; Windeatt, 241).
84. *B.M.K.*, 14–15; Windeatt, 49–50.
85. *B.M.K.*, 116; Windeatt, 153.
86. *B.M.K.*, 212; Windeatt 253.
87. *B.M.K.*, 169–70; Windeatt, 209–10.
88. Virgoe, R. (1969) 'The divorce of Sir Thomas Tuddenham', *N.A.*, 34, 406–18, reprinted in Barron, C., Rawcliffe, C. and Rosenthal, J. (eds) (1997) *East Anglian Society and the Political Community of Late Medieval England. Selected Papers of Roger Virgoe*, Centre of East Anglian Studies, University of East Anglia, 117–31.
89. Capgrave, *Liber de Illustribus Henricis*, 163.
90. Ib., 135.

Chapter 4

1. See above, 4. I owe thanks to Dr Alison McHardy for commenting on a draft of this chapter.
2. Owen, 27; *B.M.K.*, 170–2; Windeatt, 210–11.

3. Owen, 27; *Calendar of Entries in the Papal Registers. Registers relating to Great Britain and Ireland, vii, 1417–1431*, 441–2.

4. For example, Robert Salesbury, burgess of Lynn, in his will of 1429 left 6s 8d to the high altar of St Margaret's for tithes and oblations forgotten (K.L.R.O., KL/C12/11).

5. Owen, 17–28.

6. Margery was present in the choir when a Requiem Mass was being held for a married woman (*B.M.K.*, 53; Windeatt, 89). For burgesses and a knight worshipping in the chancel, see below, 79.

7. *B.M.K.*, 138–9; Windeatt, 167–8.

8. *B.M.K.*, 167; Windeatt, 207.

9. In 1402 Mayor and Congregation appointed a guardian of the jewels and ornaments of the church (Ingleby, f3). For its architecture, see Pevsner, N. (1962) *North-West and South Norfolk. The Buildings of England*, Harmondsworth: Penguin, 221–6.

10. See below, 96.

11. Owen, 28; *B.M.K.*, 169; cf. ib., 155; Windeatt, 208–9; cf. ib., 194. For Margery's relations with St Margaret, see below, 122–3.

12. Owen, 28, n 2; K.L.R.O., KL/C38/7. The gild had Masses said in St Margaret's, St James's and St Nicholas's in 1416–17 (KL/C38/10).

13. Cf. below, 94–5. *The Book* mentions an occasion when Margery was in St John's chapel (*B.M.K.*, 16; Windeatt, 51).

14. See above, 42.

15. For the presence of babies and small children in church during services, Orme, 'Children and the Church in Medieval England', 569.

16. *B.M.K.*, 14–15; Windeatt, 49.

17. E.g., below, 101.

18. *B.M.K.*, 21–2; Windeatt, 56–7.

19. *B.M.K.*, 167; Windeatt, 207.

20. *B.M.K.*, 162–4; Windeatt, 202–3; cf. *B.M.K.*, 327.

21. P.R.O., C47/43/275; Westlake, *Parish Gilds*, 198; *C.P.R., 1413–16*, 238. For the wills, N.R.O., 79 Surflete (Clerk),103 Surflete (Game), 33 Surflete (Candeler). The poll tax return of 1379 shows that there were some mercers, shipmen and specialist craftsmen among the inhabitants of South Lynn. There is an absence of very rich people; the majority were taxpayers at the basic rate of 4d (text in Owen, 235–6).

22. Watkin, A., (ed.) (1948) 'Archdeaconry of Norwich. Inventory of Church Goods temp. Edward III', *Norfolk Record Society*, xix, part ii, 208, 222.

23. Harrod, 30. In 1421 Joanna Catefeld was the anchoress at the Carmelite friary, and Anne Whyote outside the East Gate (Gilchrist, R. and Oliva, M. (1993) *Religious Women and Medieval East Anglia: History and Archaeology c. 1100–1540*, Norwich: Centre of East Anglian Studies, University of East Anglia, 97). Joanna may have been the widow of Thomas Catefeld who held her husband's former tenement near St Margaret's (Owen, 182). John Jobbard, chaplain, paid rent for the year 1425–6 to the mayor

and community for the hermitage and chapel outside the East Gate (Owen, 186–7).

24. *B.M.K.*, 226, 228; Windeatt, 270–2, 291–2.

25. Owen, 27. An old print showing the incorporation of parts of the crossing and transepts in the later St James' Workhouse is reproduced in Richards, *King's Lynn*, 85.

26. Pevsner, 226–7.

27. Owen, 28–9.

28. Ib., 135–9.

29. *B.M.K.*, 372–3; *Calendar of Papal Registers . . . Papal Letters, vii, 1417–1431*, 441–2; Owen, 140. Bishop Morgan's Register apparently does not survive.

30. *B.M.K.*, 373–4; Owen, 140–1; *H.M.C., King's Lynn*, 162. In 1428 the mayor, John Permonter, and community supported Richard Waterden's attempt to procure permission for a font in St James (KL/C7/2, 227–8).

31. *B.M.K.*, 58–60; Windeatt, 94–6.

32. *B.M.K.*, 148–52; Windeatt, 187–91.

33. *Chichele Reg.*, iii, 404.

34. K.L.R.O., KL/C12/9 (Silsden); N.R.O., 83 Wylbey (Cook).

35. Pevsner, 228.

36. Capgrave, *Liber de Illustribus Henricis*, 139. There were thirty-eight friars listed as resident in 1382 (Owen, 117–19).

37. Aston, *Arundel*, 285; Harrod, 104, 106.

38. Gransden, 'A fourteenth-century chronicle', 276; College of Arms, London, 'Processus in Curia Constabularii et Marescalli Anglie inter Reginaldum Grey militem Dominum Hastings et Edwardum Hastings pro Armis familie', MS 1, ff 514–19; Jack, R.I. (1965) 'Entail and descent: The Hastings inheritance, 1370 to 1436', *Bulletin of the Institute of Historical Research*, xxxviii, 1–3, 12–13; Wight, J.A. (1972) *Brick Building in England from the Middle Ages to 1550*, London: John Barker, 327. For the Bardolf family, see above, 32. The Carmelite church contained an image of St Christopher, before which the burgess John Slegge willed to be buried in 1414 (*Chichele Reg.*, iii, 410).

39. *Derby's Expeditions*, 278; Goodman, A. (1992) *John of Gaunt*, London and New York: Longman, 244–8; *C.P.R. 1413–16*, 25; Capgrave, *Liber de Illustribus Henricis*, 37–9.

40. K.L.R.O., KL/C12/11 (Salesbury); N.R.O., 83 Wylbey (Cook); ib., N.P., 2 Aleyn (Slynghelant); ib., 119 Surflete (Guybon).

41. N.R.O., 66, 67 Doke (Martenet); ib., 121 Doke (Spycer); Lucas, P.J. (1993) 'A bequest to the friars in the will of John Spycer 1439–40: John Capgrave O.S.A. (1393–1464), William Wellys O.S.A. (*fl.* 1434–40) and Augustinian learning in Lynn in the fifteenth century', *Norfolk Archaeology*, xli, 482.

42. Gransden, 'A fourteenth-century chronicle', 270–8; Oxford, Bodl. MS. Lat. th. d. 1; cf. Little, A. (1943) *Franciscan Papers, Lists and Documents,*

NOTES

Manchester; U.P. 244–7. Little printed one of the sermons (ib., 247–56). For discussion of a marginal annotation in *The Book* which suggests an identification of the visiting friar who forbade Margery's attendance at his sermons at St James as William Melton, *B.M.K.*, 321.

43. Goodman, *Gaunt*, 37, 119; Lynn, Nicholas of, Eisner, S. and MacEoin, G. (eds) (1980) *Kalendarium*, Athens: University of Georgia Press.
44. Way, A. (1843–65) *Promptorium Parvulorum sive Clericorum, by Fratre Galfrido*, London: Camden Society, xxv, liv, lxxxix; Orme, N. (1973) *English Schools in the Middle Ages*, London: Methuen, 97.
45. See below, 95–6.
46. Worcestre, *Itineraries*, 356–7. The editor surmises that 'Lyme' = Lynn. Bishop Despenser's ordinances of 1373 had forbidden a priest or anyone else to teach boys in the parish church and the two detached chapels (text in Owen, 133–5).
47. Seymour, M.C. (1996), 'John Capgrave', in id. (ed.) *Authors of the Middle Ages*, iii, Aldershot: Variorum, 207–33; Emden, A.B. (1963) *A Biographical Register of the University of Cambridge*, Cambridge: U.P., 121–2. It is not clear how long Capgrave was away from Lynn. He left there for the *studium generale* in London in 1417 and he went to Cambridge in 1422 (Seymour, 219–20). For his life of St Katherine of Alexandria, see below, 122–3, 196, and for his pilgrim guide to Rome, below. Capgrave was sustaining a tradition of learning in the Lynn house. In 1382 two of the friars were styled *professor* of theology, and three of them *lector* (Owen, 119).
48. *B.M.K.*, 167; Windeatt, 206.
49. *B.M.K.*, 79; Windeatt, 115. In 1433 she received a warm welcome, and approval of her intentions as divinely inspired, from a Franciscan, a Doctor of Divinity, in Norwich (*B.M.K.*, 227–8; Windeatt, 271–2).
50. *B.M.K.*, 209; Windeatt, 250.
51. *B.M.K.*, 17–18, 43–5, 46–7, 142; Windeatt, 52, 79–80, 82, 181. Katherine Curson, in her will dated 18 September 1415 (proved 14 October following), bequeathed 40d to an anchorite at the Dominicans – perhaps the successor to Margery's supporter (*Chichele Reg.*, iii, 404). A Dominican Doctor of Divinity, Master Custawns, visiting Lynn for a chapter of his Order, tried to boost support for her among the Lynn clergy (*B.M.K.*, 165–6; Windeatt, 204–6). For an identification of this friar as one residing in the Norwich house in 1423, *B.M.K.*, 327.
52. Ib., 21–2; Windeatt, 56–7. Master Aleyn may have been the Carmelite who first offered to write her book (*B.M.K.*, 6; Windeatt, 38; cf. ib., 302).
53. *B.M.K.*, 136; Windeatt, 175.
54. *B.M.K.*, 150; Windeatt, 189.
55. *B.M.K.*, 167–70; Windeatt, 207–10. Netter was chosen as provincial in 1414 and held office until his death, c. 1430. It was a testimony to Margery's orthodoxy that Netter, theological opponent of the Lollards and expert on the history of their movement, relaxed his ban on her association with Master Aleyn (Knowles, *Religious Orders*, ii, 146–8).

56. *B.M.K.*, 268; College of Arms, Grey v. Hastings, f516. Gaywood gave his age as fifty-nine in 1408, which tallies approximately with the date of birth which Emden gives for Alan of Lynn.
57. Emden, *Cambridge*, 181–2; Knowles, ii, 152–3.
58. *B.M.K.*, 171, 370–1; Windeatt, 211.
59. Dr McHardy has pointed out to me similarities between the parochial organisation of the port of Boston (Lincs.) and Lynn. In Boston, like Lynn a borough not of ancient foundation, where there was only one parish church, there were numerous parochial chaplains in the later fourteenth century (McHardy, A.K. (1992) *Clerical Poll-Taxes of the Diocese of Lincoln 1377–81*, Woodbridge: Boydell for Lincoln Record Society, 11, 115, 157). Apropos relations between seculars, monks and friars in Lynn, in 1361 the Augustinian prior had made an agreement to end an issue of contention with the prior of St Margaret's. He and his successors would hand over a quarter of all funeral offerings made at the friary, as the Dominicans and Franciscans already did with theirs (Owen, 116–17).
60. *B.M.K.*, 150–63; Windeatt, 189, 202; KL/C10/2/f49v. In documents of 1427 and 1436, Spryngolde was described as Bachelor in Decrees (Owen, 140; Virgoe, 'The divorce of Sir Thomas Tuddenham', 122). Spryngolde is the priest most frequently mentioned in *The Book*.
61. *B.M.K.*, 60; Windeatt, 96.
62. *B.M.K.*, 136; Windeatt, 175.
63. *B.M.K.*, 139; Windeatt, 179.
64. *B.M.K.*, 162–4; Windeatt, 203–4.
65. *B.M.K.*, 226; Windeatt, 270.
66. *B.M.K.*, 246–7; Windeatt, 291–2.
67. For instance, Christ's promise to her about Master Robert, *B.M.K.*, 216; Windeatt, 257–8.
68. *B.M.K.*, 4–6, 152–4, 221; Windeatt, 35–7, 38, 191–3, 265.
69. *B.M.K.*, 58, 153; Windeatt, 93, 192.
70. *B.M.K.*, 168, 328; Windeatt, 208.
71. *B.M.K.*, 142–4; Windeatt, 181–2.
72. See references in n 70 above.
73. *B.M.K.*, 148–52; Windeatt, 187–91.
74. *B.M.K.*, 219; Windeatt, 260.
75. Certificates were listed by Westlake, *Parish Gilds*, 192–9; texts of certificates written in English were printed in Toulmin Smith, *English Gilds*, 45–109. For the Latin texts of the certificates for the gilds of St Mary Damgate and St James, Owen, 321–2. Westlake omitted to mention the gild of St Nicholas (cf. Toulmin Smith, 97–9).
76. Owen, 324–6.
77. The gilds were taxed a sum total of £163 3s 5d in 1371; they had been rated at half the assessed value of their chattels. Some of the identifications of these gilds with ones which returned certificates in 1389 may be mistaken.

78. There were ten gilds whose chattels were valued at between £24 and £10, thirty-six at between £8 10s and £1, twenty-one at between 19s 8d and 4s.

78. There were ten gilds whose chattels were valued at between £24 and £10, thirty-six at between £8 10s and £1, twenty-one at between 19s 8d and 4s.
79. For variations in cults of the Blessed Virgin, see below, 234, n 105.
80. Toulmin Smith, 47–8, 62–3; Westlake, 197–8.
81. Toulmin Smith, 80–2, 94–5, 97–9.
82. Westlake, 192.
83. P.R.O., C47/42/239 (coifmakers), C47/43/274 (young scholars); Toulmin Smith, 51–3, 54–7; Westlake, 192–4.
84. Ib., 197.
85. Watkin, 'Inventory of Church goods', 123: 'baculus Sancti Thome martyris quem in mare gestabit'.
86. Toulmin Smith, 62–3; Westlake, 194, 196. There was also a gild of St Peter and All Saints (ib., 197).
87. C47/43/279; Westlake, 199. In 1392 John Brunham, as mayor, with the community procured licence for the alienation in mortmain by John Waryn and Richard Dun of properties to the community, in part to provide lights to burn daily in honour of Corpus Christi (*C.P.R., 1391–6*, 157). For the fraternity's role in urban ceremony, see above, 31, 48.
88. C47/43/261 (St Margaret); Toulmin Smith, 97–8 (St Nicholas); C47/43/254 (Decollation); Westlake, 194 (Nativity of St John); Toulmin Smith, 54–7 (Exaltation).
89. Westlake, 193–4.
90. Toulmin Smith, 47–8, 100–2.
91. Ib., 74–7; Westlake, 194. In 1389 the gild had chattels worth £4 3s, a larger amount than most other Lynn gilds then admitted to possessing. The valuations put on gilds' chattels in 1371, at the community's rather than the Crown's behest, were probably more realistic. In 1402 the Crown granted licence for the foundation of a gild of St George in Lynn. It is not clear whether these letters patent referred to an existing gild (*H.M.C., Lynn*, 204).
92. Goodman, A., 'Introduction', in Goodman and Gillespie, J.L. (eds) (1999) *Richard II. The Art of Kingship*, Oxford: Clarendon Press, 10–13.
93. Parker, 12.
94. C47/43/267; Westlake, 197. The gild had a male aldermen and brethren in 1389. The saint is portrayed on rood screens at Somerleyton and Westhall, Suffolk (Woodforde, C. (1950) *The Norwich School of Glass-Painting in the Fifteenth Century*, Oxford: U.P. 88–9).
95. Owen, 321–2; Westlake, 197.
96. C47/43/272; Westlake, 198.
97. C47/42/249; ib., 250; Westlake, 194.
98. Toulmin Smith, 47–8 (a gild of St Thomas of Canterbury).
99. Westlake, 192.
100. For example, the officers of the gild of the Decollation of St John, founded in 1361, could be fined for negligence (C47/43/254).

101. Toulmin Smith, 54–7; Westlake, 193; passage from penitential manual cited by Pantin, W.A. (1955) *The English Church in the Fourteenth Century*, Cambridge: U.P., 205, 209.

102. For instance, the gild of St Mary and the Exaltation of the Holy Cross in 1389 had John Sponer as alderman, and the *custodes* Walter Glou', William Wodehill, skinner, Simon Sadeler and John Cestrefeld, holding the gild's chattels, valued at 51s, in equal portions (C47/43/263). Glou' and Wodehill were also among the *custodes* of the gild of St Mary and St George (C47/43/264).

103. Toulmin Smith, 51–3; Westlake, 193.

104. The gild of Holy Trinity, St Mary, St Thomas and All Saints met 'in the drinking place' (*in loco potacionis*) before processing to St Margaret's (C47/43/278). Some gilds met quarterly. The gild of St Mary and St George had four annual *colloquia* to discuss and make decisions for the common interest of the gild. Brothers and sisters who failed to attend were liable to a penalty of 4d (C47/43/264).

105. Feasts of the Blessed Virgin were popular in both 1371 and 1389, but in 1371 dedications to the Assumption (seven out of ten) were unrivalled in popularity, which no longer seems to have been the case in 1389, when only four gilds solely devoted to feasts of the Blessed Virgin made returns, celebrating the Conception, the Annunciation and (two) the Purification. For feasts of the Virgin, see Pfaff, R.W. (1970) *New Liturgical Feasts in Later Medieval England*, Oxford: Clarendon Press. The feast of the Visitation was instituted by Boniface IX in 1389: Margery's insertion of herself into the scene may have reflected its growing popularity in England and in particular its early celebration by the Carmelites (ib., 40–7; *B.M.K.*, 18–19; Windeatt, 53).

106. For Margery's visit to the Jordan, see below, 193–4.

107. In 1371 there were dedications to some early saints which do not appear in the 1389 returns – Mary Magdalene, Bartholomew, Christopher, Helen, Martin, Patrick and Stephen. There were two St Edward gilds in 1371, one of them certainly honouring the Confessor.

108. Gilds of the Annunciation, St Mary and St George, St Nicholas and St Thomas of Canterbury.

109. Gilds of Holy Trinity, St Mary in Damgate, St Mary and Holy Cross, All Saints and the Purification, St John the Baptist, St Peter, St James, St Giles and All Saints, Saints Giles and Julian, St Leonard.

110. Other gilds in St Margaret's were in honour of the Conception of the Virgin; Holy Trinity, St Mary, St Thomas of Canterbury and All Saints; Saints Antony; Katherine; George; Laurence; Margaret; Thomas of Canterbury; William of Norwich.

111. See above, 64.

112. Toulmin Smith, 54–7; Westlake, 193.

113. Toulmin Smith, 49–50; Westlake, 196.

114. Toulmin Smith, 94–6.

115. See below, 142.
116. KL/C7/2, 237. Wythe and Springwelle were prominent burgesses and office-holders in Lynn, and T. Chevele had been appointed common clerk of the borough in 1428 (KL/C7/2, 209–11).
117. Tanner, N.P. (ed.) (1977) *Heresy Trials in the Diocese of Norwich, 1428–31*, London: Royal Historical Society, Camden fourth series, xx, 73–4.
118. *B.M.K.*, 40, 320; Windeatt, 36.
119. *B.M.K.*, 132; Windeatt, 170.
120. See below, 141.
121. See above, 81.
122. See above, 32–3, 35.

Chapter 5

1. *B.M.K.*, 6–9; Windeatt, 41–3. I owe thanks to Dr Gary Dickson for his comments on this chapter.
2. The tentative dating is based on the documentary evidence for John Kempe's involvement in brewing; see above, 70.
3. *B.M.K.*, 9–16; Windeatt, 43–50.
4. *B.M.K.*, 49, 52, 87, 126, 215, 253; Windeatt, 85, 164, 256, 297. Dame Julian cited *Romans*, viii, 26 to Margery; this applied more aptly to her way of life than to the latter's (*B.M.K.*, 43, 173; Windeatt, 78, 213).
5. *B.M.K.*, 16–17; Windeatt, 51. The chapel was probably that of St John the Baptist, and if so it was an appropriate place for the re-ordering of her asceticism. The Wilton Diptych (National Gallery, London), painted in the 1390s, represents him characteristically as unkempt and scantily clad in a rough skin.
6. *B.M.K.*, 17; Windeatt, 51–2.
7. *B.M.K.*, 18–20, 38–9; Windeatt, 52–5, 73–4.
8. *B.M.K.*, 39; Windeatt, 75. For Margery as wife and mother, see above, 66ff. For devotional works that helped to inspire and mould her piety, see below, 114ff.
9. *B.M.K.*, 143–4; Windeatt, 181–2.
10. *B.M.K.*, 17–18; Windeatt, 52. For Margery's relations with the Dominicans at Lynn, see above, 88. For the *topos* of Christ as mother, strikingly developed in Dame Julian's Revelations, see Julian of Norwich, Spearing, A.C., 'Introduction', in id. (ed.) and Spearing, E. trans. (1998) *Revelations of Divine Love*, London: Penguin, xxi–xxvii.
11. *B.M.K.*, 168, 217–18; Windeatt, 207, 259. For Master Aleyn, see above, 88–9; for Spryngolde, see above, 90.
12. *B.M.K.*, 29; Windeatt, 65; cf. *B.M.K.*, 142; Windeatt, 181.
13. For the interviews with some of these prelates, see below, 129ff.
14. *B.M.K.*, 32; Windeatt, 67–8.
15. For Dame Julian, and for Margery's relations with her, see below, 138–9.

16. *B.M.K.*, 159–60, 172–3, 199, 213–14; Windeatt, 199, 212–13, 254–6 (deathbeds and the sick); *B.M.K.*, 176–7; Windeatt, 216–17 (lepers); *B.M.K.*, 75; Windeatt, 111 (Lazarus). For a description of St Hugh the Bishop's compassion for lepers, Orme, N. and Webster, M. (1995) *The English Hospital 1070–1570*, New Haven and London: Yale U.P., 24. In the prayers of Margery which terminate Book Two, the raising of Lazarus is given an exemplary significance, and her visit to Bethany is referred to (*B.M.K.*, 253; Windeatt, 297).

17. Owen, 215. In 1429 Robert Salesbury, burgess of Lynn, bequeathed 20d each to the leperhouses of Magdalen, Gaywood, Harwick, Setchey and West Lynn (K.L.R.O., KL/C12/11). In 1410 William Silisden, burgess, left 3s 4d to the poor people in leperhouses (KL/C12/9), Stephen Guybon of North Lynn in 1433 12d to each leperhouse near Lynn (N.R.O., 118, 119 Surflete), and John Cook of Lynn in 1447 20d to the lepers of St Mary Magdalene and 12d to each leperhouse within three miles of the town (N.R.O., 83 Wylbey). For the constitution of the hospital of St Mary Magdalene, Page, W. (ed.) (1906) *Victoria County History of Norfolk*, London, 441–2. It was on the causeway leading from the borough to Gaywood. In Damgate there was the general hospital of St John the Baptist (ib., 441).

18. See above, 67.

19. *B.M.K.*, 13, 16; Windeatt, 48, 51.

20. *B.M.K.*, 68–9; Windeatt, 104–5.

21. For the words used to describe the phenomenon, see below, 107–8, 140.

22. *B.M.K.*, 137–8; Windeatt, 176–7.

23. *B.M.K.*, 88–9; Windeatt, 124–5. A description of a manifestation which occurred on Good Friday, apparently in Lynn after her great pilgrimages, noted that this recurred on that day for ten years (*B.M.K.*, 139–41; Windeatt, 178–9). Elsewhere she speaks of her weeping becoming softer and easier, and the fire of love increasing in fervour after the pilgrimages, as her understanding of the nature of the divinity grew (*B.M.K.*, 209; Windeatt, 250). For a mention of the sensation of 'a flame of fire about her breast full hot and delectable', *B.M.K.*, 219; Windeatt, 260. Whilst she was occupied with writing 'this treatise, she had many holy tears and weepings, and often times there came a flame of fire about her breast full hot and delectable' (*B.M.K.*, 219; Windeatt, 260). For the *topos* of 'the fire of love', see below, 114–15.

24. For the admission of 'Margery Kempe' to the Holy Trinity Gild, see above, 105. However, the 'Margery' of *The Book* said that Christ's visitations to her and her holy contemplations (with which 'crying' is often associated in *The Book*) had being going on for twenty-five years when it was written (*B.M.K.*, 214; Windeatt, 255–6).

25. The vision which Margery is described as having on Mount Calvary, of Christ on the Cross, is particularly vivid. She received this 'before her in her soul ... truly by contemplation' (*B.M.K.*, 68; Windeatt, 105–6). For

her artistic sensibility, see her reactions to a Crucifixion in a church in Leicester (a Rood Cross?) and to a *pietà* in a Norwich church (*B.M.K.*, 111, 148; Windeatt, 148, 186–7). Some idea of one sort of sacred painting with which Margery may have been familiar (from the top end of the artistic market) can be gained from the Despenser Retable in Norwich cathedral, whose panels depict the Resurrection (for whose provenance, see above, 26). For a contextualisation of Margery's responsiveness to visual imagery, see Wallace, D. (1984) 'Mystics and followers in Siena and East Anglia. A study in taxonomy, class and cultural mediation', in Glasscoe, M. (ed.), *The Medieval Mystical Tradition in England*, iii, Woodbridge: Boydell and Brewer, 182–5.

26. *B.M.K.*, 184–5; Windeatt, 224–5. For the 'ghostly sights' which she had every Palm Sunday and Good Friday, *B.M.K.*, 187–90; Windeatt, 228–31. Hildegard said that her visions were experienced not in dreams or whilst sleeping or in a trance, 'nor with the exterior ears of man or in hidden places, but by God's will [she] beheld them wide awake and clearly, with the mind, eyes and ears of the inner man' (cited in Lagorio, V.M. (1984) 'The medieval continental women mystics: an introduction', in Szarmach, P.E. (ed.), *An Introduction to the Medieval Mystics of Europe*, Albany: State Univ. of New York Press, 164). For Julian's distinction between bodily and spiritual visions, *Revelations*, 7–9.

27. *B.M.K.*, 47; Windeatt, 83. Christ promised that she would be rewarded in Heaven for as many times as she took the Sacrament at the altar with many holy thoughts (*B.M.K.*, 209; Windeatt, 250). With her bodily eyes, she often saw bright white specks, multiple and mobile, which Christ told her were a sign of the presence of guardian angels around her (*B.M.K.*, 88; Windeatt, 124). For her experience of sweet, unearthly odours, *B.M.K.*, 87; Windeatt, 124.

28. *B.M.K.*, 131; Windeatt, 169–70.

29. *B.M.K.*, 87–8, 185, 219; Windeatt, 124, 225–6, 260. If *The Book* was being referred to here as having been written in 1436, the phenomenon presumably started to appear in 1411. It is said to have happened frequently in Rome (1414–15). In the context of the writing of *The Book*, Margery mentioned that 'she heard many times a voice of a sweet bird singing in her ear, and often times she heard sweet sounds and melodies that passed her wit for to tell them' (*B.M.K.*, 219; Windeatt, 260).

30. An example is the vision which occurred when she was participating in the Holy Thursday procession (presumably in Lynn), when she fell down in the field among the people and cried, roared and wept as if she would have burst (*B.M.K.*, 174; Windeatt. 214).

31. Cf. above, 101.

32. *B.M.K.*, 30; Windeatt, 66.

33. *B.M.K.*, 86–7; Windeatt, 122–4.

34. *B.M.K.*, 210–11; Windeatt, 251–2.

35. *B.M.K.*, 31, 68; Windeatt, 66, 104. For plays in Lynn, see above, 62.

36. *B.M.K.*, 198; Windeatt, 239.
37. *B.M.K.*, 138; Windeatt, 177.
38. See above, 236, n 23.
39. *B.M.K.*, 69; Windeatt, 105.
40. *B.M.K.*, 68; Windeatt, 104.
41. *B.M.K.*, 69–70; Windeatt, 105.
42. *B.M.K.*, 198–9; Windeatt, 239–40.
43. *B.M.K.*, 89; Windeatt, 126.
44. *B.M.K.*, 205; Windeatt, 246; cf. *B.M.K.*, 30–1, 199; Windeatt, 66, 240.
45. *B.M.K.*, 69; Windeatt, 105.
46. *B.M.K.*, 40, 69, 185; Windeatt, 75, 105, 225.
47. William Sowthfeld, Carmelite of Norwich, is described as reassuring her about the divine nature of her spiritual experiences (*B.M.K.*, 41; Windeatt, 76–7).
48. See above, 93.
49. Cf. above, 216, n 28.
50. *B.M.K.*, 29–30; Windeatt, 65.
51. *B.M.K.*, 11, 89, 102, 134–5; Windeatt, 46, 125, 140, 173, 287–8; Brucker, G. (ed.) and Martines, J. (trans.) (1967) 'The Diary of Buonaccorso Pitti', in *Two Memoirs of Renaissance Florence*, New York, Evanston and London: Harper and Row, 19–106. For 'Merry England', Furnivall, F.J. (ed.) (1866) 'The Twelve Letters that shall save Merry England', *Political, Religious and Love Poems*, E.E.T.S, xv, 1–3 (dating from Edward IV's first reign, 1461–70).
52. Goodman, 'Introduction', in *Richard II. The Art of Kingship*, 11–13.
53. For Christ's assurance, see in particular Chapter 2 of Book One (*B.M.K.*, 9–11; Windeatt, 86–8).
54. Ib. The edifying scenario which Christ forecasts for Margery's deathbed is a good illustration of the desire for a 'good death'.
55. Du Boulay, R.H. (1970) *An Age of Ambition. English Society in the Late Middle Ages*, London: Nelson.
56. 'Sad and sober' was the right demeanour for a wife (*B.M.K.*, 178–9; Windeatt, 218–19).
57. Owen, 422.
58. Ragusa, I. (trans.) and Green, R.B. (ed.) (1961) *Meditations on the Life of Christ*, Princeton, N.J.: U.P. The *Meditationes* were promoted especially by the Franciscan Order and became very popular in England, whence forty-three of the surviving one hundred and thirteen Latin texts originate. Shortly before 1410 an abridged version in English, *The Mirrour of the Blessed Lyf of Jesu Christ*, was made by Carthusian Nicholas Love, prior of Mount Grace (for which house, see above, 1–2). This had one of the widest circulations of any devotional manuscript in late medieval England; around fifty manuscripts survive (Wallace, 'Mystics and followers in Siena and East Anglia', 177–81; Lovatt, R. (1968) 'The Imitation of Christ in late Medieval England', London: *Transactions of the Royal Historical Society*, fifth series, xviii, 97–9). It is not clear whether Margery knew Love's version.

59. *B.M.K.*, 99; Windeatt, 136. Dame Julian cited from St Jerome to Margery (*B.M.K.*, 43; Windeatt, 78).

60. See below, 128–30.

61. Menzies, L. (trans.) (1953) *The Revelations of Mechthild of Magdeburg 1210–1297: or, The flowing light of the Godhead*, London and New York: Longmans, Green, xvii–xviii; Beer, F. (1992) *Women and Mystical Experience in the Middle Ages*, Woodbridge: Boydell and Brewer, 7.

62. *B.M.K.*, 74, 86, 112; Windeatt, 110, 123, 150.

63. *Revelations of Mechthild*, xix–xxxix.

64. For German and Flemish mysticism, see H.E. Allen's Prefatory Note to the edition of *The Book*, *B.M.K.*, liii–lxviiii, and Appendices IV–V, 376–80. For citations in the text of *vitae* of Mary of Oignies and St Elizabeth of Hungary, *B.M.K.*, 152–4; Windeatt, 191–3. Master Custawns, a Dominican visiting Lynn for a general chapter of the Order, cited an unnamed *vita* of a holy woman (*B.M.K.*, 165–6; Windeatt, 205). For Italian parallels to *The Book's* piety, Wallace, op. cit.

65. Surtz, R.E. (1990) *The Guitar of God. Gender, Power and Authority in the Visionary World of Juana de la Cruz (1481–1534)*, Philadelphia: Pennsylvania U.P., 1–8.

66. *B.M.K.*, 152–4; Windeatt, 191–3. Cf. Vitry, Jacques de, (trans.) King, M.H. (1987) *The Life of Marie d'Oignies*, Toronto: Peregrina, 31–4, chapters 17–19, e.g. 'such an abundance of tears was pressed out by the wine-press of Your Cross in the Passion that her tears flowed so copiously on the floor that the ground in the Church became muddy with her footprints'. A priest who rebuked Mary for her tears in church the day before Good Friday, leading to her withdrawal, had a demonstration, according to her prayer, that this sort of weeping was involuntary. Celebrating Mass, he almost suffocated with tears and, despite his efforts to repress them, drenched himself, the book and the altar cloths (ib., 31–3).

67. Rolle, Richard, (trans.) Wolters, C. (1972) *The Fire of Love*, Harmondsworth: Penguin, 46–7; Beer, 112–28.

68. Ib., Chapters 14 and 15.

69. Hilton, Walter, (trans.) Sherley-Price, L. (1957) *The Ladder of Perfection*, Harmondsworth: Middlesex, 9–12; Milosh, J.E. (1966) *The Scale of Perfection and the English Mystical Tradition*, Madison: University of Wisconsin Press, 3–32.

70. *Ladder of Perfection*, 2.

71. Ib., 3.

72. *B.M.K.*, 95, 134–5; Windeatt, 132, 173.

73. *B.M.K.*, 47; Windeatt, 83.

74. *B.M.K.*, 245–6; Windeatt, 290–1. See below, 159, for Margery's Baltic travels.

75. Harris, M.T. (ed.), Kezel, A.R. (trans.), Nyberg, T. (intro.) (1990) *Birgitta of Sweden. Life and Selected Revelations*, New York: Paulist Press, 13–51 (introduction).

76. 'The Life of Blessed Birgitta by Prior Peter and Master Peter' in *Birgitta of Sweden*, 83, 86–9. Margery may have been emboldened to emphasise in *The Book* how she had supposedly criticised particular archbishops and a bishop to their faces because of Christ's revelation to Bridget about aspects of episcopal conduct, though Margery's criticisms were unsolicited, whereas Bridget's revelation was made at the request of Bernard de Rodez, archbishop of Naples ('The Seventh Book of Revelations', in *Birgitta of Sweden*, 177–80).

77. *The Book* merely says that when she came to London, 'she was sped of her letter anon of the Archbishop of Canterbury' (*B.M.K.*, 136; Windeatt, 175).

78. Knowles, D. (1955) *Religious Orders*, ii, 175–81; Wylie, *Henry the Fourth*, ii, 451–4; Dahlerup, T. (ed.) (1989) *Danmarks Historie*, vi, *De fire staender, 1400–1500*, Copenhagen: Gyldendalske Boghandel (etc.), 62–3. I owe thanks to Ms Tina Eriksson for translating passages from this.

79. Ib., 63.

80. See above, 19.

81. Capgrave, *Liber de Illustribus Henricis*, 117.

82. Worcestre, *Itineraries*, 192–3; *Danmarks Historie 1400–1500*, 62–3. The churches are Horsham St Faith's (Norfolk) and Westhall (Suffolk) (Duffy, E. (1992) *The Stripping of the Altars*, New Haven and London: Yale U.P., 86, 171).

83. *Birgitta of Sweden*, 10, 256 (wash basin episode cited from Prior Peter's *Vita*), 37–8 (citing references to Karl in her *Revelations*); B.M.K., 137; Windeatt, 175.

84. *B.M.K.*, 110–11; Windeatt, 148; Coad, J.G. (1970) *Hailes Abbey Gloucestershire*, London: Historical Buildings and Monuments Commission for England; Brown, A. (1997) 'Civic ritual: Bruges and the counts of Flanders in the later Middle Ages', *E.H.R.*, cxii, 280–4.

85. Cited in *Birgitta of Sweden*, 21 from her *Revelations*, Book 1, Chapter 53.

86. Margery reacted strongly to St Mary Magdalene's unworthiness, the intensity of her love for Christ and His compassionate treatment of her; see, for example, *B.M.K.*, 49, 73, 75, 174, 176, 193–4, 197, 253; Windeatt, 85, 109, 111, 214, 216, 234, 237–8, 297. For her visit to the house of Mary and Martha at Bethany, *B.M.K.*, 74–5; Windeatt, 111. For Mary Magdalene's healing powers, see above. For Margery's devotion to St Mary the Egyptian, see below, 193–4.

87. B.M.K., 30; Windeatt, 65.

88. Duffy, 171; Woodforde, *The Norwich School of Glass-Painting*, 177.

89. *B.M.K.*, 39; Windeatt, 75.

90. *B.M.K.*, 50–1; Windeatt, 86.

91. *B.M.K.*, 52; Windeatt, 87–8.

92. Lewis, K. (2000) *The Cult of St Katherine of Alexandria in Late Medieval England*, Woodbridge: Boydell and Brewer, 249–56. I owe thanks to Dr Lewis for drawing my attention to the significance of the cult of

St Katherine in the context of *The Book*. For these episodes of apparent persecution, see below, 130, 141–5.

93. Goodman, A. (1994) *Katherine Swynford*, Lincoln: Honeywood Press, 27. For the significance of Duchess Katherine's badge of the Katherine Wheel, Lewis, 67, 69–70.
94. British Library, Royal MS 2 A XVIII, f15v, 16r–v.
95. *B.M.K.*, 111–12; Windeatt, 149; cf. below.
96. *B.M.K.*, 216; Windeatt, 257.
97. *B.M.K.*, 108; Windeatt, 145.
98. *B.M.K.*, 41; Windeatt, 76–7.
99. Pantin, W.A. (ed.) (1976) 'Instructions for a devout and literate layman', in Alexander, J.J.G. and Gibson, M.T. (eds) *Medieval Language and Literature. Essays Presented to Richard William Hunt*, Oxford: Clarendon Press, 398–400. I owe thanks to Dr Andrew Brown for pointing out to me the relevance of this text.
100. Modern text in Myers, A.R. (ed.) (1969) *English Historical Documents*, iv, *1327–1485*, London: Eyre and Spottiswoode, 837.
101. Mayor, J.E.B. (ed.) (1876) *The English Works of John Fisher*, London: E.E.T.S., extra series, xxvii, 293–5. In 1494 Margaret commissioned the printing of Hilton's *Ladder of Perfection*; for this, and for her piety in general, see Jones, M.K. and Underwood, M. (1992) *The King's Mother. Lady Margaret Beaufort, Countess of Richmond and Derby*, Cambridge: U.P., 174–80. I have benefited from discussing Lady Margaret's piety with Mr Harry Schnitker.
102. See above.

Chapter 6

1. *B.M.K.*, 311. I owe thanks to Professor Barrie Dobson for his comments on this chapter.
2. Ib., 202; Windeatt, 243. The nuns of Denney were drawn mainly from substantial burgess and gentry families (*V.C.H., County of Cambridge and Isle of Ely*, ii, 295–302).
3. See below, 116. Margery went on pilgrimage to the Augustinian priory at Walsingham (*B.M.K.*, 227; Windeatt, 271).
4. For comments on the accounts of these interviews, see Catto, 'Religious change under Henry V', in Harriss, *Henry V. The Practice of Kingship*, 112–13. No such particulars are given about her visits in 1417–18 to seek privileges from Repingdon and Archbishop Chichele.
5. The suggestion that Margery met Repingdon at Sleaford is based on the dating clauses in his mandates (*Reg. Repingdon*, ii, 302, 308, 311, 316–18, 320, 322).
6. Knowles, *Religious Orders*, ii, 186–7; McFarlane, *John Wycliffe*, 102–3, 108–15; Hudson, A. (1988) *The Premature Reformation*, Oxford: U.P., 70–2, 73 and note.

7. *Reg. Repingdon*, i, xviii, xxi, xxxiii, l–li.

8. *B.M.K.*, 36–7; Windeatt, 69–71. Repingdon even gave Margery money to buy white clothes. Knowles, ii, 188–9, gives an account of their dealings.

9. *B.M.K.*, 36–7; Windeatt, 71–2. *The Book* does not make clear whether Arundel authorised Repingdon to give Margery the mantle and ring and permission to wear white clothes. He provided a letter authorising her to choose her confessor and to receive communion every Sunday. So *The Book* passes in silence over the ceremony of the mutual vows which must have initiated her life as a vowess.

10. See Aston, *Arundel*; Davies, R.G. (1973) 'Thomas Arundel as Archbishop of Canterbury', *J.E.H.*, 24, 9–21.

11. Hudson, 82ff.

12. Aston, *Arundel*, 39–43.

13. For Love, Oguro, S., Beadle, R. and Sargent, M.G. (eds) (1997) *Nicholas Love at Waseda* (etc.), Cambridge: U.P. For Margery and the *Meditationes*, see above, 112.

14. *B.M.K.*, 108–9; Windeatt, 146–7. Meech and Allen identified the place to which Peverel summoned Margery as the episcopal manor at Henbury (Gloucs.) near Bristol (*B.M.K.*, 309). The last date in Peverel's Register which indicates his probable whereabouts (Hillingdon, Berks.) is 31 March 1417; he had been staying at his London *hospitium* for some time, from 1 January (Worcestershire Record Office, b. 716. 093-BA. 2648/5 (ii), ff157–63). The church where Margery waited for and knelt down before the bishop may have been Henbury parish church, which has fine, predominantly thirteenth-century features. The 'Bishops hall' where she had been brought, and berated his fashionably clad servants, and the place where she ate and tarried with him may have been on or near the possible site of the vicarage nearby.

15. McFarlane, *John Wycliffe*, 176–8 for the rebels from Bristol. In *The Book*, the hostile man of Bristol is capitalised as 'Richeman' and 'Rycheman', whereas Margery, in her rejoinder to him, invoking Christ, plays on the words 'ryche man', 'good man' and 'meke man' (*B.M.K.*, 108). Could Richeman have been his surname? There was a burgess family in Bristol of that name in the early fourteenth century, but I have not traced the name there in this period.

16. *B.M.K.*, 109; Windeatt, 147.

17. Emden, *Biographical Register . . . Cambridge*, 1472–3. Peverel had been bishop of Ossory (1395), Leighlin (c. 1398) and Llandaff (1398).

18. *B.M.K.*, 109–10; Windeatt, 147. Cambridge University Library, EDR, F5/33, an ecclesiastical formulary, contains notes from diet accounts of Peverel's household in 1413 (cf. Woolgar, C.M. (1992) *Household Accounts from Medieval England*, i, Oxford: U.P., 710). Total expenditure for five months and eight days (£200 7s 8d) suggests that Peverel then maintained a household of less than fifty (cf. Mertes, K. (1988) *The English Noble Household 1250–1600*, Oxford: Blackwell, 117).

19. *B.M.K.*, 163; Windeatt, 125.
20. *B.M.K.*, 122–8; Windeatt, 161–6; Borthwick Institute, University of York, Registers 17 and 18, Register of Henry Bowet, Archbishop of York 1407–23, f299v.
21. *B.M.K.*, 131–5; Windeatt, 170–3; Reg. Bowet, f60r–f60v. The chapter was held on a Wednesday; Margery was examined on a Friday.
22. Emden, *Biographical Register . . . Cambridge*, 83–4. For Bowet's library, *Test. Ebor.*, iii, 76–7. Professor J.A.F. Thomson has remarked that Bowet emerges from the account in *The Book* 'as a man of marked dignity and no little patience' (op. cit., 195 and note).
23. *Chronica et Annales*, 408–10; McKenna, J.W. (1970) 'Popular canonization as political propaganda: the cult of Archbishop Scrope', *Speculum*, xlv, 608–23; York Minster Library, MS Add. 2, Horae Eboracenses (The Bolton Hours), f. 100; Pattison, I.R. and Murray, H. (2000) *Monuments in York Minster*, York: Friends of York Minster, 18–19.
24. *Test. Ebor.*, i, 398–402; Pattison and Murray, 20–2.
25. Gibson, P. (1979) *The Stained and Painted Glass of York Minster*, Norwich: Jarrold, for Dean and Chapter of York, 21; Brown, S. (1999) *Stained Glass at York*, London: Scala, 77–8; Kirby, *Henry IV*, 202; Wylie, *Henry IV*, ii, 451 n. For Bowet's devotion to St Peter and St Paul, see the opening sentence of his will, *Test. Ebor.*, i, 398–9.
26. *B.M.K.*, 133; Windeatt, 172–3; Eubel, C. (1898) *Hierarchia Catholica Medii Aevi* (etc.), Munster, 481–2 and 482 n. For ordinations carried out by the bishop of Soltaniyeh at Cawood on 18 September and 18 December 1417, and on 19 February 1418, Reg. Bowet, f398r, and v, f399r; for Bowet's commissions against Lollards in 1411, ib., 305. He had other suffragan bishops active in 1417–18. Emden identifies the Dr Paris who received Bowet's commission in 1411 with John Paris, O.P., D. Th. by 1376, who was vicar general of the English province in 1378 and took part in the Blackfriars council which condemned Wycliffe in 1382 (*Biographical Register . . . Cambridge*, 441–2).
27. *C.P.*, xii, part ii, 544–7 and 547 n. Lady Westmorland may have helped to finance Margery's pilgrimage to Jerusalem. For the countess's character, Dobson R.B. (1973) *Durham Priory 1400–50*, Cambridge: U.P., 185–7.
28. *C.P.*, vi, 195–7 and 197 note.
29. *Reg. Chichele*, ii, 355–4. For Exeter's connections with Lynn, see above, 33–5.
30. Worcestre, *Itineraries*, 56–7.
31. *S.A.C.*, 114; Meale, C.M. (1997) 'The early ownership of Love's *Mirror*, with special reference to its female audience', in Oguro, Beadle, and Sargent (eds) *Nicholas Love at Waseda*, 23, note 16, discussing Bodl. MS e Musaeo 35. Beaufort may have been on pilgrimage at Walsingham in 1411 or 1412 (K.L.R.O., KL/C39/48).
32. *B.M.K.*, 173–4; Windeatt, 213–14. Margaret Beaufort saw a religious play in Lynn when she was entertained there in 1410–11 (see above, 35).

33. *B.M.K.*, 108; Windeatt, 145.

34. *B.M.K.*, 108; Windeatt, 145–6. Marchale possessed vernacular literacy (*B.M.K.*, 111; Windeatt, 149). For trade between Lynn and Newcastle-upon-Tyne, see above, 19. Meech and Allen deduced from Marchale's itinerary that he was more likely to have hailed from Newcastle-under-Lyme (Staffs.) (*B.M.K.*, 309). No one called Marchale appears in the minutes of elections of borough officers from 1369 to 1411 printed by Pape, T. (1928) *Medieval Newcastle-under-Lyme*, Manchester: U.P., Appendix F, 142–75. In Bristol, Thomas Marchall (d. 1434), vicar of All Saints in 1392 and for a long time after, and notable among a list of vicars and other priests who were benefactors of the church, does not fit the description in *The Book*, not least because he was a cleric, a status which Margery appears to have generally recorded (Strong, P.L. (1967) 'All Saints' City, Bristol. Calendar of Deeds Part 1: Introduction and Text', Diploma in Archive Administration, University of London, 119–21; Bristol Record Office, P/A S/Ch W/1, 'Minutes of All Saints' Parish in the Reigne of Edward IV', f78.)

35. Margery received a generally frosty reception in Hull (*B.M.K.*, 129; Windeatt, 167).

36. *B.M.K.*, 157; Windeatt, 119.

37. *B.M.K.*, 60; Windeatt, 25.

38. *B.M.K.*, 160; Windeatt, 122.

39. *B.M.K.*, 120–1; Windeatt, 158–9. Perhaps Margery had decided to stay on in York until the feast of the Translation of St William (10 January 1418).

40. *B.M.K.*, 157; Windeatt, 119.

41. *B.M.K.*, 162–7; Windeatt, 124–38.

42. Wilson, C. (1977) *The Shrine of St William of York*, York: Yorkshire Museum. I owe thanks to Dr Elizabeth Hartley, Keeper of Archaeology at The Yorkshire Museum, for sending me a copy of this work and for allowing me access to the remains of the shrine, as rebuilt in the later fifteenth century, which are kept in the museum.

43. Toy, J. (1985) *A Guide and Index to the Windows of York Minster*, York: Dean and Chapter of York.

44. I am much indebted to Ms Smith, of the York Glaziers Trust, for discussing the St William window and for allowing me to read a draft chapter of her forthcoming thesis on the iconography of the window. See also Nilson, B. (1996) 'A reinterpretation of the St Willliam Window in York Minster', *Yorkshire Archaeological Journal*, lxviii, 157–79; Brown, 74. St William of York is depicted in a window of the later fifteenth century in the church of St Peter Mancroft, Norwich (Woodforde, *Norwich School of Glass-Painting*, 20).

45. *B.M.K.*, 21–3; Windeatt, 56–8.

46. St William Window, F 81–2, F 93–5 (Nilson, 174).

47. Jennings, B. (1999) *Yorkshire Monasteries*, Otley: Smith Settle, 127–9; Knowles, ii, 117–18; *Chronica et Annales*, 388.

48. *B.M.K.*, 121; Windeatt, 159. Thomas Greenwood, canon of York, refers to a keeper of Scrope's tomb in his will of 1421 (*Test. Ebor.*, iii, 361). Meech and Allen doubted whether *The Book* referred to Scrope's tomb (*B.M.K.*, 313–14). For the Bardolf family's connection with Lynn, see above, 32.
49. Warren, *Anchorites*, 36–7, 39.
50. Deansely, *The Incendium Amoris*, 38–9; cf. above.
51. Beer, *Women and Mystical Experience in the Middle Ages*, 122–3.
52. Deansely, 63–4.
53. *Test. Ebor.*, i, 264–71; Deanesly, 74. Two other copies of *Incendium Amoris* were owned by St Mary's abbey, York (ib., 54).
54. *Test. Ebor.*, iii, 33 note.
55. Ib., 91 note.
56. The Bolton Hours, f107v.
57. Brown, 64–70.
58. Windeatt, 305, suggests that the Kempes may have attended the Corpus Christi plays on their visit to York in 1413.
59. There were forty-six parish churches in Norwich in the 1520s (Tanner, *Church in Late Medieval Norwich*, 20).
60. Ib., 88–90.
61. See above, 95–6.
62. *B.M.K.*, 140–1, 189–92, 204, 250; Windeatt, 178–9, 230–3, 245, 294.
63. Tanner, 58–64; Gilchrist and Oliva, *Religious Women in Medieval East Anglia*, 71–5.
64. Ib., 76–7.
65. Beer, *Women and Mystical Experience*, 130; Tanner, 58–60.
66. *B.M.K.*, 42–3; Windeatt, 77–9.
67. *B.M.K.*, 102–3; Windeatt, 140–4. In Lynn, Margery experienced hostility from two clerics who had come from Norwich, one a monk from the cathedral priory transferred to St Margaret's, the other the friar who preached at St James's (see above, 79, 88, 92).
68. *B.M.K.*, 38–40, 147; Windeatt, 73–4.
69. Tanner, 231–2.
70. *B.M.K.* 41–2, 278; Windeatt, 76–7.
71. *B.M.K.*, 104; Windeatt, 141–2. It appears that her benefactor bought the cloth and had it speedily made up into a gown, hood, kirtle and cloak.
72. *B.M.K.*, 102; Windeatt, 139–40. The offerings were probably made in the cathedral, dedicated to the Holy Trinity.
73. *B.M.K.*, 227–8; Windeatt, 271–2.
74. *B.M.K.*, 107; Windeatt, 144–5.
75. *B.M.K.*, 110; Windeatt, 148.
76. *B.M.K.*, 111; Windeatt, 148.
77. *B.M.K.*, 245; Windeatt, 289–90.
78. *B.M.K.*, 107–8, 110; Windeatt, 144–5, 148.
79. *B.M.K.*, 107, 245–6; Windeatt, 144–5, 290–1.
80. *B.M.K.*, 245; Windeatt, 290.

81. *B.M.K.*, 27–9; Windeatt, 64.
82. *B.M.K.*, 36; Windeatt, 71–2.
83. *B.M.K.*, 111–12; Windeatt, 148–9.
84. *B.M.K.*, 120; Windeatt, 158.
85. *B.M.K.*, 123–4; Windeatt, 162. For Cawood as the location, *B.M.K.*, 122, 131; Windeatt, 160, 170.
86. *B.M.K.*, 129; Windeatt, 168.
87. Thomson, *Later Lollards*, 8, 99, 195 and 195 note.
88. Hudson, *Premature Reformation*, 82–5.
89. Thomson, 220.
90. McFarlane, *John Wycliffe*, 150–2; McNiven, P. (1987) *Heresy and Politics in the Reign of Henry V. The Burning of John Badby*, Woodbridge, Suffolk: Boydell, 81–6, 89.
91. McFarlane, 160–4.
92. *B.M.K.*, 122; Windeatt, 160.
93. Aston, M. (1980) 'Lollard women priests?', *J.E.H.*, xxxi, 441–61, reprinted in id., *Lollards and Reformers*, 39–70.
94. McFarlane, 166–71; Thomson, 4–7.
95. Ib., 220.
96. Hudson, 77, 132.
97. *B.M.K.*, 112–13; Windeatt, 150–1.
98. Somerville, *Duchy of Lancaster*, i, 563.
99. Storey, R.L. (1961) *Thomas Langley and the Bishopric of Durham 1406–27*. London: The Society for Promoting Christian Knowledge, 151.
100. *S.A.C.*, 114; Capgrave, *Liber de Illustribus Henricis*, 140; Thomson, 13, 16; Wylie, J.H. and Waugh, W.T. (1929) *The Reign of Henry V*, iii, Cambridge: U.P., 87–8.
101. Reg. Bowet, f321v–f322r; Storey, 151; Wylie and Waugh, iii, 92. See Bowet's Register, *passim*, for the dating sequence of his letters in the summer and autumn of 1417.
102. *B.M.K.*, 117–19; Windeatt, 154, 156–7. Margery intended to set out from Leicester to Lincoln, perhaps because she had heard that Repingdon was there (*B.M.K.*, 117; Windeatt, 155). Repingdon dated letters at Sleaford on 1, 9, 16 August, from 10 to 30 September and on 4 and 18 October. On 12 November he dated one at Huntingdon, presumably when on his way to London, where he appears to have been staying in the Old Temple between 20 November and 11 December (*Reg. Repingdon*, iii, 185, 189, 190, 194, 210–12). For a discussion of when Margery may have arrived in York, see *B.M.K.*, 312.
103. *B.M.K.*, 129, 131–5; Windeatt, 147–8, 170–3.
104. Aston, M. (1982) 'William White's Lollard followers', *Catholic Historical Review*, lxviii, 469–97. Reprinted in *Lollards and Reformers*, 71–100.
105. Tanner, *Heresy Trials in the Diocese of Norwich, 1428–31*, 9.
106. Cf. above, 98.
107. Ib.

108. Thomson, 102; Aston, M. (1960) 'Lollardy and sedition, 1381–1431', *Past and Present*, lxxi, 1–44, reprinted in *Lollards and Reformers*, 1–47.
109. *B.M.K.*, 244–5; Windeatt, 288–9.
110. *B.M.K.*, 118; Windeatt, 159.
111. *B.M.K.*, 136; Windeatt, 175.
112. *B.M.K.*, 120; Windeatt, 158.
113. *B.M.K.*, 114; Windeatt, 151.
114. *B.M.K.*, 116; Windeatt, 153.
115. *B.M.K.*, 130–1; Windeatt, 169.
116. *B.M.K.*, 245; Windeatt, 290.
117. *B.M.K.*, 121; Windeatt, 158–9.
118. *B.M.K.*, 125; Windeatt, 163.
119. *B.M.K.*, 121–3; Windeatt, 159–61.
120. *B.M.K.*, 128; Windeatt, 167; *Chronica et Annales*, 210. Jacqueline Goodman suggests that the political disturbances in Lynn may have induced equivocal reactions to Margery elsewhere.
121. Hindle, P. (1998) *Medieval Roads and Tracks*, Princes Risborough: Shire Publications, 20–35.
122. *B.M.K.*, 106; Windeatt, 143.
123. Cf. the dialogue between Margery and her confessor in 1433 about suitable male company for her and her daughter-in-law on the journeys between Lynn and Ipswich (*B.M.K.*, 225–6; Windeatt, 270).
124. *B.M.K.*, 117–19; Windeatt, 148, 155, 157. Patryk may have been the man from Wisbech mentioned *B.M.K.*, 113; Windeatt, 151.
125. *B.M.K.*, 128; Windeatt, 166.
126. *B.M.K.*, 118; Windeatt, 155; Melbourne Hall, Melbourne, Derbyshire, X94, Lothian Box 34/1 (1411 and ?1415 references) and 34/2 (1416). I owe thanks to Professor Christopher Dyer for alerting me to the existence of this archival material on Melton Mowbray, and to Dr Laughton for her great generosity in allowing me to use her researches into the archive (for a project on East Midland towns, in conjunction with Professor Dyer), and for calendaring for me the references in the port moot rolls to the Paterike family in the fifteenth century. I am indebted too for her comments on the status of the family. There are further references to one or more John Paterikes in the rolls (in whose sequence there is a gap from 1416 to 1424) down to 1454. By the mid-1430s they were well established in the town: on 15 November 1434, John Paterike was named second of four capital pledges in the Court Baron (Box 34/3).
127. *B.M.K.*, 242–3; Windeatt, 287.
128. For Margery's visits to the nuns of Denney, see above, 18.
129. *B.M.K.*, 111; Windeatt, 148–9.
130. *B.M.K.*, 130–1; Windeatt, 169.
131. *B.M.K.*, 242; Windeatt, 287.
132. *B.M.K.*, 96; Windeatt, 149.
133. *B.M.K.*, 78; Windeatt, 133.

134. *B.M.K.*, 112; Windeatt, 157.

135. *B.M.K.*, 119; Windeatt, 168.

136. *B.M.K.*, 243–5; Windeatt, 287–9.

Chapter 7

1. Westlake, *Parish Gilds*, 198. For reverence in the parish of South Lynn in the early fifteenth century for the altar of the Holy Trinity there, see above, 81–2. I owe thanks for comments on this chapter to Professor Christopher Allmand, Dr John Law and Professor Nicholas Orme.

2. Ib., 193. For gilds of St Thomas of Canterbury at Lynn, see above, 94–5.

3. *B.M.K.*, 127; Windeatt, 165.

4. Vaughan, R. (1966) *John the Fearless*, London: Longman, 161. Professor John Thomson informs me that provision for the safe passage of pilgrims occurs frequently in diplomatic negotiations with Flanders, and sometimes with France and other countries.

5. Carus-Wilson, E.M. (ed.) (1937) *The Overseas Trade of Bristol in the Later Middle Ages*, Bristol: Bristol R.S., nos 66–71. For licences granted in 1428, ib., nos. 56–60. Travel abroad without royal licence had been forbidden in 1416; a principal motive was to prevent the export of bullion. A parliamentary Act of 1423 confirmed the prohibition of its export. Pilgrims were expected to take only what was reasonable for their expenses (Barber, M.J. (1957) 'The Englishman abroad in the fifteenth century', *Medievalia et Humanistica*, xi, 69–71; Carus-Wilson, *Overseas Trade*, no. 58; *Rotuli Parliamentorum*, iv, 252b).

6. Lodge, E.C. and Somerville, R. (eds) (1937) *John of Gaunt's Register 1379–83*, London: Royal Hist. Soc., Camden third series, lvi, vol. I, no. 381.

7. *B.M.K.*, 180; Windeatt, 220. For contemporary criticisms of pilgrimage, Finucane, R.C. (1977), *Miracles and Pilgrims. Popular Beliefs in Medieval England*, London: Dent, 199–201.

8. Lodge and Somerville, no. 252.

9. Duffy, *The Stripping of the Altars*, 191–5; *B.M.K.*, 79; Windeatt, 115. *The Book* specifies where plenary remission was to be gained on Mount Sion and in the Church of the Holy Sepulchre, and mentions that, on the journey back from Jerusalem to Ramle, Margery wished that she could return to Jerusalem, in part to gain more indulgences (*B.M.K.*, 72, 75; Windeatt, 108, 111). For the pardon granted to her at Ramle, *B.M.K.*, 175–6; Windeatt, 215: for the indulgences which Margery is likely to have received in Rome, see below, 195, 197.

10. *B.M.K.*, 32; Windeatt, 67.

11. *B.M.K.*, 72; Windeatt, 108.

12. *B.M.K.*, 224; Windeatt, 268.

13. Lincolnshire Archives, Bishop's Register XII, Register of John Buckingham, Bishop of Lincoln 1363–98, f 350 v; *Reg. Repingdon*, i, 122. Multon and Copildik both had landed interests in Lincolnshire.

14. Dickinson, J.C. (1956) *The Shrine of Our Lady of Walsingham*, Cambridge: U.P., 7–9; Ashdown-Hill, J. (1997) 'Walsingham in 1469: The pilgrimage of Edward IV and Richard, Duke of Gloucester', *The Ricardian*, xi, no. 36, 2–16. For a visit by Margery to Walsingham to 'offer in worship of our Lady', *B.M.K.*, 227; Windeatt, 271. William Wey, Fellow of Eton College, presented many informative mementoes of the Holy Land to Edington priory, Wiltshire (Order of Bonshommes), for the embellishment of its chapel of the Holy Sepulchre and other parts of the church. Among his gifts were 'a mappa of the Holy Lond, wyth Jerusalem in the myddys. Also ii levys of parchement, on[e] wyth the tempyl of Jerusalem, another wyth the holy movnte of Olyvete'. There was a collection of 'other thyngys of the holy lond made in bordys' – presumably wooden models or kits. One may have been either a full-scale model of the Holy Sepulchre or a board marked with the key measurements. Made of boards, there was a model of the chapel of Calvary (in the Church of the Holy Sepulchre), one of the church of Bethlehem, and a third of the Mount of Olives and the Vale of Jehosophat (Bandinel, B. (1857) *The Itineraries of William Wey . . . to Jerusalem, A.D. 1458 and A.D. 1462, and to Saint James of Compostella, A.D. 1456*, London: Roxburghe Club, xxviii–xxx).
15. Stewart, A. (trans.) (1892–3), *The Book of the Wanderings of Brother Felix Fabri*, 2 vols, London: Palestine Pilgrim's Text Society, i, 2–4.
16. Ib., i, 48–50.
17. Vaughan, 169–70, 195–7. Duke John fled from Paris on 23 August 1413; in 1414 his opponents, the Armagnacs, invaded Artois and threatened Flanders. A royal mandate (29 July 1413) for the proclamation of the truce concluded with Flanders was recorded by William Asshebourne, the common clerk of Lynn (Asshebourne, no. 21).
18. I owe thanks to Mr Schnitker for allowing me to cite from his paper, 'Margery Kempe in Zeeland'. Cf. *B.M.K.*, 60–1; Windeatt, 96–7, where Zierikzee is described as a 'great town'.
19. I owe thanks for the suggestion about Sigismund's war with Venice to Dr John Law.
20. Gregorovius, F. (trans.), Hamilton, G.W. (ed.), Morrison, K.F. (1898) *History of the City of Rome in the Middle Ages*, London: G. Bell, vii, part ii, 630–3; Law, J., in Hay, D. and Law, J. (1989) *Italy in the Age of the Renaissance*, London and New York: Longman, 235. John XXIII left Florence, arriving in Bologna on 12 November 1413; after an internal political coup, Bologna had recently once more submitted to papal rule.
21. Morris, C. (1997) 'Bringing the Holy Sepulchre to the west: S. Stefano, Bologna, from the fifth to the twentieth century', in Swanson, R.N. (ed.) *The Church Retrospective. Studies in Church History 33*, Woodbridge, Suff., and Rochester, N.Y.: Blackwell, 31–59.
22. *B.M.K.*, 100–2; Windeatt, 138–40; Schnitker, op. cit. The fact that Margery returned home via Norwich suggests that her company landed at an East Anglian port.

23. *The Itineraries of William Wey*, x–xi.
24. *B.M.K.*, 110; Windeatt, 147–8. Wey spent a comparable amount of time on pilgrimage to Santiago in 1458. Sailing from Plymouth on 17 May, he reached La Coruña on the 21st; he re-embarked there on 5 June, and reached Plymouth on the 9th (op. cit., xxvi). Perhaps both Margery and Wey went to other places associated with Santiago in Galicia, such as El Padron (cf. Letts, M. (ed.) (1957) *The Travels of Leo of Rozmital*, Cambridge: U.P., Hakluyt Society, cviii, 109–10, 114).
25. *S.A.C.*, 9.
26. *Travels of Leo of Rozmital*, 102–3, 115–17; Letts, M. (ed.) (1946) *The Pilgrimage of Arnold von Harff* (etc.), London: Hakluyt Society, second series, xciv, 274–5 and 274 n.
27. Storrs, C.M. (1998) *Jacobean Pilgrims from England to St James of Compostella*, London: Confraternity of Saint James, 114.
28. *B.M.K.*, 226–9; Windeatt, 270–3. Ipswich had a well-known devotional attraction which doubtless drew Margery there – a shrine of Our Lady with (as at Walsingham) some of her milk (Finucane, 198).
29. *B.M.K.*, 229–33; Windeatt, 273–7.
30. Bartos, F.M., Klassen, J. (eds) (1986) *The Hussite Revolution 1424–37*, Boulder: Columbia U.P., 104–5, 18; Worcestre, *Itineraries*, 306–7.
31. *B.M.K.*, 231–3; Windeatt, 268, 275–6.
32. *Travels of Leo of Rozmital*, 23.
33. *B.M.K.*, 235–8; Windeatt, 279–82.
34. *B.M.K.*, 238–41; Windeatt, 283–5.
35. Sommé, M. (1970), 'Les déplacements d'Isabelle de Portugal et la circulation dans les Pays-Bas bourguignons au milieu du XVe siècle', *Revue du Nord*, lii, 183–97; Wey, op. cit., xviii. Wey's route from Calais to Aachen went through Gravelines, Dunkirk, Nieuwpoort, Bruges, Ghent, Termonde, Mechelen, Aerschot, Diest, Hasselt and Maastricht. I owe thanks to Dr Graeme Small for the reference to Sommé's article.
36. Duffy, 191.
37. Storrs, Chapter 8, 1.
38. Warren, *Anchorites*, 242–5.
39. The window is now in the redundant church of All Saints, Pavement, York.
40. The altarpiece is kept in the Capela das Reliquias in the cathedral of Compostela. It has five panels (from left to right): (1) Christ preaching to three figures in a fishing boat; (2) Christ (?) preaching to a crowd; (3) St James in pulpit – centrepiece; (4) St James's execution; (5) St James's body in sailing boat, being transferred to Galicia.
41. Westlake, 194; cf. above, 82, 94, 96. In 1389 there was a gild of St James in the parish of North Lynn, outside the borough (Westlake, 200).
42. *B.M.K.*, 232; Windeatt, 276.
43. Nicolas, N.H. (1826) *Testamenta Vetusta*, i, London: Nichols and Son, 196. Arundel, who was from Northumberland, was a chamber knight of

Henry IV early in his reign (Given-Wilson, *Royal Household and King's Affinity*, 195, 230).

44. Tanner, *Church in Late Medieval Norwich*, 87.
45. van Herwaarden, J. (1978) *Opgelegde Bedevaarten*, Amsterdam, 410. The Holy Land was not specified, but Cyprus (42) and Bari (33) were. I owe thanks for this information to Mr H. Schnitker.
46. Sumption, J. (1975) *Pilgrimage. An Image of Medieval Religion*, London: Faber and Faber, 282–3. Dr Sumption cites the report by the Faculty of Theology of the University of Erfurt (c. 1445) on the miraculous blood, to be found in Bodl. MS Lat. th. e. 2, f61–f65. In her will of 1411, the Danish princess Margrete, widow of Hakon VI of Norway, made a bequest to Wilsnack; the shrine was attracting royal and noble Danish patronage in the later fifteenth century (*Danmarks Historie 1400–1500*, vi, 31, 33, 224, 244, 273). I owe thanks to Ms Tina Eriksson for translating the relevant passages of this last work.
47. Furnivall, F.J. (ed.) (1867) *The stacions of Rome: and the pilgrims sea-voyage* (etc.), London: E.E.T.S., original series, xxv, 37–40.
48. *B.M.K.*, 102; Windeatt, 139.
49. *B.M.K.*, 110; Windeatt, 147. The threat to throw Margery overboard may well not have been invented, or its seriousness exaggerated, since it related to deeply held superstitions about the bad luck which the presence of women on ships could bring. It had been alleged that when in 1379 a military expedition, commanded by Sir John Arundel (brother of the archbishop who treated Margery kindly), was blown off course en route to France and was being battered by terrible storms, those who had abducted as many as allegedly sixty women blamed them for their misfortunes and, as the monastic chronicler unfeelingly puts it, threw them to the fishes. They included nuns! (*Chronicon Angliae*, 249–51.)
50. *B.M.K.*, 242; Windeatt, 286–7.
51. Usk, Adam, Given-Wilson, C. (ed. and trans.) (1997) *The Chronicle of Adam Usk 1377–1421*, Oxford: Clarendon Press, 152–4. On his return from Rome in 1406, Usk 'was almost frozen to death by the snow', when travelling over Mont Cenis (ib., 210–11).
52. *B.M.K.*, 65; Windeatt, 101.
53. *B.M.K.*, 62; Windeatt, 98.
54. *B.M.K.*, 100–1; Windeatt, 137–8. For the desolate nature of the country around Rome in the period, see Stinger, 15–17.
55. *B.M.K.*, 238; Windeatt, 282–3.
56. *B.M.K.*, 234; Windeatt, 277–8.
57. *B.M.K.*, 77; Windeatt, 112–13.
58. Usk, 154–5.
59. *B.M.K.*, 79; Windeatt, 115.
60. B.M.K., 235–7; Windeatt, 279–82.
61. *B.M.K.*, 238–40; Windeatt, 282–4.

62. *B.M.K.*, 240–1; Windeatt, 285. The text does not make clear whether Margery feared that the friar would molest her, though he is throughout referred to favourably. He would have been unable to give her effective protection; he had been robbed himself.

63. The principle of hospitality was maintained by monasteries and pilgrim hospices (Sumption, 198ff). For the Hospice of St Thomas at Rome, see below, 199.

64. *B.M.K.*, 65; Windeatt, 101.

65. *B.M.K.*, 234–5; Windeatt, 278–9.

66. *B.M.K.*, 235, 237, 241, 243; Windeatt, 279–81, 286–7.

67. *B.M.K.*, 32; Windeatt, 67.

68. *B.M.K.*, 60; Windeatt, 96.

69. *B.M.K.*, 105–6, 108, 110; Windeatt, 143, 145–6, 147.

70. *B.M.K.*, 134; Windeatt, 173.

71. *B.M.K.*, 64; Windeatt, 100.

72. *B.M.K.*, 64–6; Windeatt, 100–3.

73. *C.C.R.*, *1422–9*, 483. Cf. the letters of exchange made by Alesander de Ferentinis of the fellowship of the Albertini in London to two Lynn friars, the Augustinian William Rodnale in 1422, and the Dominican John Tydde in 1428 (ib., 478; *C.C.R.*, *1429–35*, 377). Dr Law suggests that the fellowship may have been to the Alberti Company of Florence. For Belle, see above, 154–5.

74. A.S.V., Cancelleria Inferiore, Notzi, busta 94. I am indebted to Dr Stefano Piasentini for this reference, and to Dr Law for his comments on it.

75. *B.M.K.*, 91–7; Windeatt, 128–34.

76. *B.M.K.*, 102; Windeatt, 139–40. As Margery intended to use part or all of the three halfpence for an offering to the Trinity in Norwich, it is likely that she was anticipating hospitality and help with travelling expenses from friends in the city. The offering was presumably made in the cathedral, dedicated to the Holy Trinity.

77. *B.M.K.*, 232, 236; Windeatt, 276, 280.

78. *B.M.K.*, 239, 241; Windeatt, 283, 285.

79. *B.M.K.*, 243; Windeatt, 287.

80. *B.M.K.*, 60–1; Windeatt, 96–7.

81. *B.M.K.*, 66–7; Windeatt, 102–3.

82. *B.M.K.*, 61, 66; Windeatt, 97, 102.

83. *B.M.K.*, 61; Windeatt, 97.

84. *B.M.K.*, 80, 84; Windeatt, 115–16, 120. This priest may have been the one who disputed possession of a sheet with her on board the galley (*B.M.K.*, 67; Windeatt, 103).

85. *B.M.K.*, 97, 102; Windeatt, 134, 140.

86. *B.M.K.*, 76–7, 80, 92, 106; Windeatt, 111–13, 116, 128–9, 144.

87. *B.M.K.*, 111, 113, 117–18; Windeatt, 148, 151–2, 155–6. One of these companions, Patryk, seems to have acted after Margery's return to England as her servant and hired help (and perhaps also to Thomas Marchale). If

he can be identified with John Patryk of Melton Mowbray, he was clearly of lower status than Margery (see above, 149). A pilgrimage might be a means of making useful mundane connections and gaining patronage and employment, through the process of bonding in unfamiliar and often uncomfortable surroundings.

88. *B.M.K.*, 61–2; Windeatt, 97–8. Margery was not entirely friendless; a male companion 'who loved her well' acted as intermediary with the others.

89. *B.M.K.*, 62; Windeatt, 98.

90. *B.M.K.*, 66; Windeatt, 102–3.

91. For communication by Margery and devout Italian women through behaviour and gesture, B.M.K., 77–8; Windeatt, 113–14.

92. See below, 190–1, 193–4.

93. Cf. below, 200–1.

94. *Chronica et Annales*, 395–6.

95. *B.M.K.*, 85; Windeatt. Professor Angus MacIntosh notes that 'we have good written evidence for well over a thousand dialectically differentiated varieties of later Middle English' ('Word Geography in the Lexicography of Medieval English' (1973), *Annals of the New York Academy of Sciences*, ccxi, 55). I owe thanks to Dr Margaret Laing for advice about works on the subject.

96. *B.M.K.*, 232; Windeatt, 276. For Margery's German confessor in Rome, see below, 199–200.

97. Power, E. and Postan, M.M. (1933) 'The economic and political relations of England and the Hansa from 1400 to 1475', in Power and Postan (eds), *Studies in English Trade in the Fifteenth Century*, London: Routledge, 116; Fudge, J.D. (1995) *Cargoes, Embargoes and Emissaries*, Toronto: U.P., 11. In 1434 the Hansetag, meeting at Lübeck, planned retaliatory measures; the Grand Master of the Teutonic Order threatened the expulsion of the English from Prussia.

98. *B.M.K.*, 236; Windeatt, 280–1. For an allusion by a fellow townsman of Margery to the insult about tails, see Capgrave, *Chronicle of England*, 284. Jacques de Vitry (c. 1170–1240) had castigated the scholars of Paris for insulting their various nations: the English, it was said 'were drunkards and had tails' (Schachner, N. (1962) *The Mediaeval Universities*, New York: A.S. Barnes and Company, Inc., 78).

99. *B.M.K.*, 240–1; Windeatt, 284–5.

100. Munro, J.H. (1970) 'An economic aspect of the collapse of the Anglo-Burgundian alliance, 1428–42', *E.H.R.*, lxxxv, 225–44; Bolton, J.L. (1980) *The Medieval English Economy*, London: Dent, 299.

101. Thrupp, S.L. (1957) 'A survey of the alien population of England in 1440', *Speculum*, xxxii, 262–73.

102. Owen, 457–9, printing the return of aliens resident in Lynn and other places in Freebridge hundred from P.R.O., E179/149/126. For Slynghelant's will, N.R.O., Consistory Court of Norwich, N.P.2, Aleyn. For brief lists of aliens in Lynn liable to pay fines in the 1420s, KL/C7/2, 119, 241.

103. Ingleby, f81r.
104. *B.M.K.*, 97; Windeatt, 134–5. I owe thanks to Ms Andrea Briehle for discussing the varieties of the German language with me.
105. Warner, G. (ed.) (1926) *The Libelle of Englysshe Polycye. A Poem on the Use of Sea-Power, 1436*, Oxford: U.P.; modern version cited from Dunham, W. and Pargellis, S. (1938) *Complaint and Reform in England 1436–1714*, Oxford: U.P., 3–30. Cf. Holmes, G.A. (1961) 'The "Libel of English Policy"', *E.H.R.*, lxxvi, 193–216.
106. See above, 19–20.
107. Professor Orme has pointed out to me that a benevolent view of Christendom is often found in fifteenth-century English romances.
108. *B.M.K.*, 137–8; Windeatt, 176–7.
109. *B.M.K.*, 97; Windeatt, 115.

Chapter 8

1. Lane, F.C. (1934) *Venetian Ships and Shipbuilding of the Renaissance*, Baltimore, Johns Hopkins Press; Tucci, U. (1991) *I Servizi marittimi veneziani per il pellegrinaggio in Terra santa nel Medioevo*, Venice: Università degli Studi di Venezia. I owe thanks to Dr Stefano Piasentini for the reference to Professor Tucci's work, and for his great generosity in providing me with the references cited below from the Archivio di Stato and the Biblioteca Marciana, Venice. Dr Patricia Allerston kindly advised me on relevant categories of holdings in the Archivio. I have benefited from the advice of Dr Gianfranco Dogliani and Dr Richard Mackenney about Venetian history. I owe thanks to Professor Christopher Allmand, Dr John Law and Professor Nicholas Orme for commenting on the chapter, and to Dr Mackenney for commenting on the section on Venice.
2. *Derby's Expeditions*, lxiii.
3. *B.M.K.*, 65; Windeatt, 101.
4. Wey, *Itineraries*, xi.
5. *B.M.K.*, 66; Windeatt, 102.
6. *B.M.K.*, 65; Windeatt, 101–2.
7. *B.M.K.*, 18–19; Windeatt, 52–3.
8. Fabri, *Book of the Wanderings*, i, 101–2.
9. Newett, M.M. (ed.) (1907) *Canon Pietro Casola's Pilgrimage to Jerusalem in the Year 1494*, Manchester: U.P., 136–7. I owe thanks to Professor Michael Angold and Dr Mackenney for introducing me to this text.
10. Von Harff, *Pilgrimage*, 51.
11. Information from Dr Piasentini.
12. Fabri, i, 93, 110–11.
13. Casola, 137.
14. Ellis, H. (ed.) (1851) *The Pylgrymage of Sir Richard Guylforde to the Holy Land, A.D. 1506*, London: Camden Soc., li, 7.
15. *Derby's Expeditions*, lx–lxi, 275–7.

16. Fabri, i, 93, 110–11.
17. Casola, 129–32, 143–5.
18. Mansueti, *Miracle of the Reliquary of the True Cross in San Lio*; Bellini, *Miracle of the Cross at the Bridge of San Lorenzo*, Gallerie dell' Accademia, Venice, the latter reproduced in Chambers, D.S. (1970) *The Imperial Age of Venice 1380–1580*, London: Thames and Hudson, pl. 76.
19. For the Ascension Day ritual, ib., 136; Fabri, i, 98–100.
20. Ib., 108–9.
21. For her appreciation of the admirable qualities of a variety of folk in Lynn, see above, 111–12.
22. *B.M.K.*, 65–6; Windeatt, 101–2.
23. Cherry, J. (1969) 'The Dunstable Swan Jewel', *Journal of the British Archaeological Association*, third series, xxxii, 48–9; Goodman, A. (1986) 'John of Gaunt', in Ormrod, W.M. (ed.) *England in the Fourteenth Century*, Boydell: Woodbridge, 73 and references in notes 38–40; *Derby's Expeditions*, lx, lxvii.
24. This much reproduced illumination is in Oxford, MS Bodley 264, f. 218r.
25. Version from Dunham and Pargellis, 13–14.
26. *B.M.K.*, 66–7; Windeatt, 102–3.
27. Lane, 29–30; Wey, 6.
28. Fabri, i, 88 (clause 7 of contract).
29. Ib., 83–91; Wey, 4–6; Casola, 153–4.
30. Fabri, i, 91; Wey, 4.
31. Ib., 4.
32. Account Book of Francesco Quirini, A.S.V., Miscellanea atti diversi manoscritti, busta 134; *Derby's Expeditions*, cii–ciii. In 1436, in bills of exchange, Venetian ducats were valued at between 3s 3d and 3s 5^1/2d (Spufford, P. and Wilkinson, W. (1977) *Interim Listing of the Exchange Rates of Medieval Europe*, Keele, 252).
33. Fabri, i, 126–7.
34. Lane, *Venetian Ships*, 15–17.
35. Casola, 161.
36. *B.M.K.*, 67; Windeatt, 103. Fabri (i, 127ff) and Casola (155ff) provide vivid descriptions of the galleys they travelled in and of living conditions aboard. For a summary of the supplies taken on board Derby's galley and references to the furnishing of his cabin, see *Derby's Expeditions*, lxi–lxii.
37. Wey, 5. The 'spices' which a German priest put in Margery's mouth when she appeared to have been taken ill on the way from Ramle to Jerusalem had probably been stored in his chest (*B.M.K.*, 67; Windeatt, 103).
38. Fabri, i, 130–1.
39. Casola, 155–61; cf. Fabri, i, 129. Dr Mackenney pointed out to me that the rowers were exempt.
40. Quirini, f. 47; Orme and Webster, *The English Hospital*, 194–5. In 1478 William Worcestre found a record in the Dominican friary at Truro that a Ralph Reskymer had died in 1465 (*Itineraries*, 99).

NOTES

41. Quirini, ff. 35, 47; Watt, D.E.R. (1977) *A Biographical Dictionary of Scottish Graduates to A.D. 1410*, Oxford: U.P., 398–9. I owe thanks for the identification of Moffat to Dr Stephen Boardman.

42. Biblioteca Marciana, Venice, Positivo Marciana, n. 38, 'Cronaca di Antonio Morosini', i, 836.

43. *B.M.K.*, 67, 66; Windeatt, 103.

44. A.S.V., Senato Misti, registro 50, c. 150.

45. Wey, xiii.

46. Chapters 28–30.

47. *B.M.K.*, 189; Windeatt, 230.

48. *B.M.K.*, 132; Windeatt, 170–1.

49. Fabri, i, 316–17; *B.M.K.*, 78; Windeatt, 114.

50. Dull, S., Luttrell, A. and Keen, M. (1991) 'Faithful unto death: the tomb slab of Sir William Neville and Sir John Clanvowe, Constantinople, 1391', *The Antiquaries Journal*, lxxi, 174–90; Worcestre, *Itineraries*, 355, 359; N.R.O., Consistory Court of Norwich, 20, 30 Coppinger. Carbonell died before 18 November 1430, when a writ to the escheator of Norfolk and Suffolk was dated, ordering him to hold an inquisition post mortem (*Calendar of the Fine Rolls*, vol. xvi, *1430–7* (1936), London: Stationery Office, 1–2). On 16 October 1429 Alexander de Ferentinis of the fellowship of the Albertini, dwelling in London, had received royal licence to make a letter of exchange for £20, payable to him (*C.C.R., 1429–1435*, 378). Perhaps this was intended to help finance Carbonell's pilgrimage. The same banker had been licensed to make a similar bill out to him, for £40, in 1427 (ib., 375).

51. *Chronica et Annales*, 377–8.

52. Frans Halsmuseum, Haarlem; Centraal Museum, Utrecht.

53. Fabri, i, 24.

54. See above, 154.

55. *Derby's Expeditions*, 299–300, 302. For Willoughby (c. 1370–1409), see *C.P.*, xii, part ii, 661. In a Lynn chamberlain's account for 1410–11, 3s 4d was accounted for as payment for a tun of wine granted to Willoughby and his lady when they were last in the town, for its honour (K.L.R.O., KL/C39/47). Erpingham (1357–1428) was one of those appointed in 1403 to settle the disputes between Bishop Despenser and the borough (see above, 27).

56. *C.P.*, xii, part ii, 3, 79.

57. *B.M.K.*, 35; Windeatt, 70.

58. See above, 141.

59. Cf. above, 112.

60. Wey advised that thirteen or fourteen days would be spent in the Holy Land and provided an itinerary which mostly corresponds with Margery's (op. cit., 6–7, 19).

61. Burgoyne, M.H. (1987) *Mamluk Jerusalem*, London: World of Islam Festival Trust, 53, 59–60; Peters, F.E. (1985) *Jerusalem*, Princeton, N.J.:

U.P., 427, 436; cf. Fabri, i, 247–55. I owe thanks to Professor Michael Angold for the reference to Burgoyne's book.

62. *B.M.K.*, 73–4; Windeatt, 109–10.
63. Fabri, i, 282–4.
64. I have relied heavily for impressions of the Holy Land on the vivid water-colours and romantic description in Fulleylove, J. and Kelman, J. (1912) *The Holy Land*, London: Adam and Charles Black.
65. Fabri, i, 88–9; ib., ii, 4–5.
66. Peters, 436; Fabri, ii, 8–10.
67. *Guylforde*, 18.
68. Fabri, ii, 84–5.
69. *Guylforde*, 39. William Wey was an avid collector of relics from the holy places: he got a stone apiece from the Mount of Calvary, the Holy Sepulchre, the hill of Tabor, the pillar at which Christ was scourged, the place of the Invention of the Cross and the holy cave of Bethlehem (*Itineraries*, xxix).
70. *B.M.K.*, 118; Windeatt, 156. The friars gave her 'many great relics'.
71. Von Harff, 152.
72. *B.M.K.*, 77–8; Windeatt, 113.
73. Peters, 435; Fabri, i, 241–4. 257–8, 267, 269.
74. *B.M.K.*, 75; Windeatt, 111; Fabri, i, 284–5.
75. Ib., i, 224; *Guylforde*, 16.
76. Fabri, i, 265. For an account of the terrors of a dust storm, ib., 266. *The Book* puts Ramle only in a devotional context (see below, 194).
77. Ib., i, 279–82.
78. *B.M.K.*, 67; Windeatt, 103. Fabri says that the asses which his company had hired were sure-footed on mountain tracks and that the women rode boldly (op. cit., ii, 11).
79. *B.M.K.*, 67–71; Windeatt, 104–7.
80. *B.M.K.*, 72; Windeatt, 107–8.
81. *Guylforde*, 22.
82. *B.M.K.*, 72–3; Windeatt, 108.
83. *B.M.K.*, 73; Windeatt, 109.
84. *B.M.K.*, 74; Windeatt, 111; Fabri, ii, 3–4, 11–23, 66–7. For the plenary indulgence on offer there, and the perils of the pilgrimage, including those incurred in bathing in the Jordan, Von Harff, 222 and n.
85. *Golden Legend*, i, 227–9.
86. *B.M.K.*, 74; Windeatt, 110; *Golden Legend*, i, 227.
87. Von Harff, 224–5; Fabri, ii, 42–3, 46, 48–9, 53, 54, 57; Wey, 7; *B.M.K.*, 74; Windeatt, 110. The Mount of Temptation was called Mount Quarantine, referring to the forty days of Christ's temptation (ib., 314).
88. *B.M.K.*, 74–5; Windeatt, 110–11; Wey, 14–15; Von Harff, 221; Fabri, i, 78.
89. *B.M.K.*, 75; Windeatt, 111.
90. Gregorovius, vi, part ii, 634–40, 652–3; Partner, P. (1972) *The Lands of St Peter: the Papal State in the Middle Ages and the Early Renaissance*, Berkeley: California U.P., 391–33; Law in Hay and Law, 202–5.

91. *The stacions of Rome*, 1–24.
92. *B.M.K.*, 95–6; Windeatt, 132; Capgrave, John, (ed.) Mills, C.A. (1911) *Ye Solace of Pilgrimes* (etc.), London; British Archaeological Society of Rome, 85–155.
93. *B.M.K.*, 29, 42, 87, 215; Windeatt, 75, 137, 256.
94. *The stacions*, 2–3; Sumption, 249–50; Stinger, 37–8. I owe thanks to Dr Gary Dickson for pointing out to me the importance of the *sudarium* as a relic.
95. *The stacions*, 8–11.
96. *B.M.K.*, 82; Windeatt, 118.
97. *The stacions*, 16–17.
98. *B.M.K.*, 99; Windeatt, 136.
99. *B.M.K.*, 80–2; Windeatt, 116–18. Meech and Allen identified this church as one known to them as Sta Caterina in Ruota (*B.M.K.*, 299).
100. Stinger, 24.
101. *B.M.K.*, 86–9; Windeatt, 122–4.
102. *B.M.K.*, 92–3; Windeatt, 129.
103. Usk, 200–3; *Incontro dei pellegrini col papa Ciriaco sotto le mura di Roma*, Gallerie dell' Accademia, Venice.
104. Sumption, 148. Cf. Stinger, 46ff, on how the magnificence of religious ceremonies in Rome declined in the decades after Margery's visit.
105. Law, in Hay and Law, 201–3.
106. Usk, 188–9.
107. Stinger, 21–7; cf. Law, in Hay and Law, 207.
108. *B.M.K.*, 95; Windeatt, 132.
109. *B.M.K.* 80; Windeatt, 116. For some recent comments on the English Hospice, and on the background to Margery's experiences in Rome, see Harvey, M. (1999) *The English in Rome 1362–1420. Portrait of an Expatriate Community*, Cambridge: U.P., 55–76, 129–30. I owe thanks for this reference to Dr Richard Mackenney.
110. Allen, J. (1962) 'Englishmen in Rome and the Hospice 1362–1474', *The Venerabile*, xxi, 43–81.
111. *B.M.K.*, 94–5; Windeatt, 121–32.
112. Allen, 112.
113. Pilgrim lists (May 1479–May 1484) are printed in Hay, G. (1962) 'Pilgrims in the Hospice', *The Venerabile*, xxi, Appendix 12, 109–44. There were usually in this period only a few pilgrims from the same shire resident at a time, often just one or two. Some were husbands and wives together; there were also women named separately. Most of the pilgrims were men.
114. Allen, 54–5; A.V.C.I.R., Liber 16/30/X21/5, 'Liber acquitanciarum de Anglia et fratrum receptoram in Roma' (text printed by Allen, 68–81). This book was started in 1446. The donors, listed by diocese, were from those of Exeter, Carlisle, Rochester and from the Welsh dioceses. The only entry from the diocese of Norwich (dated 16 March 1492) comprised a

married couple, the prioress of Campsey, and eight other ladies (f8). In 1425 Archbishop Chichele had authorised collections of the 'Firma Angliae' for the Hospice and granted an indulgence to penitent donors (*Chichele Reg.*, iv, 256–9). I owe thanks to Mr Christian Daw, formerly archivist of the Venerabile Collegio Inglese, Rome, for his helpful response to my enquiries, and to his successor as archivist, Mr Nicholas Schofield, for his help and scholarly advice.

115. A.V.C.I.R., Membranae, m 179 (Richardson), m 188 (Warner), m 183 (Rodgerson).
116. Allen, 54. By 1431 the Hospice owned thirty-one houses and received 280 ducats in annual rent.
117. Ib., 45, 48–9, 59–60.
118. Thomassen was guardian in 1407 and 1418 (A.V.C.I.R., mm 91, 183), and Newton was clerical chamberlain in 1408 and 1418. John Croat was lay chamberlain in 1408 (ib., mm 91, 183).
119. Surviving lists of *confratres* date only from 1446 onwards (see above, 258, f114). Peter de Ragon was the Hospice's *procurator et syndicus* in 1408, and a certain Roger was *confrater* in 1418 (A.V.C.I.R., mm 91, 183).
120. Information in letter from Mr Nicholas Schofield.
121. *B.M.K.*, 85–6; Windeatt, 122. Before and after serving the old woman, Margery was staying at the house of a host (*B.M.K.*, 92; Windeatt, 128). Presumably at the English Hospice a rule enforcing a limited length of stay was being applied (see above, 199).
122. *B.M.K.*, 92–4; Windeatt, 128–31.
123. Allen, 47.
124. *B.M.K.*, 80–1, 92; Windeatt, 116–17, 128–9.
125. Stinger, 15–17; Law, in Hay and Law, 209–10; *B.M.K.*, 99–101; Windeatt, 137–8. Margery received Christ's reassurance that she and the company would be safe, and was able to allay the fears expressed a little way out of Rome by her priestly patron.
126. Burgoyne, 61–74.
127. *Test. Ebor.*, ii, 419–20.

Chapter 9

1. *B.M.K.*, 126–8; Windeatt, 164–6; Owen, 404–5; Harrod, 72. Dr Owen transcribed Hunte's present (from Asshebourne's copy) as 'a litill yonge horsbeer'. I owe thanks to Mrs Katherine Parker for consulting the text and providing me with the correct version. The countess of Warwick kept a bear in 1420–1 (Woolgar, *Household Accounts*, ii, 25). I owe thanks to Dr Adam Fox for discussing the presence of bears in towns with me.
2. *B.M.K.*, 16–17; Windeatt, 51–2.
3. I refer to the cults of St Thomas of Canterbury, St William of York and St John of Bridlington; see above, 135–6, 141.
4. See above, 24–5, 29–30.

5. For the disrespect shown to a royal sergeant-at-arms in Lynn in 1416, see above, 44–5. To treat one of these feared trouble-shooting agents of the Crown in this contemptuous way was a bold act of defiance. For their past roles and reputations, see Partington, R. (2001) 'Edward III's enforcers: The king's sergeants-at-arms in the localities', in Bothwell, J.S. (ed.), *The Age of Edward III*, Woodbridge: York Medieval Press/Boydell, 89–106.

6. Westlake, *Parish Gilds*, 195.

7. Baldwin, F.E. (1926) *Sumptuary Legislation and Personal Regulation in England*, Baltimore: Johns Hopkins Press, 76ff, 85, 91–2.

8. Woodforde, *The Norwich School of Glass-Painting*: for the wall-painting at Broughton, 185 and plate xli; for the background, Chapter 7 (182–92). Christ thanked Margery 'specially for thou mayest suffer no man to break my commandments nor to swear by me but if it be a great pain to thee and for thou art always ready to reprove them of their swearing for my love' (*B.M.K.*, 160; Windeatt, 199).

9. Bokenham, Osbern, Serjeantson, M.S. (ed.) (1938) *Legendes of Hooly Wummen*, London: E.E.T.S. Bokenham (?1392–?1447) was an Augustinian friar of Stoke-by-Clare (Suffolk) who made these verse translations to present to friends and patronesses.

SELECT BIBLIOGRAPHY

Manuscript sources

BRISTOL
Bristol Record Office
P/AS/Ch W/1   'Minutes of All Saints' Parish in the Reigne of Edward
                     IV'

CAMBRIDGE
Cambridge University Library
EDR, F5/33   Ecclesiastical formulary, with notes from diet accounts
                     of Bishop Peverel of Worcester's household, 1413

KING'S LYNN
Muniments of the borough of King's Lynn
KL/C6/2   Hall Rolls, 1399–1403
KL/C7/29   Ingleby, H. (trans.) (1924) 'King's Lynn corporation
                     minutes. Book 1. 1422–1450' (KL/C7/2: Hall
                     Book)
KL/C10/2   The book of William Asshebourne
KL/C12/9   Will of William Silisden (1410)
KL/C12/10   Will of Henry Bachecroft (1421)
KL/C12/11   Will of Robert Salesbury (1429)
KL/C12/12   Will of Gilbert Watson (1479)
KL/C17/14   Leet and Hustings Roll, 1403–4
KL/C17/15   Leet and Hustings Roll, 1404
KL/C38/7, 10, 11   Accounts of Holy Trinity Gild, 1406–7, 1416–17,
                     1421–2
KL/C39/42, 43, 45, 47, 48   Borough chamberlain's accounts, 1398–9,
                     1401–2, 1404–5, 1410–11, 1411–12
KL/C50/203, 233, 236.   List of deeds to corporate estates

LINCOLN
Lincolnshire Archives
Bishop's Register XII   Will of Sir John Multon (1388), Register of John
                     Buckingham, Bishop of Lincoln, 1363–98, f 350v

LONDON
College of Arms
'Processus in Curia Marescalli', MS1; process between Sir Reginald Grey and
                     Edward Hastings

· 261 ·

Public Record Office

C47/42; C47/43 — Chancery Miscellanea: gild certificates for Lynn (1389); those in English printed by Toulmin Smith, op. cit.

E101/93/31 — Exchequer, Accounts Various; particulars of account of subsidy, Lynn, April 1389 to November 1391

KB27/580, Rex, m 5 — King's Bench Roll, 1406; indictment for riot at Lynn

KB9/188, m 9–11 — King's Bench Roll, 1416; indictment for riot at Lynn

MELBOURNE, DERBYSHIRE
Melbourne Hall (see Preface)
X94, Lothian Box 34/1–4 — Portmote rolls for Melton Mowbray, 1411–52 (with gap in sequence, 1416–24)

NORWICH
Norfolk Record Office
Lynn wills proved in consistory court of bishops of Norwich (registers of Surflete, Doke, Wylbey, Aleyn and Coppinger)

ROME
Muniments of Venerabile Collegio Inglese
Liber 16 30 X21.5 — 'Liber acquitanciarum de Anglia et fratrum receptarum in Roma'
Membranae — property deeds, 1404–1

VENICE
Archivio di Stato (see Preface)
Cancelleria Inferiore, Notzi, busta 94; Notzio Giacomello Girardo, Protocolo, carta 21 (26 April 1393): bill of exchange of Daffydd ap' Jevan and his companions
Miscellanea atti diversi manoscritti, busta 134: account book of Francesco Quirini for voyage to the Middle East, 1414
Senato Misti, registro 50, c. 150: notice of departure of Lorenzo Priuli's galley for Jaffa, 4 September 1414
Biblioteca Marciana (see Preface)
Positivo Marciana, n. 38 — Gallovich, G. and Cecchetti, B., transcribed, 'Cronaca di Antonio Morosini', vol. 1

WORCESTER
Worcestershire Record Office
b. 716. 093 – BA. 2648/5 (ii) — Register of Thomas Peverel, Bishop of Worcester, 1407–19

YORK
Borthwick Institute, University of York
Registers 17 and 18 — Register of Henry Bowet, archbishop of York, 1407–23
York Minster Library
MS Add. 2 — Horae Eboracenses; 'The Bolton Book of Hours'

Dissertations and other unpublished sources

Clark, J.G., 'Thomas Walsingham reconsidered: books and learning at Late Medieval St Albans', forthcoming , *Speculum.*

Dunn, A.J. (2000) 'The endowment and disendowment of lay magnates in England and the Welsh marches, 1396–1408', University of Oxford D.Phil.

Kettle, A.J., 'Kempe, Margery (c. 1373 [–] c. 1439)', to be published in Loades, D. (ed.), *Reader's Guide to British History*, London: Fitzroy Dearborn.

Myers, M.D. (1996) 'Well-nigh ruined?: Violence in King's Lynn 1380–1420', Notre Dame University, Indiana, Ph.D.; copy in King's Lynn Record Office.

Parker, K. (2001) 'Lordship or liberty? Counting the cost in King's Lynn: 1399–1406'.

Schnitker, H. (2000) 'Margery Kempe in Zealand'.

Smith, J. (2000) Thesis on the iconography of the St William window, York Minster: draft chapter on the canons, the Roos family and the commissioning of the window; for University of York Ph.D.

Strong, P.L. (1967) 'All Saints' City, Bristol. Calendar of Deeds Part 1: introduction and text', University of London Diploma in Archive Administration.

Published and calendared documents

Archer, M. (1963–82) *The Register of Bishop Philip Repingdon 1405–1413*, 3 vols, Lincoln Record Society, lvii, lviii, lxxiv.

Calendars of Close Rolls (1909–33) 1360–1435, nineteen vols, London: Stationery Office.

Calendars of Inquisitions Miscellaneous, 1377–1388, 1392–1399, 1399–1422 (1957–68) London: Stationery Office.

Calendars of Patent Rolls (1895–1916) 1370–1436, sixteen vols, London: Stationery Office.

Isaacson, R.F. (trans.), Ingleby, H. (ed.) (1919–20), *The Red Register of King's Lynn*, 2 vols, King's Lynn; Thew and Son.

Jacob, E.F. (ed.) (1938–47) *The Register of Henry Chichele, Archbishop of Canterbury, 1414–1443*, 4 vols, Oxford: Clarendon Press.

Kirby, J.L. (ed.) (1978) *Calendar of Signet Letters of Henry V*, London: Stationery Office.

Legge, M.D. (1941) *Anglo-Norman Letters and Petitions*, Oxford: Blackwell.

Owen, D.M. (ed.) (1984) *The Making of King's Lynn. A Documentary Survey*, London: British Academy.

Owen, D.M. (ed.) (1981) *William Asshebourne's Book. King's Lynn Corporation Archives 10/2*, Norwich: Norfolk Record Society, xlviii; calendar of KL/C 10/2.

Pantin, W.A. (ed.) (1976) 'Instructions for a devout and literate layman', in Alexander, J.J.G. and Gibson, M.T. (eds) *Medieval Language and Literature. Essays Presented to Richard William Hunt*, Oxford: Clarendon Press, 398–400.

Register of Edward the Black Prince, iv, 1351–65, London: Stationery Office.

Tanner, N.P. (ed.) (1977) *Heresy Trials in the Diocese of Norwich, 1428–31*, London: Royal Historical Society, Camden fourth series, xx.

Testamenta Eboracensia (1836–65) 3 vols, London and Durham: Surtees Society, iv, xxx, xlv.

'The manuscripts of the corporations of Southampton and King's Lynn' (1887) *Historical Manuscripts Commission. Eleventh Report*, Appendix X, part iii: London.

Toulmin Smith, J. and Toulmin Smith, L.T.S. (ed.) (1870) *English Gilds*, London: E.E.T.S.

Toulmin Smith, L. (ed.) (1894) *Expeditions to Prussia and the Holy Land made by Henry Earl of Derby*, London: Camden Society, new series, lii.

Twemlow, J.A. (ed.) (1906) *Entries in the Papal Registers relating to Great Britain and Ireland. Papal Letters*, vii, 1417–31, London: Stationery Office.

Literary works

Bandinel, B. (ed.) (1857) *The itineraries of William Wey . . . to Jerusalem, A.D. 1458 and A.D. 1462; and to Saint James of Compostella, A.D. 1456*, London: Roxburghe Club.

Capgrave, John, Hingeston, F.C. (ed.) (1858) *Liber de Illustribus Henricis*, London: Rolls series.

Capgrave, John, Hingeston, F.C. (ed.) (1858) *The Chronicle of England*, London: Rolls series.

Capgrave, John, Mills, C.A. (ed.) (1911) *Ye solace of pilgrimes* (etc.), London: British Archaeological Society of Rome.

Deanesly, M. (1915) *The Incendium Amoris of Richard Rolle of Hampole*, Manchester: U.P.

Ellis, H. (ed.) (1851) *The Pylgrymage of Sir Richard Guylforde to the Holy Land, A.D. 1506*, London: Camden Society, li.

Furnivall, F.J. (ed.) (1867) *The stacions of Rome: and the pilgrims sea-voyage* (etc.), E.E.T.S., original series, xxv.

Galbraith, V.H. (ed.) (1937) *The St Albans Chronicle 1406–1420*, Oxford: University Press.

Gransden, A. (1957) 'A fourteenth-century chronicle from the Grey Friars at Lynn', *E.H.R.*, lxxii, 270–8.

Harris, M.T. (ed.), Kezel, A.R. (trans.), Nyberg, T. introduced (1990) *Birgitta of Sweden. Life and Selected Revelations*, New York: Paulist Press.

Hilton, Walter, Sherley-Price, L. (trans.) (1957) *The Ladder of Perfection*, Harmondsworth: Penguin.

Julian of Norwich, Spearing, E. (trans.), Spearing, A.C. introduced (1998) *Revelations of Divine Love*, London: Penguin.

Letts, M. (ed.) (1946) *The Pilgrimage of Arnold von Harff Knight* (etc.), London: Hakluyt Society, second series, xciv.

Letts, M. (ed.) (1957) *The Travels of Leo of Rozmital*, Hakluyt Society: Cambridge University Press, second series, cviii.

Mechthild of Magdeburg, Menzies, L. (trans.) (1953) *The Revelations of Mechthild of Magdeburg, 1210–1297: or, The flowing light of the Godhead*, London, New York: Longmans Green.

Meech, S.B. and Allen, H.E. (ed.) (1940) *The Book of Margery Kempe*, London: E.E.T.S., original series, 212.

Newett, M.M. (ed. and trans.) (1907) *Canon Casola's Pilgrimage to Jerusalem in the Year 1494*, Manchester: U.P.

Ragusa, I. (trans.), Green, R.B. (ed.) (1961) *Meditations on the Life of Christ*, Princeton: U.P.

Riley, H.T. (ed.) (1866) *Johannis de Trokelowe . . . Chronica et Annales*, London: Rolls series.

Rolle, Richard, Wolters, C. (trans.) (1972) *The Fire of Love*, Harmondsworth: Penguin (for Latin text, see above, under Deanesly).

St Bridget, Cumming, W.C. (ed.) (1929) *The Revelations of Saint Birgitta*, London: E.E.T.S., original series, clxxviii.

Stewart, A. (trans.) (1892–3) *The Book of the Wanderings of Brother Felix Fabri*, 2 vols, London: Palestine Pilgrims' Text Society.

Thompson, E.M. (ed.) (1874) *Chronicon Angliae*, London: Rolls series.

Usk, Adam, Given-Wilson, C. (ed.) (1997) *The Chronicle of Adam Usk 1377–1421*, Oxford: Clarendon Press.

Vitry, Jacques de, King, M.H. (trans.) (1987) *The Life of Marie d'Oignies*, Toronto: Peregrina.

Voragine, Jacobus de, Ryan, W.G. (trans.) (1993) *The Golden Legend. Readings on the Saints*, vol. 1, Princeton: U.P.

Way, A. (ed.) (1843–65) *Promptorium Parvulorum sive Clericorum*, by Fratre Galfrido, London: Camden Society, xxv, liv, lxxxix.

Windeatt, B.A. (ed.) (1994) *The Book of Margery Kempe*, London: Penguin.

Worcestre, William, Harvey, J.H. (ed. and trans.) (1969) *Itineraries*, Oxford: U.P.

Secondary sources

Allen, J. (1962) 'Englishmen in Rome and the Hospice 1362–1474', *The Venerabile*, xxi, 43–81.

Ashdown-Hill, J. (1997) 'Walsingham in 1469: The pilgrimage of Edward IV and Richard, Duke of Gloucester', *The Ricardian*, xi, no. 36, 2–16.

Aston, M. (1960) 'Lollardy and sedition, 1381–1431', *Past and Present*, lxxi, 1–44, reprinted in id. (1984) *Lollards and Reformers*, London: Hambledon, 1–47.

Aston, M. (1967) *Thomas Arundel*, Oxford: U.P.

Aston, M. (1980) 'Lollard women priests?', *J.E.H.*, xxi, 441–61, reprinted in *Lollards and Reformers*, 49–70.

Aston, M. (1982) 'William White's Lollard followers', *Catholic Historical Review*, lxviii, 469–97, reprinted in *Lollards and Reformers*, 71–100.

Aston, M. (1984) 'Devotional literacy', in *Lollards and Reformers*, 101–33.

Barber, M.J. (1957) 'The Englishman abroad in the fifteenth century', *Medievalia et Humanistica*, xi, 69–77.

Beer, F. (1992) *Women and Mystical Experience in the Middle Ages*, Woodbridge: Boydell and Brewer.

Brown, S. (1999) *Stained Glass at York*, London: Scala.

Brundage, J.A. (1993) *Sex, Law and Marriage in the Middle Ages*, Aldershot: Variorum.

Burgoyne, M.H. (1987) *Mamluk Jerusalem*, London: World of Islam Festival Trust.

Cameron, H.K. (1979) 'The fourteenth-century Flemish brasses at King's Lynn', *Archaeological Journal*, cxxxvi, 152–66.

Catto, J. (1985) 'Religious change under Henry V', in Harriss, G.L. ed., *Henry V. The Practice of Kingship*, Oxford: U.P., 97–115.

C[okayne], G.E., Gibbs, V. *et al.* (ed.) (1910–59) *The Complete Peerage of England, Scotland, Ireland and Great Britain and the United Kingdom*, 13 vols, London: St Catherine's Press.

Cullum, P.H. (1996) 'Vowesses and female lay piety in the province of York, 1300–1530', *Northern History*, xxxii, 21–41.

Dickinson, J.C. (1956) *The Shrine of Our Lady of Walsingham*, Cambridge: U.P.

Duffy, E. (1992) *The Stripping of the Altars*, New Haven and London: Yale U.P.

Emden, A.B. (1957–9) *A Biographical Register of the University of Oxford to 1500*, 3 vols, Oxford: Clarendon Press.

Emden, A.B. (1963) *A Biographical Register of the University of Cambridge to 1500*, Cambridge: U.P.

Finucane, R.C. (1977) *Miracles and Pilgrims. Popular Beliefs in Medieval England*, London: Dent.

Fulleylove, J. and Kelman, J. (1912) *The Holy Land*, London: Adam and Charles Black.

Gibson, P. (1979) *The Stained and Painted Glass of York Minster*, Norwich: Jarrold, for Dean and Chapter of York.

Gilchrist, R. and Oliva, M. (1993) *Religious Women in Medieval East Anglia: History and Archaeology c. 1100–1540*, Norwich: University of East Anglia.

Gregorovius, F., Hamilton, G.W. (trans.), Morrison, K.F. (ed.) (1898) *History of the City of Rome in the Middle Ages*, vi, part ii, London: G. Bell.

Harrod, H. (1874) *Report on the Deeds and Records of the Borough of King's Lynn*, King's Lynn.

Hay, D. and Law, J. (1989) *Italy in the Age of the Renaissance 1380–1530*, London and New York: Longman.

Hay, G. (1962) 'Pilgrims in the hospice', *The Venerabile*, xxi, Appendix XXI, 109–44.

Hudson, A. (1988) *The Premature Reformation*, Oxford: U.P.

Kelman, J.: see Fulleylove, J.

Kettle, A. (1984) 'My wife shall have it: marriage and property in the wills and testaments of later medieval England', in Craik, E.M. (ed.), *Marriage and Property*, Aberdeen: U.P.: 89–103.

Kirby, J.L. (1970) *Henry IV of England*, London: Constable.

Knowles, D. (1955) *The Religious Orders in England*, ii, *The End of the Middle Ages*, Cambridge: U.P.

Lagorio, V.M. (1984) 'The medieval continental women mystics: an introduction', in Szarmach, P.E. (ed.), *An Introduction to the Medieval Mystics of Europe*, Albany: State University of New York.

Lane, F.C. (1934) *Venetian Ships and Shipbuilding of the Renaissance*, Baltimore: Johns Hopkins Press.

Law, J.: see Hay, D.

Lewis, K. (2000) *The Cult of St Katherine of Alexandria in Late Medieval England*, Woodbridge: Boydell and Brewer.

Leyser, H. (1995) *A Social History of Women in England 450–1500*, London: Orion Books.

McFarlane, K.B. (1952) *John Wycliffe and the Beginnings of English Nonconformity*, London: English Universities Press.

McKenna, J.W. (1970) 'Popular canonization as political propaganda: the cult of Archbishop Scrope', *Speculum*, xlv, 608–23.

Nilson, B. (1996) 'A reinterpretation of the St William Window in York Minster', *Yorkshire Archaeological Journal*, lxviii, 157–79.

Oliva, M.: see Gilchrist, R.

Orme, N. (1973) *English Schools in the Midde Ages*, London: Methuen.

Orme, N. (1994) 'Children and the Church in medieval England'. *J.E.H.*, xlv, 563–87.

Orme, N. (1995) 'The culture of children in medieval England', *Past and Present*, cxlviii, 48–88.

Orme, N. (1999) 'Children and literature in medieval England', *Medium Aevum*, lxviii, 218–46.

Ormrod, W.M. (1990) *The Reign of Edward III*, London: Guild Publishing.

Parker, V. (1971) *The Making of King's Lynn: secular buildings from the eleventh to the seventeenth century*, Chichester: Phillimore.

Pattison, I.R. (2000) *Monuments in York Minster*, York: Friends of York Minster.

Peters, F.E. (1985) *Jerusalem*, Princeton: U.P.

Powell, Edgar (1896) *The Rising in East Anglia in 1381*, Cambridge: U.P.

Powell, Edward (1989) *Kingship, Law and Society. Criminal Justice in the Reign of Henry V*, Oxford: U.P.

Richards, P. (1997) *King's Lynn*, Chichester: Philimore.

Roskell, J.S. *et al.* (1992) *The History of Parliament. The House of Commons 1386–1421*, 4 vols, Stroud: Alan Sutton for The History of Parliament Trust.

Scott Stokes, C. (1999) 'Margery Kempe: her life and the early history of her book', *Mystics Quarterly*, xxv, nos 1–2.

Seymour, M.C. (1996) 'John Capgrave', in id. ed., *Authors of the Middle Ages*, iii, Aldershot: Variorum.

Stinger, C.L. (1985) *The Renaissance in Rome*, Bloomington: Indiana U.P.

Stork, N.P., 'Did Margery Kempe suffer from Tourette's syndrome?', *Medieval Studies*, lix, 261–300.

Storrs, C.M. (1998) *Jacobean Pilgrims firom England to St. James of Compostella from the Early Twelfth to the Late Fifteenth Century*, London: Confraternity of Saint James.

Sumption, J. (1975) *Pilgrimage. An Image of Medieval Religion*, London: Faber and Faber.

Surtz, R.E. (1990) *The Guitar of God. Gender, Power and Authority in the Visionary World of Juana de la Cruz (1481–1534)*, Philadelphia: Pennsylvania U.P.

Tanner, N.P. (1984) *The Church in Late Medieval Norwich 1370–1532*, Toronto: Pontifical Institute of Medieval Studies.

Thomson, J.A.F. (1965) *The Later Lollards 1414–1520*, Oxford: U. P.

Toy, J. (1985) *A Guide and Index to the Windows of York Minster*, York: Dean and Chapter of York.

Tucci, U. (1991) *I servizi marittimi veneziani per il pellegrinaggio in Terra santa nel Medioevo*, Venice; Università degli Studi di Venezia.

Wallace, D. (1984) 'Mystics and followers in Siena and East Anglia, a study in taxonomy, class and cultural mediation', in Glasscoe, M. (ed.), *The Medieval Mystical Tradition in England*, ii, Woodbridge: Boydell and Brewer, 169–91.

Warren, A.K. (1985) *Anchorites and their Patrons in Medieval England*, Berkeley, California: University of California Press.

Westlake, H.F. (1919) *The Parish Gilds of Medieval England*, London: Society for Promoting Christian Knowledge.

Wilson, C. (1977) *The Shrine of St William of York*, York: Yorkshire Museum.

Woodforde, C. (1950) *The Norwich School of Glass-Painting in the Fifteenth Century*, Oxford: U.P.

Wylie, J.H. (1884–94), *History of England under Henry the Fourth*, i–ii, London: Longmans Green.

Wylie, J.H. and Waugh, W.T. (1929) *The Reign of Henry the Fifth*, iii, Cambridge: U.P.

INDEX

Aachen, 159, 163
Aleyn, Master, 88–9, 93, 103
aliens, 19, 99, 171–3
All Saints church, South Lynn, 81–2, 152
Alnwick, William, bishop of Norwich, 76, 83–4, 98
amanuenses of *The Book of Margery Kempe*, 5–6, 8–10, 90–1
anchoresses, 26, 73, 82, 126, 134–5, 136, 150, 229n
anchorites, 82, 88, 102, 126, 134, 136, 160
apparel, *see* clothing; hair shirts
Arundel, Sir Richard, 160
Arundel, Thomas, bishop of Ely, archbishop of Canterbury, 18, 32–3, 39, 47, 69, 103, 129, 142, 169, 209
Asshebourne, William, 19, 42–4
Assisi, 87, 117, 174
Augustinian friary, King's Lynn, 40, 207; *see also* Capgrave

Babthorpe family, 144–5
Bad Wilsnack, 121, 152, 159, 160–1, 164, 251n
Bardolf family, 32, 136
  Thomas, Lord, 32, 34
bears, 205
Beauchamp, Richard, Earl of Warwick, 188
Beaufort, Henry, bishop of Winchester, cardinal, 33, 42, 44, 51, 132, 146
Beaufort, Joan, Countess of Westmorland, 126, 132, 133
Beaufort, John, Earl of Somerset, 123

Beaufort, Margaret, Countess of Dorset, Duchess of Exeter, 35, 244n
Beaufort, Thomas, Earl of Dorset, Duke of Exeter, 30, 33–5, 39, 41, 47, 87, 133, 187, 243n
Bedford, Duke of, *see* John of Lancaster
beguines, 138
Belleyetere, Edmund, 27, 38, 223n
Bergen, 19, 119
Bethlehem, 193
Beverley, Yorkshire, 106, 130, 145, 147, 149–50
bills of exchange, 165
Bilney, John, 39, 41, 42–4
Blessed Virgin Mary
  communications from, 105, 193
  cults of, 94–5, 109
  feasts of, 250n
  relics of, 154, 155, 159, 174, 197
  visions of, 88, 102, 105–6, 107, 176
Blocke, Joanne, 60
Bologna, 156, 157
Boston, Lincolnshire, 150, 232n
Botekesham, Robert, 35, 36, 37, 38
Bowet, Henry, archbishop of York, 13, 56–7, 98, 122, 130, 131, 132, 141–2, 144, 145, 148, 164, 205, 207
Brandon, John, 27, 34, 223
Braunche, Robert, 15
Brekeropp, John, 38, 44, 66, 220n
brewing, 70
Bridlington priory, Yorkshire, 134, 135; *see also* St John of Bridlington
Bristol, 129, 140, 153, 242n, 244n
Brunham, Edmund, 222n